THE STATE AND ILLEGALITY IN INDONESIA

VERHANDELINGEN
VAN HET KONINKLIJK INSTITUUT
VOOR TAAL-, LAND- EN VOLKENKUNDE

269

THE STATE AND ILLEGALITY IN INDONESIA

EDITED BY

EDWARD ASPINALL AND GERRY VAN KLINKEN

KITLV Press
Leiden
2010

Published by:
KITLV Press
Koninklijk Instituut voor Taal-, Land- en Volkenkunde
(Royal Netherlands Institute of Southeast Asian and Caribbean Studies)
PO Box 9515
2300 RA Leiden
The Netherlands
website: www.kitlv.nl
e-mail: kitlvpress@kitlv.nl

KITLV is an institute of the Royal Netherlands Academy of Arts and Sciences (KNAW)

KONINKLIJKE NEDERLANDSE
AKADEMIE VAN WETENSCHAPPEN

Cover: Creja ontwerpen, Leiderdorp

Cover photos: Front: A *pendekar* (strongman) of the Betawi Brotherhood Forum.
Photo by Ian Wilson
Back: Members of the Betawi Brotherhood Forum at the group's headquarters in Cakung, Jakarta
Photo by Ian Wilson

ISBN 978 90 6718 371 0

Contents

Acknowledgements

This volume is the product of an extended and intensive process of collaboration in which many individuals participated. It has its genesis in a panel at the European Association for Southeast Asian Studies (Euroseas) conference in Naples, Italy, on 12-15 September 2007. Several of the papers in that panel were published in a special edition of *South East Asia Research* in 2008 (Volume 16, Number 2). A second workshop on the State and Illegality in Indonesia brought together some of the Naples authors with a considerably enlarged group of researchers a year later. It was hosted by the Australian National University in Canberra on 22-24 September 2008. Participants presented and debated their draft chapters. We would like to thank the Australia Netherlands Research Collaboration (ANRC) for generously funding this workshop.

Above all, we the editors would like to thank all contributors, who brought their diverse backgrounds to this elusive yet important topic, and did so in a highly collaborative manner. We found it a delight to take part in a series of meetings where participants contributed their ideas so creatively and generously. Afterwards, it was gratifying to work with authors who approached the task of writing and revision with such seriousness. In addition, we would like to thank other participants in the conference panel and workshop who liberally shared their research experiences and insights. They included Najib Azca, Laurens Bakker, Lois Bastide, Michael Buehler, Luky Djani, Andreas Harsono, David Jansen, Barak Kalir, Akhiruddin Mahjuddin, Akiko Morishita, Loren Ryter and Sophie Schuette.

At the Australian National University, Allison Ley and Lyn Ning provided invaluable assistance in organizing the research workshop. Allison Ley also helped to prepare the glossary and bibliography. The index was prepared by Angela Grant. At KITLV Press, we thank Ireen Hoogenboom for careful fine editing, and Kees Waterman for so enthusiastically supporting the project through to completion. We also thank two anonymous reviewers appointed by the press.

Edward Aspinall and Gerry van Klinken

Canberra and Leiden

October 2010

About the authors

Edward Aspinall is Head of the Department of Political and Social Change, School of International, Political and Strategic Studies, College of Asia and the Pacific, Australian National University. His latest books are *Islam and nation; Separatist rebellion in Aceh, Indonesia* (2009) and *Problems of democratisation in Indonesia; Elections, institutions, and society* (2010) (edited with Marcus Mietzner).

Simon Butt is Senior Lecturer at the University of Sydney where he teaches Indonesian law, intellectual property, dispute resolution in Asia, and law and investment in Asia. He has published widely on a number of areas of Indonesian law and is currently working on several research and book projects relating to Indonesian legal institutions and Indonesian law. His research and consultancy interests include law-making, policy and law, corruption, Islamic law, human rights law, the judiciary, the rule of law and the legal implications of regional autonomy in Indonesia.

Robert Cribb is Professor of Asian Politics and History in the School of Culture, History and Language at the Australian National University. His research focuses on the history of Indonesian identity, problems of mass violence, historical geography and environmental history. He is the author of the *Digital atlas of Indonesian history* (2010) and editor (with Michele Ford) of *Indonesia beyond the water's edge; Managing an archipelagic state* (2009).

Howard Dick is Professorial Fellow in Management and Associate of the Asian Law Centre at the University of Melbourne and Conjoint Professor in Business and Law at the University of Newcastle, New South Wales. His research into governance has focused on the shadow economy, law reform and anti-corruption strategies, and he co-edited with Tim Lindsey *Corruption in Asia* (2002).

Michele Ford chairs the Department of Indonesian Studies at the University of Sydney, Australia, where she teaches about politics, social activism and human rights in Indonesia and other parts of Asia. Michele's research is focused on social movements in Southeast Asia and the Indonesia-Singapore borderlands. Her publications include *Workers and intellectuals; NGOs, trade unions and the Indonesian labour movement* (2009) and *Indonesia beyond the water's edge; Managing an archipelagic state* (2009) (co-edited with Robert Cribb).

Jun Honna is Professor in the Faculty of International Relations, Ritsumeikan University in Kyoto, Japan. His research interests include civil-military relations, security policies and democratization in Indonesia. He is the author of *Military politics and democratization in Indonesia* (2003).

Gerry van Klinken is Senior Researcher with the KITLV/Royal Netherlands Institute of Southeast Asian and Caribbean Studies in Leiden, the Netherlands. His interests have included human rights, ethnicity, post-authoritarian transition, and historical memory. His most recent sole-authored book is *Communal violence and democratization in Indonesia: small town wars* (2007).

Professor Tim Lindsey is Director of the Asian Law Centre and Director of the Centre for Islamic Law and Society, both in the Law School at the University of Melbourne, where he is also an ARC Federation Fellow. He publishes widely, and is the editor of *Indonesia; law and society* (2d ed, 2008), and *Law reform in developing and transitional states* (2007).

Lenore Lyons is Research Professor in Asian Studies at the University of Western Australia. Recognized as the leading scholar on the feminist movement in Singapore, she is the author of *A state of ambivalence; The feminist movement in Singapore* (2004). She recently completed a major study of citizenship, identity and sovereignty in the Riau Islands of Indonesia (with Michele Ford) and is currently working on a project that examines migrant worker activism in support of female domestic workers in Malaysia and Singapore.

John McCarthy lectures in the Australian National University's Crawford School. He researches agrarian change, land tenure, environmental governance and natural resource policy. He has carried out various assignments with agencies in Australia and Indonesia including AusAID and the Centre for International Forestry Research (CIFOR). He currently has an Australian Research Council grant to research agrarian change and oil palm expansion in Malaysia and Indonesia. He is the author of *The fourth circle; A political ecology of Sumatra's rainforest frontier* (2006).

Ross McLeod is an economist with the Indonesia Project at the Australian National University. He has been working in and on Indonesia as postgraduate student, consultant and academic researcher since 1978, and has been editor of the ANU's *Bulletin of Indonesian Economic Studies* since 1998. He is the joint editor, with Andrew MacIntyre, of *Indonesia; Democracy and the promise of good governance* (2007).

Marcus Mietzner is Lecturer in Indonesian Studies, School of Culture, History and Language, College of Asia and the Pacific, Australian National University, Canberra. He is the author of *Military politics, Islam, and the state in Indonesia; From turbulent transition to democratic consolidation* (2009) and editor (with Edward Aspinall) of *Problems of democratisation in Indonesia; Elections, institutions, and society* (2010).

Jeremy Mulholland is a PhD candidate in the Department of Management and the Asian Law Centre at the University of Melbourne on the topic 'Intra-elite rivalry in Indonesia; A new institutional economics perspective'.

Gerben Nooteboom is Lecturer and Researcher at the Department of Anthropology and Sociology, the University of Amsterdam. He teaches state and society, social theory, Southeast Asia, and the anthropology of development. His research has been on social security, poverty, inequality, ethnic violence, livelihood, migration, child labour, illegality and human adaptation in East Java and East Kalimantan. He wrote his PhD dissertation at Radboud University Nijmegen, the Netherlands, on 'A matter of style; Social security and livelihood in upland East Java' (2003).

J. Danang Widoyoko is the Coordinator of Indonesia Corruption Watch (ICW), a respected anti-corruption NGO in Indonesia. He has written numerous investigative reports on corruption cases, for example involving government budgets, state-owned enterprises, the public service, oil and extractive industries, and forestry. He also conducts training on investigative reporting, public service monitoring using report cards, and budget analysis. Danang graduated in electronic engineering from Satya Wacana Christian University, Salatiga. He serves as chairperson of the board of INFID (International NGO Forum on Indonesia Development), an NGO coalition that focuses on monitoring the impact of development and foreign debt.

Ian Wilson is a Research Fellow at the Asia Research Centre and Lecturer in the School of Social Sciences and Humanities, Murdoch University, Western Australia. His research interests include gangs, militias and non-state sources of violence, informal street economies and political corruption. He has published extensively on gangsters, organized crime and political violence in Indonesia in journals such as *Critical Asian Studies* and *Nationalism and Ethnic Politics*.

EDWARD ASPINALL AND GERRY VAN KLINKEN

The state and illegality in Indonesia

In July 2007, at the height of a government military operation against separatist rebels in the Indonesian province of Aceh, a short but curious article appeared in the local newspaper.[1] It quoted the Aceh military commander, Major General Endang Suwarya, warning members of the public not to be hoodwinked if they received a telephone call from someone claiming to be him and asking for money. Apparently, a group of swindlers had been telephoning rich people in the province, with one first pretending to be Endang's adjutant. After ascertaining the identity of the person being called, the 'adjutant' would hand over the telephone to 'the commander' who would then ask for hundreds of millions of rupiah in order to help pay for the military operation. A number of local officials and businesspeople had apparently already fallen for the trick, and transferred large sums to the bank accounts in Jakarta nominated by the swindlers. Endang was angry: 'For as long as I've been serving here, I have never telephoned anyone to borrow or ask for money.'[2] Yet this was not the first time, nor the last, that confidence tricksters had pretended to be members of the security forces in order to extort money from people in Aceh; on the contrary, there have been repeated reports of individuals pretending to be police officers, army soldiers or agents of the State Intelligence Agency (Badan Intelijen Negara, BIN) for this purpose.[3]

There is, of course, an unspoken irony in such stories. Here we have ordinary civilians engaging in what are apparently acts of pure criminality that do not involve abuse of state office or misuse of state funds, but in order to do so, they find it most convenient to imitate corrupt state officials. Everybody involved apparently takes it for granted that this act of imitation is logical, even crafty. Neither the military officers being imitated, nor the police officers in charge of investigations, nor those being swindled, nor the reporters, ques-

1 Small parts of this introductory chapter are based on Van Klinken 2008. The authors thank Ian Wilson, Howard Dick, Ross McLeod and Robert Cribb, and the two anonymous reviewers, for their very helpful comments on earlier versions.

2 'Mayjen Endang Suwarya dicatut untuk memeras', *Serambi Indonesia* 22-7-2003.

3 See for example 'Rekan tersangka BIN gadungan dipanggil polisi', *Serambi Indonesia* 27-6-2007; 'Coba memeras geuchik, lima BIN gadungan dibekuk di Langsa', *Serambi Indonesia* 22-4-2009.

tion the effectiveness of the trick. And little wonder: the swindle is entirely plausible. Everyone in Aceh at the time of the story described above knew that military personnel were involved in all sorts of extortion rackets, as well as engaging in a variety of other 'off-budget' fundraising techniques, involving skimming off money from government development budgets, extracting protection payments from large companies, and participating in all manner of legal and semi-legal activities ranging from the marijuana trade to illegal logging. Ordinary soldiers and policemen routinely demanded payments from drivers of vehicles who drove through their checkpoints, or they stole money, household goods, livestock and other valuables from ordinary citizens' homes and farms when they raided villages in their hunt for separatist rebels. Hence the logic of the swindle: in order to be a criminal, so it seems, it helps if you are first a state official, or at least can pretend to be one. And although such swindles were especially common in Aceh, where the security forces were until recently an overwhelming presence, they also occur throughout Indonesia. National and regional newspapers frequently run stories about extortion scams by 'fake police' (*polisi gadungan*), fake soldiers, fake intelligence agents, fake prosecutors, fake anti-corruption commissioners and many other varieties of fake state officials.[4]

Empirical and theoretical starting points

The concept of legality is inherent in the modern concept of the state. It is the state that defines what is legal and illegal and invests that distinction with legitimacy. The state also has the power to enforce the law, using violence if necessary, at least in theory if not always in practice. Every state that joins the United Nations subscribes to these ideas. Yet in reality state officials are themselves also not infrequently implicated in illegality of various kinds. This simple observation, which certainly holds true for Indonesia, is the starting point for the explorations in this volume.

Throughout Indonesia, as in many other countries of the world, the involvement of state officials in illegal activity is both ubiquitous and a matter of public knowledge. At the upper level of the state are the major scandals that habitually excite public opinion when evidence comes to light of senior government officials stealing from the public purse, striking shady deals with private entrepreneurs, or fleecing money from them. Very often the logic of illegality in such cases is nakedly self-serving and predatory, summed up by the Supreme Court judge in Tim Lindsey and Simon Butt's chapter in this

4 See, for example, 'KPK gadungan ditangkap', *Kompas* 18-7-2006, 'Polisi gadungan ditangkap karena diduga memeras', *Pikiran Rakyat* 21-1-2010.

volume whose questions to a supplicant's lawyer are blunt: 'Do you have money or not? If you don't, I'll make an offer to your adversary.' As we move down, the same predatory dynamic underpins much official illegality, ranging from the policemen who extort money or sexual favours from suspects if they want to be released without trial, through to the impecunious elementary school teacher who charges the parents of his or her pupils unofficial but obligatory fees. However, as the naked greed of the wealthy senior official gives way to the more modest demands of the lower civil servant, who levies fees only in order to maintain a humble lower middle-class lifestyle, social attitudes toward such behaviour often change, with the demands of the less senior official frequently viewed as reasonable and sometimes even regarded with sympathy. Moreover, as some of the contributions in this volume make clear, illegality by state officials often also serves useful functions for large groups of ordinary citizens, thus not only for those who are cut special deals at the expense of others (such as rival ligitants in court cases). As a result, such illegality is often viewed as entirely legitimate by large sectors of society. Consider, for example, the helpful immigration officials in the Riau Islands who sell migrants 'real but fake' travel documents cheaply so the latter can move on quickly to Malaysia or Singapore and who, as Michele Ford and Lenore Lyons explain in their chapter, are seen by local people as resisting an unjust and unworkable legal regime imposed on them by Jakarta.

It is when we begin to consider the social approval that such illegal behaviour often evokes that the censorious and normatively charged tone that surrounds much discussion of corruption, defined conventionally as the 'misuse of public office for private gain', begins to come under strain. This conventional understanding of corruption is also strained when we find examples of illegality that are ostensibly for 'public' purposes, such as a dramatic case in 1999 that involved some of Indonesia's most senior military officers counterfeiting Rp 19.2 billion (US$2 million) in Rp 50,000 notes in order to buy weapons for pro-integration militia in East Timor. According to one of those charged in the case, this activity was carried out with the approval of officials at Bank Indonesia (BI), so long as 'the amount printed did not exceed Rp 200 billion. The numbers and series were to be given by BI, the quality of the printing had to be good, and the fake notes were not to circulate outside East Timor.[5] As both Ross McLeod and Howard Dick and Jeremy Mulholland make clear in their contributions to this volume, state officials routinely violate their own cumbersome and opaque rules just to ensure the regular functioning of the bureaucracy. To further complicate matters, many state officials are also involved in 'ordinary' illegality that occurs in the societal domain and does not involve as its main focus the predation of state resources. Wherever one goes in Indonesia, state

5 'Investigation: smiling – all the way to the bank', *Tempo* 10-16 July 2001.

officials are especially likely to be involved in criminal activities that involve a high degree of organization, such as extortion and protection rackets, smuggling, illegal logging, and the narcotics trade, while law enforcement officers enjoy close and murky relations with everyday criminals.

Before we go further, a qualification is in order. We certainly do not believe that illegality is the exclusive preserve of state officials, nor that state officials never take action to uphold legal order. Much illegal activity in Indonesia is carried on entirely by individuals who are not directly connected with the state. Indonesia has its share of robbery by taxi drivers, enslavement of domestic servants by wealthy entrepreneurs, tax dodging by restaurateurs and the full range of mendacity, cruelty, crimes of passion and of desperation that modern societies are capable of generating. Moreover, the state employs a large number of functionaries to police the rules it sets for society. We do not wish to create the impression that state officials never uphold these rules. Many police detectives, prosecutors, judges, jailers, as well as teachers, social workers, and other public moralists do in Indonesia more or less what they do in other countries to control this kind of behaviour. Indonesia is by no means a Hobbesian jungle. According to (somewhat problematic and dated) comparative official statistics (Arthur and Marenin 1995), homicide, rape and robbery rates in Indonesia have historically been among the lowest in the world. But we have chosen not to focus primarily on these state successes in maintaining legal order. The reason is not that we dispute their reality. Rather it is that control of crime is so often overshadowed by other forms of illegal activity in which state functionaries collaborate or are even the directing agents.

Why, then, did we write this book? In the first place, phenomena that so constantly undermine public faith in the state cry out for morally engaged comment and analysis. The popular 1998 *reformasi* movement that brought down President Suharto's New Order regime demanded above all an end to illegal practices by state officials, from military human rights abuses to nepotistic investment policies. This movement created as its main rallying cry the condemnation of Corruption, Collusion, Nepotism (Korupsi, Kolusi dan Nepotisme, KKN), a phrase that has remained central to public political discourse to this day. The problem of corruption, which in public perception seems to trump all other forms of illegality, has stimulated a flood of advice to every government since that of Suharto, both from within and outside the country. Yet today corruption and other illegal practices by state officials have proven more resistant to reform than people had hoped. Many new anti-corruption regulations have been created, new institutions built, elections have introduced a measure of accountability for parliamentarians and elected executives, and the much lauded Corruption Eradication Commission (Komisi Pemberantasan Korupsi, KPK) has made spectacular arrests. Yet Indonesia has crept up only slowly on international corruption lists. It has gone from 2.0 to 2.8 (on a scale of 0 to 10) between 1998 and 2009, according to Transparency International's corruption perception index (admittedly an index that has been widely criticized for the methods that it uses).[6] According to the World Bank, Indonesia had by 2008 improved to 31% on 'control of corruption' from an absolute low of 9% in the chaotic year of 1998, but it has still not quite returned to its late New Order level of 33% measured in 1996.[7] Public opinion surveys in Indonesia itself likewise record alarmingly low levels of trust in public institutions, and a common view that corruption is all-pervasive. Indonesia's public political domain is still characterized by animated discussion of corruption and the abuse of power by public officials: this alone makes a scholarly treatment of this topic urgent and appropriate.

This ubiquity and resilience of corruption and other illegal practices by state officials points to a second reason why we wrote this book. As many reports have put it, corruption and other forms of state illegality in Indonesia are 'entrenched'. We argue it is precisely this entrenched character that requires attention. Rather than add to the flood of advice with another survey of the list of things that should be, could be, or had already been done to combat illegal practices, we wanted to do some serious intellectual work on the problem of entrenched illegality. What is state illegality entrenched in and how does it become entrenched? Answering this question involves first studying actual cases of state illegality, and trying to understand them, as far as possible, from the standpoint of the participants. In particular, as will become apparent through this volume, it especially requires studying closely the webs of relationships that run in all directions, both within and beyond the state. Within the state, for example, a senior teacher has to bribe his or her Education Department superior if he or she wants to be appointed school principal (as related in Danang Widoyoko's chapter). The 'backing' (*beking* or *deking*) that petty gangsters enjoy from military patrons who help to enforce their protection rackets among Jakarta's street vendors cross the formal boundary between state and society (see Ian Wilson in this book). Motorcycle thieves, pirates, drug dealers, prostitutes, illegal timber cutters, their clients and financiers, who sometimes appear to operate purely within society, are often protected by state actors. Comparative statistics throw little light on these relationships. Only detailed case studies of the kind included in this book can do that.

A third goal of the volume, therefore, was to see what inquiring into the nature of illegal activities by state officials would tell us about the nature of the state itself. Much discussion of corruption and other forms of illegal behaviour by state officials takes a highly normative view of the state, see-

6 http://ww_w.transparency.org/policy_research/surveys_indices/cpi/2009. For one criticism see Galtung 2006.

7 Kaufmann et al. 2008: Table C6. Continually updated rankings available on full dataset, available through http://info.worldbank.org/governance/wgi/ (accessed 8-3-2010).

ing them as deviations from an ideal bureaucratic machine bound by legal rationality. Even the words we use to describe this sort of behaviour betray these assumptions: misconduct, misuse, misdemeanours and so on. By looking at both the broad patterns and micro processes of state illegality, we wish to describe and understand the state as it is, not as we believe it should be. Taking this approach does not entail abandoning the moral engagement that underpins our work, but is simply necessary for thinking clearly about the state and illegality. Clear thought is especially necessary in circumstances where, as we explain below, there is a large gap between activities that are formally in contravention of state law and hence illegal and those which are the target of social opprobrium and hence illicit. Our observations of actual practices led us to rethink some fundamental ideas about the nature of the state in Indonesia, especially regarding its socially embedded character.

In noting the ubiquity and entrenched character of corruption and state illegality, and its centrality to how the state operates, we are of course not breaking entirely new ground in the study of Indonesian politics and society but instead building on a long tradition of close observation of illegal practices built up during the New Order and before it. Studies by Harold Crouch (1979), Richard Robison (1986) and others on the centrality of corrupt patronage distribution to the functioning of the New Order have become classics in the field. In the late New Order years, a growing focus on the state's links with criminal groups,[8] and historical research on the anti-communist pogroms of 1965-1966 (Cribb 1990) opened researchers' eyes to the illegal violence the state perpetrated. To mention just one other example, in a striking essay written in the aftermath of the collapse of Suharto's New Order regime, Tim Lindsey (2001:284) wrote of the New Order as a 'criminal state' in which 'the real structures and systems by which the New Order operated were illegal'. We have learned much from these and other prior research efforts, and present this volume as a contribution to an ongoing discussion about the nature of the state and illegality in Indonesia.

Studies of state actors' entanglement in illegality in Indonesia, and beyond, can be conveniently divided into four broad streams: marketist, culturalist, statist and strategic-relational approaches. The first category is the dominant one in writing on corruption, and has surprisingly little to say about the state except as the field in which corruption takes place; the final three are distinct approaches to the study of the state that imply different emphases and postures regarding the study of illegality by state functionaries. While the boundaries between the approaches are somewhat fuzzy, each has a distinct view on how to explain the sources and motivations of the intermeshing of state and illegality in countries like Indonesia.

8 Especially in the so-called 'Petrus', or 'mysterious shooting', killings of 1983 (Bourchier 1990, Siegel 1998).

The first interpretation, which is dominant in the international scholarly literature on corruption, posits that state officials operate according to a market logic. Illegality by state officials – like all forms of crime – is a consequence of rational choice, in which participants balance the likely benefits of crime against the risk of being apprehended. Individual officials act like rational entrepreneurs seeking to maximize their 'rents'. There is nothing inherently problematic with the state in this view, except that it is sometimes too weak to enforce its rules on all its members all the time. The Africanist Colin Leys (1965) wrote a pioneering paper articulating this viewpoint. He urged the study of corruption not primarily as a moral problem but as one involving material incentives for officials operating in an impoverished and poorly disciplined state. The political scientist James Scott was another pioneer of this approach with his observation that corruption was a businesslike affair (Scott 1969) (although Scott also emphasized the nature of the regime that dispensed corrupt patronage and thus foreshadowed the statist interpretation). On the assumption that people act collectively only if it brings them a private return (Olson 1971), neo-liberal economists subsequently developed a theory of rent-seeking behaviour that remains influential. In this view, officials enjoy discretion in the way they collect or spend the large sums of state money that pass through their hands. If their salaries are low, if they are under pressure from all sides to do more than they can realistically achieve, or if hardly anyone looks over their shoulder while they work, so the argument goes, they are likely to collude with the taxpayers or recipients of government funds to cream off some of those funds on the way. Governments that implement regulations, for example, to restrict imports or license businesses, merely create opportunities for corruption that, on balance, cost society more than having no regulation at all (Krueger 1974). The implications were not only that corruption was more costly to society than previously thought, but also that the way to solve the problem was to reduce government intervention in the market, thus reducing the opportunities for state officials to act corruptly. The economist James M. Buchanan won the 1986 Nobel prize for developing these fundamentally anti-state ideas into a field of study known as public policy (Buchanan, Tollison and Tullock 1980). The approach long remained agenda-setting in anti-corruption prescriptions produced by multilateral agencies like the World Bank. By the late 1990s, however, the emphasis was shifting from pushing back government intervention, regulation and discretion to improving government discipline (Rose-Ackerman 1999). The World Bank, USAID, the United Nations Development Program and other international agencies have produced numerous expert 'good governance' reports over the last decade advising the Indonesian government how to reform its institutions to improve free market competition, reduce government red tape, protection and subsidies, and strengthen checks and balances. Most of

Indonesia's governance reforms since the International Monetary Fund intervention in 1997 have been technically informed by this advice. Yet the marketist approach has been criticized by many authors, including some in this book (see in particular the chapter by John McCarthy) on a range of grounds. One criticism has been that by locating the motive for corruption and other forms of state illegality in individual greed it misses wider contexts. For example it closes its eyes to the very embeddedness of such practices in state institutions, the often political motivations that guide such behaviour, and the social and cultural codes that govern and legitimate it.

The second approach, which we call culturalist, imagines that illegality by state officials is rooted not in rational calculation but in a moral order that legitimates certain forms of behaviour by officials even when they contravene the state's formal laws. Individuals act not primarily according to calculations of potential personal benefit balanced against the risk of exposure and punishment, but according to a coherent set of moral values. Very often, the roots of such a moral order are depicted as lying in the precolonial past. The Africanist J.P. Olivier de Sardan (1999) has explained contemporary corruption with the logic of a 'moral economy of corruption', in which tribal chiefs expect tribute, private and public affairs are indistinguishable, and ordinary folk are not citizens with rights but subjects who must ingratiate themselves with the chief to get anything done. Illegality disappears from this literature as an inappropriate alien imposition. At most, it persists as a theatrical device in discourses aiming to discredit rivals; but everyone understands that such talk is hypocritical. Africanists find the culturalist argument so compelling because the modern state south of the Sahara is often so weak that it resembles a thin institutional veneer over a society whose roots lie far deeper (D.J. Smith 2006). In Indonesia the state is far less dysfunctional than in, say, Sierra Leone, yet here too it is much more thinly spread than in a developed economy. This is evident from statistics of, for example, civil servants as a proportion of the population, or the state budget as a proportion of GDP.[9]

Scholars studying weak states and resurgent authoritarianism in Southeast Asia in the 1960s and 1970s began to describe elite behaviour in terms of a return to a precolonial template. Several took an interest in the role of patronage in providing internal coherence to these states, in the power of the patrimonial values behind authoritarian and corrupt bureaucratic practices, and in the precolonial origins of both the values and the practices (Resink 1975; T.M. Smith 1971; Wertheim 1964). Indeed, the Austrian ethnologist Robert Heine-Geldern had helped found modern Southeast Asian studies in the United States with a 1942 paper on Southeast Asian notions of kingship

9 Indonesia's central government tax revenue was 12.8% of GDP in 2001, less than a third of the 38.2% in the Netherlands, while 2.0% of the total population worked for the Indonesian government in 1997, less than half the 4.6% in the Netherlands in 1995 (Tables 1 and A.4 in UNPAN 2002).

(Heine-Geldern 1956). This led Benedict Anderson to write his influential paper on the resurgent influence of allegedly traditional Javanese values of deference on contemporary Indonesian politics, in which he ascribed official corruption to 'the residual influences of the appanage system [of precolonial times] in contemporary administrative behavior' (Anderson 1972:48). Harold Crouch, in his analyses of New Order military politics, likewise drew on the idea that precolonial styles of personal rulership had experienced a revival in the postcolonial state. Sharing insights common in Africanist and Asianist circles, he saw the bureaucracy as a highly personalized hierarchy of neo-patrimonial relations, in which 'traditional modes of thought and behavior have often continued to influence the workings of apparently modern institutions' (H. Crouch 1979:194). The idea of a 'culture of corruption' rooted in Java's feudal traditions remains strong in journalistic circles (Loveard 1999), and above all in Indonesian public discourse. For example, some years ago, the Indonesian historian Djoko Suryo wrote:

> Under the Javanese kings the word corruption did not exist. But that doesn't mean behaviour similar to corruption did not exist. Tribute beyond taxation was one example. That was normal at the time [...] Probably the regents of those days only realized this was wrong after Multatuli in [the novel] *Max Havelaar* harshly criticized their tribute practices.[10]

During the late 1970s and 1980s serious doubts began to arise among scholars of Indonesia about such an approach, under the impact of both Marxist-oriented structuralism (see especially Robison 1981) and Edward Said's powerful critique of Orientalist scholarship, much of which, in Said's view, presented an ahistorical and essentialized understanding of the East and its culture. For Indonesianists these doubts were expressed in an important book by John Pemberton (1994), which showed that Javanese political culture had not remained static since precolonial times. On the contrary, it was largely constructed out of the interaction between the Javanese courts and the growing Dutch state during the nineteenth century. The manipulation of 'culture' continued during the New Order, when the regime invoked themes of Javanese subservience to enforce its authoritarian rule. Pemberton did not intend by this observation to replace the power of culture with that of the state, but rather to contextualize it. Thus, while culturalist explanations for involvement by state officials in illegal behaviour can often be revealing, they need to avoid reifying culture as static and somehow isolated from the behaviours they seek to explain. Rather, the cultural codes governing illegality are best seen as themselves embedded in and constructed out of dynamic

10 'Pamomong: budaya 'korupsi' di Jawa (1)', *Suara Merdeka* 14-8-1997.

interactions between state and societal actors.

The preceding two interpretations of the state's entanglement in illegality – the one marketist, the other culturalist – tend to think of the modern state as largely unable to discipline its members. The first sees state actors as primarily acting out of their own material interests, and the second sees them as mainly motivated by a complex of cultural obligations. A third interpretation, sometimes called the statist approach, attributes a great deal of autonomy to the state as a unit. Rather than seeing it as being too weak to prevent illegality, or as confounded by competing moral values, it views the state itself as a predatory institution designed to extract benefits for the people who control it.[11]

The dominant image of the state in the study of Indonesian and Southeast Asian politics and history is of an alien and sovereign force imposing its will upon society. The injurious effects of a relatively autonomous colonial bureaucratic machine upon an agrarian society became a major theme in Southeast Asian studies, notably at Cornell University under the influence of Oliver Wolters and Benedict Anderson. The model was attractive for many observers for a long time because colonial and independent states that lacked legitimacy and acted violently formed a pattern throughout the region in much of the twentieth century. Anderson took this approach to its apogee in an influential essay that posited something resembling a zero-sum contest between state and society in Indonesia. He described the New Order regime as representing little less than the victory of state over nation (Anderson 1983). This approach, which tends to see the state as a leviathan, undifferentiated and monolithic, gave rise to many revelatory studies of Indonesian politics. It especially helped explain instances of gross violence perpetrated by state officials against citizens (Anderson 2001). But this approach is arguably less useful for explaining the quotidian practices of everyday corruption and petty illegality with which this book is mostly concerned. Borrowing from Robert Cribb, we might also argue that this approach has little to say about the motivations behind state illegality, except to point to 'personal lust for extraordinary power – and a drive to maintain that power'.[12]

A fourth approach to the study of the state that has been gaining ground in recent years has sometimes been called 'strategic-relational'.[13] In this approach, illegal behaviour by state officials is best understood as a product of competitive strategizing among the heterogeneity of interests and actors that populates the state. While wanting to retain a central place for the state

11 We are grateful to Robert Cribb for this formulation.

12 Cribb 2009:2. Cribb made this comment in relation to early studies showing participation by Western states in clandestine and illegal activities, such as the heroin trade in Southeast Asia, pointing to the difficulties the insights conferred by such research had in meshing with conventional political science analysis.

13 Jessop 2007. An alternative nomenclature would be derived from what Migdal (2001) calls a 'state-in-society' approach.

in their analysis even in developing countries, the scholars who formulated the strategic-relational approach have preferred to see the state less as an autonomous actor and more as an arena that favours certain kinds of strategic action while obstructing others, and where multiple players compete for influence, make alliances, and expropriate resources. One of the most influential authors in this field, Joel Migdal (2001:15-6), defines the state as 'a field of power marked by the use and threat of violence and shaped by (1) *the image of a coherent, controlling organization in a territory, which is a representation of the people bounded by that territory,* and (2) *the actual practices of its multiple parts*'. Viewing the state as 'field of power' is central to this emerging revisionist political science literature. Abandoning the conventional Weberian ideal type of the autonomous, bureaucratic state 'firing on all cylinders' (as Migdal 2001:14 put it), it proposes simply studying actual state practices with the eye of the ethnographer, minus the Weberian assumptions. It no longer sees the state as a 'thing', but as a relational arena. In this view, the essence of the state is relationships and strategies, developing through time and space, rather than static structures or impersonal rules.[14] The basic argument is to envision the state as a competitive arena and site of strategic struggle for the ultimate rule-making authority. The 'ideal' state, meanwhile, should be studied for what it is, namely an ideological construct or, in Migdal's term, an image, deployed by both state officials and their opponents in society. Another thrust of this thinking is that the homogeneity of the state, and its autonomy from social forces – themes prominent in writing about Indonesia during the New Order – have been greatly exaggerated. Instead, the study of the state is increasingly being reinserted into the study of society, and anthropologists, political scientists and others are becoming more alert to the ways in which state actors seek out and collaborate with societal allies, often to such an extent that the boundary dividing state from society may be blurred almost to the point of erasure, especially at the local level.

A strategic-relational approach helps illuminate the problem of illegality and the state in several ways. It can throw light on the ways in which the socially embedded character of the state shapes and impels certain forms of illegality. An example may be drawn from Gerben Nooteboom's study in this book of the relationships between police officers and Madurese migrant entrepreneurs, including ones engaged in illegal activity, in East Kalimantan.

14 The theoretical political science literature on the state is too voluminous to trace here. One of us (Van Klinken) co-authored two introductory chapters tracing its links with writings about the state in Indonesia from the 1950s to the 2000s (both in Van Klinken and Barker 2009). A powerful statement rejecting the concreteness of the state and calling for an ethnographic study of actual state practices in all their fragmentedness is Abrams (1988). Van Klinken owes a debt to Bob Jessop's 'strategic-relational' approach to the study of the state (Jessop 2007). Jessop develops at length a provocative statement by Nicos Poulantzas that 'the state is a social relation', by which he meant that we cannot study the state without having a clear grasp of what we mean by society.

Here we see a complex web of relationships in which state actors not only threaten and exploit, but also depend upon, societal actors. As Nooteboom writes 'The police in Samarinda need to permit a certain level of criminality in order to keep criminality under control.' Police officers who collaborate with petty criminals while tolerating and profiting from certain forms of illegal behaviour can gain access to criminal networks. They need access to obtain the information, resources and agents they need to act against other forms of illegality they consider more serious. Here engagement by state actors in illegality is not so much a sign of venality or of the overbearing power of the state over society as it is of the state's dependence on societal actors. Seeing the state as an arena in which competing forces contend for power and resources also provides a political motive for state actors to engage in activity that can be illegal according to the state's normative rules. An example is drawn from Marcus Mietzner's chapter on illegal funding practices by political parties. We cannot understand this behaviour simply through a marketist lens, for there must be easier and less risky ways of making quick money than running a public election campaign. Nor will cultural deference to patrons do as an explanation, for frequently the relationships are quite businesslike. And, of course, by disaggregating the state into smaller units that often compete against each other, the strategic-relational approach avoids the statist trap of assuming the state is a single 'leviathan'.

The authors of this book debated these fundamental issues about the state and illegality at two workshops. We did not seek to reach a common view, but some commonalities did emerge. One of these is a certain theoretical ecumenism. Most of us feel the pull of all four approaches discussed above, and we believe all have made durable contributions to our understanding of the problem of the state and illegality. We are not necessarily trying to burst any paradigms, or to create new ones. There is, as we have indicated, a rich tradition of studying the state and illegality in Indonesia, even if it does not always use the same terminology and nomenclature that we use here. We want to contribute to this growing tradition. Before we explain how we hope to do so in conceptual terms, it is necessary to explore the methods contributors to this book used in their research.

Methodological challenges

Illegality is notoriously difficult to study directly. In most situations, illegal activities are either fully or partly hidden. Individuals involved in illegal behaviour typically have strong interests in concealing that involvement, because they fear legal sanction, social opprobrium or both.[15] Their individual interests in concealment are typically reinforced by strong collective codes of silence in institutions and networks involved in the illegal behaviour, codes that can be policed socially, by exclusion from the benefits of illegality or by physical violence. Even where participants know that certain forms of behaviour (petty corruption, for example) are highly unlikely to invite juridical punishment, even a small risk is typically enough to discourage them from breaking their habit of silence to discuss their involvement openly with non-participants. Where the illegal activity in question, such as logging in state forests or unofficial border crossing, is locally socially acceptable or legitimate, and takes place more or less in the public eye, participants can be more willing to talk. But even then they are likely to fear that open acknowledgment to a researcher or journalist might invite the unwelcome attention of outside law enforcement officials. Moreover, illegal behaviours are often conducted in a highly coded language that can be next to impossible for non-initiates to penetrate.

In general, secretiveness increases in tandem with both the illicitness and illegality of the behaviour in question, and with the risk and magnitude of punishment. It is easier to research petty corruption than grand corruption, and easier to research, say, the smuggling of contraband where it is everyday and visible (for example, ordinary trade goods on the Thai-Burma border) than where it is highly secretive (for example, the smuggling of narcotics through major airports). Finally, and of particular concern for this book, illegality involving state officials is almost by definition difficult to research because, as already indicated, modern bureaucratic states are based on the principle, or at least the fiction, that they are rule-bound and disciplined organizations. Hence, no matter how ubiquitously state officials engage in corrupt and other illegal practices, they are typically unwilling to acknowledge them publicly.

As a result of this combination of circumstances, directly researching illegality can be both difficult and risky for researchers and those who help them. Investigative journalists and other researchers who have looked into organized crime in some countries have been killed; some Indonesian journalists who have dug too deeply into corruption cases have suffered the same fate. Many others have been subject to non-fatal forms of violence, or threats of it. The more common problem is that of information failure: the frustrating experience of coming up against a blank wall, of knowing that a particular form of illegal behaviour is everywhere around you, but learning that nobody will even acknowledge its existence in anything but the most platitudinous terms. Little wonder, therefore, that so much literature on illegality ends up relying on data produced by law enforcement agencies or on anonymous

15 For interesting comparative discussions of the practical, ethical and methodological challenges of researching criminality, see Ferrell and Hamm (1998).

surveys and other forms of arms-length research.

How did the contributors to this volume try to get around these problems? What kinds of methods did we use and what lessons might be drawn from our approaches to benefit scholars studying similar phenomena in different countries and contexts? Answers to these questions begin with three observations.

The first observation is that many of the contributors to this volume did not become interested in the topic of illegality by design. Instead, many of us were drawn into it as a by-product of other research on a highly diverse range of subject matters ranging from party system institutionalization to migrant risk-taking cultures, from armed insurgency to local politics. That so many of us ended up becoming concerned with illegality is itself indicative of the centrality of this phenomenon, especially corruption, in Indonesia's economic, social and political structures.

But this background also had implications for the methods that many of us used in researching illegality. In most of the cases in this book where the interest in illegality arose as part of a wider research agenda, researchers were able to use the local or sectoral knowledge, expertise and contacts they had built up over long periods to gradually learn more about illegality. Some contributors had spent long periods getting to know informants from particular locations and/or sectors: Madurese brick makers in East Kalimantan (Nooteboom), former guerilla fighters in Aceh (Aspinall), political party leaders in Jakarta (Mietzner), senior officials in state security bodies (Honna) and so on. We were, in other words, able to draw on relations of familiarity and trust built up over long periods of fieldwork – sometimes totaling years – to slowly learn more about the illegal behaviours that are the subject of this book. If expressed schematically, we might say that our research typically progressed through phases: first, becoming generally familiar with a topic area, research site and set of actors; next, learning about the 'public transcript' (Scott 1985) of legally sanctioned activity concerning that topic; then, gradually picking up second-hand stories and rumours about the shadow world of corruption and illegality; and, finally, being able to discuss under-the-table details of such illegal behaviours directly with participants.

In one respect, therefore, this book is founded on what is typically called an area studies approach. Contributors to the book include persons trained in various disciplines (anthropology, economics, political science, sociology and history), but those of us from outside Indonesia have all spent long periods of training on the language, history, culture and politics of the country, and have spent years acquiring the research skills needed to conduct fieldwork there. The techniques most of the contributors used to research their chapters will be familiar to area specialist scholars with a variety of disciplinary backgrounds: long immersion in field sites, participant observation, semi-structured interviews, intensive utilization of local press reports, and so on.

As one of our contributors, Howard Dick, put it, our research often involved asking the basic question of all fieldwork: 'What do people do and why do they do it?' Curiosity about the social, economic and political interactions we witnessed around us prompted us to inquire into illegal practices, but doing so would have been impossible without knowledge of local culture, politics and language. Such knowledge was essential for at least beginning to understand the often subtle signals associated with illegal behaviour and to begin to penetrate the largely hidden world of illegality.

In some respects, therefore, this book may be read as a defence of area studies approaches, or at least as a demonstration of what theoretically informed area studies scholarship can produce. Indeed, we suspect that the skills that area studies training provides are essential for collecting data on, understanding, and theorizing about the sorts of behaviours discussed in this book. This comment applies not only to Indonesia: the inter-penetration of state and illegality discussed in this book is not just an Indonesian phenomenon but is strikingly similar to patterns described by scholars working in diverse settings in Africa, Latin America, Asia, Eastern Europe and the former Soviet states, and in parts of the developed world. The 'shadow state' is close to being a universal phenomenon, at least in the developing world (Wilson and Lindsey 2009). New understandings of the state that take into account this reality are almost exclusively products of area studies scholarship. Without the insights that grew from applying our area studies skills, we would still be constrained by highly stylized and abstract notions of the state that bear little resemblance to the state's actual workings.

A second observation is that, for most of us, conducting fieldwork research on illegal practices also meant adopting a considered approach to our informants, whereby we guaranteed their anonymity and safety and avoided judging them personally for participating in the activities we set out to study. Scholars who have researched similar topics in other places have been required to adopt a similar posture. Giorgio Blundo and Olivier de Sardan (2006:9), for example, in the introduction to their study on the everyday politics of corruption in Africa note that 'it was important that, *as researchers,* we refrained as far as possible from all moral condemnation and normative judgment throughout the duration of the study'. This posture derives from practical considerations flowing from the imperative that, if we are to understand it, corruption and state illegality 'has to be studied from the viewpoint of the participants' (Olivier de Sardan 1999:25). Research on illegality most often fails because informants seek to maintain secrecy. Both in order to overcome this challenge and for ethical reasons we were required to ensure confidentiality of sources to ensure that none of our informants or the persons close to them were harmed directly or indirectly because they assisted our research. This could at times lead to uncomfortable situations for the researcher. By not stating disapproval of illegal acts, the informant might assume the researcher approves of them or might even wish to participate. Thus, one of our number (Ian Wilson) was once unexpectedly asked to address a group of about 200 petty gangsters, with police in attendance, to explain why he thought the group was within its rights to demand 'taxes' from businesses. Those present assumed that he would be a public advocate on their behalf.[16]

A third observation about the contributions in this volume is that many of their authors were informed by or made use of what some readers may consider to be a surprisingly large array of material available from public sources, especially from the Indonesian media. Especially since the fall of the Suharto government in 1998 (but even before that), the media have been full of reports about corruption and other impropriety by state officials. Indeed, we might say that exposing corruption has become the major concern of especially the quality print press over the last decade. The pervasiveness of this sort of reporting is itself a product of two contradictory features of illegality (especially corruption) in contemporary Indonesia that have already been remarked upon: its ubiquity, pervasiveness and centrality in virtually all forms of state activity on the one hand, and the social illegitimacy of much of it on the other. This combination of circumstances means, for one thing, that there has been an enormous volume of public reporting on corruption and other illegal behaviour by state officials, even if relatively little of this reporting is deeply investigative, and if there remain many silences and inconsistencies in it. The silences are due in part to what is commonly called the 'envelope culture' in the media itself – so named for the most common method for conveying cash payments to journalists. Yet the envelope culture has not silenced some extremely revealing public reports about corruption. The story of involvement by state intelligence officers in mass-scale counterfeiting near the start of this introduction is one of them. Highly detailed stories abound about bribes and commissions paid by aspiring politicians in the regions to legislators or party officials whom they believed would further their ambitions. Almost all the contributors to this book have learned a great deal about their topics from the Indonesian media and we should acknowledge our debt.

Even with the combination of sources, skills and methods elaborated upon above, the contributors to this volume still faced a set of challenges that we suspect are common to researchers on the state and illegality anywhere in the world. These challenges can constrain the approaches that researchers take to their topics and limit the information they acquire. Some of these limitations are evident in this book, perhaps not so much in what it does contain as in what it does not touch upon.

A first limitation concerns sources. It remains very difficult to conduct

16 Our thanks to Ian Wilson for sharing this experience with us.

research on illegality and the state by obtaining information directly from state officials involved in illegality. Most of the scholars in this book approached their topics from the margins. There were exceptions, but our overall tendency was not to seek or obtain information from state officials involved in illegal activities, but from people who had dealings with them. We spoke with Madurese migrants struggling to establish themselves economically, rather than with the police officers who levy fees on them; with ex-combatants trying to make it in the contracting industry, rather than the government officials they bribe and intimidate; with petty gangsters rather than the police officers with whom they cooperate, and so on. Sometimes we were able to cross-check information from other sources, such as the press and NGO reports. Most respondents naturally show a bias determined by their position in the system of relations in a particular illegal activity, so the ongoing problem is how we can obtain a full picture. Where illegal behaviours are locally legitimate and carried on more or less in full public view, it can be less difficult to access state officials. Thus Michele Ford and Lenore Lyons had greater success in speaking directly with state officials engaged in irregular border crossing in the Riau Islands than did most of the researchers who contributed to this book. By contrast, Ian Wilson chose, for his research on relations between gangsters and police in Jakarta, to interview retired police officers rather than active ones. This technique has also been long used by researchers working on the Indonesian military.

Our preferences are part of a broader pattern. With only a few exceptions, scholars have not been able to observe closely the everyday operations of state officials in such a way as to attain direct insights about their involvement in formally illegal activities. (One notable exception is Joshua Barker, who wrote a PhD dissertation on the police and local security in West Java: Barker 1999a). This is not only because state officials tend to be reticent about such activities, but also because of a wider culture of secrecy in the bureaucracy that makes it difficult to obtain official permission to conduct such research. One participant in the workshop that led up to this volume, but who did not end up contributing a chapter, had achieved the rare feat for a foreign researcher of building close research relationships with police officers in one Indonesian town. He observed that he did not want to make inquiries of them or other informants about police involvement in corruption because he believed that such inquiries would jeopardize his relationships and lead to them cutting off all contact. Another participant (Gerben Nooteboom), whose field research touched directly upon illegal activity by police officers, did not attempt to even make contact with those officers, fearing this would attract unwelcome attention. Many other participants agreed that they deliberately minimized their direct contacts with state officials – especially those from law enforcement and security agencies – because they feared that if their research interests became known the authorities could take action to interrupt or stop their research, or even have them expelled from the country. As a result of such practical difficulties, in Indonesia as elsewhere, we still have a long way to go in understanding what might be called the internal modalities of state officials' involvement in illegal activities, especially the norms and moral codes governing that involvement.

A second limitation concerns the range of topics we address in the book. Certain types of activity remain very difficult to research and are hardly touched upon in this book. One contributor, Ian Wilson, remarked that while he found it possible to observe the daily activities of small-scale gangsters running local protection rackets in Jakarta, as soon as his inquiries began to touch upon the activities of much more secretive, violent and wealthy gangs known to be involved in more highly organized criminal activities such as the narcotics trade, he was immediately warned off in a threatening manner. Petty gangsters themselves also warned him he would end up 'out of his depth'. In his research on contracting activity in post-conflict Aceh, Edward Aspinall found it much easier to obtain information about the activities of relatively poor, low-ranking and unsuccessful ex-combatants than about how their leaders were managing to strike deals with senior government officials. As a result of such difficulties, where high-scale elite corruption or illegality in Indonesia is discussed publicly, the discussion tends to be either highly charged and condemnatory (in the media or advocacy literature) or, in the scholarly literature, rather formal and abstract. Where flesh is put on the bones of such analyses, it is common to rely on a relatively small number of cases that have been exposed by the media or anti-corruption NGOs, or which have been prosecuted. As a result, while we have a relatively clear picture of the ubiquity of corruption in the upper echelons of the state, we often get little more than glimpses of its fine mechanics there or how it is comprehended by the participants. When close studies are made of the lived experiences of corruption and state involvement in illegality (and this book is one of the first concerted efforts to do this for Indonesia), the tendency is to focus on the petty rather than the grand, the everyday rather than the spectacular, the local rather than the national. Thus, this book contains discussions of small-scale street gangsters, but nothing on high-level organized crime; we have a chapter about the important topic of massive illegal border crossing by people, but not about the smuggling of narcotics; we learn about how low-ranking police officers interact with impoverished migrants in Kalimantan, but not how their most senior leaders exchange fees and favours with politicians in Jakarta.

All of this leads to an obvious point: we hope that this book will be a spur for future research efforts to comprehend more fully the relationship of state and illegality in Indonesia. We believe that we have only begun to scratch the surface of many of the most intriguing and perplexing questions in the field. Key among them are those regarding the way state involvement in illegality is understood and legitimated by participants, how it is regulated by them, what systems of norms govern it, and how participants themselves draw the line between tolerated and excessive illegality.

The approach of this book

Most of the authors gathered in this volume are university academics (one is a member of an important Indonesian anti-corruption organization). None are directly engaged in making policy or advising government. This gives us less access to the inner workings of government, but arguably a sharper eye for the unexpected twists and ironies that policy inevitably brings about. The academics all consider themselves social scientists – historians, anthropologists, political scientists, and economists – and at the same time area specialists. No doubt with some of the conceit that comes from enjoying what we do, we feel we have something to contribute that the well-funded multilateral agencies are missing.

The following pages sets out what we consider to be the main messages of this book. The starting point for our project was our agreement that illegal activities by state officials are best understood, not as an aberration external to the normal workings of the state, but as somehow part of its very logic. Others had explored this line of reasoning before us (Heyman 1999), but not for Indonesia. It implied a research agenda of looking for contexts and processes that cut across the state-society divide. Doing that led us to fresh insights, and thence to the thematic chapter division.

The book begins with a set of essays which contextualize the problem of illegality and the state historically and theoretically. Robert Cribb begins by arguing that a central problem in Indonesia is not that law does not matter, but that there is an elaborate 'system of exemptions' that means it does not apply to many persons, especially state officials. 'Indonesia is not a lawless society, but rather one in which law is unevenly implemented', he writes. Understanding this system, he argues, requires paying attention to three factors – state weakness, the disjuncture between law and popular moral values, and the fragility of a tradition of social contract. Each of these he traces back to the colonial era and the early decades of Indonesian independence when state criminality was necessary to ensure the state's survival. Next, we have an analysis that contextualizes the current period of pervasive state corruption by looking back to the three decades of President Suharto's New Order regime (1966-1998). In this period, argues Ross H. McLeod, Suharto constructed a 'franchise system [...] the fundamental purpose of which was to use the coercive power of government privately to tax the general public and redistribute the revenue to a small elite'. The 'franchisees' in the system – virtually all state officials – were allowed to exploit the economic opportunities their positions brought for their own benefit, but they also had to make payments to the 'franchisor' to secure their positions in the system. A key to the system's resilience was the low formal remuneration paid to civil servants, making them permanently dependent on the system of private taxation in which they participated, and in a state of permanent political dependence on their superiors and, ultimately, Suharto himself. Howard Dick and Jeremy Mulholland, viewing the state as a 'political marketplace' draw particular attention to the use of slush funds to buy the loyalty of associates, rivals and subordinates within the state. Analysing the chief varieties of such slush funds, they trace the transition from a system under Suharto in which their use was arranged in a hierarchical pattern, to a much more fluid and complex Reformasi pattern of horizontal intra-elite rivalry and competitive party politics. In both periods slush funds play a key role in achieving an 'elite consensus that moderates intra-elite rivalry and the social divisions that would flow from it'.

The second section of the book consists of a set of closely observed case studies on state illegality in various sectors of Indonesian government. Each one of these studies also raises broader conceptual and analytical issues about the relations between state and illegality. The first two essays in this section both illustrate how local regimes of legality/illegality can come into conflict with those imposed from the centre. The first essay, by John F. McCarthy, looks at the vexed topic of 'illegal logging' in Indonesia. He points to a 'mismatch between legal logic and everyday practices' in the management of Indonesia's natural resources. He does this by describing instances in which local people exploit the forest 'more in keeping with local perceptions of justice than the formal law', and instances when, following Indonesia's democratic and decentralizing reforms from the late 1990s, local administrations authorized forestry activities that technically violated existing state laws. Michele Ford and Lenore Lyons illustrate the extent and pervasiveness of the phenomenon of local state illegality as they explore a sprawling but efficient web of migration agents and public servants in the Riau Islands. They cooperate to assist would-be 'illegal' migrants to obtain 'real but fake' documents that help them to cross the international border to Singapore and Malaysia to find employment. This system of illegality is understood by its participants not as something exploitative or oppressive, but as a helpful response to local needs as well as the needs of migrants, in the face of an alien and unjust migration regime imposed on them by the national government in Jakarta.

If Ford and Lyons describe state illegality from the perspective of some of the most marginalized and disempowered people in regional Indonesia – undocumented labour migrants – Marcus Mietzner, by contrast, looks at the apex of political power in the regions. He details how aspirants for state office at the local level – candidates in direct elections for local government heads – systematically and flagrantly disregard the legal regime governing campaign finances. They raise money from private donors, to whom they remain indebted after winning office. Gerry van Klinken and Edward Aspinall take up the same theme of the intermeshing of local economic and state power by examining the construction sector, which in Indonesia is the source of income for a hugely politically influential class – contractors – who are dependent upon state largesse for their success. In the Suharto era, relations between state actors and contractors were organized through formal corporatist organizations. Since democratization, contractors have remained tightly bound to the state, but now through complex and informal webs of influence and exchange. The pervasive system of corruption that results has proven resistant to attempts to reform construction and clean up government procurement. J. Danang Widoyoko explores corruption in the education sector. His analysis identifies four levels of corruption, from the Ministry of National Education and the national parliament in Jakarta, down to the principals and teachers at the school level. As with the preceding two chapters, Widoyoko also illustrates the intrinsically political nature of corruption. Everyone, from officials at the Ministry of National Education in the centre down to school principals in the villages, needs extra money. Whether they gain it from the national budget or from fees they illegally levy on students, they use it partly to buy political support and pay off superiors and potential adversaries. The recipients range from obstreperous legislators able to sabotage Ministry policy at the centre, to local bureaucrats able to transfer principals to remote and poor schools. In the last piece in this section, Simon Butt and Tim Lindsey provide a detailed exploration of illegality in the judicial system. Given the central role of the judiciary in upholding legality, this is clearly a crucial case study. Yet the judiciary is itself deeply implicated in illegality in Indonesia. Butt and Lindsey distinguish between 'internal illegality' and 'external illegality'. The former covers illegal actions by judges themselves in the discharge of their judicial functions, typically in the form of deciding cases not on their merits but on the basis of corrupt payments. The latter concerns the judicial endorsement of illegal acts performed by other agents of the state. On the one hand, external illegality may have declined in the post-Suharto period: the judiciary has become more inclined to find that certain actions of state officials are illegal. (Human rights abuses by military officers constitute an important exception.) Internal illegality, on the other hand, is as entrenched and pervasive as ever, with judges fighting hard to resist attempts to impose external accountability mechanisms on them.

Finally, the connection between insecurity and illegality was strong enough that we placed the essays dealing with this problem in a third section of their own. The poverty of the good governance approach to the problem of illegality is nowhere more evident than in its inability to sense the extent to which people's actions are motivated by fear. Conversely, insecurity is central to our political approach to the problem. It is the logical consequence of the internal competition that characterizes the state. Hence, the very marginality and legal tenuousness of many of the business activities engaged in by Madurese migrant entrepreneurs in East Kalimantan is what drives them into the arms of the police as both protectors and exploiters (Nooteboom). The racketeers Ian Wilson describes are not simply entrepreneurs engaged in a benevolent market. They are engaged in a frequently violent struggle for political mastery over territory. Nor does it help to view their activities as evidence that the state is weak. On the contrary, they owe their strength to the superior repressive capacities of their 'backers' within the state apparatus. The irony of predatory violence emanating from the state whose most basic function is to keep citizens safe is a most pressing reason to review mainstream views of the state. The failure of the mainstream discourse on the state can have serious practical consequences. This is evident in Jun Honna's chapter on the international dialogue about transnational crime. The discourse permitted Indonesia's security agency charged with the 'war on drugs' to argue effectively for increased international funding in the name of capacity building, while shielding it from the consequences of the state's own involvement in drug crimes.

The idea in this book was not to cover every conceivable sector or aspect of illegality, but rather to explore patterns that may be common to many sectors. Readers may object that some key sectors – fisheries, for example – have been neglected. Our book also does not deal at length with certain aspects of illegality that are arguably crucial, among them gendered aspects of illegality, and the role of customary law (*adat*) as an alternative source of notions of legality. Nor, as already pointed out, did we seek to achieve a uniform view of the correct meaning of the inter-penetration of the state and illegality. Nevertheless, we think that the volume contributes a breadth of discussion that is rarely found in analyses of state illegality and corruption, suggesting new avenues for future research, and pointing toward new ways of thinking about the topic. The following pages abstract from the essays in this collection what we, the editors, think are among the most important insights into the subject of illegality and the state in Indonesia.

The ubiquity and centrality of illegality to the state

If we hope this book will convey one simple message it is this: illegality by state officials is as central to the way that the state operates in Indonesia as are the formal rules and bureaucratic structures that constitute the state on its surface. It should thus be a central task of scholars to integrate consideration of such illegal practices into the way that we conceive and analyse the Indonesian state. Although, as we have noted, much of the literature on corruption in Indonesia points to its 'entrenched' and 'pervasive' character, too often the discussion remains trapped in a limiting normative framework that takes either positive law or idealized notions of good governance as their starting points. It thus sees corrupt or illegal activities by state officials as aberrations.[17] In reality, if there are pockets in state institutions where formal bureaucratic procedures and legal rules are scrupulously observed, it is these pockets that are the aberrations, not the illegal practices that are so ubiquitous. The levying of illegal taxes on students by school principals who need the money to buy protection or promotions from their supervisors; the collusive networks that determine how government construction contracts are awarded, the cooperative arrangements that local police officers systematically build with local gangsters: these practices are not just an aberration or an undermining of the state, they are the state.[18]

The political character and functions of illegality

Another lesson to be derived from this book is that it is essential to understand illegality by state officials through a political, rather than merely a legal, lens. Political structures and arrangements shape the 'syndromes of corruption' (Johnston 2005) that are experienced in different countries, and Indonesia is no exception. Of course, involvement by state officials in illegal behaviour frequently involves personal enrichment as one of its goals, but making this mundane observation does not get us very far. More importantly, our contributors also show that such illegality almost invariably occurs as part of collective, patterned, organized and collaborative acts, linked to the competition for political power and access to state resources. Understanding illegality in this way is helped by viewing the state less as a bureaucratic machine and more as a field of power characterized by competition and insecurity. Particular instances of illegality by state officials can almost always be viewed as connected to the distribution of material resources and political opportunities. These goods pass up, down and sideways through and along the patron-client networks and alliances that pervade state institutions and that crisscross the boundary between state and society. Some of the contributions in this volume demonstrate this dynamic clearly. The political problem of purchasing internal cohesion in an insecure system riven with competing fac-

17 As already noted, one important exception is Lindsey 2001; see also Lindsey and Dick 2002.

18 The authors would like to thank Ward Berenschot for this formulation.

tions is central to Ross McLeod's evocative essay on the 'Suharto franchise'. In McLeod's analysis, the New Order strongman encouraged officials to 'live off the land' in order to retain their loyalty. Since all of them were guilty of legal transgressions, he could easily threaten to exclude any of them from these perks by waving the rule book. As in a commercial franchise, incumbents were free to use their wits for their own self-advancement, while preserving the trappings of uniformity. In Howard Dick and Jeremy Mulholland's essay on political slush funds, rivalry between elite factions is again the operative principle, with slush funds providing the fuel that powers that rivalry, but also the resources that buy elite cooperation and social peace. Many of the close local case studies in the book also point to the ubiquity of political motives in illegality: petty gangsters act as muscle in electoral and other political conflicts (Wilson, Nooteboom), small-time contractors are drawn into political networks and fund election campaigns if they want to succeed in the construction field (Mietzner, Van Klinken and Aspinall). Indeed it might be possible to argue that the vast majority of illegality by state officials in Indonesia concerns the construction of political networks, specifically involving the purchase of political protection or access from above, or the purchase of political support or acquiescence from below, or to exclude rivals laterally.

There is of course also an exclusionary element and a class dimension to these bureaucratic politics that we should not lose sight of. Those with power to allocate state resources not only distribute them to buy support from above and below, but in doing so, they inevitably block access to actors who lack such privileged access. Those who are not part of the network find it hard to get jobs, their communities receive school buildings and bridges that crumble before their time, and they resent those who do manage to build privileged access. It is precisely for such reasons that condemnation of corruption remains a powerful rallying cry in Indonesian political life. It explains why local anti-corruption groups try to focus their campaigns on increasing community awareness about the effects of corruption and on opening up channels for them to participate more fully in the political process.

The benefits of illegality

Yet awareness of the exclusionary and hierarchical framework that organizes much illegal behaviour by state officials should not blind us to the wider integrative and stabilizing functions that such behaviour may also have. Indeed, one of the revelations that was shared by most participants in the workshops that gave rise to this book was that many of the illegal practices we discussed had aspects that could be described as socially beneficial. Particularly at the lower end of the social ladder, they sometimes seemed essential to the proper functioning of the state and provided benefits even to marginal groups. Sometimes those benefits occur in an exploitative context: the petty collusion between police and small-time entrepreneurs in East Kalimantan that Gerben Nooteboom describes costs the latter 5-15% of their turnover; but it also helps them get around many obstacles that would otherwise impede their activities. Police collaboration with criminals also, as Nooteboom argues, allows the police 'to keep criminality under control', an outcome that arguably has wider social benefits. Collusive favouritism and networks of illegality can provide working solutions to difficult problems. These include how to facilitate the speedy and convenient exit from Indonesia by would-be migrant workers (Ford and Lyons), or how to ensure that volatile and potentially violent ex-combatants are satisfied with the outcome of a peace process by giving them a stake in the existing system (Van Klinken and Aspinall). Indonesia's shadow state may be an alternative to a smoothly functioning, Weberian taxation and policing system. Precisely because it is a state that is based on personal contacts and networks rather than impersonal hierarchies and rules, it is also a system that gets lots of things done.

The blurring of the state-society boundary

The next point follows logically from our earlier one about how much illegal activity by state officials takes place in networks that both pervade the state but also cut across the boundary separating formal state institutions from society. If we view the hidden illegal practices of the state as being as central to its functioning as the bureaucratic structures and procedures that appear in the formal sphere – and we do hold this to be so – and if these practices involve alliances, networks and partnerships that cross the state-society divide, then it follows that our conceptual boundary between state and society begins to break down. At the very least, thinking seriously about state involvement in illegality helps us to think of the state as being socially embedded. As Joel Migdal has written, the presence of behaviours like 'corruption' and 'criminality' by state officials might in fact reflect the influence of alternative moral codes derived from society. This might lead us to re-think our image of the state:

> Various parts or fragments of the state have allied with one another, as well as with groups outside, to further their goals. Those practices and alliances have acted to promote a variety of sets of rules, often quite distinct from those set in the state's own official laws and regulations. These alliances, coalitions, or networks have neutralized the sharp territorial and social boundary that the first portrayal of the state [that is, as a dominant and integrated entity that monopolizes rule-making in a given territory] has acted to establish, as well as the

> sharp demarcation between the state as preeminent rule maker and society as the recipient of those rules. (Migdal 2001:20.)

Certainly, the following pages provide many illustrations of this dynamic at play. In particular, they illustrate just how many state (or at least state-like) functions in Indonesia (for example, the levying of 'taxes', the redistribution of material resources, the maintenance of order and suppression of certain forms of criminality) are carried out not simply by state institutions in their formal, bureaucratic mode, but by networks of state and societal actors, in which both sides are engaging in activities that are formally illegal.

The licitness of illegal activities

Another theme that recurs in the chapters that follow therefore concerns the social legitimacy or 'licitness' (Abraham and Van Schendel 2005) of much of the illegal behaviour that we discuss. Many of our contributors draw attention to what we have already indicated is one of the striking characteristics of illegal behaviour by state officials: its often brazen openness. As Marcus Mietzner puts it in his chapter on elections: 'many politicians, entrepreneurs and rent-seekers simply ignore the law and expect that nobody will notice or care'. In some cases, as in those depicted by Mietzner and by Widoyoko, political apathy on the part of citizens accounts for their passive acceptance even of activity that may be disadvantageous to themselves. They are habituated to a system where everybody knows the formally illegal acts in question are unlikely to be punished. In such cases, state illegality may be illicit, or socially disapproved, yet still ubiquitous and open. However, another explanation is provided in chapters by John McCarthy and by Michele Ford and Lenore Lyons. These explore how societal actors and state officials in Indonesia's regions cooperate to build mutually beneficial local regimes, for example to regulate logging and migration. Both parties view the central government's rules as intrusive and antagonistic to local needs. Both of these accounts portray the central state as a predatory outsider, a hostile leviathan, that does not understand or connect with the real social world at the grassroots, a world in which low-ranking local state officials are immersed, adopting its rules and seeing its interests as their own. In such accounts we see conflict between local regimes of licitness and state legality, as well as conflict between the state's commanding heights at the centre and its socially embedded functionaries at the local level. In yet other chapters licitness differs between insiders and outsiders. Simon Butt and Tim Lindsey point to modes of illegal behaviour in and around the judicial organs where insiders apparently adhere to reasonably well-regulated rules and norms, while outsiders, from whom these behaviours are hidden, regard them disapprovingly and call their practitioners the 'judicial mafia'. In such cases we may perhaps speak of 'insider's licitness'. All of this is to reinforce a point we have already made above, namely, that we hope this book will help to prompt future research into the internal modalities that shape state officials' involvement in illegal activities and, we might add, how those modalities intersect with broader societal norms concerning the licitness of such activities.

Policy implications

Few of the contributors to this book are deeply engaged in the work of making policies or building institutions designed to combat corruption or other forms of illegal activities by state officials. As students of the deep structures, quotidian practices and social embeddedness of state illegality in Indonesia, it is perhaps not surprising that when we turned to the global discourse of good governance that has now become so dominant in shaping the fight against corruption in the country, the overwhelming instinct of most participants in this project was to stress the difficulties that beset that fight and the ironies that occur when the global good governance discourse is translated into practice. Most good governance anti-corruption strategies aim to depoliticize the state, to reduce the 'fight' to a technical operation. Here, cleanliness is to be achieved by separating vested interests from decision-making processes and by empowering oversight and investigatory agencies to enforce the law and police the probity of state officials (see Dick 2002). We feel the pervasiveness of illegality makes this a process fraught with difficulty. Very often the new regulations and institutions simply end up providing new opportunities for predation. No clearer example exists in Indonesia than the decentralization legislation passed in 1999. The legislation was intended to bring government closer to the people and thus make it more accountable, more responsive and, by implication, cleaner. Yet, as is widely known, decentralization also provided manifold new opportunities for local actors to engage in novel forms of predation. A similar example, given in this volume, is reform of school governance in the education sector (Widoyoko). Moving control of funds to the schools simply shifted the locus of corruption to the school level. Reform of government procurement is another case (Van Klinken and Aspinall). By creating a new class of supervisory consultants empowered to ensure that projects proceed on track, it created a new layer of predators in the system. In a slightly different vein, global discourses of good governance and crime prevention, and the funding support they promote, can readily be turned by state actors to their own, often particularistic interests. We see this in Jun Honna's analysis of how Indonesian security agencies seized upon new international discourses about transnational crime to expand their own authority.

Instead of trying to depoliticize corruption and the fight against it, we argue for accepting that both are political processes. The key to progress – even if it is by necessity very slow progress – will be in making politics accountable to a broader public. This requires greater politicization, not less. As Michael Johnston (2005:3) has argued,

> [opposing corruption] is a matter not only of improved public management but of justice. It requires 'deep democratization': not just elections but vigorous contention over real issues among people and groups capable of defending themselves politically, and of reaching settlements sustained by their own lasting interests.

Combating corruption and other forms of illegality thus requires what has been called in another context a transition 'from clientelism to citizenship' (Fox 1994). Such a transformation – still in many respects a distant dream in Indonesia – would require a new form of socially embedded state: one that is embedded not in webs of clientelism and particularistic dependency, but in a politically engaged citizenry.

Theoretical and historical perspectives

ROBERT CRIBB

A system of exemptions

Historicizing state illegality in Indonesia

If Weber had been thinking of law rather than violence when he addressed the University of Munich in 1918, he might well have described the state as 'a human community that (successfully) claims the monopoly of the right to determine what is legal and illegal within a given territory'.[1] Although it is commonplace to say that the power of the state ultimately rests on violence, it might plausibly be argued that the creation and administration of law is more central to the nature of the state even than control of violence. The right to determine what is legal and illegal is a complex attribute, including the right to declare law, the right to investigate (suspected) breaches of the law, the right to determine guilt and the right to punish. Whereas some of these rights may be claimed (successfully) by other sections of society, only the state possesses the full range of these powers over legality and illegality. Indeed, so closely entwined are the concepts of state and law that a state which makes no claim to administer law is probably not to be regarded as a state at all.[2]

Classic conceptions of law interpret this right to determine legality and illegality in terms of the state's presumed capacity to translate the general interests of society into a legal system. According to Williams (1994:11), for instance, crime is:

1 Weber, of course, actually referred to the state's 'monopoly of the legitimate use of physical force'; see Max Weber, 'Politik als Beruf', ('Politics as a vocation'), *Gesammelte politische Schriften* (München, 1921), pp. 396-450. Originally a speech at Munich University, 1918, published in 1919 by Duncker and Humboldt, Munich. http://www2.pfeiffer.edu/~lridener/DSS/Weber/polvoc.html.

I should like to thank Gerry van Klinken, Antje Mißbach and two anonymous readers for their helpful comments on an earlier draft of this chapter.

2 This issue is not a trivial one in the Indonesian context. At various times in Indonesian history, notably during the first weeks of the national revolution in August-September 1945, many groups of people claimed to represent organs of the Indonesian Republic, even though they had no connection with what were then the exceedingly rudimentary institutions of the new state. The argument in this chapter focuses on those periods when the state is powerful enough to grant and to withhold exemptions. A different kind of analytical framework is needed for circumstances in which state power is diffuse and subordinate to other sources of power.

> a wrong to society involving the breach of a legal rule which has criminal consequences attached to it (that is, prosecution by the State in the criminal courts and the possibility of punishment being imposed).

For a rather long time, however, observers have been aware that the law also tends to uphold the social order, falling unevenly on different social groups. Anatole France (1905:87) memorably summed up this insight at the end of the nineteenth century: 'The poor must work [...], in presence of the majestic quality of the law which prohibits the wealthy as well as the poor from sleeping under the bridges, from begging in the streets, and from stealing bread.' The Foucauldian approach takes this insight still further: the law can be seen as an arbitrary tool of authority, important less for its content than for the fact that it is law, to which people are subjected.

Remarkably sparse in the analysis of law, however, has been an appreciation of the role of discretion in determining the social impact of law. Discretion refers to the fact that the implementation of the law never fully follows the letter of the statutes, decrees or whatever other written or oral form the law may take. Rather, the law is always administered selectively, differentially, partially. Discretion on the part of police, prosecutors and judges is an essential part of the humane and effective administration of the law. At very least, discretion avoids clogging the legal system and afflicting the population with prosecution for actions which, although they may technically be illegal, are in fact trivial and not worth the attention of the legal apparatus.[3] At its more creative, it may recognize that the breaker of a law may have been acting under unusual compulsion or that the prospects for rehabilitation would not be served by giving a criminal record to a young offender. Discretion, however, is also a key element in the use of law to uphold or change the social order. In every system, at least some of the decisions about which cases to pursue and which to ignore are made on the basis of social impact – certain individuals and groups who are considered in some way to be socially 'valuable' are protected from the force of the law while others, considered to be less useful or even dangerous, are not.

In every legal system, therefore, there is a gap between written law and the law that is actually applied in society. In Indonesia, this gap appears to be particularly wide. Other chapters in this book suggest the scope of the phenomenon. Politicians and government employees accept bribes, inducements, favours, commissions and kickbacks in a variety of forms in exchange for making decisions that favour one party over others in a dispute, examination or competition. They solicit and receive payment for overlooking regulations, and for providing routine government services, including licences. State

3 In the legal context, the principle is known as de minimis non curat lex (the law is not concerned with trifles).

funds are embezzled directly or are extracted by means of legal or quasi-legal devices such as commissions and uncompetitive pricing. Funds that might otherwise flow to the state are channelled into private pockets. State property and state facilities are used for private purposes. State security forces remain largely immune from prosecution for illegal acts of violence in the past against other citizens. All this illegal activity leads some observers into the impression that law matters little in Indonesia. This is a mistaken impression. The central characteristic of the Indonesian system is that law matters, but only to some people and only in some circumstances. Indonesia is not a lawless society, but rather one in which law is unevenly implemented. The legal system managed by the Indonesian state is above all a system of exemptions.

Understanding this system of exemptions requires attention to a range of underlying features of Indonesian society which work in favour of exempting some people from the full force of the law. These elements are: the weakness of the Indonesian state and its institutions; a mismatch between law and moral values; and the weakness of a sense of social contract in the Indonesian political order. None of these features is in any way inherent to Indonesian societies or cultures, but they are connected with features of Indonesian culture that have been reinforced by historical circumstances. For this reason, they do not lend themselves to simple remedies. In addition, the system of exemptions needs to be understood as a form of economic behaviour which persists not just for historical reasons but because it delivers profitable outcomes. Seeing exemption as an economic device highlights its connections with the current political order and suggests potentially useful remedies.

State weakness

For a complex range of historical, geographical and social reasons, Indonesia lacks the capacity to implement law evenly across the whole of its territory. Lack of state revenue, shortages of personnel, lack of equipment and training, and the social and geographical complexity of the country all make it difficult for Indonesia to carry out that suite of activities – statute drafting, surveillance, record-keeping and coordination, investigation, prosecution and punishment – that normally underpins a modern system of legal order. Laws and regulations are often not drafted with sufficient care so as to be readily implemented, or they may be inconsistent with other laws or regulations. Dutch colonial rule left Indonesia with relatively few trained lawyers and building a strong legal profession was never a high priority after independence. Knowledge of the law is weakly and unevenly spread though society. The police force has historically been understaffed and underfunded. Indonesia's rate of incarceration is 45 per 100,000 of national population, one of the lowest in the world,[4] but this rate reflects a lack of capacity to incarcerate rather than low levels of major crime. During the six decades since independence, moreover, Indonesia has come under domestic and international pressure to expand its repertoire of prohibitions. Colonial Indonesia was a relatively under-governed society, but the years since 1945 have seen the promulgation of laws prohibiting various activities in the name of environmental protection (pollution, toxic waste, endangered species), human rights and morality (trafficking in people, prostitution, extra-marital sex, drugs, gambling, medicines), heritage (protection of antiquities) and citizenship and residence. In addition new opportunities have emerged for criminal activity as a result of the closing of the resource frontier (making the theft of natural resources lucrative in a way that it has not been before). The expansion of welfare and development funding has also created a flow of funds available to be tapped criminally. Every legal system faces problems of capacity, and it typically cuts its losses by deciding not to devote resources to every sector. Over the whole of the period since independence in 1945, however, Indonesia's capacity to administer law has fallen dramatically short of what the law itself would seem to demand. Unevenness in law-keeping across the archipelago has been the consequence.

Law vs moral values

A second reason for the system of exemptions is a sense of mismatch between law and moral values. We see in many other countries that laws implementing values not shared by society are simply ignored. In some cases, the law may go beyond what is considered improper behaviour by the community at large and will thus be disregarded. Offending laws may simply be relics of past times whose values no longer apply. In other cases, thoughtlessly drafted laws arising from hasty over-reaction to a crisis may simply not be able to be implemented in a way that is consistent with social values. Conversely, laws may not go far enough to reflect social values. Then sections of society may take the law into their own hands if they feel that the legal system is failing to address some wrong to society. It is unlikely that there is a greater sense of mismatch between law and moral values in Indonesia than in many countries. Rather, it appears that Indonesians are more willing than many peoples to allow moral values to trump the letter of the law when a conflict becomes apparent.

The principle that law was subject to moral review was embedded into the legal system of independent Indonesia as early as 10 October 1945, when

4 By contrast, the incarceration rate per 100,000 of national population in Sweden is 82, in The Philippines 108, in Australia 126, in Singapore 350 and in the United States 738 (2006 figures). See Walmsley 2008.

Government Regulation no. 2 provided that laws promulgated in the colonial era would be valid only as far as they were consistent with the Constitution (Linnan 2008:75). Since the Constitution was a brief, often vague, document, this provision meant that the application of law was formally subject to political considerations. Sharp evidence of the gap between law and public morality includes the prevalence of market-place lynchings (*pengeroyokan*) of suspected thieves and Islamist attacks on bars and brothels (Colombijn 2002; Welsh 2008). This sense of mismatch was also evident in the decade-long reluctance to prosecute former President Suharto for his various economic and political crimes on the grounds that he had also made great contributions to the state. There was no doubt in the minds of citizens and opinion-leaders that Suharto had carried out many illegal acts during the course of his presidency, but proponents of leniency argued that his achievements on behalf of the nation ought to be set against these crimes and to render them unworthy of prosecution. In more recent times it has been argued publicly that the Corruption Eradication Commission (Komisi Pemberantasan Korupsi, KPK) should be bridled because its work is hampering the development process. The illegality of the acts that it pursues is not in question, but the proponents of a bridle believe that the application of law ought to be dependent on some external judgement of the likely consequences. We can recognize such arguments as self-serving, of course, but the fact that they can be made publicly indicates that there is in Indonesia a widespread belief that external arguments can trump legality. (Contrast this with the phenomenon, relatively common in the West, of otherwise competent politicians whose careers are ended by some form of misdemeanour unrelated to their overall performance.)[5]

The conviction that moral values ought to prevail in any mismatch between law and moral values probably has its origins in the colonial history of Indonesia. In contrast with most other colonial rulers, the Dutch in Indonesia were slow to move towards a system of universal law. Instead of a single set of statutes applying to all in the colony, they partly preserved, partly constructed a baroquely complex legal system which recognized a multitude of indigenous laws and separate indigenous legal jurisdictions under the broad heading of *adatrecht* (Von Benda-Beckmann and Von Benda-Beckmann 1980). This system had originally been a matter of convenience and parsimony for the Dutch East India Company (Verenigde Oost-Indische Compagnie, VOC); it spared the company the cost of running a legal system which would service all the people within their possessions. Over time, however, it became a matter of strategy: abjuring any idea of a civilizing mission, the Company, and the Dutch colonial state that succeeded it at the end of the eighteenth century, believed in the principle of ruling people as far as possible by their

5 The legal maxim in this case is fiat justitia, ruat coelum (let justice be done, though heaven falls).

own laws and under their own rulers. Most of these laws addressed family, property and religious issues, but the idea of culturally determined law even stretched into criminal law (Cassutto 1927). The existence of these multiple legal systems within the Netherlands Indies undermined the tendency, which universalist legal systems encouraged, to regard the law as an expression of common human moral values. Created by the colonial state for its own purposes, modern law in Indonesia bore its Western origins more obtrusively than did the law in many European colonies. As a consequence, when Indonesian national identity began to assert itself, the legal system lacked the moral authority which would have made obedience to it a natural consequence of citizenship.

The consequences of legal pluralism were exacerbated by the fact that the Dutch colonial administration paid relatively modest attention to administering law to Indonesians. Although the colonial state was vigorous enough in applying legal sanctions to its political enemies, it paid relatively little attention to the role of the law as an arena for arbitration between subjects and still less to its role as a forum within which subjects might obtain redress against the state. In consequence, Indonesians in general lacked day-to-day experience of a Western legal system. The vast majority of Indonesians simply did not feel the statute book, even indirectly, as a direct influence on their lives. This system encouraged the assumption that law should relate to specific local values, rather than to universal principles. It left open a strong sense of the appropriateness of correcting social injustice and unfairness without recourse to law.

When Indonesia achieved independence, therefore, the law was exceptionally weak as an arena for resolving social disputes. Most Indonesians had very little reason to imagine that the law would either punish them for infractions or come to their aid if they were being afflicted. Colonial Indonesia lacked a social class of lawyers and bush lawyers who would have made it their business to know the law and to turn it to their own advantage and to the advantage of their clients. Legal consciousness, in other words, and the penetration of legal skills in society were both weak. The law was distant and ill-defined, moral values were close and familiar. Small wonder that moral values prevailed.

If moral values had been shared, such a situation might naturally have produced a stable social order, but during the closing decades of the colonial era, the legal pluralism that had its roots in the VOC was matched by an increasingly explicit moral pluralism in politics. In the earliest years of the Indonesian nationalist movement, it had seemed to some Indonesian leaders at least that the aspirations of the non-European inhabitants of the archipelago would be satisfied if the Dutch would only treat everyone by the same standard. The 1912 essay by Soewardi Soerjaningrat, 'Als ik eens Nederlander was' ('If I were a Dutchman'), was a rebuke to the colonial hypocrisy which would allow the Dutch in the colony to celebrate the centenary of their own liberation from Napoleonic rule while at the same time suppressing the freedom of colonized peoples (Soewardi Soerjaningrat 1913). Yet its tone implied at least a faint optimism that the Dutch would see the injustice of their ways and would accept a shared political morality with their Indies subjects. During the three decades that followed, however, such hopes were repeatedly dashed, as the colonial authorities adopted strategy after strategy to thwart the growth of nationalist strength.

The colonial authorities defined sedition in broad terms that made much nationalist activity illegal, and the political style of the figures who were to lead Indonesia after independence was shaped by the reasonable assumption that laws might need to be broken to achieve results. More specifically, one of the most important tools of Dutch political repression in the colony was a formalized system of executive discretion known as the extraordinary powers (*'exorbitante rechten'*) of the Governor-General to remove any European from the colony and to impose internal exile on any indigenous colonial subject. These powers dated from the nineteenth century and were explicitly intended to address the difficulty and expense of prosecuting political opponents of the colonial order. Initially they were employed against insubordinate local rulers and rebellious Islamic leaders, but in the twentieth century they became the device by which the colonial government exiled hundreds of communists to the Boven Digul settlement in New Guinea following the 1926-1927 communist uprisings, and by which the most prominent nationalist leaders – Sukarno, Hatta and Syahrir – were consigned to isolated corners of the archipelago for the last decade of the colonial era. This assumption was all the more deeply embedded by the armed struggle for independence in the 1940s. In the four-year tangled political and military struggle to secure independence that followed the foundation of the Indonesian Republic in 1945, nationalists operating in territories occupied by the Dutch routinely and unselfconsciously characterized their work as not legal (*'tidak legaal'*), as indeed the Dutch resistance to Nazi rule in the occupied Netherlands had called itself the legality (*illegaliteit*). Legality and illegality were thus political categories, not deeper moral ones. The experience of nationalist struggle and independence war thus helped to embed assumptions that legitimized a high degree of discretion in implementing laws.

Weakness of the social contract

A third reason for the system of exemptions has been the weakness of ideas of social contract in Indonesia. At the heart of this concept is the idea that the sovereign people delegate to the state the right to govern in exchange for good government. Although we should not suppose the social contract really underpinned the relationship between state and society in the West, the rhetoric and imagery of the contract was a powerful element in the emergence of state legitimacy in the West. In particular, it encouraged a discourse of government responsibility to the people which included a moral responsibility to behave properly in positions of authority. The social contract also replaced the notion that the ruler owned the state with the more modest notion that the ruler was entitled to proper recompense and respect for the task of governing; the very term 'contract' implied an economic dimension to the relationship. The Netherlands Indies of the nineteenth century, however, was a direct heir to the Dutch East Indies Company in its insistence that the sole purpose of the colony was profit. The open description of the colony as a region of profit (*wingewest*) persisted until the introduction of the Ethical Policy at the beginning of the twentieth century. There was virtually nothing in the idiom of colonial rule before the twentieth century that seriously suggested the colonial state's responsibility for the welfare of those it ruled.[6]

The colonial state's lack of quasi-contractual responsibility to its subjects was reinforced by its reliance on indigenous aristocratic elites as the formal source of political legitimacy for colonial rule. This reliance rested in turn on the convenient fiction that the indigenous peoples of the archipelago were less advanced than their European masters. They were scattered, so it was said, at various points on the scale of human development, from Stone Age to Mediaeval, but all these stages were located conveniently before the era which had led in European history to the emergence of the social contract idea. This is not to say that pre-colonial polities in the Indonesian archipelago lacked any notion of the rulers' responsibility to his (or occasionally her) subjects. Rather, such responsibility was conceived principally in terms of personal, patrimonial bonds, with indigenous aristocrats offering protection and favour in exchange for support and material tribute. But such benevolence was imagined in terms of the individual character of a particular ruler, rather than in the abstract terms of a social contract. Within the already lightly administered legal order of the Netherlands Indies, therefore, the colonial authorities were consistently indulgent towards the patrimonial privilege of indigenous aristocratic elites. They interpreted the patrimonial system as permitting traditional rulers considerable license to treat their subjects as they wished, as long as they did not exceed some indefinite, but always rather high, threshold of barbarity, greed or incompetence. The colonial native district chiefs (*demang, bupati*) and other indigenous office-holders of the regions did not enjoy a formal immunity from prosecution or litigation, but in practice they were brought to court only in the most extreme of cases.

6 Through much of the nineteenth century, there were strong criticisms of colonial rule from Dutch observers who did subscribe in one way or another to the notion of a social contract. Their criticisms, however, had no serious influence on government policy.

It is true that the Ethical Policy, announced by the Netherlands government at the opening of the twentieth century, had many of the characteristics of a social contract view of politics. Indeed, the essay that stood most clearly for the ethical approach in colonial policy was entitled 'A debt of honour' (Van Deventer 1899:205), implying precisely the kind of contractual relationship that was presumed to exist in Western polities. The Ethical Policy, however, was short-lived, undermined by the Depression and by its own inflated expectations, and its intellectual legacy was weak. In consequence, by the end of colonial rule in 1942, Indonesia had experienced only the early stages of the inevitable collision between traditional ideas of patrimonial government and modern universal law. In patrimonial government, there was no presumption of equality between citizens or subjects and a pronounced blurring, by contrast, of the distinction between public office and private interest that modern societies identify as corrupt. This blurring was most pronounced in the regions of the Netherlands Indies that were under indirect rule, but it applied also within the indigenous section of the Binnenlands Bestuur, the central organ of the colonial administration. It should be emphasized that the colonial system did not leave Indonesians tolerant of corruption as such, but rather that it left intact the cultural assumptions of privilege which led to corruption. The working out of the contradiction between assumptions of privilege and probity, which no society resolves quickly or easily, had barely begun when Indonesia achieved independence.

Villains and Heroes

The three sections above argue that the Indonesian state has been institutionally and politically weak, primarily for historical reasons, when it comes to consistently implementing the law. The state has been unable to marshal the government apparatus needed to implement law effectively, thus leaving serious gaps in the rule of law. The state has lacked unambiguous popular legitimacy to apply written law because the colonial tradition of legal pluralism, in combination with the legal expediency of the anti-colonial struggle, hampered the emergence of a sense of the universal moral value of law. And the colonial order failed to make a serious start with combating patrimonial assumptions about government, with the result that political values indirectly conducive to corruption, exemption from punishment and other forms of special treatment have tended to persist.

These arguments accord with the conventional view that the state, as the institution which creates law and defines crime, has a natural interest in implementing law and combating crime. In this view, a state's failure to do so is necessarily a consequence of weakness. The description of such weakness typically refers both to structural weakness of the kind suggested above and to the role of what are commonly called 'rogue elements' (*oknum*[7]), individuals and groups who calculatingly exploit state weakness. The conventional view makes it almost impossible to imaging the state committing acts which it defines as criminal (unless the state as a whole has become a 'rogue state'). It provides no framework for analysing the systematic complicity of the state in illegal or criminal activity.

In recent times, Timothy Lindsey has made an important contribution to understanding this issue with his coining of the term '*preman* state' to characterize the Indonesian state. *Preman* is one of the common terms for Indonesia's vigorous community of (semi-)criminal toughs (Lindsey 2001, 2006). Lindsey's central proposition resembles parts of the argument set out earlier. He suggests that Indonesia missed out on the political presumptions surrounding the social contract and that the apparatus of state is a tool for the enrichment of power holders. This analysis is influenced by Lindsey's lawyerly instinct to look at the Indonesian Constitution to discern the essential character of the state. In examining that document, and the intellectual environment which produced it, he came to the disturbing conclusion that the basic document which is supposed to determine Indonesian governance demonstrates no real interest in the state's role as an arbiter between citizens, in other words, no real interest in keeping social order except as it relates to the state's own interests. The legitimacy which the state might have obtained by providing social order was, in his view, replaced by an ideological claim to state legitimacy as the embodiment of national identity and the popular will. In other words, the Indonesian state came into being with the presumption that it could by definition do no wrong.

The pioneers of national independence, therefore, paid little or no attention to creating a court system which might stand up for individuals against the state. This neglect had the consequence that the court system was unable to prevent a massive recruitment of state institutions to private purposes. In Lindsey's view, the whole of government in Indonesia came to resemble the territory of a *preman*, with officials collecting rent or tribute for whatever activity passed through their domain and enjoying something close to legal impunity while doing so.

Although Lindsey's argument suggests an important mechanism by which corporatist ideology could lead to self-serving individualism on a vast

7 The term *oknum* has a curious etymology. *Uqnum* is a Christian Arabic term originally used to translate the Greek '*hypostasis*', a term referring to the separate characters of the three elements in the Christian trinity. It does not appear in any recognizable form in the Malay Concordance Project (http://mcp.anu.edu.au/Q/mcp.html), which indexes most early Malay language texts; Indonesian-English dictionaries of the 1960s translate it innocuously as 'person', but by the 1980s it acquired an increasingly negative connotation and was used to refer only to people with bad intentions.

scale, his analysis remains broadly within the 'rogue elements/rogue state' framework. Because Lindsey's analysis rests on a broad characterization of the ideas underlying the Indonesian state, it implies a sweeping negative judgement of the Indonesia venture. It also implies a basically heroic solution. Indonesia will be redeemed, if that is possible, by individuals who are able to construct a legal system and a set of political assumptions that will shift the balance of power between the individual and the state. It is a tall order.

In portraying a world of (scarce) heroes and (numerous) villains, Lindsey accurately reflects a widespread Indonesian perception of corrupt officials as evil, or at least morally weak. This perception is a common one throughout the world and may be reasonably accurate, at least in its gentler form, but in Indonesia it tends to be paired with a somewhat unrealistic expectation of what it should mean not to be corrupt. The difficult years of nationalist agitation against an entrenched and obdurate colonial government, and the harsh challenges of armed revolution, entrenched a culture of self-sacrifice in Indonesian public life. There were no material rewards for being a nationalist leader in the colonial era. Those who campaigned for their country's independence gave up hope of government employment and faced harassment and exile. During the revolution against the Dutch, many lost all they owned and survived the struggle eating frugally, wearing old clothes, living simply. Those who resisted the Dutch often faced harsh conditions, and risked loss of life or crippling injury in an armed struggle in which they were almost always poorly supplied with weapons and ammunition. Indonesians in this era were capable of great sacrifice for the sake of their nation, and those who sacrificed much were deeply admired by their fellow Indonesians.

These examples of self-sacrifice, together with the absence of a social contract notion of proper reward for high government service, meant that Indonesians have tended to believe that holders of public office ought to serve from conviction and should not expect substantial material rewards for their service. This sentiment is common, of course, in most modern democracies, but it was particularly acute in Indonesia because the independence struggle had set such high standards of self-sacrifice. There was no attempt in post-revolutionary Indonesia, therefore, to set salaries for politicians or senior officials at a level that would enable them to maintain an elite lifestyle without engaging in some form of additional, often corrupt, means of income-seeking. These perceptions have led to an assumption that all that is needed to improve the situation is heroic behaviour, rather than attention to the structures that promote state criminality. It would be surprising, however, if criminality were only a consequence of a lack of heroic spirit. What, then, are the structures that promote state criminality? Specifically, what is the economic logic of the Indonesian system of exemptions?

State structure and the economic logic of exemption

To explain the economic logic of exemption, it is necessary to depart from the main conventional views of crime. The modern criminological understanding rests uneasily on two different paradigms. One is basically microeconomic: it sees each crime as an act carried out on the basis of a cost-benefit analysis, in which the key considerations are the likely benefit to be had from the crime, the likelihood of success in relation to effort, the risk of detection and the severity of punishment. Within this paradigm, the key to control of crime is to shift the cost-benefit calculation as far as possible against committing a contemplated crime. This shift is predicted to be achieved by enhancing prevention (through surveillance and physical barriers), by detection (through police work, forensics and the court system) and by deterrence (through punishment). The second paradigm is that crimes are committed by the 'bad, sad and mad', in other words by those who for some reason fit poorly with society. Such people commit crimes not out of any intention to profit but out of some flaw in their nature. The remedy for crime that this paradigm proposes is either reform (redemptive punishment, changes in the social environment that stimulates crime) or removal (normally execution, exile or incarceration, occasionally mutilation so as to make the criminal physically incapable of repeating his or her crime). Both these paradigms focus on the individual and therefore do not lead further than the 'rogue elements' argument which we have found wanting in the analysis of state crime.

An alternative approach is to shift the focus from criminals and criminal acts to what might be termed criminal niches, by analogy with the concept of ecological niches which support particular kinds of organism. The decision by a state to prohibit an activity does not make everyone cease to be interested in doing it, but rather raises the threshold for entry into that particular market. In effect, the state creates a criminal niche and paradoxically, by its policing activities, protects the criminals who are clever enough and powerful enough to occupy that niche from competition by other sections of society.

One would normally expect the state to have no involvement in the economic functioning or social life of these criminal niches. Indeed, the very absence of the state sometimes gives these criminal niches a state-like character: without a legitimate state to provide basic government services, criminal bosses themselves sometimes have to set up rudimentary systems to provide basic social services to their followers. There are three circumstances, however, in which a state might become complicit in activities that it has banned.

First, a state may recognize that a stable, segregated regime within an identifiable criminal niche is preferable to chaos. This argument helps explain, for instance, the long-term historical relationship between Chinese states and the warlike nomads beyond the northern frontier. Chinese emperors generally preferred to deal with a single powerful Mongolian khan and a regulated system of protection payments which kept the nomadic hordes on their side of the Great Wall, rather than face a multitude of ambitious war leaders, each tempted to obtain fame and fortune by mounting an expedition against China (Barfield 1989; Waldron 1990).

Second, the state may have some additional use for the organizations which develop to exploit a criminal niche. This reason is particularly relevant in Indonesia, where the state has a long tradition of using criminal organizations as a violent auxiliary to state power. Although there is some evidence that the colonial state connived in violent clashes between the Islamic and communist nationalists in the 1920s in order to deploy violence that the state did not want to take public responsibility for, the long golden age of criminal recruitment to politics began early in the armed revolution against the Dutch, when the new Republican government found the violence of former criminal gangs a valuable element in their campaign for international recognition. Only by recognizing the Indonesian Republic, went the argument, would the international community assuage the anger of the Indonesian masses against colonialism that was leading to mass slaughter and the destruction of property (Cribb 1991). From that time on, there has been a consistent pattern in Indonesian politics of recruiting gangsters to carry out armed actions that the state authorities can deny responsibility for (Ryter 1998; Bourchier 1994; Cribb 1984). Bearing in mind the political value of these gangs, the state has diminished incentive to attempt to smash them.

Even more important, state connivance in illegality, particularly various forms of bribery, has permitted Indonesia to sustain a government apparatus very much larger than could have been supported out of legitimate forms of revenue. This dependence on extra-budgetary funding had its origins in the national revolution, when the new Indonesian Republic was simply unable to access the traditional sources of state revenue that had sustained the Netherlands Indies government. The central government could resort to devices such as the unrestrained printing of currency and the trade in opium (Cribb 1988), but most sections of the government, including the armed forces, depended for their continuing operations on the collection of contributions from local communities and from local business activities. Pressing need in the revolutionary era came to be institutionalized as routine practice in the 1950s, especially in the absence of strong countervailing ideological or social forces, and this routine practice was reinforced again during the economic chaos of the 1960s. Even when the resources boom of the New Order meant that these practices were no longer crucial to the survival of the government apparatus, they were so deeply entrenched that they did not disappear.

Third, the state's prohibition of an activity may be a device to restrict the market. In other words, the state exempts itself and its associates from rules that it applies in other parts of society and uses that exemption as a source of profit. Put slightly differently, the state creates rules, sometimes primarily, sometimes incidentally, as an opportunity for its officials to collect rents (that is, unproductive levies on social activity). The vast system of exemptions – characterized by Lindsey as the *preman* state, by Ross McLeod (in this volume) as the Suharto Franchise and by just about everyone as rampant corruption – is an exercise in economic protectionism. Its enduring seductive power and its great political strength, lie in the competitive advantage that it gives to insiders. The underlying driving force behind the involvement of government officials in illegal activity is the consciousness of the huge advantage that state protection confers on any kind of economic activity. The advantage is the same whether those fields are legal or illegal.

The system of exemptions that still dominates the Indonesian political order is sustained by three distinct but inter-related factors. First is the durable sociocultural environment of state weakness, moral pluralism, and the weakness of the social contract described in the first part of this chapter. This complex factor profoundly undermines the institutional and moral capacity of the Indonesian state to attack illegal state activity. Nonetheless, the significance of this sociocultural heritage is diminishing with the strengthening both of state capacity and of political discourses favouring moral universalism and social responsibility. Second, state criminality is institutionalized. Having been necessary for the survival of the state for much of the Republic's first two decades of existence, the official habit of creating and exploiting exemptions from the law became too deeply entrenched to eradicate with simple measures. This second factor too, however, is diminishing in importance. There is a growing consensus that corruption cannot be defended as a form of subsidiary state finance and serious efforts are being undertaken to reduce it. Only the third factor remains undiminished. The simple advantage that comes from using state power to restrict the marker for private gain is a seductive one throughout the world. Except through enhanced surveillance and punishment, Indonesia is unlikely to be able to reduce this temptation.

ROSS H. McLEOD

Institutionalized public sector corruption

A legacy of the Suharto franchise

Policy analysts in Indonesia are familiar with the formal hierarchy of various kinds of state laws.[1] The Constitution is the highest law of the land, followed in turn by laws enacted by the Indonesian parliament (Dewan Perwakilan Rakyat, DPR), government regulations, presidential decrees, and regional government regulations (Law no. 10/2004 on the Formulation of Laws, Article 7). But in reality another law outranks all of these, despite lacking any means of enforcement: namely, the economic law of supply and demand, according to which the prices of goods and services and assets adjust so as to bring supply into balance with demand. When governments create laws that are in conflict with the law of supply and demand, this inevitably generates illegal behaviour.

Examples abound. Since long ago, governments around the world have legislated against activities such as prostitution, gambling, and the consumption of recreational drugs, but have never succeeded in eliminating them: in each case, demand always finds sources of supply. At various times countries have tried to legislate their exchange rates, only to see a black market emerge in which both buyers and sellers are happy to do business. In the current Indonesian context, regulations that set fuel prices well below world market levels result in outward smuggling of fuels, and regulations that seek to prevent imports of rice result in inward smuggling of that commodity. In the labour market, the fixing of minimum wage rates above free market levels results in bribery of labour inspectors to turn a blind eye to infringements. In short, laws that attempt in some way to maintain prices different from those that would result from the unfettered interaction of supply and demand are virtually guaranteed to result in behaviour that is illegal in terms of those laws.

This same principle applies in the case of laws and regulations that determine the basic salaries of civil servants. The relevant law (Law no. 43/1999 on the Civil Service, Article 7) states simply that civil servants 'have the right to

1 This chapter draws heavily on McLeod 2008a. Useful feedback on this earlier paper from participants in the workshop on which this volume is based is gratefully acknowledged.

Figure 1. Managerial level remuneration in public and private sectors

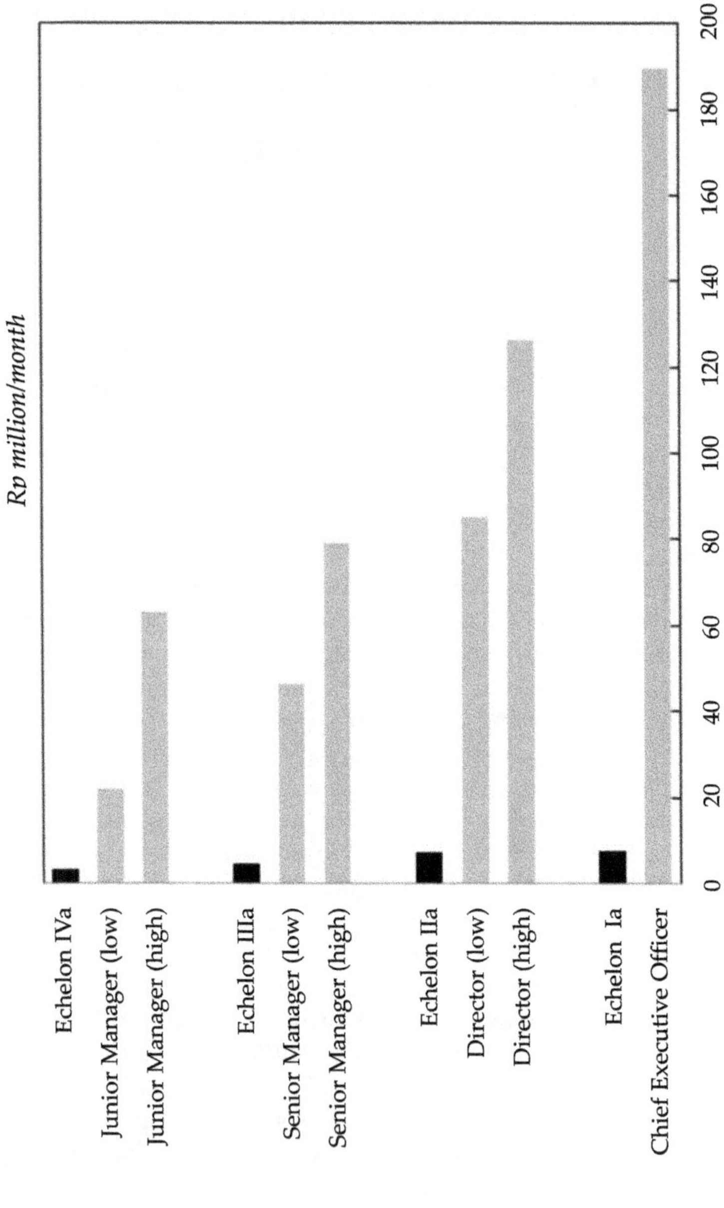

Note: The black bars are for the civil service; grey bars are for the private sector.
Source: Private sector remuneration data were taken from a report in SWA Magazine, 15-28 February 2007, of a survey by the Hay Group.

a fair and reasonable salary commensurate with their work and responsibilities'. While this aspect of the law cannot be faulted, the actual basic salaries set out in the related government regulations are deeply in conflict with the law of supply and demand. The individuals who comprise the civil service (and indeed the entire public sector workforce) supply services in return for remuneration, the 'fair and reasonable' level of which is indicated by the interaction of supply and demand in the private sector.[2] It can be expected that public sector salaries will be somewhat lower because of the much higher degree of job security, the promise of a pension after retirement, and the provision of a range of fringe benefits – not to mention the willingness of some individuals to sacrifice self interest in the service of the nation. The size of this gap in Indonesia, however, particularly at higher levels of management, vastly exceeds any realistic estimate of what is reasonable, as we shall see.

Similar to other cases in which state law conflicts with economic law, the consequence here is that public sector employees are bound to devote a significant part of their energies to finding ways to make their total incomes broadly comparable with what otherwise would be determined by the forces of supply and demand. Indeed, over the course of several decades, the civil service and other parts of the public sector have developed a variety of mechanisms to minimize the gap between private and public sector remuneration. In the specific case of the civil service, the most obvious of these is the proliferation of allowances (*tunjangan*) of various kinds. These include family allowances, rice allowances, structural allowances (for holders of managerial positions), functional allowances (for employees with certain professional skills), and so on; there is even an allowance for civil servants who for whatever reason do not receive structural or functional allowances (Presidential Regulation no. 12/2006). The purpose of all these allowances is to bring total remuneration levels closer to those of individuals in the private sector with similar qualifications and experience.

This effort still falls well short of what is required for higher level officials, however, even though the sum total of allowances far exceeds their basic salaries. Figure 1 compares managerial level remuneration in Indonesia's public and private sectors. The public sector data refer to the totals of basic salaries plus structural allowances at the senior upper levels of Echelons I-IV, which are assumed to be roughly equivalent to Chief Executive Officers, Directors, Senior Managers and Junior Managers, respectively, in the private sector. It can be seen that the gaps are enormous – and increasingly so, the higher the level of management responsibility. In other words, private sector salaries have a high degree of progressivity with respect to increasing levels of re-

2 The elucidation of the law interprets 'fair and reasonable' salary levels as those that avoid a gap between the welfare of public and private sector employees.

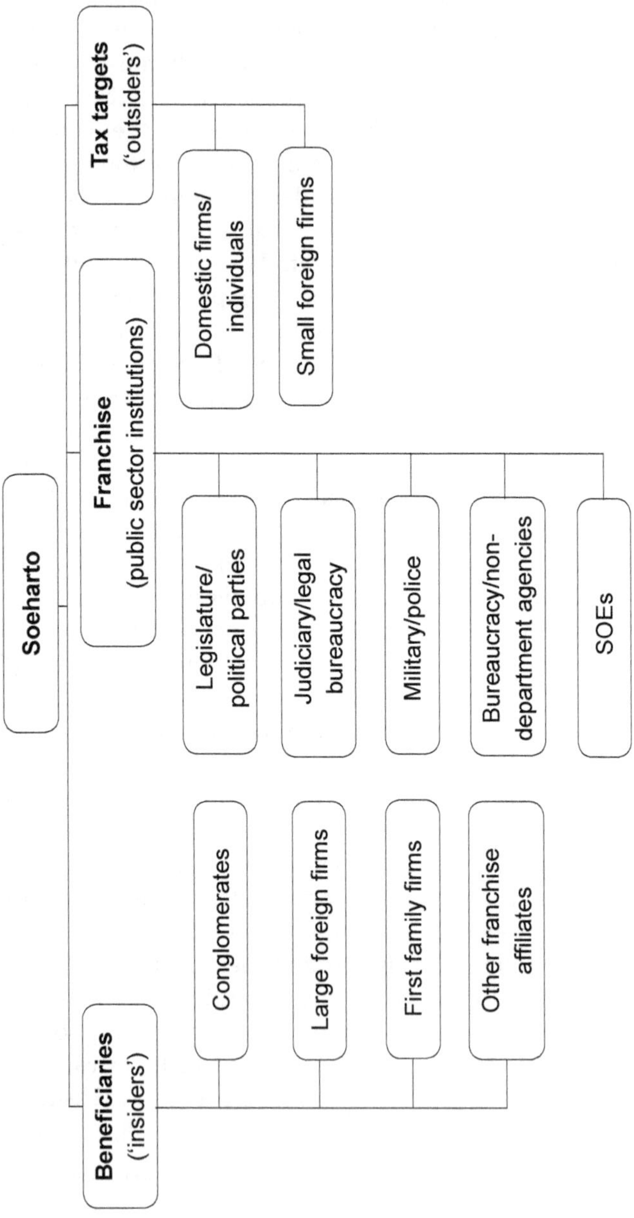

Figure 2. Suharto's franchise system

sponsibility, whereas the civil service structure is very flat by comparison.[3]

When the overall package of basic salary and formal allowances is clearly inferior to that available in the private sector, many government officials can be expected to react to the failure of their employer to pay them a 'fair and reasonable salary commensurate with their work and responsibilities' by finding ways to generate additional income from the opportunities that present themselves – including those that involve corruption. As a consequence, informal – and often illegal – practices have been introduced over the years, the effect of which is to make a public sector career far more attractive than formal remuneration levels would suggest. Many high-level officials exploit these opportunities to the full, becoming extremely wealthy in the process. In short, governments' attempts to defy the law of supply and demand – both in their regulation of private sector activity, and in relation to remuneration of their own employees – result not only in patterns of illegal behaviour in the private sector, but also in the public sector itself.

The foregoing discussion suggests that it is unhelpful to view endemic corruption simply in terms of unprincipled behaviour on the part of the individuals who comprise the public sector workforce. A large proportion of these individuals see nothing wrong in their routine acceptance of additional payments that may be technically illegal, knowing that their formal entitlement to remuneration falls short of their private sector peers' incomes. At the same time, many members of the general public are usually not too concerned by the petty extortion they encounter in their dealings with the public sector. On the contrary, it is by no means unusual for them to make small gifts to officials they deal with from time to time – much like tipping waiters in restaurants – because they know that official remuneration is unrealistically low. Rather than being seen as individual impropriety, corruption is best understood in terms of institutional weakness. More specifically, it is a product of entrenched personnel management practices that ignore market realities. The main focus of the discussion that follows, therefore, is the central role played by these practices in the public sector during the Suharto New Order era (1966-1998).

The Suharto franchise

I argue that former president Suharto moulded the five major components of the public sector into a 'franchise' system (Figure 2), the fundamental purpose of which was to use the coercive power of government privately to tax the gen-

[3] By contrast, remuneration for new tertiary graduates to the civil service is much closer to private sector levels. Here the shortfall is of the order of 50%, but this gap would be partly offset by fringe benefits of various kinds.

eral public and redistribute the revenue to a small elite. Government was not 'of the people, by the people and for the people', but rather 'of the people, by and for the controlling elite'. The discussion that follows provides a detailed interpretation of how this system came to operate under Suharto. It is not intended to suggest that he came to the presidency armed with a full-fledged blueprint for this 'franchise', but rather that it evolved under his direction through a process of trial and error over a period of several years, and building on his own previous experience and observations of aspects of government both under the Dutch colonialists and under former President Sukarno.

The first branch of the franchise encompassed the legislature and the political parties. There were only three parties, one of which was Suharto's election vehicle, Golkar. The other two were tame parties that had been formed by forced amalgamations of a greater number of parties that had existed in years gone by. The second branch of the franchise comprised most of the bureaucracy – that is, most ministries, plus a number of non-department agencies. The third element was the judiciary and the associated legal bureaucracy, such as the Attorney General's office and the Department of Justice. Fourth was the military, which, under Suharto, also included the police.[4] Finally, we come to the numerous state-owned enterprises (SOEs) that were spread over a wide range of sectors of the economy, such as banking and finance, natural resources, transportation, retailing, plantation agriculture and so on.

The core activity of this giant franchise was located in the bureaucracy and, to a lesser extent, the state enterprises. One of the key functions of the bureaucracy was to implement policies that would generate rents on behalf of the beneficiaries of the franchise system. These 'insider' beneficiary firms included the so-called 'conglomerates' (that is, large, diversified business groups owned by cronies of the president, most of which were owned by ethnic Chinese); a number of large foreign firms permitted to operate in Indonesia, almost always in partnership with some local entity favoured by the regime; companies owned by the first family (that is, relatives of the president himself);[5] and companies owned by franchisees (numerous officials at various levels within the public sector institutions) and their families. Rents could be generated in countless ways by the bureaucracy for each of these beneficiary groups. A simple example from the early days of the regime was the granting of exclusive rights to import cloves – the all-important special ingredient in Indonesia's famous clove cigarettes, or *kretek* – to just two firms, one owned by the president's half-brother, Probosutedjo, the other by one of his closest cronies, Liem Sioe Liong (Backman 1999:114). Another type of

4 In recent years, the police force has been separated from the armed forces.

5 This group became increasingly important and significant in the economy as Suharto's children grew to become adults and began to establish businesses of their own, rather than in partnership with their father's cronies.

monopoly was that enjoyed by individuals – often serving or retired military officials – designated as concessionaires with the sole right to undertake logging in large parts of Indonesia's vast rainforests.[6]

Monopolies and concessions of one kind or another were just two of the means by which the beneficiaries of the franchise could be virtually guaranteed to earn very high profits, which were then to be shared with Suharto and his family members, and with highly placed members of the franchise.[7] The state-owned enterprises were also used as a means of enriching the beneficiaries of the franchise system, most obviously the conglomerates and first-family companies. Firms in these groups engaged in business transactions with SOEs at artificially determined prices favourable to themselves. Loans from state banks carried below-market interest rates, and often had the enormous added benefit of not having to be repaid. Fuel could be purchased at below-market prices from the giant state oil company, Pertamina. Airport space and facilities could be rented from state-owned airport operators at below-market rates, again with the added bonus of perhaps indefinitely delayed payment.

The same kind of symbiotic relationship as that which existed between the president and big business was replicated on a smaller scale at ministerial level and below, as well as in regional governments throughout the country. Provincial governors, mayors and heads of districts, subdistricts and even villages, along with their bureaucrats and administrators, were encouraged – indeed, expected – to act in similar manner. When opportunities existed for government officials at any level to use their authority in ways that generated excess profits for favoured businesses, this was precisely what occurred. Obvious examples include awarding overpriced contracts for the construction of public works, government buildings and so on, or for the supply of equipment and materials to government offices, schools and healthcare facilities, and even for catering for official gatherings of one kind or another. Enterprises and banks owned by lower level governments were also used to generate excess profits for favoured private sector businesses.

While insider firms harvested the rents generated for them by the bureaucracy, other 'outsider' private sector firms and individuals served instead as targets for predation. Franchisees within the bureaucracy, the military and police were expected by Suharto to generate additional income via extortion from these firms and individuals, including smaller foreign firms, and to share the proceeds with him. Bureaucratic extortion usually took the form of requiring bribes as a condition for the issue of licences, the delivery of normal

6 Barr 1998:4-6. These were monopolists in the sense that they were simply awarded concessions by government fiat, rather than needing to bid in competition with other firms for the right to log the concession areas.

7 Two important techniques for rent sharing were donations by the insider firms to a number of non-transparent and non-taxable foundations controlled by the regime, and the issue of shares in these firms, free of charge, to family members of the franchisor and franchisees.

public services, and so on, while extortion of a more overtly criminal nature, involving the use or threat of violence, was undertaken by the military,[8] often working through private sector sub-contractors – gangs of thugs known as *preman* (Wilson 2006). The military also generated large amounts of income through involvement in victimless crime – gambling, prostitution and drug trafficking – and through illegal exploitation of the nation's natural resources, such as forests, minerals and fisheries (Rieffel and Pramodharwardani 2007).

The relationship of the public sector with outsiders was parasitic, while that with insiders was symbiotic. But in both cases it was the general public that ended up paying the 'tax'. The prices of products it purchased and of those purchased on its behalf by the government from the insider firms were artificially high; and the prices of goods and services sold to insider firms by state enterprises were artificially low. The payments made by individuals in response to bureaucratic, military and police extortion differed only in that they were quite transparent to the 'taxpayer'.

The 'product' offered by the Suharto franchise was the right to make use of the coercive power of government to impose this 'private taxation' on the general public, whether by means of bureaucratic or conventional extortion, or by artificially boosting the profitability of insider firms at the expense of the general public (and then sharing the excess profit harvest with the beneficiary companies). The revenues collected were for the private benefit of individual members of the franchise and their subordinates and of the 'owner' of the franchise, Suharto. In order to join the franchise or to move to a higher level within it – for example, by being appointed as a provincial governor or district head, or to a position of authority in one of the ministries, or to a court in one of the main commercial centres, or to a management position in one of the state enterprises – the individual was required to make a payment in some form, directly or indirectly (through higher level franchisees) to the franchisor. This can best be considered as the upfront payment of a share of revenues expected to be received in the future by virtue of the exercise of the power to extort individuals and firms, or to generate and share in rents harvested by insider firms.[9]

8 Suharto himself had previously been involved in such activity, and 'was dismissed from his position as commander of the Diponegoro Division in Central Java in October 1959 for demanding money from local businesses' (Rieffel and Pramodharwardani 2007:31).

9 Note that whereas a large part of the early public choice literature (see, for example, Buchanan and Tullock 1962; Krueger 1974; Posner 1974) focuses on 'rent-seeking', the emphasis here is on 'rent generation and harvesting'.

Explaining success

By any measure, the Suharto franchise was spectacularly successful in its objective of generating wealth for its members and cronies. Pre-crisis estimates of the net worth of the Suharto family run to many billions of dollars, while cronies such as Liem Sioe Liong became among the richest individuals in Asia. Countless high-level bureaucrats, military officials, state enterprise managers and judges became fabulously wealthy relative to their miserably small official salaries. One of the keys to success was the fact that the regime was able to maintain a very high average annual rate of economic growth (well over 7% in real terms) over some three decades; very few countries in the world are able to boast a similar achievement. Of course, the regime collapsed in fairly spectacular fashion during the Asian financial crisis in 1998, and the economy plunged into a very deep recession. But although economic output fell by 13% in that year, conditions were able to be stabilized quite quickly after the regime change, and by 2000 the economy had returned to growth at annual rates of around 5%. Even taking into account this major setback, Suharto left Indonesia's economy, and most of its people, considerably better off than they had been when he first came to power, notwithstanding the large-scale redistribution of income from the general public to the elite.

Elsewhere I have argued that the important distinction between Suharto and most other developing country dictators is that he had an implicit understanding of the logic behind the so-called 'Laffer curve': that maximizing tax revenue (whether public or private tax) involves keeping the rate of taxation modest, since high tax rates have the effect of encouraging tax avoidance and evasion, or even driving the taxed activity out of existence (McLeod 2000:105-6). The Suharto franchise owed its success to a strategy of imposing private taxation at relatively low rates on a very wide tax base – effectively the entire economy and its supporting natural resources. In other words, most kinds of economic activity were taxed in some way, but relatively lightly, so as not to destroy incentives for their continued expansion. The contrast with highly destructive dictatorial regimes such as those in developing countries like Nigeria and Zimbabwe, where private taxation was levied at high rates that took no account of their longer term implications, could not be more stark.

Since the effectiveness of any organization depends on the behaviour of the individuals that comprise it, Suharto's principal concern as 'owner' of the franchise was to create a set of incentives for individuals within it that would guarantee its success. An important concern of this chapter is to elaborate the nature of these incentives.

As is the case with commercial franchises in the world of business, the basic incentive to high performance on the part of franchisees is the monetary return this brings. Countless individuals were able to achieve huge increases in their net worth during their working careers by virtue of their success as Suharto franchisees. The strong financial incentives they faced are clearly reflected in the fact that there have always been numerous applicants for positions in the civil service and the military relative to the number of such positions available at any time, and that individuals have always been willing to make under-the-counter payments to the relevant 'gatekeepers' to secure such positions, or to secure promotions and transfers to more lucrative positions once inside the system (Kristiansen and Ramli 2006).

Another similarity with ordinary business franchises was the existence of a process of 'natural selection' that contributed to overall success. Individual performance relative to the objectives of the franchise was constantly monitored, and franchisees were continuously assigned and reassigned to positions that reflected their performance. The less successful franchisees found themselves shifted sideways as they were replaced by others willing to bid more for their positions, or who had persuaded officials at higher levels that they were capable of superior performance – and therefore of making greater financial and other contributions to the franchise – than those of the incumbents.

Public sector employees as threats to the regime

The Suharto era version of the Law on the Civil Service (no. 8/1974) required individuals employed in the bureaucracy to sacrifice their own interests in the service of the state and their fellow citizens (Article 3). In reality, it seems unlikely that the prospect of a lifetime of self-sacrifice would have held much appeal to most public sector employees, who presumably hoped simply to earn a reasonable day's pay from an honest day's work – just like those who took up private sector employment. It also seems unlikely that public sector employees would have been happy with the notion of government as an instrument for redistributing income to the elite, however. One of the key problems Suharto faced, therefore, was to ensure that civil servants would at least acquiesce in the face of common knowledge as to what the franchise was about, and certainly not actively oppose it.

A key part of the solution to the problem of ensuring loyalty to the franchise can be seen in Suharto's approach to determining the structure of employee remuneration.[10] The 1974 Law required that salaries be determined bearing in mind the financial capacity of the state (Elucidation, Article 7), which provided a pretext for keeping them low. In fact, if they had been set at levels comparable with those in the private sector, the public sector could

[10] For earlier discussions of the nature, structure and consequences of public sector employee remuneration, see for example, Smith 1975; Gray 1979; and Clark and Oey-Gardiner 1991.

have been staffed perfectly adequately for the purpose of undertaking what are commonly regarded as the legitimate responsibilities of government.[11] However, this would surely have resulted in the recruitment of large numbers of individuals who would have baulked at the abuse of the powers of government that characterized the Suharto regime. The franchise could hardly have been successful under such conditions.

Instead, the approach was to maintain a compensation structure that provided market-comparable incomes at the lower levels of the civil service (where opportunities for supplementing one's income were limited), but which kept earnings increasingly far below those for similarly qualified and experienced individuals in the private sector at the higher levels (where such opportunities were widespread). Thus, as we have already noted, the remuneration structure was greatly compressed: ratios of high-level to low-level incomes were much smaller than in large private sector organizations.

At first glance, this would appear to have made a career in the civil service thoroughly unattractive, except perhaps for those who did not aspire to promotions significantly beyond the lower ranks; and yet there were always far more applicants for civil service positions than there were jobs available. To some extent this could be explained by applicants having unrealistic perceptions as to the possibility of being recruited despite their limited educational achievements. The prospect of lifetime employment, a government pension beyond that, plus various other benefits such as subsidized family access to health services, free transport to the place of work and so on, was also important. More important, however, was the widespread and well-founded perception that the income-earning potential of positions in the public sector was far greater than the pattern of formal remuneration and other benefits suggested. In other words, it was well-known that one could expect to receive a wide range of additional allowances of one kind or another, and that if one were so inclined there would be ample opportunity to be involved in lucrative corrupt activity.

The history of the judiciary under the New Order clearly illustrates the key features of the Suharto strategy for ensuring that most members of the franchise institutions would support the franchise, and that few would oppose it (Pompe 2005). The imposition of very low salaries relative to comparable private sector levels ensured that judges would be forced to play by the rules of the franchise if they were to enjoy a standard of living commensurate with their professional status. Members of the judiciary who were unwilling to do the bidding of the regime – including, as Aspinall and Van Klinken put it in the introduction to this volume, by endorsing 'illegal acts performed by

11 Just as in the private sector, the socially optimal size of the bureaucracy is defined by the margins at which the gain to society from employing additional personnel just matches the cost of doing so, evaluated at market-determined salaries. Getting this balance right is a matter of adjusting numbers of employees, not salary levels.

other agents of the state' – found themselves languishing indefinitely in far distant outposts, with few fringe benefits, little work to occupy their time or hone their skills, and no hope for a 'successful' career in any sense of the term.[12] At the other end of the spectrum, those who, like the president himself, enthusiastically embraced the notion of taking advantage of their positions to achieve personal enrichment, were only too willing to do what was asked of them by the regime (see Butt and Lindsey, in this volume). Among the latter, those who were most effective were appointed to highly lucrative positions in the most active big city district courts, and some were promoted to the high court or the supreme court.

With salaries and formal allowances kept low, public sector institutions needed only to be provided with limited funding from the budget to cover their personnel costs. The practical implication was that managers of these institutions had to find additional, off-budget sources of funds if they were to get things done and to provide additional income to their employees in order to secure their loyalty and support. Inevitably this would involve engagement in various forms of activity that were either clearly corrupt, or at least were located within the fuzzy boundary that delimits corrupt and non-corrupt activity. Thus, for example, despite the importance of the military's contribution to maintaining Suharto's political monopoly,[13] on which the success of the franchise depended,

> the military won little in the way of budget resources during the Soeharto era. [...] By withholding budget funds, [Suharto] gave military commanders a strong incentive to engage in income-generating activities. At the same time, his ability to grant or deny access to these activities fostered a high degree of loyalty and dependence among these commanders. (Rieffel and Pramodhawardani 2007:32.)

In other words, Suharto secured the loyalty of the military not by allocating government revenue to it, but by appointing its commanders as franchisees – granting them the right to collect private tax revenues and to allocate them as they saw fit, including to their own pockets. The similarity with the case of the judiciary discussed above is obvious.

Within the bureaucracy, management would ordinarily devote part of the so-called 'development' budget, largely deriving from bilateral and multilateral aid agencies, to the payment of various allowances over and above

12 Widoyoko in this volume, discusses the same issue in relation to school principals.

13 The threat of military-sanctioned violence was not limited to the purpose of extortion, but also as a means of repressing potential opposition to the regime. The army had given a green light to the killing of hundreds of thousands of alleged communists and communist sympathizers as a prelude to Suharto's appointment as president, and this served as a vivid reminder of the likely fate of any who dared too openly to criticize the New Order government. Discussion of these aspects of Suharto's rule is beyond the scope of this chapter, however.

the formal entitlements – for example, to people who served on project committees (and, through them, to both their superiors and subordinates in the same area). More obviously corrupt was the practice of awarding government contracts at inflated prices to firms that agreed to kick back a suitably large portion of the excess over reasonable market value to the officials or committees that awarded the contracts.[14] These illicit payments were typically used as slush funds for topping up the incomes of other employees of the government entity in question. The key point to note here is that the rents were shared widely within the relevant part of the bureaucracy. In this manner, large numbers of officials became dependent on the continued operation of the system. It was highly unlikely that any individual would blow the whistle on such practices, because to do so would be to put at risk not only a significant part of one's own overall income, but also that of one's peers. Lack of transparency within the system for transfers and promotions meant that such individuals could be severely punished by denying them promotion and access to informal allowances in cash and in-kind to which they had no formal entitlement, or moving them to bureaucratic backwaters.

In short, the kind of salary structure chosen for public sector institutions was such as to discourage the entry of highly principled individuals (which is not to deny that many such were recruited, nevertheless), and correspondingly to encourage that of people who at least would not concern themselves too greatly about the sources of their special allowances and other salary supplements – or, better still, of those predisposed to engage actively in the work of the franchise. This is the only plausible explanation for the fact that individuals were willing to pay for the privilege of embarking on, and persevering with, a career characterized by increasingly large shortfalls below market salary levels the higher one rose in the hierarchy.

Decisions had to be made not only about the public sector salary structure, but also about the number of employees. Indonesia's civil service under Suharto was never particularly large,[15] and yet, in relation to the fairly narrow objectives of the franchise, the number of public sector employees seems at first glance to have been unnecessarily great. This impression is no doubt heavily influenced by the obvious degree of underemployment within the bureaucracy, which was quickly apparent to visitors to virtually any government office building. Early in the New Order, Suharto decided to adopt personnel management practices within the bureaucracy that mirrored those he had been used to in the army. One aspect of this was a rigid pyramidal hierarchy, in which the commanding officer would have a fixed number of subordinates reporting to him, each of whom would have a fixed number re-

14 The chapter by Van Klinken and Aspinall in this volume is much concerned with such practices.

15 In 1997 (Suharto's last year in office), Indonesia had 4.1 million civil servants, equivalent to just 2% of the population.

porting to him, and so on down to the level of private. Thus all battalions, all regiments and so on would have the same number of individuals at each level in the hierarchy. Whatever its merits in the military context, such an approach made little sense within the bureaucracy, because different agencies were involved in widely varying activities, and their staffing needs differed correspondingly (Synnerstrom 2007:164-5). Nevertheless, the benefit to the franchise was that this approach typically resulted in excessive numbers of bureaucrats at low levels[16] and insufficient numbers of them at high levels. The rampant underemployment of staff just mentioned was in fact a characteristic only of low-level employees; by contrast, those at high levels were quite often heavily overworked. The implication was that relatively few at the low levels could expect rapid promotion, and yet promotion was the only way to gain access to the more lucrative opportunities for supplementing one's income with special allowances and other top-ups paid from slush funds or derived from participation in corrupt activity. In these circumstances, individuals desirous of promotion had strong incentives to compete with their peers – especially for promotion into positions in the 'wet' areas, where the availability of off-budget funds was greatest (Kristiansen and Ramli 2006).

Such competition took a variety of forms, and working hard was by no means the only one. The process for determining promotions and transfers within the bureaucracy lacked transparency and objectivity, and relations with one's own superior were, in practice, the crucially important deciding factor – hence the prevalent culture of *asal bapak senang* – 'as long as the boss is happy' – within Indonesian public sector institutions. Management of franchises at the local level is typically delegated to the franchisee, who is then more or less free to choose which of his subordinates to promote or transfer to positions of greater authority, and which to leave where they are or to shift to positions of little influence. In the context of the Suharto franchise, in which the primary objective was regressive redistribution of the national income rather than the delivery of services to the public, it is hardly surprising that competition also often took the form of bidding for desirable positions.

In Indonesia, most civil service positions are for sale, rather than being acquired in open competition based on merit. The practice of selling civil service jobs goes hand in hand with corruption more generally – from one perspective, the investment needed to obtain a position needs to be recovered; from another, the likelihood of access to lucrative opportunities for self-enrichment makes such an investment worthwhile (Synnerstrom 2007:174).

The winners of the competition were those who bid the highest prices for promotion or appointment to particular positions, and these were typically those who had the greatest confidence in their ability to abuse these prospec-

16 The problem persists to this day, including at local government level (McLeod 2008b:204).

tive positions of authority to generate cash inflows. That is, just as the salary structure encouraged recruitment of the kinds of individuals who would serve the franchise well, so the hierarchical structure within the bureaucracy reinforced this tendency by promoting the same kinds of individuals after they had had a chance to demonstrate their capacity and willingness to contribute to the objectives of the franchise.

There was perhaps one additional reason for recruiting what may seem like excessive numbers of high school and university graduates to the public sector.[17] The regime had decided to increase significantly the number of children and young people attending schools and universities, since this was clearly a way of generating support from the public and thus offsetting concerns that the government cared only about its big business friends. But students have always been a potent political force in Indonesia (Aspinall 2005: Chapter 5), so it made sense to hold out the enticing prospect of a well-remunerated career in the public sector following graduation, because students – and their parents – would have been well aware that involvement in student activism directed against the regime would very likely ruin any chance of being recruited. The strategy of offering eventual access to lucrative positions in the franchise to those who demonstrated their willingness to accept it for what it was thus extended even to potential public sector employees.

Allowing members of the bureaucracy and SOE branches of the franchise to tap into foreign aid flows and to collude with private sector firms engaged in economic transactions with the public sector constituted useful and effective means of allowing public sector employees to top up their formal remuneration and thus to ensure their support for the broad objectives of the franchise. But there were, of course, additional means of doing this. Recall here the distinction introduced earlier between insiders and outsiders. The insiders were the privileged firms that cooperated with the franchise so as indirectly to tax those outside the elite in one way or another. The outsider firms and individuals, on the other hand, were the targets rather than the beneficiaries of such taxation, and they were taxed by way of extortion 'unofficial imposts' (*pungutan liar* or *pungli*). Broadly speaking, the bureaucracy created a wide range of regulations with which firms needed to comply, and then found ways of forcing firms to pay bribes in order to obtain certification of such compliance. In addition, it accepted bribes from firms wishing to reduce, or avoid altogether, their payments of legitimate taxes, such as customs duties, value added tax and income tax. Outsider firms and individuals were also subject to extortion by the military and police, involving the employment of violence or the threat of violence to persuade them to contribute to their own 'protection'. The small but relatively wealthy ethnic Chinese community was always particularly vulnerable, and some of its members found it pru-

17 In 1997, 83% of civil servants were graduates of senior high school or tertiary institutions.

dent to try to keep local military officials favourably disposed to it (Susanto 2006). But indigenous (*pribumi*) citizens were also targets.

It is because of the heavy emphasis on public sector extortion of firms and individuals that Indonesia has such a poor image in relation to corruption and bureaucratic inefficiency (Kaufmann, Kraay and Mastruzzi 2008; World Bank 2008; see further discussion below). Indonesia's rapid economic progress under Suharto is somewhat paradoxical when viewed against this background. The paradox is readily resolved, however, when we recall the existence of insider firms, which collectively accounted for a very large share of the modern sector of the economy, and which were not only broadly immune to such extortion but in fact benefited strongly from their privileged relationship with the bureaucracy, the state enterprises and the public sector in general.

Post-Suharto reform

The Asian financial crisis that began in mid-1997 suddenly created turmoil in Indonesia, depriving the New Order regime of its legitimacy as a sound economic manager. In turn, this simultaneously emboldened opponents of the regime and dramatically weakened Suharto's ability to maintain discipline within the franchise, such that its various branches and members no longer continued to act in a mutually supportive fashion. As a result, he was pushed out of office in May 1998, and reformers then moved quickly to overturn several key features of the regime he had built up over the previous three decades. Relatively little progress has been made in reforming the bureaucracy, however, which remains highly dysfunctional.

The law on the civil service was amended in 1999 so as to replace the previous naïve requirement for civil servants to sacrifice their own material well-being in the interests of the state and the people with a more realistic emphasis on the need for comparability of public sector remuneration with that in the private sector. This perfectly sensible restatement of principle has not been accompanied by an equally sensible restructuring of remuneration packages, however: as we have seen, these remain far removed from the realities of the private sector market for professional and managerial labour. Inevitably, the failure to remove the conflict between state law and economic law has meant that corrupt behaviour remains endemic in Indonesia's public sector.

Surveys such as those undertaken by Transparency International suggest that Indonesia is one of the most corrupt countries in the world (ranked at equal 126th out of 180 countries in Transparency International's Corruption

Perceptions Index for 2008, with a score of just 2.6 on a scale of 1-10).[18] Other sources, such as the World Bank's *Governance Matters* and *Doing Business* reports (Kaufmann, Kraay and Mastruzzi 2008; World Bank 2008) show clearly that it is also very inefficient, and emphasize the deleterious impact of this inefficiency on the business and investment environment. For example, Indonesia was ranked only in the 42nd percentile in terms of 'government effectiveness' in 2007 in the *Governance Matters* report.[19] At the same time, its world ranking on a number of important standardized indicators of the ease of doing business (as this relates to the influence of the bureaucracy) can also be seen to be very low (Table 1).

Table 1 Ease of doing business in Indonesia: selected sub-indices and components

Indicator	Measure	Rank (among 181 countries)	
Overall ease of doing business			129
Starting a business			171
Time	76 days	165	
Cost (% of income per capita)	77.9%	146	
Employing workers			157
Difficulty of Hiring Index (0-100)	61	153	
Difficulty of Firing Index (0-100)	60	157	
Firing costs (weeks of wages)	108 weeks	168	
Paying taxes			116
Time	266 hours	103	
Registering property			107
Time	39 days	75	
Cost (% of property value)	10.7%	143	
Dealing with construction permits			80
Time	176 days	75	
Cost (% of income per capita)	221.1%	176	

Source: World Bank (2008).
Note: The closer the numerical rank to 1, the easier it is perceived to do business.

18 See http://www.transparency.org.

19 On this index, the lower the percentile rank, the less effective government is perceived to be.

The bureaucracy succeeded in generating consistently high economic growth during the New Order period because this was in the interests of the franchise, and because there were strong incentives for success within it. The franchise prospered by taxing virtually the entire economy, so the faster the economy grew, the greater the pay-off. But in the entirely different context of post-Suharto democratic Indonesia the bureaucracy as economic policy maker has been found wanting. The franchise no longer exists, since there is no longer a franchisor capable of imposing discipline on all of its branches: this became an impossibility once Suharto's monopoly on the presidency came to an end. Its collapse following Suharto's demise is directly analogous to the breakdown of a cartel as a result of its individual members' failure to restrict their output to agreed quotas: cartels cannot survive in the absence of internal discipline. In post-Suharto Indonesia officials still have an incentive to abuse their authority to their own advantage, but they now do so in uncoordinated fashion, competing with each other rather than playing defined, mutually supportive roles within the giant organism that is the Indonesian public sector.

To the extent that current and future governments in Indonesia perceive government as an instrument for improving the efficiency of the economy rather than one for redistributing income in favour of sections of the elite, it seems clear that removing the conflict between state law and economic law is of crucial importance. This should not be interpreted to mean that merely improving the formal remuneration of public sector employees is all that is needed, however. Remuneration comparable with that in the private sector must be accompanied by other human resource management practices that are also comparable with those in the private sector. This should be taken to include a strong emphasis on performance evaluation as the key determinant of promotions (and therefore remuneration), and the opening up of vacant positions to competition among the widest possible range of applicants. In short, if individuals are to be paid market salaries, then they must also be obliged to compete on equal terms for positions within the public sector with all others who think themselves worthy of filling those positions.

Conclusion

In this chapter, I have attempted to show how the Suharto regime managed the economy and polity of Indonesia for the benefit of the dominant elite, rather than for Indonesian citizens in general. I have argued that his New Order 'franchise' was extraordinarily successful in terms of its own objectives, and that this reflected the strategies employed to provide appropriate incentives to individuals within the various branches of the public sector.

Suharto set total formal remuneration for more senior personnel very low relative to market levels. At the same time, however, franchisees were effectively granted the right to collect private taxation, backed by the full resources of the franchise. Positions as franchisees were thus eagerly sought after by those who had no qualms about using the coercive power of government for their personal benefit. Others who wanted nothing more than fair and reasonable – that is, private sector-comparable – remuneration were obliged to suppress their moral concerns about the functioning of the franchise unless they were prepared to be left to languish in positions where they would have no real influence on the processes of government, and where their earnings would be far below that of their private sector peers.

The conflict between the law on the civil service as implemented and the law of supply and demand resulted in a constant search by franchisees for ways to supplement their incomes, inevitably drawing them towards corrupt activity – thus making them dependent on, and unlikely to challenge, the status quo. Paradoxically, low salaries enabled Suharto to buy support for the corrupt practices of his franchise. If significant progress is to be made in minimizing corruption and improving the performance of the bureaucracy it will be essential to remove this conflict by more closely aligning remuneration and personnel management practices with those of the private sector.[20]

[20] While the present government of Susilo Bambang Yudhoyono does not see this as a priority, there is, nevertheless, a desire on the part of at least some members of his cabinet to move in this direction. Foremost among these is the Minister for Finance, Dr Sri Mulyani Indrawati; details of the far reaching bureaucratic reforms taking place in the finance ministry are discussed in McLeod (2008a).

HOWARD DICK AND JEREMY MULHOLLAND

The state as marketplace

Slush funds and intra-elite rivalry

Why is the state so weak and erratic in enforcing legislated sanctions against corrupt and criminal behaviour?[19] This question is usually referred to as the problem of 'implementation', as though the failure was simply one of administrative competence or a confusion of priorities. Critics also frequently cite 'lack of political will', which is no more insightful. Such rationalizations blur the essential distinction between the state as it should be and the state as it is. Corruption and crime invariably co-exist with the state.

This messy and unsatisfactory situation can be explained and analysed in terms of the behaviour of the elites who control the state and access to it. The state is the arena for contestation (Migdal 2001; Day 2002). We refer to this as the elite game of power, wealth and status. New Institutional Economics (NIE) usefully distinguishes between formal and informal 'rules of the game' whereby informal rules or norms of behaviour regulate the formulation and application of formal rules, including legislation (North 1990). For example, there are many reasons why allegations of criminal or corrupt behaviour may not result in legal convictions: hearsay allegations may not be brought to public notice because of fear of retribution; police and prosecutors may not proceed with charges; evidence may not substantiate them; witnesses may refuse to testify; restitution may be made before prosecution; courts may be influenced; or appeals may overturn convictions. In short, illegality becomes a matter for negotiation under a complex interaction of formal and informal rules. Contestability is seen also in the way informal rules serve to redistribute power, wealth and status. A useful perspective on the state is therefore that of a transactional space in which the rules of the political system are constantly being tested and renegotiated. The state may not work in accordance with the constitutional and legislative façade but the informal rules of the game, however inscrutable to outsiders, help to maintain and enrich the often fractious power elite.

19 Research for this chapter was assisted by an Australian Research Council grant.

By a next logical step, the state may be construed not just as a transactional space but as a political marketplace, in which access to authority and property rights to economic resources are traded in the process of elite contestation. Trading occurs most obviously through negotiation over the relevant formal and informal rules. But money and prices may become an explicit part of the negotiation over political outcomes within the state itself, as well as between state actors and the rest of society. The essential difference between such a political market and an economic market is that monetary payments in the former are only part of the transaction, a balancing item or 'side-payment', not its summation. Nevertheless, a fruitful line of research is to follow the 'money trail' or, perhaps even better, the 'money chain' because the need for concealment often gives rise to a series of intermediate transactions between the principals. Along this transactional chain flows an exchange of money for favours. The direction and pattern of the chain are never random. Networks and personal influence map the pattern and channel the flows.

This chapter attempts to follow the money chain and informal modes of behaviour in Indonesia during the transition since 1998 from authoritarian to democratic regime. It thereby seeks to throw some light on the unexpected outcome that a revolution intended to overthrow the highly corrupt Suharto regime has led to a democratic regime in which corruption is even more pervasive and apparently less well-ordered (MacIntyre 2001). Notwithstanding neo-liberal orthodoxy that the state should withdraw from direct economic involvement, democracy makes it more likely that ideological and policy battles within the elite may result in the state becoming more interventionist because elites need insulation from markets in order to generate the rents that keep them in power or fund their ambitions.

NIE is a powerful body of theory that relates power to contestation for resources and property rights through formal and informal rules and their legitimating ideology (North 1990, 2005). Yet while sometimes endorsing (Mokyr and Nye 2007; Jones 2006), sometimes belittling the significance of intra-elite rivalry (Acemoglu and Robinson 2006), NIE does not incorporate it explicitly into its theory of political and economic change (North, Wallis and Weingast 2009). There is no need to reinvent the wheel, however, because the disciplines of sociology and political science have already done the work. Mills (1956) identified and Putnam (1976) deconstructed the elite in its monopoly of power, wealth and status. At the apex of every society is a small power elite (ruling clique): the president and ministers, generals and top bureaucrats plus close confidants and business leaders. Clustering around the power elite is the several thousand strong ruling elite within which individuals and groups called 'elite members' fight against each other and make strategic collaborations. Thus the elite is not singular but plural (Higley and Burton 2006; Pakulski 2006). Elite individuals and groups are in a constant state of flux between cooperation and competition for the spoils of power, wealth and status.

In Indonesia, intra-elite rivalry was a feature of democratic politics (1950-1957), to be deftly manipulated by President Sukarno during the era of Guided Democracy (1957-1966), then suppressed under President Suharto under the New Order (1966-1998) before bursting forth again with the new party politics of Reformasi. Political analyses of Indonesia have almost invariably addressed intra-elite rivalry and personality politics but this focus has still not been well translated into theory. Based upon the Weberian model which Fred Riggs (1966) had applied to Thailand, Karl Jackson and Lucian Pye (1978) portrayed New Order Indonesia as a 'bureaucratic polity'. The particular emphasis upon bureaucracy might have been appropriate in the colonial era but was curiously anachronistic after independence when bureaucratic power was eroded by the successive assaults of party politics, martial law, executive authority and military supremacy. Elite polity would have been a better formulation. Applying neo-Marxist theory with Weberian elements, Richard Robison (1986) put forward a more nuanced model of bureaucrat-capitalism in which the bourgeoisie is a harmonious alliance of indigenous politico-bureaucrats and Indonesian-Chinese business conglomerates. Yet here again, as in later works such as Robison and Hadiz (2004) and Chua (2008), the emphasis upon 'bureaucrat' seems too narrow and too much agency is attributed to ethnic Chinese business leaders, who institutionally and ideologically are still shut out of political power. Causation surely runs the other way with state powerholders using their leverage to negotiate rent-sharing access to the means of production.

Ross McLeod (this volume, preceding chapter; 2000) presents an elegant 'franchise' model of the hierarchical distribution of rents during the New Order, which looks to be an exemplary case of 'well-ordered corruption'. Nevertheless, this system was not so much a product of Suharto's brilliant design as the gradual outcome of improvisation, muddle and improvement. The regime evolved, along with Suharto's own power and stature, from a broad-based elite coalition to military-technocratic dictatorship to family business, then collapsed like a house of cards in mid-1998. Explanation of historical continuity therefore directs attention to how that rivalry was suppressed by the rewards and sanctions of an increasingly centralized, patronage-based and hierarchical system of government, then with regime change gave way to a more contested system.

This chapter addresses two different ways in which the Indonesian state may be understood as a political marketplace by exploring patterns of routine informal behaviours. First, it looks at the role of 'slush funds' as the unaccountable revenues and expenditures that underpinned the Suharto hegemony but carried over into the era of Reformasi. Here the emphasis is upon the informal rules governing relations between state actors who extract slush funds and their 'clients' who seek favours and/or control resources. Second, it considers how the shift after 1998 from an authoritarian to a democratic regime has influenced the dynamics of intra-elite rivalry. Here we pay particular attention to informal rules governing the new relationship between the executive and parliament. The former demonstrates the continuity of informal rules between regimes, the latter change and discontinuity. In both cases, corruption is seen to be intrinsic to the state, whether authoritarian or democratic.

Slush funds

'The state does not produce its own subsistence' (Dick 1993:5). Even to maintain the state apparatus, the state must extract resources from the rest of society. In the first instance, this can be done by taxation. Control of the state, the so-called 'monopoly of violence', confers rights of taxation (Levi 1990; Bates 2008). However, systematic taxation has the notable disadvantages to rulers of requiring an effective bureaucracy and of being transparent and accountable under the state budget. As Paul Collier (2007) points out, it also tends to erode the popularity and legitimacy of weak governments.

While budgetary revenues finance some state functions, rulers also need to find resources to 'buy' and maintain the loyalty of associates, rivals and subordinates, both within the elite and among the populace at large. Despite some scope for 'pork-barrelling', budgetary revenues are not readily deployed for 'political' purposes, certainly not for those where secrecy is paramount and perhaps also where the amount and timing are unpredictable (Lambsdorff 2007; Johnston 2005). Hence there is a need for off-budget, non-accountable and discretionary revenues that we denote here by the generic term 'slush funds' – the term is more journalistic than academic but it has common currency and best describes their nature and purpose. Powerholders need slush funds because they are discretionary, not bound by the formal rules, procedures and accountability that govern budgetary revenues and expenditures. At the very least, they provide a cushion against what is expected of officeholders from limited resources and improve their chances of securing favour and promotion. As explained in greater detail below, they may also be ploughed into official projects, fund personal emoluments, reward subordinates and provide gifts to superiors and patrons. They may also be used for political purposes. The opaqueness or muddiness of slush funds, is their raison d'être.

Historically in Southeast Asia, rulers generated slush funds through landholdings and commerce (Reid 1993:245-51). In the tiny sultanate of Brunei Darussalam, state revenues are still not formally separated from the royal household: foreign oil companies provide a ready source of revenue, there is minimal taxation and everything flows from the sultan's munificence. In Indonesia, former presidents Suharto and Habibie both benefited from commerce through the extensive business interests of close family members, who in turn benefited from their proximity to the centre of power (Aditjondro 2006). The Reform era has seen private wealth become a springboard for political careers. Susilo Bambang Yudhoyono's 2004 presidential campaign was supported among others by business magnate Aburizal Bakrie, who became a senior minister in his government. Jusuf Kalla's family fortune helped him to become leader of the Golkar Party and subsequently Vice-President with no disadvantage to his family's diverse business interests (Aditjondro 2009). In 2009 former general Prabowo Subianto's campaign for the Gerindra Party and, unsuccessfully, for the presidency was financed by his brother, Hasjim Djojohadikusumo.

In the modern state, enormous creativity goes into generating many other forms of slush funds. The informal mechanisms by which the Indonesian state apparatus generates off-budget and unofficial revenues are multifarious and the result of continual innovation. Nevertheless, at least five different types of behaviours or extractive mechanisms may usefully be distinguished. The five types overlap and are therefore something less than a typology but the point is not so much to classify as to identify the different mechanisms of extraction, all of which characterized the New Order period but have carried over into the era of Reformasi.[20] These streams of fungible revenues flow into broader and muddier rivers of 'slush funds'.

Levies are informal taxes and imposts for state services, sometimes referred to as unofficial imposts (*pungutan liar* or *pungli*). Thus police, customs or immigration officers and many other bureaucrats require small payments for signatures for the issuing of permits, licences, approvals and so on over and above the official charges. These levies are captured by the official concerned and often placed in a common pool for distribution according to agreed formulae with shares being scaled down the hierarchy according to rank (Goodpaster 2002:93, 97-8).

Leaks are funds siphoned informally from budgetary or project revenues. At each step along the way in the collection of revenues and the disbursement of expenditures in and out of the state budget, a percentage is extracted as something like an unofficial fee for service. In 1993 economist and former minister Sumitro Djojohadikusumo estimated that the national budget incurred leakages of around 30% each year.[21] In 2003 Minister for Planning Kwik Kian Gie more conservatively estimated budget leakages as at least 20%

20 Our approach differs from that of MacIntyre (2000), whose analysis of off-budget funds and rent-seeking distinguished 'command lending', 'private contributions' and 'hidden government funds'.

21 *Biografi Prof. Dr. Sumitro* 2009. The same figure was later cited by Jeffrey Winters as applying to leakages from World Bank loans to Indonesia (Winters 1997:29).

(Kwik 2003). A significant proportion of these leaks are distributed as a top-up of official salaries and/or the operating expenses of their respective offices.

Deals are one-off arrangements to generate informal revenues, making state officials or their nominees party in their own right to transactions with private interests. Typical examples are kickbacks on contracts (public works, procurement), the issuing of licences (especially in forestry and mining), the sale of public land or the rezoning of private land. Generous commissions have also been paid in relation to the privatization of state assets – one notorious set of deals immediately after the Suharto presidency was the Indonesian Bank Reconstruction Agency (IBRA) in its disposal of nationalized bank assets.

Gift loans are non- or part-repayable loans from state banks with less than commercial levels of collateral and perhaps also concessional rates of interest. President Suharto's children were prime beneficiaries of such arrangement, usually in response to a personal note (*surat sakti*) or informal advice from the president or his close advisers. By the 1990s, however, as the children became more active, they more often made direct approach to bankers, who just assumed presidential approval and granted the requested loans.

Rents are contrived income streams to state powerholders who have leveraged their position to become stakeholders in productive or financial assets. During the Suharto era it was common practice for foreign multinationals setting up in Indonesia to allocate equity holdings to well-connected members of the Indonesian elite, in the early years often to military interests, later more frequently to members of the President's extended family. Typically the Indonesian party made no capital contribution but enjoyed the dividends on these sleeping equity holdings as the price of political protection. After the early 1990s the government's new divestment policy for foreign investment created a market in which it was easy for political insiders to acquire substantial shareholdings at a discounted price. Rental streams could also be created by the allocation to favoured individuals and their companies of privileged monopoly contracts to operate public facilities (for example, airport services, toll roads) or to provide services to foreign multinationals. The Freeport gold and copper mine in Papua exemplifies both practices (Leith 2003:68-76). These contrived rents usually accrued to senior powerholders but the money trail was often disguised through beneficiaries such as family members or non-profit foundations (*yayasan*).

Besides these five mechanisms of extraction, there are the issues of how slush funds are stored and how they are disbursed. If funds are collected in cash, they may be deposited in bank accounts, more or less opaque, earning interest until disbursement. In Suharto's Indonesia, funds for presidential use were commonly held on account by foundations (*yayasan*), whose purposes were ostensibly charitable but whose accounts were never properly audited (Aditjondro 2006). Not all funds, however, needed to be collected in advance of their use. Since the need for funds was unpredictable, the patronage system worked in such a way that those who held office by presidential favour, as also those who enjoyed the benefits of state licences or contracts, necessarily incurred contingent obligations. The powerholder granting a favour could demand its return, whether in money or in-kind at any time and to any amount within the capacity of the recipient. To refuse would be proof of gross disloyalty and incur certain punishment through the withdrawal of favour and loss of position, perhaps even charges of corruption, trial and imprisonment.

The best examples of the working of this patronage system were state enterprises and agencies (Badan Usaha Milik Negara, BUMN). The trusted subordinates appointed as heads of state enterprises were expected not only to direct a proportion of revenues to powerholders but also to respond to periodic requests from the responsible minister or even the president himself. In return, they siphoned off revenues for their own purposes. With the notable exception of the state oil company Pertamina, most state enterprises therefore ran at a loss, the amount being reimbursed from the state budget.[22] In this way budget revenues were routinely diverted into non-official channels. Loosely supervised state enterprises were therefore broadly equivalent to the older notion of appanage, a grant to a powerholder of the surplus entitlements of an area of land and its villagers. We denote these consolidated rental streams as fiefs.

For Suharto, loyalists like Ibnu Sutowo at the state oil company Pertamina and a series of trusted subordinates at the state logistics agency Bulog were also like personal bankers, ever expected and able at short notice to extend an overdraft. Thus Pertamina might be asked as the need arose to undertake or underwrite a 'national project' such as a new manufacturing plant or industry or to fund infrastructure. As with state banks themselves, the device by which President Suharto made his requests was a polite, ambiguous request known as *surat sakti* (literally 'sacred letter'). A loyal subordinate took the hint and responded to the request, checking if need be with presidential advisers. If the job was done well, reward or promotion would follow – if not, presidential favour could be withdrawn without further explanation.

The logic of slush funds extended from the president down to the bottom of the bureaucratic hierarchy. A variant of the section's opening axiom might be 'the state provides no more than a subsistence'. In Indonesia after independence it became common for ministers to reward followers by granting them positions in their department, whether at the central or local level, or by allocating them contracts to generate rents from informal collaborations with businesspeople. After 1957 the state's seizure and nationalization of most of the modern sector of the economy gave enormous scope for arbitrary use of

22 Pertamina itself went spectacularly bankrupt in the mid-1970s, leading to the fall from grace of Suharto confidant Ibnu Sutowo (McCawley 1978). It still has the reputation of leaking revenue like a sieve.

power, extortion and smuggling in state enterprises and the bureaucracy. As inflation became rampant, rising from some tens to hundreds of percent per annum by the mid-1960s, civil service positions became valued simply for their monthly rations in-kind, mainly rice, sugar, cooking oil, salt and textiles. The civil service ballooned as a patronage-based relief organization, the beneficiaries hardly being expected to do actual work but simply to report, then carry on whatever other employment would earn the necessary balance of an income (Feith 1967). Of course the incentive system was entirely pernicious. Civil servants had every incentive to maximize bureaucratic complexity to extract funds from whoever could afford to pay, which in practice meant mostly private business, but also state enterprises, and to some extent the impoverished general public.

The New Order in its early years sought to trim the size of the bloated bureaucracy but never cut it back to a merely functional size. The excess staff, including the so-called honorary appointments (*honorair*), was maintained by keeping the basic monthly salary very low and allowing civil servants and the military (including police) to find extra revenues to meet administrative needs and private incomes. From top to bottom, a civil service position was therefore equivalent to a 'hunting licence', subject to various informal rules as to what type of exactions and how much was acceptable.

The disbursement of informal revenues or slush funds can be divided into three broad categories. First is to fund the operation of the department or agency. The routine budgets of most civil service departments are still low, not only in wages and emoluments but also in the funds allocated for office buildings, fit-out and even such essentials as stationary and utilities. In other words, official funds may suffice for only a few months of the year. A good department or section head has therefore not only to try and manipulate the best possible budget but also to secure top-up funding. One expedient, quite effective in terms of utilities, is simply not to pay the bills to the responsible state agencies and let the government sort it out. But other sources of revenue have also to be found. Under the New Order, the most important were not illegal or quasi-legal sources of funding but development projects, funded partly from the state budget but mainly from development aid. Thus bureaucratic politics revolved very much around competition for projects and all their associated benefits: better offices, computers, vehicles, travel, extra salary, and so on. Astute heads knew how to squeeze budgets ('leaks') so that the maximum amount was retained by the office and the least amount was spent on the project consistent with its successful completion. At the end of the Suharto era a figure of 30% was widely quoted as a conservative World Bank estimate of the leakage of aid funds (McCarthy 2002:42-3).

The second category of disbursement is the support of a state official's family to provide an adequate standard of living and lifestyle. Given the reality of low official salaries and emoluments, every official has long been allowed some discretion in generating additional income. The means are not necessarily extractive or illegal. While some officials such as police, customs and immigration have been notorious for greed and lavish lifestyles, civil servants can also quite legitimately earn attendance money for meetings or seminars or per diems for travel. They can engage in second jobs. Thus doctors in public hospitals run after-hours private practice, teachers give private tuition, academics at state universities teach also at private universities or engage in consultancy projects, mostly for government departments or donor agencies. As the economy has expanded, the means have increased, but so also have the demands. Indonesia is a highly status-conscious society, so the growth of a middle class highly dependent upon the state and with a more and more westernized and luxurious lifestyle has meant that the modest growth in civil service salaries could never keep pace with rising expectations. Strong informal sanctions underpin these informal norms: an official reluctant to take advantage of his/her position or to share the rents may be condemned as too idealistic, even stupid, unworthy or stingy.

The third category may be described broadly as political disbursements. In the Suharto era, these payments would pass up the hierarchy as the 'rent' on patronage, though perhaps more typically they would be contingent and would involve making payments or providing services or projects on demand, whether for a covert political object, in the 'national interest' or for the purposes of 'development'. Under Reformasi, when political competition has become more intense, these slush funds are aptly referred to as 'tactical funds' (*dana taktis*) (Bayuni 2005).

In these various ways, following the money trail of slush funds reveals an informal or shadow state that only partially coincides with the formal state apparatus. Part of the explanation for the divergence is that the state is chronically underfunded by the formal budgetary system, so that deficits have to be made good by informal means. A deeper explanation is that the rational bureaucratic state as portrayed in organizational charts is subverted by networks of patron-client ties. Powerholders within these networks may take advantage of their position to raise and distribute informal revenues for non-state purposes. The following section will consider in more detail how the shadow state has evolved from the hierarchical system of the Suharto era to the more democratic and contested system of the Reform era. Particular attention will be paid to the new relationship between the executive and parliament, the emergence of political markets and the role of informal institutions in moderating intra-elite rivalry.

Regime change

Some scholars, such as Higley and Burton (2006) and Pakulski (2006), maintain that tension and conflict between elite individuals and groups drives political and economic change. When an elite group gains control of the state apparatus, it can institutionalize its informal norms and view of the world throughout society. Suharto's New Order (1966-1998) was an archetypal case of what Higley et al. (1998) refer to as an 'ideologically unified elite' or, more precisely, a dictator and his ruling clique that over time impose a master ideology limiting and concealing intra-elite rivalry. Yet within fractious elites, a shared and stable consensus over the rules governing competition for and deployment of state power is not normally to be expected. Many countries have post-colonial histories of chronic instability. Indonesia looked to be following the same path until the three decades of stability under the New Order, whose sudden collapse in 1998 could confidently have been predicted to lead to renewal of fierce intra-elite rivalry and bloodshed. Instead the outcome was confounding.

The most remarkable thing about the transition from the authoritarian New Order to the representative and procedural democracy of the Reformasi era is that it was accomplished with relatively little violence and bloodshed, at least at the centre (King 2003; Emmerson 1999). After the riots that convulsed Jakarta and several other cities in May 1998, President Suharto resigned with quiet dignity and there was an orderly transition. Notwithstanding some horrific outbreaks of communal and separatist violence on the periphery and much random criminality on Java, it was still a marked contrast to the wave of mayhem and mass murder that followed the collapse of the Sukarno regime in 1965-1966 (Roosa 2006; Van Klinken 2007; Sidel 2006). Over the next six years there were three changes of president through parliamentary and electoral means and various changes in the composition of coalition governments, all achieved without bloodshed or any force of arms, then a full five-year term of stable and quite effective coalition government under President Susilo Bambang Yudhoyono (SBY) and Vice-President Jusuf Kalla (JK), again without repression.

The stability of the SBY-JK government was therefore of a very different kind from that of Suharto's long term in office. Whereas the New Order was characterized by centralized control, patronage and repression, the Reformasi era has seen continual and intense intra-elite rivalry between parties and within factions for access to state power. Since many of the leading actors and parties are the same as in the New Order, this sudden change in the dynamics of the game of power, wealth and status is at first sight illogical and demands explanation. Clearly, as New Institutional Economics would suggest, there has been a reconfiguration of the 'rules of the game'. Moreover, the stability of those new rules suggests, in Higley's terminology, a new elite consensus that imposes limits on the extent of conflict and allows for effective cooperation to mutual benefit.

This chapter addresses one important aspect of the new political consensus, namely the modes and mechanisms of competition for access to resources as the means to buying and defending power in the state. Here there is an essential difference between the New Order and the Reformasi era. Under the New Order, as described by McLeod in the preceding chapter, intra-elite rivalry was channelled through a hierarchical patronage network controlled ultimately by Suharto himself through allies and subordinates. By contrast, under the parliamentary democracy of the Reformasi era, the power of the executive has been diluted by the necessity of coalition government and the demands for accountability to parliament. Hence there is much more horizontal competition and jostling between parties and factions, as also a much more lively public debate cutting across any dominant political ideology.

Structurally the most important change has been the emergence of the legislature as an independent power centre. Until 2004 the president was elected by the People's Consultative Assembly (Majelis Permusyawaratan Rakyat, MPR) and appointed a coalition government that would enjoy support of a majority of legislators in the People's Representative Council (Dewan Perwakilan Rakyat, DPR), Indonesia's main legislative body responsible for passing laws and approving the state budget. Since the introduction of direct presidential elections in 2004, the president has enjoyed an independent popular mandate but still requires DPR approval for the passage of legislation and budget. The eleven DPR standing committees (*komisi*) have also acquired strong bargaining power in the drafting of legislation and budget, as also in the questioning of ministers and officials over matters of public accountability. Christianto Wibisono argues that parliament has become 'a monster' that has no compunction about squeezing the executive, a view that is widely shared among Jakarta's political elite. [23]

Also significant has been the formal independence of the judiciary. Since 1957, first Sukarno and then Suharto had intimidated, subordinated and corrupted the judiciary to become a mere instrument of state power (Lev 1999). One of the conditions of IMF aid after the Asian Crisis was the re-establishment of an independent judiciary as part of the proper architecture of the state. Not taken into account was that independence would entrench and probably exacerbate a high level of corruption. The executive would now need to negotiate and pay for outcomes that once had simply been validated by a tame judiciary (Pompe 2005; Lindsey 2008).

These changes in the nature of political competition ought logically to be reflected in the informal flow of funds. In the Suharto era, the main use of

[23] Christianto Wibisono, interview, Jakarta, 2007.

slush funds was to maintain patronage, whether in rewarding loyalty within the state or in maintaining popular legitimacy through development projects. Under Reformasi, political parties and factions need slush funds because public funding and membership dues are minimal (Mietzner 2008a). One source is through pricing legislative outcomes: ministers, agencies and state enterprises now need to buy the passage of new legislation through parliament and even to smooth the way for favourable committee hearings, just as hostile interest groups may buy damaging questions and parliamentary votes, or perhaps just legislative delay. Within political parties, positions and parliamentary seats are allocated by internal auction, moderated by patronage and influence (Ziegenhain 2008). Parliamentarians may in turn seek to pave the way for their candidates to be appointed as ministers or officials or buy journalistic favour. Business firms including state enterprises are therefore under pressure to contribute funds in return for favours. And, of course, individuals also need support and funds in the scramble for promotion within ministries and agencies, even including Bank Indonesia. To acquire those funds and reward their own supporters, increasingly they need to belong to cliques, factions and parties. This is the world now so aptly described, after Japanese usage, as 'money politics'. No one should be surprised that the combination of parliamentary democracy and regional autonomy has led to corruption becoming more widespread and less ordered.

The presidential succession

Under the New Order, as explained above, President Suharto accumulated slush funds through various devices and deposited them in foundations (yayasan), while contingent funds were kept on hand through loyal cronies, both in state enterprises (Pertamina, Bulog) and in private business (Liem Sioe Liong, Bob Hasan) (Aditjondro 2006). Since Reformasi such informal practices have persisted but the execution has become more discreet in response to more powerful media, the threat of political exposure and the greater risk of sanctions. One clear indication that the informal rules were simply being adjusted to circumstances was the failure over a decade of half-hearted efforts to investigate Suharto's alleged wealth and the role of his foundations. To legitimize his rule and prove that he was not a Suharto puppet, Habibie at first supported the formation of an independent investigative team but backed away when Suharto's lawyer, Yohanes Yakob, threatened to lay bare everyone's secrets (O'Rourke 2002:191).

President Habibie realized from the outset that he needed to build up legitimacy and funds to be re-elected in his own right after the foreshadowed round of general elections. A campaign team (Tim Sukses Habibie) was formed to plan for this (O'Rourke 2002:245-55, 283-91). Sources of funding were readily to hand. In the wake of the Asian Crisis, many business tycoons had seen their companies nationalized and they sought by backdoor means to regain control of the billions of dollars of assets, now held by the Indonesian Bank Restructuring Agency (IBRA) as collateral for non-performing loans. The agency's mandate was gradually to sell off these assets to the highest bidder and re-inject the funds to the state budget. With so many opportunities for influencing the disposal program and generating slush funds, the chairmanship of IBRA immediately became a highly contested and fast-rotating position (Mulholland and Thomas 2002; Basri 2005). An early scandal was the Bank Bali case. The former owner of Bank Bali sought to block its sale to the British Standard and Chartered Bank and made informal payments to various political powerbrokers, in part alleged to be financing President Habibie's re-election campaign (Saydam 1999). Habibie's close ally, Minister of Cooperatives Adi Sasono, used budget and aid funds channelled through cooperatives under the social safety network program to siphon off substantial amounts. In the context of ongoing anti-Chinese violence, pressure was also applied to exact levies from Indonesian-Chinese business magnates (O'Rourke 2002:149-51; Purdey 2006:180-2).

Nevertheless, all Habibie's efforts were in vain. At the June 1999 elections, no party won an outright majority, leaving the former governing party Golkar, now a vehicle for President Habibie, and Megawati Sukarnoputri's Indonesian Democratic Party of Struggle (Partai Demokrasi Indonesia – Perjuangan, PDI-P) to face off for the presidency. The MPR eventually rejected President Habibie's accountability report and he withdrew his candidacy. After out-manoeuvering Megawati in parliamentary negotiations, a third candidate, the blind but ambitious Abdurrahman Wahid (Gus Dur), came to the presidency amidst high hopes that, as a democrat and intellectual, he would decisively break with the New Order. Unfortunately his stubbornness and erratic use of power soon alienated his coalition supporters. Gus Dur tried unconstitutionally to dissolve Parliament through presidential decree but instead was impeached in a backlash from an alliance of party bosses, allowing Vice-President Megawati to succeed him.

During the Gus Dur period (1999-2001), the government was very 'loose' (*longgar*). Business magnates such as the Eka Tjipta Wijaya and Marimutu Sinivasan of the illiquid Sinar Mas and Texmaco groups, respectively, had easy access to the president and his ruling clique as they sought to influence the outcomes of debt restructuring (O'Rourke 2002:330-9, 361-5). The most notorious example of this looseness was that Gus Dur's masseur, Suwondo was even able to 'represent' Gus Dur in establishing a company and pressuring the Bulog Director-General to transfer rents to it. Gus Dur dismissed any prior knowledge or involvement in the case but suspicions remained that he had delegated his masseur Suwondo to get funds from Bulog; this Bulog-gate scandal became grounds for his impeachment (Ridwan and Soewarno 2002; O'Rourke 2002:388-9).

Megawati's government represented a stronger and more disciplined coalition focused on her own PDI-P but, for all her popular legitimacy, Megawati was not a strong political actor in her own right. Her effectiveness depended heavily upon two astute political operators, her husband Taufik Kiemas, widely known as Mr President, who was her political power broker, and her very efficient State Secretary, Bambang Kesowo. Taufik had become a successful businessman in his own right, winning some large public works contracts (Aditjondro 2006:395-6). He formed a close relationship with Jacob Nursalim, the nephew of Sjamsul Nursalim, head of the Gajah Tunggal conglomerate and one of the leading debtors after the Asian Crisis but then in self-imposed exile in Singapore after withholding cooperation with state agencies in the debt-restructuring process. Jacob Nursalim frequently accompanied Taufik Kiemas and seems to have acted as an informal financier. In return, as IBRA's mandate was expiring, Taufik Kiemas arranged for the government at the end of 2002 to 'release and discharge' corporate debtors including Sjamsul Nursalim (Rafick 2008:51, 316-28). Marimutu Sinivasan of the troubled Texmaco group also benefited from Taufik's favour after he had been appointed to the board of that conglomerate (Aditjondro 2006). The coalition government lost one of its pillars in March 2004 when Coordinating Minister for Political and Security Affairs, Susilo Bambang Yudhoyono (SBY), resigned in consequence of growing distrust and animosity to build up popular support in his own right as a basis for winning the direct presidential election a few months later.

SBY came to the presidency in 2004 without a parliamentary majority in his own right. His own minor Democrat Party formed a rainbow coalition including the largest party, Golkar, now led by businessman-cum-politician Jusuf Kalla, who became Vice-President. As a business magnate in his own right, Kalla had reputedly bought his way to Golkar leadership against incumbent Akbar Tanjung, who had backed Megawati in her failed re-election bid. Kalla proved to be a wily politician and a powerful executive Vice-President. His influence soon led to tensions in regard to SBY's anti-corruption campaign, with a government helicopter deal through his family's Bukaka group being one of several issues taken up by the media.[24] Nevertheless, the anti-corruption drive and the growing effectiveness of the new Corruption Eradication Commission (Komisi Pemberantasan Korupsi, KPK) meant that political funds now had to be raised more discreetly, not least by the President himself. Lacking personal wealth and without the support of a large party, SBY had to rely on an inner circle of sometimes compet-

24 See 'Kisah kalla dan heli bukaka', *Tempo* 20-26 March 2007.

ing indigenous business magnates, most notably Jusuf Kalla, Coordinating Minister Aburizal Bakrie of the Bakrie group, Fahmi Idris (Kodel Group) and Tanri Abeng (Tason Group), as well as some leading figures from the Sino-Indonesian business community, especially Siti Hartati Murdaya (Central Cipta Murdaya group).[25] Slush funds were also accumulated informally in foundations such as Yayasan Puri Cikeas and Yayasan Majelis Dzikir SBY Nurussalam where they could be deployed at arm's length from the president (Aditjondro 2009).

This brief review of the several changes in government since 1998 points to a fairly rapid turnover in governing coalitions, ministers and backers. At the same time, many of the leading figures remain the same and there is a good deal of circulation. Thus intra-elite rivalry is a good deal more complex than a zero-sum game. In the rest of this section we explore how the working of parliament and its relations with the executive and state apparatus are shaped by informal behaviours and lubricated by slush funds.

Parliament

Nowhere is the state-as-marketplace more apparent than in Indonesia's national parliament, the DPR. Coalition governments looking to re-election are highly vulnerable to parliamentary obstruction because it lays them open to criticism of inaction. And within the DPR standing committees (*komisi*), there are countless opportunities for negotiation over legislation, committee hearings, projects and appointments (Haris 2007). If a powerholder or business magnate needs to do a deal with the DPR, it has to be done with money: 'They only will listen and agree to money.'[26]

Political gossip in Jakarta wittily distinguishes two kinds of parliamentary committees: 'wet' committees (*komisi mata air*) and 'dry' or 'tear drop' committees (*komisi air mata*). Lucrative committees include budgetary affairs, finance, forestry, transportation and defence. Of all 11 committees, that dealing with financial and monetary affairs (Komisi XI) is reputedly the wettest, that dealing with trade, industry and state enterprises (Komisi VI) the next, followed by Defense (Komisi I), Primary Resources (Komisi IV), Transport and Telecommunications (Komisi V) and Energy and Mining (Komisi VII);[27] the least lucrative committee is probably religious affairs (Komisi VIII).

While the powers of parliament derive from the constitution, legislation and administrative codes, the exercise of those powers is shaped by informal

25 See 'Sekoci Sang Presiden', *Tempo* 28 May-3 June 2007.

26 Adnan Buyung Nasution, interview, Jakarta, 2007.

27 See 'Pengakuan dari Komisi Mata Air', http://majalah.tempointeraktif.com/id/arsip/2002/09/30/LU/mbm.20020930.LU80999.id.html, No. 31/XXXI/30-9-2002 (accessed 1-6-2010).

norms. Five kinds of informal behaviours or, in Indonesian terms, 'common practices' (*praktek-praktek lazim*) may be distinguished. First is negotiation over the content of legislation. State ministries, departments and agencies compete for influence in the drafting of laws. For example, Bank Indonesia and the State Mint (Perum Percetakan Uang Republik Indonesia, Peruri) competed over the right to print money under the revised Finance Law.[28] Bank Indonesia had a slush fund which, among other purposes, could be drawn on for making payments to members of parliament to secure favourable consideration of legislation or to facilitate committee hearings. Exposure of this practice by the KPK led to the imprisonment of the former head of Bank Indonesia and indictments against other directors, including a deputy-director and the father-in-law of the president's son. Committees also allow outside parties such as the Chamber of Commerce (Kamar Dagang dan Industri, Kadin) or private business interests to lobby for favourable treatment, as under the prolonged negotiations over a new Shipping Law (Dick 2008). Even when drafting in committee is regarded as complete, further payments may be required before parliamentarians are willing to vote on the measure. Ministers who do not authorize payments find their legislation held up.

Second is the determination of budgetary allocations and the disbursements. In the past, the DPR did not have power over project allocations. It can now make decisions over not only national strategic allocations but down to local-level projects. Hotels around the parliamentary complex bustle with local government delegations from all over the country. The Finance Committee is the primary portal for foreign aid projects, also a gateway to influencing local government projects. The disbursement of disaster relief illustrates how the system works. There is a specified global budgetary allocation but committees can block the release of funds, thereby forcing local governments to draw upon their own resources. Local governments are obliged to inflate the required allocation, employ a broker (*calo*) to meet the relevant committee members and agree to paying committee members a substantial cut of at least 20-30% before the funds will be released, a practice tantamount to extortion (*pemerasan*).[29] Similarly, a business magnate wanting a product in the budget can use brokers to pay off members of a special parliamentary committee (*panitia khusus, pansus*) so that the company name is formally inserted into the specifications (*spek*) of the project.[30] Ever working their mobile phones, brokers meet parliamentarians along the pathways and in the corridors and canteens of the parliamentary buildings, even mingling

28 See 'Menarik pak pos ke khitah', Gatra 10-2-2003, http://www.gatra.com/artikel.php?pil=23&id=25372 (accessed 1-6-2010).

29 Confidential interview, Jakarta, 2007.

30 See 'Uang haram mengalir sampai Senayan', Gatra 10-7-2008, http://www.gatra.com/2008-07-16/artikel.php?id=116620 (accessed 1-6-2010).

in the standing committee offices – Defence Minister Juwono Sudarsono tried unsuccessfully to prevent brokers from influencing members of the Defence Committee (Komisi I).[31] Of course, the brokers also take their cut but they allow the principals to avoid the complications of direct contact.

Third is the determination of property rights and the legality of business activities. Parliamentary committees have assumed powers to issue permits and approvals that used to be at the discretion of the bureaucracy and a matter of ministerial responsibility. One example is the definition of property rights associated with land. Business magnates compete to obtain permits for amending land-use. A DPR member was recently convicted and jailed by KPK for accepting payment to alienate land in Riau province from forest to commercial use (*hak peruntukan*).[32] The DPR can also play a role determining property rights in non-land cases: the Bank Indonesia scandal referred to above revealed that executives of state banks wanting to sell shares needed to obtain 'approval' from the majority of DPR members on the Finance Committee.

Fourth is influence over appointments and promotions. Some appointments are determined by parliament, others by the government but may still require *de facto* parliamentary approval. In 2008 there was a tussle between the government and parliament over the appointment of the new Governor of Bank Indonesia, two presidential nominees being rejected before Professor Boediono was finally approved. In the same year the reappointment of KPK Vice-Chairman, Amien Sunaryadi, was rejected by parliament. A more general case was that of Minister for Oceans and Fisheries, Rokhmin Dharuri, who collected money from his departmental officials by way of leaks and levies to top up the ministerial slush fund set up by his predecessors. He then distributed the funds as patronage to members of the executive and parliament. When this became known, a big scandal ensued, leading to his arrest in November 2006 (Rafick 2008:55-7). There seems to have been no ulterior motive beyond keeping him in good favour and hopefully being rewarded with a more senior cabinet position in the next government, testimony to the informal influence of parliament on cabinet appointments, notwithstanding that the formal power to appoint cabinet members lies in the hands of the president. Dharuri simply acknowledged the new informal rules of power that govern the relations between the executive and parliament.

Fifth is influence over the dissemination of information. Not only in Indonesia is payment made for asking parliamentary questions. In Indonesia, however, payment is also made for not asking questions. Company directors are summoned to parliament nominally on grounds of accountability but

31 See 'Para makelar di seputar anggota dewan', Gatra 1-11-2007 http://www.gatra.com/2007-10-29/majalah/beli.php?pil=23&id=109150 (accessed 1-6-2010).

32 See 'Uang haram mengalir sampai Senayan', Gatra 10-7-2008, http://www.gatra.com/2008-07-16/artikel.php?id=116620 (accessed 1-6-2010).

also as a basis for negotiating payments. Thus if a director-general or head of a state enterprise wished to avoid or enjoy only mild committee scrutiny at scheduled or special hearings, payments may be issued to members of the parliamentary commission in question. An 'uncooperative' director may be ridiculed, demoted and/or fired. Contacts between members of parliament and the media are a reliable way to leak sensitive information.

These sets of informal parliamentary behaviours focus attention upon processes of negotiation between parliament, the executive, the bureaucracy, state enterprises and the private sector. Such negotiations involve political calculation, personal influence and often monetary payments. For some routine matters there are even tacitly understood schedules of prices based upon precedent, a clear sign of markets. The intrusion of money into parliamentary practice is certainly not because parliamentarians are poor. In 2005, ordinary members of parliament enjoyed monthly salaries (excluding their many perquisites) of Rp 39 million, twice that of ministers and two-thirds that of the president himself.[33] The new mode of informal money politics may be better understood as the dynamics of a party democracy in a patronage society. Parliamentarians, committee members and chairs, faction leaders and party bosses need to raise and disburse slush funds to acquire position, maintain loyalty and negotiate outcomes, as also of course to campaign in elections. These expenses are not covered by salary and perquisites or the tiny amount of public funding to political parties. The system works but it is not what would be regarded as good governance and involves a good deal of outright corruption. Several national parliamentarians and numerous provincial and local representatives have been arrested and charged by the KPK. At the trial of parliamentarian Hamka Yandhu, Corruption Court judge Hendra Yospin asked him, 'Do all laws being discussed in the House need extra money from the [Executive]?' 'There are some', was the guarded reply, seeming to confirm that bribery has indeed become a norm in parliament (Wardany 2009).

A particular feature of the new money politics is that slush funds are sometimes shared across apparently competing political parties and factions. The evidence is still circumstantial because only in the event of scandals, investigation and trials do the details ever emerge. The pattern showed up in Fisheries Minister Rokhmin Dharuri's donations across the spectrum of coalition political parties. Evidence in March 2009 by parliamentarian Hamka revealed how payments to committee members are shared between the political parties. Thus, in the case of the payment of Rp 31.5 billion (US$1.86 million) made in 2003 by Bank Indonesia to two members of the Finance and Banking Committee (Komisi XI) to smooth passage of amendments to the Bank Indonesia Law, funds were redistributed to the Committee Chairman,

33 See 'Gaji pejabat ditata ulang', *Republika* 21-2-2005.

members of the National Awakening Party (Partai Kebangkitan Bangsa, PKB), PDI-P, the Crescent and Star Party (Partai Bulan Bintang, PBB) and the National Police and Military faction (Wardany 2009). While the money politics may be crude, the political logic is sophisticated: parliamentary politics in Indonesia is not a zero-sum game. All political parties are seen as stakeholders in some degree and the committee system is one of the modes of distribution.[34] In other words, corrupt informal norms help to maintain a Higleyian elite consensus that moderates intra-elite rivalry and the social divisions that would flow from it. Marcus Mietzner's (2008a) portrayal of Reformasi party politics as 'centripetal', in contrast to the 'centrifugal' politics of the 1950s, points in the same direction, as does Dan Slater's (2004) analysis of collusive 'party cartels'. Just as a powerholder who did not share the spoils of office would be regarded as greedy and selfish, so a party which monopolized the spoils of government would be seen as an unworthy coalition partner.

Conclusion

History seeks to tease out patterns of continuity and change. 'Regime change' in Indonesia is readily apparent in drastic modification of the political system along with its constitution, laws and formal procedures. Yet regime change is also a matter of transition, during which some things remain the same. In particular, many of the people holding power in the 'new' state are those who used to hold power in the old, while much of the formal structure and organization of state institutions and bureaucracy also survives. Even more tenacious are habits of thinking and routines of behaviour. A good understanding of the democratic transition, in Indonesia as elsewhere, therefore requires study of continuity and change in informal modes of behaviour. The 'who' of political analysis and journalism is often less important than the patterns of informal norms and behaviours that constrain what does or does not happen.

This chapter has argued two propositions. First, a very important element of continuity between regimes is the widespread use within the state apparatus of 'slush funds'. While the mechanisms of raising, storing and distributing funds have been adapted to parliamentary democracy, the informal rules are much the same. The bureaucracy is still underfunded and reliant on informal leaks and levies for top-up funding. Powerholders still engage in private business, leverage corrupt deals and manipulate flows of rents with fierce competition for the most lucrative fiefs within the state apparatus. Some of the slush funds are still siphoned off into foundations which, though

34 Indonesia is not a unique case. Japan has long demonstrated similar dynamics. Even at the height of the Liberal Democratic Party hegemony, opposition parties routinely shared in the spoils, albeit in lesser degree (Bowen 2003).

managed more at arm's length from the main political actors, remain characterized by secrecy and lack of accountability. What is somewhat unusual about Indonesian democracy is that money politics applies not only to relations between the state and society but also within the state itself. Outcomes between the executive and legislature, as also between state agencies like Bank Indonesia or state enterprises and the legislature, are subject to intricate negotiations that involve monetary transfers. In other words, political horse-trading – in Indonesian ox-trading (*dagang sapi*) – is literally a matter of negotiating prices and payments as part of the outcome. Money politics in Indonesia therefore penetrates much deeper into the state than the pork-barrelling associated with electoral politics in many other countries. The informal behaviours that govern the collection and distribution of slush funds have monetized relations even between the organs of the state and created a large political marketplace at its heart. That is not to say that the state can be reduced to a market place but that patterns of routine informal behaviours have created markets within the state itself alongside the more conventional transactions between state actors and society. This has been accompanied by a marked shift in power from the executive to parliament. Slater (2004:66) nicely describes Reform-era cabinets as 'the gilded bridge between parliament and the presidency'.

Secondly, representative democracy has revived a lively intra-elite rivalry that had been tightly constrained during the New Order. The hierarchical patronage of the New Order has given way to much more horizontal competition between parties and factions. Models of a homogeneous elite are obviously no longer appropriate, if indeed they ever were. Instead the state has become a site of fierce intra-elite contestation for the political spoils. Yet the outcome has not been what might have been predicted in 1998. Fragmented parliaments and unstable coalition governments have been the bane of Indonesian democracy. The general elections of 1999, 2004 and 2009 have entrenched fragmentation but they have not resulted in unstable coalition government. After an initial five years of jostling, the 2004-2009 period saw a stable coalition with only minor cabinet reshuffles. In Higleyian terms, there has been an elite consensus. The analytical challenge is to understand how intra-elite rivalry has been moderated to maintain a workable political peace during a turbulent decade of transition.

At its most crude, our troubling contention is that this elite democratic consensus has been underpinned by a high level of corruption. After a decade of Reformasi, Indonesian democracy has achieved a degree of political stability founded on agreement over the basic formal rules and a set of informal rules to give them effect, yet in no way could the outcome be characterized as 'good governance'. Since 2004 the KPK has vigorously prosecuted top officials, ministers and parliamentarians without obviously changing modes of behaviour, except perhaps to make corruption more discreet. Notwithstanding public anger and international condemnation, corruption is proving extraordinarily resilient because its various informal behaviours are so embedded within the cultural habits of society, especially among elites. In 2009 KPK's relentless campaign provoked a backlash from within the power elite: the chairman and two commissioners were arrested and obliged to resign over murder and corruption charges that subsequently looked to have been fabricated by senior figures within the Police and Attorney-General's Department. KPK looked in vain for support from either parliament or the executive. Clearly we need much more insight into culture, society and politics before we can be confident that anti-corruption strategies will be sustainable.

Cases and sectors

JOHN F. McCARTHY

The limits of legality

State, governance and resource control in Indonesia

As anyone reading the Indonesian press or scholarly literature will inevitably note, the problem of illegality plagues discussions of natural resource management – with so much debate devoted to the problems of 'illegal' mining, logging and fishing.[1] According to reports 90% of community mining in Indonesia is regarded as 'illegal', with illegal mines employing between 465,000 and a million people, and operating in an estimated 77,000 mining sites (Lestari 2008; Manaf 1999). The extent of production is also immense, with 'illegal' mines in South Kalimantan alone extracting up to 9.4 million tons of coal per year (Manaf 1999). These mining operations involve large trucks, excavators and machinery including smelters and ships, with large illegal stockpiles of minerals standing by ports equipped with barges waiting to ship the mineral out for export. Given the very large sums of money required, these mining operations are clearly funded by large business networks. According to these accounts the ecological impacts are also extensive, with landslides, soil erosion, sedimentation in streams, acid rock drainage, together with mercury, cyanide, tailing and toxic fumes poisoning the water, land and atmosphere and affecting fishing and farming activities (Lestari 2008).

News and development agency reports have often stated that 'illegal logging' extends in a similar fashion, amounting to two-thirds of the annual timber harvest in Indonesia.[2] In 2002 one report estimated that Indonesia's illegal logging industry was worth around US$5 billion per year. At the high tide of 'illegal logging' after 1998, this involved a clientelist system extending from highly capitalized actors with extensive funding and large, industrial scale business operations, to mid-size district-based timber barons, down to the capillaries of the system which included village-based logging teams deploying buffalo and chain saws.[3]

1 Schulte Nordholt and Van Klinken 2007a; Resosudarmo 2006; Warren and McCarthy 2008.
2 DFID 2007. For discussions of the illegal logging problem see also Tacconi 2007.
3 For accounts, see McCarthy 2006, 2007b.

While these illegalities are clearly complex phenomena, in donor and policy narratives the environmental problem revolves around the question of legality. As the UK's aid agency website noted in 2007:

> A major factor that has allowed illegal logging to thrive is confusion over the law. This is why the governments of Indonesia and the UK got together in 2002 to agree on a definition of what was and was not legal. The resulting Memorandum of Understanding (MoU) set out clearly the laws on logging, making it much easier for the courts to prosecute offenders (DFID 2007).

The problem of 'uncontrolled' logging and mining is naturalized as a legal question in large part because virtually all natural resource policies, plans and projects are ultimately expressed in legal terms. In all sorts of ways state agencies set about using the law to control access and use of natural resources, in order to lead to some desired set of environmental consequences, to change people's behaviour for environmental ends, to generate revenue, and so on. The problem, as simply framed in press, natural resource management and governance narratives, is a question of legality: why can't the state implement its laws? Why does it so often fail?

While state failure in environmental management contributes to environmental decline, it also brings up the very question of the state. It is commonly observed that state legitimacy rests on avoiding political instability through administrative effectiveness and maintaining political order. State environmental management – encompassing the protection of collective resources and public health – plays a key role in establishing that legitimacy. The role of natural disasters in traditional cosmologies suggests as much, as does, more recently, the perception of environmental collapse posed by the forest fires during the legitimacy crisis that led to Suharto's downfall in 1997-1998, and the role of cyclone Katrina in the decline of President Bush. The state is considered the essential provider of key public goods through regulating natural resource management, and securing desirable environmental outcomes upon which so many livelihoods, production activities and underlying environmental services depend. The problem, as Evans (1995:5) has noted, is that 'all states would like to portray themselves as carrying out a project that benefits society as a whole, but sustaining this image requires continuous effort'.

This chapter is concerned with the question: why has the pervasive illegality in natural resource sectors persisted for so long in the face of so many campaigns, donor initiatives and legal changes aimed at its eradication? While these interventions continue to meet with limited success, the illegality narrative continues to pose the problem in the same terms. Accordingly, here I will consider a number of uncomfortable questions: what purpose does the policy narrative of illegality serve? Does it perhaps support particular political projects? What role does it play in justifying particular interventions? How does it help envision a rational-legal, bureaucratic state even when any study of illegality in this sector points to its very absence? If it does this, does it not conceal as much as it reveals? How might we reframe the legality/illegality opposition in order to more usefully understand the logic of illegality?

In the first section I discuss the question of legality with respect to the concepts of law and the state before, in the second section, considering the historical genesis of this problem in relation to the state in Indonesia. In the third section I discuss Indonesia's most recent experiment with governance approaches, focusing on the role of narratives of illegality during the decentralization reforms.

The idea of the state and the limitations of legality

Lurking behind illegality narratives are a set of Western ideas about law derived from a tradition of political thought stretching back to the Enlightenment and beyond. Reason should serve as the primary basis of authority, and law represents the most rational foundation for the social order (Griffiths 2002). In this tradition authority, centralized in the state and represented through government, is legitimate if the state 'as an organized entity is conceived to be limited by laws and by fundamental principles of legality'. In other words authority needs to accord with 'values of procedural fairness or due process' that are applied in the ways laws are enacted and implemented (Allan 1998). In contrast, an activity is 'illegal' and hence deemed unacceptable if it violates state law. In this way, in so many contemporary discussions of 'illegal logging' or 'illegal mining', the state and its laws *ipso facto* gain legitimacy merely because state law should have precedence over other possible normative orders. In other words the state, through its capacity to define (if not implement) rules, sets the parameters of the policy discourse which frames how the issue is typically considered.

For example, in policy and press narratives 'illegal logging' – known as 'anarchic', 'uncontrolled' or 'wild logging' (*penebangan liar*) – has long been considered the main critical problem to be addressed in forest management. Clearly it is indeed a major issue, especially when loggers enter into national parks and steep protection forests, as this is seen to contribute to biodiversity loss, floods, erosion, landslides and carbon emissions. Yet, arguably poorly managed but legally sanctioned extractive industries can have even more significant ecological impacts. For instance, industrial timber extraction carried out under the selective logging system developed under the framework 1967 forestry law led to significant forest degradation. According to the Ministry of Forestry's own figures, there are now 59 million hectares of 'degraded forest land' (Departemen Kehutanan 2008), mostly areas logged under the legal timber regime. Rather than sustainable production, legal timber production had dropped from 27 million cubic metres in 1990 to 5.8 million cubic metres in 2005.

Drawing on this historical inheritance, the governance discussion places 'the rule of law' alongside democracy, a free press and free and fair elections as critical achievements of modernity. This is reflected in attempts to measure the extent to which 'agents have confidence in and abide by the rules of society'. For instance, quantifiers have developed a 'World Map of the Rule of Law Index' that colours in the world map from green (in Western Europe, Australasia and North America, where we have the rule of law) to red (the bottom, predominantly African, quartile, where law is problematic). With all its problems applying state law, Indonesia finds itself painted pink – somewhere in the middle. The aim of development policy then would be to stimulate the process of evolution towards the green quartile.[4]

While without doubt the law remains a critical element in the dynamics leading to poor social and environmental outcomes, the problem with this policy narrative is that it is somewhat reminiscent of modernization theory: the assumption is that with the right assistance and governance support, the Indonesian state will evolve towards Weber's ideal typical rational-legal, bureaucratic state.[5] Yet, as earlier attempts to transplant a foreign legal culture during the time of the 'Law in Development' movement found during the 1960s, institutional arrangements are not so readily reformed.

This line of inquiry suggests that we need to bear in mind the role that the concept of legality – or what we might call a narrative of illegality – plays in relation to what Abrams (1988) called the 'idea of the state'. From Abrams' perspective the state is an ideological effect, acting to homogenize and legitimize a disparate collection of actors and institutions as 'the state'. 'The idea of the state' leads us to imagine a coherent national state extending from central government agencies to encompass local authorities, thus delocalizing a disparate set of actors and practices. It does this by applying the 'state' label to local agents who, although claiming to be working in the name of 'the state', are actually focused around localized political concerns (Gupta 1995). As Pierce writes of Nigeria, from this perspective 'the state's primary power is an ideological figure that allows government actors to present their actions as being fully rational.' Through the operation of the state-effect, 'officials can claim legitimacy for actions and projects that, were they not labelled state actions, would be wholly illegitimate'. In other words the function of the state idea is

4 Kaufmann et al. 1999; Methodologies in the Promotion of the Rule of Law http://www.passia.org/seminars/2007/Seminar 20 Nov/Methodologies in the Promotion of the Rule of Law.ppt (accessed 1-6-2010).

5 As Pierce (2006:900) has noted in an African context, the modernization idea of a modern state governing traditional peoples retains its salience.

to enable particular political projects, opening up 'possible avenues of action' while 'masking their political content' (Pierce 2006:898). The idea of the state and its concomitant legality generates 'possibilities for on-the-ground action', nowhere more so than with respect to the control of natural resources.

Illegality can then be considered a state effect: through the working of the narrative of 'illegality', paradoxically we come to imagine a coherent, rational-legal state actor as the answer to the problem. If we had a coherent state agency with ample capacity, this narrative suggests, we could clean up these 'wild' or 'chaotic' activities. In other words, the 'idea of the state' is invoked through its very absence in the regulation of logging and mining. As Pierce (2006:899) has observed in the Nigerian context, the logic of the idea of the state acts to cover the state's 'inability to act as it ought'.

Further, the narrative of 'illegality' involves labelling a disparate 'collection of individual actions and practices embedded in particular circumstances', in the process reducing these to 'a general condition' (Pierce 2006:899). In this way the illegality narrative closes discussion. For while research into extra-legal timber and mining activities point to their complex nature, the narrative simply fixes these disparate phenomena as 'illegal', reducing our need to inquire further into their causality.

The function of the illegality might be compared to the phenomenon of 'displacement' in Freud's *Interpretation of dreams*. According to Freud (1991), under the censoring influence of the moral component of the psyche, threatening impulses during dreams are displaced so that the essence of dream-thoughts only find passing and indistinct representation in dreams. In a similar way, under the influence of the dominant political forces, narratives of illegality shift policy attention away from the unacceptable topics of how access to resources is shaped by the political economy and property relations onto the comparatively safe issue of law enforcement. Accordingly, rather than unsavoury discussions of how laws open the door to a political economy linked to legal entitlements that disregard long-standing property claims (discussed later), the policy community and the press focuses on better mechanisms of law enforcement. For, if these illegal activities are simply examples of breaking the law, we need donor interventions and governance reforms to 'strengthen state capacity' (an opaque expression) and reduce corruption. But these easy assumptions – sustained by the ideological function of narratives of illegality – do not sweep the problem away.

This fissure has never been missed by regional communities. They have witnessed state-licensed timber and mining extraction in areas subject to local property claims, and the enclosure of nearby areas for nature conservation, even as their own small-scale activities were deemed 'illegal'. By the time of the economic crisis of 1997, rent-seeking combined with a highly partial use of the law to support large-scale extractive industries licensed from Jakarta –

often in disregard of local sensibilities – had worked to de-legitimize all state environmental management, including that of national parks and protected forests. This was especially the case where the considerable coercive capacity of the central state had been used by politico-bureaucratic business coalitions to over-ride locally embedded property rights. With the temporary collapse of the state coercive apparatus after 1997, this contributed to a pandemic of 'illegality' in the natural resource sector (McCarthy and Warren 2008). In contrast, a more nuanced approach would require us to unpack the legality/illegality opposition, and to examine the mismatch between legal logic and everyday practices. Such inquiries should reveal the role of 'illegality' in its wider context, where it becomes part of an underlying logic of political relationships that actually sustain it.

A social theory approach to the state and its laws suggests that the law reflects power relations. We need to study who makes the law, who uses it, and how. This perspective points to the need to investigate how the 'illegal' is constituted, how and why particular resource entitlements are legally protected while others are not. For the state system – the police, army, forestry and mining agencies – clearly sustains some entitlements while seeking to quash others. Those with these entitlements can gain access to law enforcement and dispute resolution processes such as the courts, while others remain subject to informal dispute resolution processes and extra-legal modes of resource control embedded in asymmetrical power relations.

Law is a fundamental expression of state power. On the one hand, through law the state works to create, strengthen, limit and legitimize particular patterns of resource use by granting resource entitlements legal status (for example, timber or mining concessions). On the other hand, as these legal rules are invoked in negotiating access and control of natural resources, they affect the distribution of benefits from resource extraction: state law can shape the power relations so central to resource control. Further, the state's capacity to legitimize the exercise of power and to apply this power in particular contexts clearly affects the pattern of resource use. The sociology of law suggests that we can't assume a direct relationship between a legal rule and an outcome. We need to understand interactions in the specific setting, including the strategies various actors take up and how they make use of various regulatory orders to pursue their interests. Law both constrains and is a resource. Law often 'follows rather than determines social relationships' (Crook and Houtzager 2001). The processes of interpretation and transformation that occur in local settings give law a local and a specific character.

Studying the state: placing 'illegal' practices in a historical and institutional context

In short, the foregoing discussion suggests that we need first to restore the heavily laden terms 'the state' and 'the law' to their historical context, and then consider again how applicable they are to the management of Indonesia's environment. Inevitably this leads to a discussion of state formation, the emergence and extension of state legal norms, and of the social interests that underlie particular areas of environmental regulation in history.

State law emerged in Indonesia at 'the cutting edge of colonialism' (Merry 1991:46). It was essential to the colonial project to govern its subjects and control its territories. With respect to natural resources, European law played a primary role in state objectives – including the extraction of timber, the control of land for plantation development, the creation of a wage labour force, and the redefinitions of property relations in rural domains. Yet, while the Dutch brought with them the European concept of the state and 'its corresponding institutional arrangements', as elsewhere in the colonial era, they had to contend with 'other surviving concepts and structures – different from and antagonistic to the new concept' (Nandy 1992:266).

The Dutch colonial state practice of indirect rule involved recruiting indigenous leaders, allowing that areas of life should be left to local, 'customary' or indigenous law, and repackaging indigenous institutions to incorporate them into the bottom rung of the colonial state. Inevitably, this involved allowing space for locally embedded patronage networks sustained by all sorts of payments for access to the local state and use of resources in the local domain. These 'informal' payments defied state attempts to formalize them (McCarthy 2006). Given the poor penetration of the Dutch colonial state, locally embedded institutional arrangements governing natural resources, particularly property rights, remained strong, especially in those 'remote' areas outside the core colonial economic domains.

In many respects these practices have remained, if not intact, at least normatively relevant, constituting an informal route to access that has often worked in parallel with the state system. There are two reasons for this persistence. First, after independence, the state failed to develop the fiscal capacity to support local state agencies sufficiently. Local state-based actors, including military commands and party apparatuses, needed to fund the patronage networks that kept the machinery working. Consequently, local state-based actors developed 'off budget' sources of revenue to support their operations, particularly after President Sukarno introduced the chaotic Guided Democracy period in 1959 (Obidzinski 2002). Second, the official system of resource entitlements either insufficiently provided room for local resource practices and property rights or created formal and expensive barriers to access (for example, red tape and the difficulty and expense of processing permits). This left much local mining and timber activity in the 'illegal' category.

Here it is important to bear in mind a critical tension brought to light by studies of the Indonesian state during previous decades. On the one hand, building on the vestiges of the colonial bureaucracy, Suharto was held to have forged a state with considerable coercive and autonomous capacity, an order vested in the trappings of a rational-legal, coherent bureaucracy. Here, power and governance were structured 'around institutions qua institutions' (Kuhonta 2008). On the other hand, Suharto's regime was often portrayed as dominated by powerful 'politico-bureaucrats' who were entangled with big business (Robison and Rosser 1998). Their interests penetrated the state to the extent that they hijacked natural resource policy in significant ways. The archetypical example was the capacity of Bob Hasan to dominate forestry policy (Barr 1998).

Yet, at the time of independence Indonesian nationalists, as in so many other newly decolonized states, had hailed the modern state as 'the clue to western success and political dominance' (Nandy 1992:266). Embracing the Enlightenment concept of rational governance, they embarked on an ambitious project to establish the primacy of the state system. Nationalist state building projects judged all other political arrangements only in terms of how they served 'the needs of or conform[ed] to the idea of the nation state' (Nandy 1992:267). This insistence on conformity caused serious problems for natural resource management in Indonesia.

As numerous NGO critiques of state resource management frameworks have suggested, the post-colonial state proved either unable or unwilling to expunge the colonial legal assumptions embedded in natural resource law. Rather than erasing these assumptions, in many cases the concepts were reformulated and reapplied in various ways. For instance, the colonial state had developed the concepts of state domain and idle land, concepts that had been used in various ways under the agrarian and forest laws. The 'domain declaration' (*domeinverklaring*) facilitated the development of the Dutch plantation system by allowing that all lands without statutory certified ownership (*eigendom*) remained 'waste' land not under permanent use and hence the 'free' domain of the state.[6]

Post-independence, a clause in the Indonesian constitution stated that the new nation's natural wealth should be regulated by the state 'for the welfare of the nation'.[7] During the early Suharto years this 'state right of regulation' (*hak menguasai negara*) was extended under the Basic Mining Law (UU no. 11/1967) and the Basic Forestry Law (UU no. 5/1967). The Basic Forestry Law

6 Tjondronegoro 1991; Peluso and Vandergeest 2001; Heryani and Grant 2004.

7 'Bumi dan air dan kekayaan alam yang terkandung didalamnya dikuasai oleh negara dan dipergunakan untuk sebesar-besar kemakmuran rakyat' (Clause 33, 1945 Constitution).

of 1967, as given force in the forest mapping process, built on this principle by placing approximately 70% of the national land area at the disposal of the state.[8] This opened up the possibility of a particular political project – using forest resources to underwrite Suharto's patronage machine. In the name of this 'state right of regulation', Suharto's policy facilitated extractive industries via state-licensed concessions issued irrespective of pre-existing notions of tenure and territory. Thus state laws outlawed long-established rights and practices over a huge area which lacked state permits. The state handed out concessions over this land to retired generals and others close to the regime, as rewards for services rendered.

Earlier, the new state had set out to create a single framework for the regulation of land issues for all Indonesian citizens. The objective was to overcome the pluralism of colonial land law. However, by not providing for an effective system for recognizing complex local property rights systems, and by providing a strong national interest clause that was open to abuse, the Basic Agrarian Law of 1961 at best provided only very weak protection to that majority of rural property right holders whose land remained without full certificates. The New Order then legislated to attract foreign investors, granting them more certain, state-protected property rights. Taken together, these two moves merely exacerbated the legal uncertainty and the conflicts that confound the resource sector in Indonesia. By creating distributional justice problems, such policies ultimately undermined the legitimacy of state control over natural resources while at the same time constituting many of the 'illegalities' that have plagued natural resource management.

Too often the discussion of legality in the resource sector leads into dry unresolved arguments over the constraints 'customary communities' (*masyarakat adat*) experience under state law.[9] The main point here is that, when the contemporary state attempts to exert legal control over land and surface resources, including mineral and petroleum found under the ground, it inevitably bumps up against parallel – albeit overshadowed – normative orders that have much to say about how access should be regulated and benefits distributed. The state attempts to make legitimate and enforceable decisions based on state legal assumptions that insufficiently take into account the locally embedded assumptions regarding how the benefits derived from the local domain should be distributed (McCarthy 2006). This goes some way toward explaining why the state system faces so much difficulty in making locally legitimate and enforceable regulations addressing local environmental problems.

It is tempting, at this stage, to reframe the issue in terms of 'legal com-

8 This territorial strategies involved creating what Peluso and Vandergeest (2001) have called 'political forests' – that is lands which the state declares as 'forest' (according to law) irrespective of pre-existing property rights systems.

9 For a recent overview of these debates, see Davidson and Henley 2007.

plexity', since state law operates in domains characterized by competing sets of rules derived from the plurality of legislative, executive and bureaucratic activities as well as from the local normative ordering. But this notion of legal complexity can obscure the distinction between legal norms and the power play that is so important in determining outcomes. Local officials have considerable discretion in deciding how policy gets translated into decisions and the extent to which accommodations are made with regional interests and 'local customs'. Hence, local society confronts a 'local version' of the state – that is, a 'policy interpretation' quite different from the (nominal) intentions for which the law may have been created in the distant capital (Von Benda-Beckmann 1989).

During field studies in Aceh in the 1990s I found that localized normative systems continued to regulate areas of social life outside the reach of the state. For instance, poor villagers had long met their livelihood and timber needs through logging practices, in areas informally subject to a local 'right of avail', even though they lacked formal state licences in what state foresters had mapped as conservation areas and state forest. In making decisions that might be legitimate and enforceable locally within a context of overlapping normative systems, state-based actors needed to pragmatically take into account the local moral economy. They were well placed to make use of the ideological device of the state. By threatening to apply the state law against practices that were formally illegal, they gained the capacity to extract rents.[10] Accepting bribes (or extracting 'rents') for permitting 'extra-legal' resource practices obtained degrees of local legitimacy if those practices were more in keeping with local perceptions of justice than the formal law. Moreover, extra-legal rents helped close a chronic budget shortfall. Those with power and resources had the means to acquire the required permits. Villagers living close to the subsistence line did not. They carried out their mining, logging and fishing outside the umbrella of the law. In many cases villagers then sold on their products to actors with officially recognized marketing or processing permits. Accordingly, those in possession of licences had the capacity to render the resources 'legal' and to sell them on at much higher prices, thus winning the lion's share of the benefits. At the time it was hardly surprising that it was rare for cases of 'illegal' mining or logging to get to court. Even if the village logging and mining teams were apprehended, the law enforcement agencies were reluctant to put poor people in jail for small-scale livelihood-related offences. Meanwhile, the well-connected agents behind the operations – who usually had considerable political investments – were hardly ever apprehended.

10 By outlawing local extractive practices while granting particular actors licences and permits, the system of rent seeking allows the latter to 'launder' resources extracted in the informal 'illegal' sector, in the process extracting the lion's share of rents.

From a 'post-institutionalist' perspective, outcomes emerge from processes rather than from regulatory orders. The focus shifts from the formal institutions to the complex interactions that occur when competing actors attempt to make use of particular repertoires of shifting institutional arrangements and normative orders. They deploy only those particular rules that most work to their advantage (Wollenberg, Anderson and Edmunds 2001). Rather than studying static regulations, we can understand what is occurring more readily from studying actors' expectations and strategies – including their use of law. The processes that actually shape resource outcomes can often be complex and fluid. They diverge substantially from more public forms of decision making and negotiation as set out by state laws. The *de facto* arrangements determining resource outcomes tend to be deeply embedded in the local world where such processes come into play.

This has consequences for outsiders wishing to 'craft' more functional, formally rational institutional orders. They find this state of affairs perplexing. In the social and political world in which an issue is situated, rights of access and compliance with rules are often ambiguous. Outcomes often emerge from continuous processes of dispute and negotiation. In such contexts, outsiders who wish to intervene successfully find it difficult to simply apply the law as it appears on the books. They may need to accept the dynamic nature of institutional practices, and accommodate a variety of partial and contingent solutions (Cleaver and Franks 2003).

However, as Lund (2006:700) notes in his writing on Africa, there is a paradox at work here: too much focus on the contingent, local reality can lead to an 'individualistic, voluntarist and somewhat episodic perspective'. Yet, over time the accumulation of this 'unpredictable fluidity' can lead to 'systemic, general and institutional outcomes'. As in the case of illegal logging and mining, all too often these institutional outcomes are associated with insecurity, conflict and severe environmental impacts. For this reason environmentalists wishing to put an end to such ecological tragedies can readily become nostalgic for the 'rule of law' found in the green quartile in the map discussed earlier.

This paradox can assist in understanding the persistence of illegality. On the one hand, processes of 'regularization' involve the production of 'rules and organizations and customs and symbols and rituals and categories' together with efforts to embody these in robust social forms (Moore 2000:50). These are efforts to 'fix social reality, harden it, and give it form and predictability' (Lund 2006:699). On the other hand, for many of the reasons discussed above, actors often seek to manipulate the rules, or manoeuvre between different repertoires of rules, in a fashion that leads to 'unpredictability, inconsistency, paradox and ambiguity and institutional incongruence'. This manipulation has been called 'situational adjustment'. The reality is that both regularization and manipulation tend to happen at once. So while institutions claiming to embody the state may seem to be working for formalization, this is undone by the simultaneous workings of 'corruption, political networks and powerful alliances in the same institutions' (Lund 2006:699). Lund observes that we would be in error to assume some kind of 'evolutionary development from incongruence towards congruence' in institutional terms – towards legal integration and the rule of law. Rather, he suggests, processes of situational adjustment work against these outcomes. In Indonesia, the continuing chasm between formal legal stipulations and the requirements of everyday life makes 'situational adjustment' a constant necessity.

Governance approaches

Over recent years the issues surrounding these manifold illegalities in the resource sectors have gained further salience. Since the time of the United Nations Conference on Environment and Development (UNCED) held in Rio de Janeiro in 1992, interest in the use of legal instruments to protect the environment has only grown. All governance programs in the area of natural resource management stress the importance of law. The greenhouse issue has given the problem international importance, increasing the potential for embarrassment to any state where unregulated exploitation of resources is associated with greenhouse gas emissions.

After 1998, faced by a crisis in state capacity, and under the influence of outside models, the Indonesian state embraced the vocabulary, if not the methods, of 'good governance'. While previously the state was seen as the solution to social problems and placed at the centre of decision making, it was now widely critiqued as predatory and inefficient. The alternative to state-led development was to be found in the unleashing of society-based problem-solving mechanisms. 'Governance' caused a shift in perspective regarding state-society relationships. Rather than command and control, the state was meant to work in concert with other actors to deal with collective action problems. The role of the state became one of 'enabling', establishing the regulatory framework for environmental management (among other things), using partnerships, negotiation and persuasion.[11]

The governance approach invoked in Indonesia's decentralization reform involved granting enhanced discretionary authority to regional governments, who are said to be closer to the people and thus more locally accountable. Decentralization was meant to 'bridge' the national and the local. It was envisaged as a means to overcome the state's legitimacy deficit by developing locally derived forms of accountability and representation, encompassing

11 Rhodes 1997; Tendler 1997; Pierre and Peters 2000.

more negotiation and persuasion.[12] In other words, the state took up the vocabulary of participation in order to mobilize other social actors for its purposes (McCarthy and Warren 2008).

However, for governance to work, the state needs to retain the capacity 'to make and implement policy, in other words, to steer society' (Pierre 2000). It needs to be strong enough to ensure effective regulation of the economy and social stability. To do so, the state requires sufficient infrastructural power – the capacity to penetrate civil society and to implement political decisions (Mann 1986). In other words, the state needs to retain its autonomy while being sufficiently 'embedded', or enmeshed, in the social networks that put it in close contact with private actors outside the state (Evans 1995). While the first characteristic allows states to pursue policy, the second allows them to pursue governance strategies – working in concert with other actors to deal with collective action problems.

For the Indonesian state after Suharto, governance entailed a profound shift in much more than philosophy. The problem, as Indonesia's mixed experience of decentralization suggests, is that the state system is not well fashioned to apply significant infrastructural power to obtain the collaboration of networks of groups and individuals that could lead to good environmental policy outcomes. In many areas of the archipelago, as noted earlier, state-based actors have used the idea of the state to exploit rules and relationships in the local domain for political and economic ends.

The institutional complexity of state administration exacerbated the state capacity problems. In any bureaucratic system, the state divides management problems into components and designs legal-institutional arrangements for each part (Rhodes 1997). Inevitably, different state institutions are given responsibility for different aspects of decision making and implementing the rules governing their own sector, while overlooking issues related to adjacent sectors. As state agencies have adjacent and often overlapping mandates and agendas, strong coordination is needed to avoid duplication, role confusion, competition and mistrust. Suharto had overseen the conflict between these sectoral agendas, including the contradiction between environmental regulation and the rent-seeking of powerful 'politico-bureaucrats' and their business partners, by combining a modicum of law enforcement with a firm hand that favoured those with access to the inner circle. But under decentralization, with so many different state actors creating rules according to their own agendas, with overlapping authority between different levels of government, the state has lacked a coherent form, let alone a strong coordinating hand (McCarthy 2004). Indonesian administrative arrangements elaborated

12 In natural resource management this paradigmatically extends to community governance and co-management as a social arrangement for sustainability, and to initiatives to mobilize 'social capital' (a process captured in the phrase 'community-driven development').

different logics of regulation, leading to an 'internal pluralism' of the state institutional order that works against the kind of coherence expected of states (De Sousa Santos 1992:134). The struggle over the logic of state action – between different interests, sectors and coalitions – reduced policy coherence.

In devolving authority to the district, the reforms confronted the deeply rooted state/society nexus that works according to its own logic. It encompassed, as we have seen, long-established and emergent domains of social organization, including clientelist arrangements. The central state had devolved authority to domains that already worked to their own logic, readily confounding attempts by the centre to 'steer' sub-national state and extra-state actors for policy objectives. For instance, a district head might turn a blind eye to 'extra-legal' logging or mining operations while extracting revenue, in order to increase local district revenues (Pendapatan Asli Daerah, PAD) and to develop off-budget funds for the election campaign. At the same time, increased revenues redistributed under the decentralization reforms – including natural resource rents – might be used to fund building projects that provided contracts to key clients.

These relatively autonomous domains accommodated a range of local interests. Local businessmen could make backroom arrangements with agents of local state agencies that now had greater discretionary power. At the same time, the ambiguous and contested state of affairs increased the bargaining position of actors able to use coercion or the threat of it to control access to land or resources. Corporate interests needed to court district elites, entrepreneurs and key village actors, where possible recruiting them into their processes of resource control. As localized actors became more autonomous of central control, more actors benefited. As corporate interests and investors adjusted, their strategies increasingly accommodated local actors. This meant that the fruits of resource extraction, now largely outside the control of central state administration, were now more widely distributed.

Inevitably, this caused chagrin among particular actors in Jakarta. As I will discuss further below, conflict within the state between different interests were often played out in law. Central actors disapproved of many local projects legitimized by decisions and laws passed by local administrations. A district might create its own spatial plan and issue logging and plantation licences, only to find this policy coming into conflict with decisions taken by the Ministry of Forestry. These sorts of conflicts clouded the state's monopoly over the definition of 'legality'. Inevitably, the attention of powerful actors at the centre – alongside the press and the donor community – focused now on the (previously invisible) extra-legal aspect of long-established and emergent local domains of social organization. To be sure, in the absence of effective control, monitoring and supervision, some districts had issued small-scale concession licences all over the place, often with ambiguous legality, exacerbating the rapid liquidation of the nation's forest reserves. Yet, to a large extent the narrative of localized illegality also served political ends for central state actors. It justified a retreat to older statist modes of resource control. For instance, while the decentralization reforms initially devolved authority over small-scale logging permits directly to district governments, this authority was later withdrawn.

The struggle culminated in March 2005, when during a high-profile campaign against corruption President Susilo Bambang Yudhoyono launched intensive police operations against illegal logging that had an 'immediate impact' (Soetjipto 2005). Although these operations may not initially have netted the leaders of the major timber networks, higher transaction costs for illegal logging networks due to police enforcement, combined with the increasing scarcity of timber in many places, convinced key actors to move into other comparatively booming sectors of the economy, particularly oil palm (McCarthy 2007b). Over time, Jakarta consolidated its authority over timber licences by moving against those district and provincial governments that had, under their spatial planning authority and interpretations of earlier regional autonomy legislation, been allowing exploitation within the 'forest zone'. As these licences fell in areas that the Ministry of Forestry still classified as 'state forest', technically these concessions violated existing forestry laws. Now, with the swing back to centralized control, several district and provincial heads faced charges for having issued 'illegal' permits. For instance, the governor of East Kalimantan, who had issued hundreds of oil palm plantation permits that disregarded forest boundaries, was jailed in 2006 for illegal forest destruction. [13]

The project of reworking state legitimacy by devolving areas of state authority was thus at best only partially successful. Besides the problems mentioned above, it also had yet to address the vexed question of the legal entitlements to natural resources, including the overlap between local 'customary' entitlements and concession rights issued during the previous period. In the interim, local actors had taken initiatives on their own to increase control over resources, without having these new claims formalized in law. When control shifted back to the centre, village access to resources in the local domain remained subject to state definitions of 'illegality'. As the Ministry of Forestry reasserted its control over access to trees and land in the name of the state, it reverted to its past practice of considering villagers inside the 'forestry estate' as 'forest squatters' and 'illegal loggers'.

For example, after 2003 the Ministry of Forestry gradually began to reapply its legal power over the 'forestry estate' in the province of Jambi. After 1999 ethnic Malay villagers in one district had acted on long-standing

[13] 'KPK tahan Gubernur Kaltim', *Kompas* 20-6-2006; '10 regents in Kalimantan prosecuted for illegal logging', *The Jakarta Post* 5-12-2005.

grievances over the appropriation of village land for plantations and timber concessions under Suharto. Claiming traditional *(adat)* rights over the land, they occupied plantations and opened gardens in former concession areas. Several NGOs supported them. For some time the district government turned a blind eye to local people 'illegally' opening gardens in the 'forestry estate'. However, the Ministry of Forestry retained *de jure* (if not *de facto*) control over the 46% of this particular district that was mapped as state forest land. Facing the fact that local government and local people were establishing 'facts on the ground', the Ministry allocated the area as a timber plantation concession. Eventually, to enforce this property right and effectively to re-establish the state forest status of the land, a paramilitary Police Mobile Brigade (Brigade Mobil, BRIMOB) special operations unit moved in to shift the 'forest squatters'. The villagers opening rubber or oil palm gardens on state forest land found themselves evicted as 'illegal loggers' (McCarthy 2008). In other well-established areas the Ministry was less able to regain control (Afiff et al. 2005). The Ministry sought to diffuse conflict while retaining the formal forestry status of this land by granting limited access rights to communities already in control of 'forest land'. The Ministry did this by introducing 35-year People's Timber Plantation (Hutan Tanaman Rakyat) leases to villagers over areas already under *de facto* community control (*Peoples Plantations* 2007).

District governments have retained considerable discretionary power in other areas. For instance, while the central government retains ultimate authority to issue long term concession licences (Hak Guna Usaha, HGU), districts hold the authority to issue location permits and plantation licences (*izin prinsip, izin lokasi* and *izin usaha perkebunan*). This means that control over land for investment purposes continues to be mediated via the local state, ensuring that investors have to negotiate control of land in the local domain first before proceeding to process the concession licence in Jakarta. With outside interests needing to make significant local investments within the local political domain to secure access to land, corporate interests might strategically accommodate district elites, entrepreneurs and key village actors in processes of 'freeing up' land for development.

Conclusions

Narratives of illegality provide an important frame for policy and aid interventions. The problem is that the prevalent narrative of illegality narrows policy thinking by shrinking disparate actions and practices embedded in particular local circumstances into the simple category of illegality. A rigid narrative of 'illegality' closes discussion of key issues such as the link between 'illegal' practices and the political economy, the distribution of the benefits of resource access, and property rights. By passing over underlying issues, this can lead to premature analytical closure of intricate problems, and in the process foreshadow disappointment for project and policy interventions.

These narratives help us to imagine that simply creating a coherent, rational-legal state actor is the answer to the problem. In this way they serve to underpin particular types of interventions – usually technically conceived ones that avoid confronting politically unsavoury corruption problems (for example, using satellites to capture illegal loggers in Kalimantan's jungles). Yet, as suggested here, there is no substitute for thinking through the complex dynamics and variety of causalities at work in 'illegal' phenomena. Armed with such knowledge, policy makers may be more likely to be in a position to devise strategies and evaluate their likelihood of success.

A key problem facing attempts to implement the law is state capacity. To be sure, the central state has the capacity to apply its coercive power to affect legal resource control in resource-rich enclaves where foreign investment is at stake, such as for wealthy mineral and oil concessions. However, outside these enclaves, in areas where state capacities are thinner on the ground, resource control may well be a much more negotiated affair, conducted in both formal and informal ways. Local power relations are highly clientelist in nature. Deals are made at the intersection of state legal norms, reinterpreted by local state-based actors, and what passes for 'customary orders' (McCarthy 2006). These latter modes of negotiating resource access have a degree of local legitimacy. They can lead to a wider distribution of resources locally when compared to the state-regulated resource enclaves; they provide a social safety net for the rural poor who find work in logging and mining teams deployed outside the law; and finally, they allow local access to resources that might be subject to a local 'right of avail' that remains unrecognized in state law. Unfortunately, where this 'situational adjustment' occurs in a highly clientelist way without effective governance mechanisms, this overlap between state and local institutional arrangements does tend towards resource depletion and environmental degeneration.

The loss of faith in the state as the custodian of collective resources and public goods – including the environment – in large part provided the motor behind the shift from government to governance. While governance theory suggests a decreasing reliance on formal-legal powers, the political importance of law remains evident, as any witness to the efforts various actors continue to invest in law formation processes can attest. The problem remains that unworkable existing legal definitions sustain a particular political economy of natural resources that benefit powerful actors. As legal change would require confronting these dominant interests, the required legislative and practical policy changes required for dealing with this problem remain intractable.

In governance theory, it is suggested that the devolution of authority to local authorities coupled with the provision of 'effective safeguards against arbitrary exercise of localized power and clear relations of accountability' can change the relationship between local constituents and local decision makers (Lemos and Agrawal 2006:305). By ensuring that the rule-making process reaches down to the local level, where management, enforcement, and dispute resolution occur, this theory suggests that more realistic, locally legitimate and hence more enforceable legal regimes might emerge that do away with the problem of illegality and poor resource management inherited from the past. This requires the combination of localized modes of participation and accountability with the capacity of a central state to carry out the required degree of monitoring, supervision and sanctioning to counteract the power of unaccountable local elites. It remains unclear when or how such state and society capacities will evolve in the rural contexts where most of Indonesia's natural resources exist. Meanwhile the persistent chasm between the local 'informal' social world and the state legal regime may continue to allow maximum space for powerful actors – working locally and at a distance – to use concepts of state legality to pursue political and economic projects. Where this occurs at considerable cost to the local social and natural environment, it will continue to provide the grounds for 'illegal' local adjustments to continue.

MICHELE FORD AND LENORE LYONS

Travelling the *aspal* route

Grey labour migration through an Indonesian border town

Scholarly and public policy accounts of temporary labour migration in Southeast Asia emphasize the manifold problems associated with attempts to regulate the flows of so-called 'undocumented' migrant workers throughout the region. Part of the difficulty in managing the 'illegal' movement of labour migrants is that categories used by receiving countries such as 'documented' and 'undocumented' or 'regular' and 'irregular' are extremely fluid and temporary labour migrants can move between them rapidly (Grewcock 2003). Migrants who pass through legal channels may also confront a range of practices in their home countries, such as falsified or fake documents, that blur the distinction between legal and illegal recruitment and deployment (Skeldon 2000).

While much attention has been paid to the role of people smugglers and traffickers in illegal border crossings, the part played by the state has been given less consideration. And yet, the state is clearly involved in the illegal practices associated with international temporary labour migration in all its forms. As Willem van Schendel (2005:54) has argued 'the image of states as simply reactive, responding to the growth of clandestine transnational flows, is misleading because it understates the degrees to which states actually structure, condition, produce, and enable clandestine border crossings'. Labour migrants weave their way in and out of intersecting spheres of legality and illegality as they negotiate the complex nature of the labour migration regimes that sending and host countries construct (Ford 2007).

This chapter explores the state's role in semi-legal migration flows through Tanjung Pinang, the capital city of the province of Kepulauan Riau (the Riau Islands) in the borderlands between Indonesia, Singapore and Malaysia.[1] In the Riau Islands, local officials play a pivotal role in facilitating the flow of temporary labour migrants across the border. They collaborate with a range

[1] The research on which this paper is based was funded by an Australian Research Council (ARC) Discovery Project grant *In the Shadow of Singapore: The Limits of Transnationalism in Insular Riau* (DP0557368).

of other actors involved in the labour migration process, including official and unofficial labour recruitment agents; local brokers who act as middlemen between agents, officials and prospective migrants; and numerous other private entrepreneurs who provide specialized services, such as those running 'passport bureaus'. While some of these actors are involved in legal businesses, others operate illegally but with local government sanction. Together they are part of an alternative labour migration system that sits alongside the official process, and which has both legal and illegal aspects to its operation.

As Riau Islanders are quick to observe, in the islands 'illegal doesn't mean that labour migrants travel through the *pelabuhan tikus* [illegal ports, lit. rat ports]. They have passports'.[2] As this comment suggests, locals make a distinction between 'documented but illegal' labour migrants who travel with authentic documents issued by the local immigration office, but obtained or used illegally, and 'undocumented illegal' migrants who use the services of smugglers to slip across the border undetected. The documents the first group of migrants carry are described in Indonesian as being 'real but fake' (*asli tapi palsu, aspal*), reflecting the fact that they are genuine documents obtained without going through all the processes that define formally sanctioned channels of temporary labour migration. We describe this 'grey' labour migration, where workers cross Indonesia's borders with real passports, and sometimes work permits, obtained with real or fake documents obtained through irregular channels at the point of origin, transit or departure – as the *aspal* route.

The actions of officials involved in the *aspal* route are clearly corrupt. They provide identity cards, official passports or even work permits to official and unofficial labour recruiters and other middle-men in return for payments in cash or in-kind services or as favours for friends or relatives. In doing so, they knowingly circumvent existing central government population laws and the policies and procedures of the national labour export program. However, it would be a mistake to view their behaviour solely as a matter of corruption motivated by personal gain or the desire to influence local politics. While in many cases their actions are linked to attempts to shore up their local political power bases or simply to supplement meagre wages, they are also part of a local community-sanctioned response to international migration flows through the islands. Many local people view these practices as a necessary and obvious solution to the presence in the islands of large numbers of intending labour migrants. The licitness of these illegal practices within the community has important implications for the way in which the *aspal* system operates. Significantly, it means that forms of criminality often associated with corruption in Indonesia (such as the presence of strongmen or violent coercion) are typically absent in much of the grey labour migration process.

2 Interview with NGO activist, December 2006.

This chapter traces the different practices and motivations associated with the *aspal* route in order to shed light on the nature of state illegality in Indonesia. In doing so, it seeks to go beyond simply describing modes of corruption to also examine the multiple meanings attached to the provision of 'real but fake' documents by the range of actors involved in the labour migration process. The *aspal* system is not unique to the Riau Islands or other transit areas; it is also found in provinces of origin and major urban centres like Jakarta. However, these practices become magnified in the periphery because of the vast flows of migrants into the transit provinces and across the border. Our concern with the transit provinces in general – and the Riau Islands in particular – also reflects an increasing awareness that accounts written from the perspective of the periphery offer alternative accounts of state illegality (McCarthy 2002; Wadley and Eilenberg 2005; McCarthy 2007a). Since borders act as 'pivots' (Van Schendel 2005) between territorial states and transnational flows, attention to the regulatory processes involved in managing labour migration flows in transit provinces offers both a corrective to state-centric understandings of migration and important insights into the state's involvement in irregular migration practices.

Indonesia's national labour migration system

The Indonesian state's management of temporary labour migration from Indonesia has attracted intense scrutiny over the last three decades as the numbers of Indonesians seeking work overseas continues to grow. Successive governments have been subject to sustained critiques which focus on their negligence in managing the formal process of labour migration, and emphasize the corrupt and inadequate structures of the system and their implications for individual migrant workers (see for example *Indonesian migrant workers* 2002; Human Rights Watch 2004, 2005:13-5). Less understood are those migrants who follow the *aspal* route or bypass the system altogether. Yet these migrants constitute a significant proportion of migrant flows to regional destinations. According to the government's own estimates, between 200,000 and 300,000 Indonesians working in Malaysia alone have bypassed the official system.[3]

Migrants who circumvent the official system are motivated to do so because of the very complicated processes set out under Law no. 39/2004 on the Placement and Protection of Indonesian Workers Overseas, a law ostensibly designed to improve the placement and protection of Indonesian migrant workers. Under the law, the central government – through the National

[3] Moh. Jumhur Hidayat, head of the National Agency for the Placement and Protection of Indonesian Migrant Workers, cited in *Waspada Online*. See 'Indonesia asks Malaysia not to issue working visa to individual applicants', *Waspada Online* 14-9-2008.

Agency for the Placement and Protection of Indonesian Migrant Workers (Badan Nasional Penempatan dan Perlindungan Tenaga Kerja Indonesia, BNP2TKI) – is responsible for 'regulating, guiding, carrying out and overseeing the placement and protection of Indonesian workers overseas' (Law no. 39/2004, Article 5) in collaboration with local government and other agencies. In order to be considered 'legal' under this framework, intending labour migrants must first register with the responsible local labour office, assumed – although not stated – to be in the province of origin. Workers are recruited from this pool by officially sanctioned recruitment agents. Agents must be legally constituted companies in possession of a Migrant Worker Placement Licence (Surat Izin Pelaksana Penempatan TKI, SIP) issued by the Department of Manpower and Transmigration, a recruitment agreement, a job order and a draft contract from an agent or individual in a receiving country. Workers who are selected by the recruitment agent then undergo mental and physical health checks organized by the Department of Health, receive training and undergo an assessment of their work-related competencies. The agent organizes insurance, an official migrant worker passport (which has only 24 pages rather than the normal 36 or 48), visas and payment of the US$15 fee levied by the government on intending migrant workers.

During the processing phase, intending migrant workers are housed in barracks. Immediately prior to departure, they go through a final training process and receive a copy of their employment contract and their migrant worker identity card (Kartu Tenaga Kerja Luar Negeri, KTKLN), which replaces their standard identity card whilst overseas. This card can be issued by a representative of the centrally controlled migrant labour placement office in the province of origin or at the point of embarkation. Once they have their migrant worker identity card, intending labour migrants can be issued with a letter of exemption, which removes the obligation to pay the exit tax (*fiskal luar negeri*) levied on Indonesians travelling abroad. Finally, recruitment agencies are required to report all successful placements to the local manpower office (Law no. 39/2004, Article 54). At each stage of the official recruitment process, prospective labour migrants are faced with another round of paperwork and fees they must pay. Significantly, the labour recruitment process requires intending migrant workers to remain in holding centres for between one and three months while they wait to be placed overseas.[4] The complexities of the official process, combined with the time and costs involved have created ample opportunities for rent-seeking within the formal system and a motivation for the establishment of an alternative route.

4 Under earlier regulations they could be kept in a holding centre for up to 150 days. The description that follows held true at the time of writing, but it should be noted that the system is continually changing.

Migration through the transit provinces

Many of the studies that seek to examine the nexus between migration and state illegality in Indonesia focus on the dedicated terminal for returning migrant workers at Jakarta's Soekarno-Hatta airport, Terminal 3.[5] As Rachel Silvey (2007) argues, a close study of processes within Terminal 3 demonstrates not only the complicated role of the state in migration but also the link between state-sanctioned processes and illegality. These illegal state practices may extend beyond simply 'breaking the law' to include bureaucratic incompetence, red-tape, patronage and lack of responsiveness.

Much less studied sites for examining illegal state practices in regard to the regulation of temporary labour migration are the transit provinces in Sumatra and Kalimantan through which labour migrants pass on their way to Singapore and Malaysia (Ford 2006). One such transit province is Kepulauan Riau, the province which incorporates the islands that lie to the east of mainland Sumatra. The geographical proximity of the Riau Islands to Indonesia's neighbours serves as a magnet both for internal labour migrants and for significant flows of regular and irregular labour migrants across the border.[6] International migrants pass through many ports in the islands, including the town of Tanjung Pinang, which has long been considered a strategic point from which to travel illegally to Singapore and Malaysia (Sobary 1987:5). The Riau Islands are also one of the nearest points for repatriation of large numbers of workers whose contracts have ended and undocumented migrants who have been deported from Malaysia. Tanjung Pinang alone receives hundreds of deportees almost every week. In 2006, 16,805 Indonesians passed through the Tanjung Pinang holding centre, which can accommodate up to 600 people at a time.[7] Deportees regularly arrive at the centre on a Thursday and stay a maximum of three nights before being returned by the local government to their provinces of origin.[8]

A detailed report compiled by the Indonesian Auditor General identifies a whole series of very serious problems, including endemic corruption, in its review of the labour migration process in Mainland Riau and the Riau Islands. The report identified a number of problems in the recruitment and deploy-

5 See for example Surtees 2003; Rudnyckyj 2004; Silvey 2007. Similar terminals exist in Surabaya and Solo.

6 Lyons and Ford 2007. According to the 2000 census, Singapore's 612,200 foreign workers constitute 29.2% of the total workforce (Singapore Department of Statistics 2000). About 500,000 of these workers are considered unskilled or low-skilled and Indonesians are strongly represented in low-skilled service-sector jobs and on commercial ships based in Singapore. In 2006, the total number of employed persons in Malaysia was around 10.6 million (Government of Malaysia 2007). As of the end of June 2006, there were 1.84 million registered foreign workers in Malaysia, primarily in manufacturing, services and agriculture. 64.7% of these registered foreign workers were from Indonesia (Ministry of Finance Malaysia 2007).

7 Details of this centre's operation can be found in *Daftar kedatangan* (2006a, b, c).

8 Interview with NGO worker in Tanjung Pinang, November 2006. Central government contributions to the local budget of major transit areas include an allowance for the provision of these services.

ment process including incomplete documentation,[9] and a failure to pass on over Rp one billion in charges levied on intending migrant workers to the Indonesian Migrant Worker Placement Service Centre (Balai Pelayanan dan Penempatan Tenaga Kerja Indonesia, BP2TKI) (Badan Pemeriksa Keuangan Republik Indonesia 2006:63-92). The report also identified a mismatch between the number of migrant workers registered with Pekanbaru office of the BP2TKI, which has responsibility for overseeing migrant workers in the Riau Islands, and the numbers of workers that claim exit tax-free status (*bebas fiskal luar negeri*).[10] The Auditor General found that a significant number of exit tax exemptions were issued to workers who had not followed the mandated procedure. Of the 151,762 intending labour migrants who received exit tax exemption letters in Mainland Riau or the Riau Islands in 2004-2005, 112,444 were issued tax exemption letters in the islands, yet only 43,989 exemptions were recorded with the BP2TKI (Badan Pemeriksa Keuangan Republik Indonesia 2006:87-8).

Our research shows that similar inconsistencies are evident at the local level. In 2006, 1,910 migrant workers left Tanjung Pinang on official migrant worker passports, only 310 of whom were issued exit tax exemption letters by the Department of Manpower's Tanjung Pinang office.[11] These figures suggest that instead of applying for their tax exemption letters from the local BP2TKI representative as required under Law no. 39/2004, large numbers of otherwise regular labour migrants leave Indonesia through the islands using *aspal* tax exemption letters obtained from local government agencies in the islands. In other words, they leave with authentic and appropriate documents obtained via irregular means. Our interview data and local statistics indicate that irregularities in the issuance of tax exemption letters are not the only example of *aspal* practices. For example, many labour migrants leave the islands without registering with BP2TKI at all. In 2006 alone, an estimated 2,000 migrant workers passed through the local port monthly on their way to Singapore or Malaysia despite the fact that fewer than 700 applications for placement were approved in each month.[12]

The Auditor General's report attributes such irregularities to understaffing, a lack of coordination between different agencies and between local governments in sending and receiving provinces. However, central government agencies are well aware of the involvement of local government authorities in

9 During the course of the pre-departure process, intending migrants must produce or obtain a standard identity card, school records and birth certificate, and marriage certificate where relevant; a letter of permission from their spouse, parents or guardian; a certificate of their work-related competencies; a certificate of physical and mental health; a work visa; a work placement contract; a work contract and a migrant worker identity card (Law no. 39/2004, Article 51).

10 This number does not include those with local papers, since Riau Islanders are exempt from the exit tax.

11 *Daftar calon* 2006; *Daftar PJTKI* 2006.

12 Interviews, December 2006; Department of Immigration internal documents.

the *aspal* route, a situation that it has sought to redress by establishing a dedicated team for the prevention of departures that might be designated as being 'non-procedural' according to Ministerial Decision no. KEP-14/MEN/I/2005. These ongoing efforts have had limited success in stemming the practice of issuing 'real but fake' documents, but for large numbers of labour migrants, the *aspal* system continues to be the most efficient way of crossing the border and seeking work abroad since it offers them the hope of becoming 'documented' workers in the receiving country without the costs and red-tape associated with formal system.[13] For many of the public officials responsible for issuing documents required in the labour migration process, the rewards – but also the logic – of the *aspal* route is self-evident in a context where local conditions are not taken into account in national-level decision making about Indonesia's labour export program.

Travelling the aspal route

Intending labour migrants who transit in the town of Tanjung Pinang generally seek assistance from one of three kinds of migration agents. The first group consists of companies that are officially registered with the BNP2TKI and that follow official procedures. As of November 2005, there were 24 registered agents in Tanjung Pinang, six of which had their head office in the town (Badan Pemeriksa Keuangan Republik Indonesia 2006:77). The second group of agents deliver workers with no papers to Malaysia and Singapore by boat (a practice typically referred to as 'people smuggling'). The third group consists of agents, either officially registered companies or individuals, that use local contacts to organize local identity cards and passports for workers outside the formal system either exclusively or in addition to engaging in that formal system. This third group of agents is the group associated with the *aspal* route.[14]

The *aspal* route begins when individuals are convinced or decide to migrate for work without registering with the local Manpower Office in their district of origin. This may happen because the intending labour migrant has insufficient knowledge about the formal procedures or because an acquain-

13 This reflects a structural failure in Indonesia's labour-sending system. The system relies on receiving countries accepting only those migrant workers who have followed the requirements of Law no. 39/2004, which specifies that workers can only be recruited by officially approved recruitment agents based in Indonesia. Recruitment by an Indonesian or foreign sponsor is explicitly forbidden (see Explanatory notes for Article 37, Law no. 39/2004). However, attempts by the Indonesian government in collaboration with the governments of major receiving countries to police this system have not been particularly successful. The central government has repeatedly tried to deal with the problem of direct recruitment by foreign agents or employers, most recently sending a diplomatic note to the Malaysian authorities, asking them not to issue working visas to individual applicants. See 'Indonesia asks Malaysia not to issue working visa to individual applicants', *Waspada Online* 14-9-2008.

14 Falsification of identity and many of the other aspects of the *aspal* route described here are also found within the formal labour migration system.

tance, relative or local middle-man (*calo*) suggests that the *aspal* route is a better option for them. These workers are brought by either middle-men or employees of agents based in Kepulauan Riau directly to the islands. The agent, which might be a legally registered company or an individual, then obtains a local identity card from his or her collaborators in the local administrative office under the intending worker's real name or a pseudonym in a process that can take as little as a day. In 2006 the going rate for what is referred to locally as a seasonal identity card ('KTP *musiman*') was Rp 125,000. Once a local identity card is in hand, the would-be migrant can then obtain a standard passport through regular means or more quickly through the agents' contacts in the local office of the Immigration Department. The fact that they are obtained using a local identity card means that their bearers can benefit from the province's exit tax-free status.

Although these passports are different from those issued to intending labour migrants by the Indonesian authorities, they are official travel documents that may be recognized by overseas governments issuing work visas. This means that a prospective labour migrant can use the passport to exit Indonesia and legally enter a neighbouring country. Although migrant workers are required by Indonesian authorities to hold a labour migration passport *(paspor* TKI), Indonesian citizens leaving Indonesia are unlikely to be more than summarily quizzed about the purpose of their travel when they pass through an Indonesian immigration checkpoint on a standard passport. Some of these migrants enter Singapore and Malaysia as 'tourists' on visitor's passes and then convert their visas to work permits with the assistance of a local labour placement agent. Others may be issued with work permits on arrival on the basis of *aspal* migrant labour passports issued at the point of departure. Some are turned back as potential 'illegal' workers, but many more pass through undeterred.[15]

The 'passport bureaus' that have developed to service the *aspal* route are an integral part of this system. An owner-operator of one such passport bureau, run from a shop-house in the town of Tanjung Uban, about an hour from Tanjung Pinang, specialized in providing passports for domestic workers planning to go to Malaysia and Singapore. Although he also provided passports for accredited labour agents, the vast majority of the applications he processed were for migrant workers intending to leave without fulfilling all the requirements of the official labour migration process. Between

[15] Some of those who enter on a visitor's pass may work illegally. Indonesia has signed a number of MOUs on the labour migration process with the governments of Singapore and Malaysia. These have been partially successful in addressing anomalies in the immigration regimes governing foreign workers. For example, Singapore has introduced a 'single gate policy' for the recruitment of domestic workers. Before it was introduced, domestic workers leaving Indonesia through alternative channels were not necessarily illegal in Singapore (Abdul Rahman 2003:100).

2001 and 2003, this bureau agent 'processed' several hundred passport applications per day. He obtained the 'real' passports supplied by his bureau through a contact in the local immigration office who was able to supply him with official passports using local identity cards supplied to him by his clients. Once the bureau agent received the passports, he passed them on to a range of other actors involved in the labour migration process. His clients included accredited labour agents, unofficial labour agents, casual labour brokers and sometimes intending labour migrants themselves.[16]

It is through bureaus like this that the unofficial labour-sending agents who are the mainstays of the *aspal* route obtain travel documents for their clients. An agent interviewed in 2001 was one of a large number of local 'entrepreneurs' engaged in grey labour migration.[17] He and his wife were not registered with the Department of Manpower, nor did they have a legally constituted company. They operated their business from their residence in a lower middle-class suburb of Tanjung Pinang, supplying domestic workers to a Malaysian contact. The Indonesian agent recruited women from local placement agencies in Jakarta that were not registered to supply workers for positions overseas. Once the women arrived in Tanjung Pinang, the agent used his contacts in local government and the immigration department to obtain local identity cards and passports for them. The Indonesian paperwork he provided to the women was recognized in West Malaysia, and he used appropriate permits for employment supplied by his Malaysian counterpart.[18]

Although it is now illegal for Indonesian workers to be deployed by receiving-country agents independent of the Indonesian system, these practices persist not least because of the many benefits workers derive from travelling the *aspal* route. As a Tanjung Pinang-based NGO activist observed, the *aspal* process is much faster and cheaper than the formal process because intending migrant workers get a passport, but do not have to pay for a visa (which their employer arranges once they have entered the host country), insurance or a medical check-up (mandated as part of the formal labour migration process), or the extra charges associated with obtaining these documents.[19] Most importantly, intending migrant workers do not have to wait long periods in barracks in Java or elsewhere before placement. Nor are they required to return to their province of origin before being redeployed. And although the time taken by the *aspal* process varies according to the efficiency of the agent and

16 As he was not particularly well-connected, this agent's business declined sharply in 2004 when the central government attempted to short-circuit the system by bringing in immigration officials from head office. The success of the central initiative was short-lived because the newcomers were quickly socialized into the culture of the local office and became integrated into the *aspal* system.

17 For a fuller account of this operation and details of women's motivations for using this agent see Ford 2001.

18 Malaysia's eastern states have a separate immigration system.

19 NGO interview, 13-12-2006.

the fees levied on the worker, it can be remarkably quick. Zain Zainuddin, a Malaysian journalist with the daily *Harian Metro*, claims that in 2006 workers could be deported, organize a new passport in Tanjung Pinang, and be back working in Malaysia the same day (Zain 2006). Interviews with grey migration agents in Tanjung Pinang and evidence from other transit locations confirm that such rapid processing of documents is indeed possible. In Nunukan, for example, illegal agents simply have to telephone the immigration department to obtain hundreds of passports within days.[20]

What is interesting about the *aspal* process is not that it exists, since it provides benefits for workers in a context where government corruption is taken for granted. As Nengsih – a former domestic worker who spent time in a Singapore prison for entering Singapore under a false name – reminds us, second or even third identity cards are easily obtainable anywhere in Indonesia:

> In Indonesia even if we have been deported from one country it's easy just to make another passport and go somewhere else. That's how it is here. Easy. There's nothing to stop someone having more than one passport. The government can't do anything about it. All we need to do is move from Jakarta to Batam and then from Batam to [Tanjung] Pinang. In each place we can be a different person.

What is remarkable, rather, is the high level of institutionalization and public acceptance of this alternative system. While it is illegal for temporary labour migrants to leave Indonesia without passing through formal labour migration procedures, local agents of the state are involved in the setting-up and operation of the *aspal* route. As a consequence, the production of *aspal* documents has become an established part of the immigration process in the transit zone. The *aspal* route has become such an entrenched part of local life that most locals know how the system works and who to contact to obtain the necessary paperwork. By contrast, few understand the steps involved in the official process, or could explain how or why the *aspal* system is 'illegal' beyond the fact that it may involve the payment of bribes to officials. As Nengsih's comment suggests, the payment of these bribes in itself is not regarded as a remarkable act – it is simply the way things get done.

While the local government officials involved in the *aspal* system recognize that their acts are not strictly legal, they see the grey migration system as a legitimate response to the difficulties associated with implementing the national labour migration process. Large numbers of prospective international labour migrants arrive in the Riau Islands with the hope of crossing the border into Malaysia and Singapore. They travel great distances and

20 Personal communication with Riwanto Tirtosudarmo, 14-7-2003.

endure an arduous journey before arriving in the islands. The arrival of these intending migrants in the islands poses an enormous dilemma for the local authorities. Sending them back to their provinces of origin to apply through the proper channels for an overseas job would not be practical even if the local authorities had the resources or wherewithal to do so. Given the large numbers involved, ignoring the problem is also not a solution. From the perspective of local government officials and community leaders, then, facilitating their migration by issuing 'real but fake' documents is an ideal response. It ensures a fast and efficient flow of migrants across the border (thereby mitigating against the need to feed and house the incoming migrants); provides a livelihood for members of the local community involved in the labour migration process; and affords some protection to workers once they are overseas (because they are in possession of 'real' documents). For many local officials involved in the provision of *aspal* documents, the fact that they make a side income (*penghasilan sampingan*) is a taken-for-granted aspect of their work. No one involved in the process would expect it to be any different.

Like many other aspects of state practice in the borderlands, the *aspal* route is thus at least in part a structural response to the intersection between national and local regimes – in this case the intersection between a centralized labour migration regime and a local immigration regime developed in response to the political economy of this particular borderland, characterized by close and easy physical access to neighbouring Singapore and Malaysia and the fact that islanders are exempt from the national exit tax. To fully comprehend the nature of 'state corruption' in labour migration flows, therefore, we must pay attention not only to the ways in which individual claims to licitness intersect with state practices, but also to the interstices of such competing regimes. What this points to is a need to invoke the concept of scale not only in terms of establishing the importance of the borderlands as periphery, but also in relation to the state itself. In particular, we need to consider differences (and similarities) in the ways that local, provincial and national level governments and officials respond to labour migration flows.

Migration, illegality and the state

Given the systemic involvement of Indonesian government officials in illegal practices, it is not surprising that corruption has emerged as a significant problem in policy making and academic research on the Indonesian state (Schulte Nordholt and Van Klinken 2007b). Indeed, a growing number of detailed studies of the 'webs of political, economic, and social exchange' (Migdal 1988:247) in which grassroots politicians, bureaucrats and strongmen are involved conclude that corruption is endemic in contemporary Indonesia.

One of the enduring explanations for widespread corruption in Indonesia is that there exists an in-built, structural requirement for the bureaucracy and the military to raise funds to support its own activities and pay wages (Mietzner 2008b). As these accounts suggest, in such a system officials extract as much 'informal' income as they can. Other accounts point to the lack of formal channels for meaningful participation in government decision-making processes, arguing that this encourages individuals to pursue their interests using informal networks built on personal ties (H. Crouch 1975, 1978, 1979; Robison 1981, 1986). This view, which suggests that corruption is part of an elite-sponsored system to shore up power and draw attention away from the regime's own complicity in illegal practices, has fed into more analyses that focus on idea of a 'shadow state' – a concept that describes the part of the state that lies outside formal state structures, in which political authority is drawn from the ability to control the informal economy (Harriss-White 2003).

The literature on the shadow state suggests that while control of the informal economy may sometimes depend on the use of actual physical force by strongmen, more often stakeholders exert influence through market monopolies, as state actors invite non-state actors to join in the shadow state network they build and provide them with protection from formal state authority (Erman 2007; Hidayat 2007; Migdal 1988). Those involved in the shadow state use formal institutions for private ends, including corruption, collusion and forced privatization of state assets. Schulte Nordholt and Van Klinken (2007b:7) argue that as a consequence of these practices, the 'boundaries between (legitimate) state violence and (illegal) criminality, and between formal institutions and semi-informal criminal gangs' become increasingly blurred. Corruption thus provides the 'space collective state actors need to build political coalitions with societal partners against perceived rivals' (Van Klinken 2008). However, the problem with these accounts of state corruption or involvement in illegal activities is that they assume that state actors regard corruption as a form of criminal behaviour.

In contrast to this view, many of those involved in so-called corrupt practices, including state officials, may consider themselves legitimate entrepreneurs or leaders and be recognized as such in the eyes of the local community. Far from being 'strongmen' or belonging to 'criminal gangs', they may be legitimate community leaders seeking to address what they see as inequities in a system which works in favour of the central government and its cronies. John McCarthy's (2002, 2007) work on illegal logging in South Aceh and Central Kalimantan, in which he begins to unpack the difference between legality and what he calls 'legitimacy', examines the role of local strongmen and the development of local extralegal systems which act to compensate for a system in which 'state agencies working with nation wide organizational rules are often unable to accommodate the interests of diverse groups and the variety of variables involved in local settings' (McCarthy 2002:880). In the case of Aceh, McCarthy (2002:873) asserts that local leaders were able to claim legitimacy for many of the illegal practices he observed because 'outside interests and central government gain the lion's share of economic rents derived from legal logging concessions'. Illegal logging employs many people in the local community and beyond, including those in retail and service sectors as well as the wide network of district official raising taxes and *oknum* receiving payments. Thus, the local community benefits considerably. This dynamic, combined with other factors (notably, a fall in prices for other local products), produced a situation in which logging became legitimate.

Similarly, in their work on logging in West Kalimantan, Reed Wadley and Michael Eilenberg (2005) use the term 'illegal' in inverted commas to suggest that although logging is seen by both the Indonesian government and the international community as an illegal activity, the local communities see it as a negotiated sale of timber from their traditionally managed forests and thus a legitimate act. As Anne Casson and Krystof Obidzinski (2002:2148) argue, 'illegal' logging can be viewed as a structurally important element of life in rural Kalimantan, and in some cases, it is no longer considered to be 'illegal'. In other cases, confusion over what constitutes 'illegal logging' is further heightened as a result of attempts by the central and provincial governments to re-assert national laws. Whereas previously little attempt was made to enforce the national laws, heightened concerns by the central government about the practice of 'illegal' logging led to an active process of criminalizing such acts through arrests and court procedures (Wadley and Eilenberg 2005). It is no surprise then that local border communities are confused about what is considered legal and illegal, and have a heightened mistrust towards state laws and regulations (Eilenberg 2008:8).

These examples demonstrate that the involvement of local government authorities in illegal practices cannot be regarded as simply a matter of entrenched nation-wide corruption that manifests itself at all levels of bureaucracy. Instead, we need to explore particular expressions of corruption and its meanings for local officials and other stakeholders. Itty Abraham and Willem van Schendel (2005) have used the concept of 'licitness' to take into account the gap between the state's understandings of criminal activity and those understandings deployed by individuals themselves. They call for the need to identify the origins of regulatory authority and distinguish between political authority (whether something is legal or illegal) and social authority (whether it is licit or illicit). In other words, to use the example of labour migration, persons involved in the management of cross-border flows, as well as migrants, may or may not share the state's categorization of their activities as criminal (Abraham and Van Schendel 2005). As Horstmann and Wadley point out, differences between regulatory authority and social authority are accentuated in border zones because of the presence of dense webs of connection that link individuals on either side of the border – connections that prompt frequent cross-border flows of objects, peoples and practices (Horstmann and Wadley 2006). When this is combined with the vast geographical distances between the centre of state political authority (usually located in the nation's capital) and life in the margins, the state's categorization of certain kinds of cross-border movements as 'illegal', may be deemed by borderlanders themselves as a 'way of life'.

We find the heuristic device of (il)legal/(il)licit also useful when describing flows whose trajectories extend beyond the borderlands because it allows us to challenge commonsense understandings of the boundaries between legal and illegal flows across international borders. For example, in her study of Indonesian women who migrate to Malaysia as undocumented domestic workers, Diana Wong (2005) argues that while the receiving state may view their arrival as a problem of human smuggling (an illegal activity), the majority of international migrants see it as a natural response to Malaysia's demand for cheap, low-skilled labour (an activity which is perfectly licit). The fact that their work may be deemed 'illegal' or that they enter the country as 'irregular' migrants is blamed on the Malaysian government's unfair migration system. This commonsense view of the 'illegal but licit' nature of the presence of large numbers of 'illegal migrants' in Malaysia, is supported by research which shows that in situations where a high demand for labour is combined with a highly restrictive migration regime, there is an increased likelihood of irregular migration, trafficking and human rights violations (Hugo 2005; Kelly 2005; Athukorala 2006). In these situations, there is also heightened capacity for rent-seeking on the part of bureaucrats and local authorities who regulate labour migration in both sending and host states. These practices further blur the line between the illegality and legality of state practices.

Within Indonesia, migrant workers pay unofficial charges even when using official government channels (Hamim 2003). In the face of the activities of state bureaucracies, individuals may determine that the laws governing temporary labour migration are simply 'bad laws' (Vásquez-León 1999) and thus 'illegal' migration is a rational choice.[21] Indeed, as we noted earlier many people who leave Indonesia through the transit provinces see irregular labour migration as attractive precisely because of the complexity, slowness and high cost of government-sanctioned processes.[22] In the eyes of many of

21 Vásquez-León (1999:255, footnote 2) defines the informal economy 'as that part of the illegal economy that results in legitimate economic activities that have to be undertaken illegally because of bad state laws and regulations, which make them too costly if undertaken legally or make legal activity non-viable for many low-income entrepreneurs'.

22 Spaan 1994; Ford 2001; Abdul Rahman 2003; Idrus 2008. McCarthy (2002:870) describes a similar rationale behind the actions of 'illegal' loggers – the process of obtaining legal logging papers in Aceh was so time

these migrants, as well as local bureaucrats and leaders in the transit zones, it is the national laws and those who create them that are corrupt. According to this view, laws to protect migrants appear designed to squeeze money out of poor workers who incur large debts and lengthy repayment schedules. This suggests that in order to understand the nature of state involvement in illegal practices, attention must first be given to the ways in which certain acts come to be identified as being illegal. In the case of Indonesia's labour migration program, this would require an approach that examines how a system that has been established ostensibly to assist and protect hundreds of thousands of low-skilled workers in fact makes criminals out of those same workers and the officials that try to help them.

The case of the Riau Islands also demonstrates that in order to understand the nature of corruption we should not only take into account the structural factors that support (or inhibit) state involvement in illegal acts, but also consider the meanings attached to those acts by different individuals and communities. It is clear from our interviews and from other studies (Idrus 2008) that grey migration agents and the intending labour migrants who choose to use their services – and the passport bureaus that support them – believe that their activities are licit. But the fact that grey migration agents and *aspal* passport bureaus have formalized, and openly promote, their collaborative relationships with government agencies suggests that grey labour migration also has a degree of licitness for local agents of the state. For many of these officials, the *aspal* solution is a necessary and inevitable response to flaws in the national labour migration system.

Conclusion

This discussion of the *aspal* system in the Riau Islands points to the complexities surrounding attempts to theorize the form and nature of state involvement in illegal activities. Disjunctures between the ways the official labour migration system is supposed to assist migrant workers and the reality of its impact on those workers and on communities create opportunities for the *aspal* system to emerge and flourish. The ways that individuals respond to the grey labour migration system – including the 'corrupt' practices of local government officials – reflects their understanding of a number of factors including the legitimacy of central government policy (and authority), the impact of such policy on the local community, and the saliency of local expressions of identity. In the case of the Riau Islands, on the whole the local

consuming and complex, that local entrepreneurs would give up and provide payments to local officials to 'turn a blind eye'.

community regards the *aspal* system as an inevitable outcome of the central government's failure to understand life in the border zone. Most local people also see the behaviour of local officials and their private partners in the grey migration system as a legitimate response to the flows of migrant workers into the islands.

An examination of the intersections between legality and licitness in labour migration processes in different sites opens up possibilities for re-thinking the nature of state illegality, not just the dissonances between society and state. If we are to understand the corrupt practices of local government officials with regard to labour migrants passing through the transit zone we require an approach that accounts for the structural factors that support or inhibit corruption as well as the meanings associated with different forms of illegal behaviour. As the visibility and community acceptance of the *aspal* route implies, the motivations behind ostensibly very similar forms of state involvement in illegal practices in different sites may vary considerably. In the case of the Riau Islands, corrupt practices around the issuing of travel documents are in part a local community-sanctioned response to managing the impact and limitations of a central government policy that fails to take local conditions into account. Like the local ecologies of legitimacy that surround illegal logging in other parts of Indonesia, this case suggests that attention to scale is important in the study of the motivations and manifestations of the Indonesian state's engagement with illegality.

MARCUS MIETZNER

Funding *pilkada*

Illegal campaign financing in Indonesia's local elections

One of the most intriguing features of illegal activity in Indonesia's post-Suharto state has been the unashamed 'transparency' with which political actors have violated existing laws and regulations. Far from developing sophisticated schemes that outsmart investigators and the public, many politicians, entrepreneurs and rent-seekers simply ignore the law and expect that nobody will notice or care. Mostly, the perpetrators can be confident that their actions will be met with apathy, indifference or – as Aspinall and Van Klinken note in their introduction to this book – even 'social approval'. Indeed, there are entire policy fields in which no effective regulation takes place, with relevant laws deliberately overlooked by both violators and state prosecutors. One such policy field is that of political financing in general and campaign funding in particular. Since 1999, Indonesia's electoral laws have set detailed limits for the amount of donations that political parties and individual candidates are allowed to receive, and have obliged them to submit audited reports on income and expenditure to the authorities. However, parties and nominees have developed a habit of reporting only a fraction of their donations and costs, with prosecutors showing little interest in investigating these transgressions. In interviews with the media, politicians have regularly mentioned much higher numbers for the costs of their campaigns than stated in their financial reports, and except for a small number of civil society groups, neither the public nor the state have aggressively questioned these discrepancies (IFES 2004). Apparently, most Indonesians have come to view illicit campaign financing as an inevitable side effect of political activity, and thus are not overly concerned about the legal violations involved. In fact, many political commentators seem to prefer illegal party self-financing to a more effective system of control, which would reduce the overall income of parties and encourage them to request more money from the state.

This chapter discusses illegal campaign financing in Indonesia's direct local elections (or *pilkada*),[1] which have seen a particularly high level of unreported donations from lobbyists and wealthy entrepreneurs. At the national level, financial underreporting and illicit fundraising has been rampant as well (Mietzner 2007), but the need for a centralized campaign organization and the scrutiny from Jakarta-based media has had a moderating effect on parties and candidates. In the regions, however, the lack of financial contributions from Jakarta, the absence of strong control mechanisms through the media, and the personality-focused nature of direct elections have aggravated the problem significantly. This chapter approaches the issue of illicit financing of campaigns in local ballots in three steps. First, it explains the regulatory framework for political fundraising and spending in Indonesia, outlining the legal parameters which sponsors and politicians alike find so easy to violate. In the second section, this set of legal norms is contrasted with the reality of campaign financing in local elections. Faced with exploding campaign costs and provided with almost no public subsidies, parties and candidates have decided to ignore the official caps on donations that, if adhered to, would dramatically cut into their funding base. Having established the illegality of these actions, the third part of this chapter evaluates the impact of prohibited campaign funds on the quality of democratic institutions and the outcome of elections. While there is sufficient evidence that the current campaign financing system fuels corruption, it does not seem to seriously distort the result of local ballots, as claimed by some authors (Choi 2005; Hadiz 2007). Finally, I explain how the inherent pragmatism of the Indonesian elite vis-à-vis illegal activity has contributed to the post-Suharto polity's perception of itself as a transitional and 'preliminary' state. Conveniently, this concept has allowed the elite to use the state as a forum to unabatedly compete for power while still upholding Weber's ideal of a positivist, unbiased regulator.

Campaign financing in Indonesia: laws and regulations

When Suharto's authoritarian regime fell in 1998, the reform of Indonesia's campaign financing laws was viewed as one of the most crucial preconditions for the development of a competitive and transparent democracy. Under the New Order, the government had not only used the military to control political activity, but it had also shifted so many financial resources to its electoral machine Golkar that no meaningful competition at the ballot box could take

1 *Pilkada* is the Indonesian acronym for *pemilihan kepala daerah* (election of chiefs of regions). In order to distinguish them from the previous elections through local legislatures, the *pilkada* were initially called *pilkadasung* or *pilkada langsung* (direct election of chiefs of regions). But *pilkada* is now the more commonly used acronym.

place (Suryadinata 1989). The authorities provided Golkar with impressive office buildings, and all government officials and civil servants were expected to support the party with funds and development projects. In addition, Suharto personally managed a foundation that helped to finance Golkar's operations and electoral campaigns – at the time of his resignation, that foundation still controlled funds of over Rp 900 billion (about US$90 million).[2] By contrast, Golkar's competitors were only given small offices and equally meagre allowances, and they were not allowed to be politically active below the district level.[3] Against this background, the post-autocratic party system emerging after 1998 urgently needed fair and strict campaign financing laws, which would guarantee a level playing field for all contestants and neutralize the privileges accumulated by Golkar over the course of three decades. Accordingly, the political elite agreed to limit the amount of money parties could routinely collect, and to require them to report their expenditures to relevant state bodies. For electoral campaigns, separate regulations were issued, which set different levels of allowed income and obliged the contestants to submit audited reports on their campaign funds to the electoral commission shortly before and after the ballot.

Despite frequent revisions to the laws on political parties and general elections, there are three principles of post-Suharto campaign financing that have remained largely constant.[4] To begin with, Indonesia is primarily concerned with imposing income limitations, not expenditure caps. The current regulations explicitly refrain from regulating the maximum amounts politicians can expend during campaigns, making it impossible for the authorities to detect possible discrepancies between reported income and spent funds. Given that expenditures are generally of a public nature and thus easier to scrutinize than donations, Indonesia's decision to focus its relevant laws exclusively on income figures has rendered its campaign financing controls largely ineffective. Second, Indonesia's lawmakers have refrained from defining enforceable sanctions for possible violators of campaign financing regulations. While the state threatens those who exceed the allowed amount of donations with stiff prison terms and fines, its laws are deliberately vague on how such transgressions can be verified. Most importantly, the regulations only discuss the possibility of parties or candidates obtaining too many donations on their officially registered bank accounts – but remain silent on the obviously much

2 Interview with former Golkar chairman Akbar Tandjung, Jakarta 17-12-2007. Suharto discontinued funding for Golkar after his fall.

3 Golkar was able to establish offices everywhere, including in villages. Through a bizarre but effective legal construction, Golkar was not classified as a political party, which meant that restrictions that applied to parties did not affect Golkar.

4 The first post-authoritarian laws on political parties and on general elections were passed in 1999. The party law was subsequently revised in 2002 and 2008, while the electoral laws were rewritten in 2003 and 2008.

higher chance of such payments going into private accounts or being handed over in cash. Third, Indonesia's system of campaign financing supervision operates in an environment in which parties and candidates receive only small amounts of subsidies from the state. While the level of public party financing has fluctuated significantly over the years, it has consistently covered only a small percentage of the real expenditures of electoral contestants.[5] As a result, Indonesia's party financing laws have not only encouraged, but in fact forced participants in elections to raise the bulk of their campaign funds from external sponsors.

These three main pillars of campaign financing in post-Suharto Indonesia were also used to develop the regulatory framework for the direct elections of governors, regents and mayors, which began in June 2005. In the 2004 law on local government, it is regulated that nominees can raise funds for the elections from three sources only: first, from their own pockets; second, from the political parties that nominated them; and third, from donations by individuals or corporations (paragraph 81-1). The law grants no state subsidies for the candidates, who presumably are expected to utilize the small amounts of public funding made available to political parties under other laws and presidential decrees. Based on the funding formula laid out there, each year central party leaderships receive Rp 21 million (US$2,100) per seat obtained in the last elections at the national level. Similar arrangements are in place for the party boards in provinces and districts. Given the low sums paid out under this mechanism, it has been very difficult for parties to make ends meet. For example, between 2004 and 2009 the medium-sized National Awakening Party (Partai Kebangkitan Bangsa, PKB) received an annual subsidy of only Rp 1.092 billion (US$110,000) for its central board. At an average of 100 local elections per year during that period,[6] the party thus had a mere US$1,100 to hand out to each of its district or province-level candidates – assuming, of course, it had no other operational costs to cover. The regulations on external donations in local ballots are equally 'idealistic'. Individuals are allowed to donate Rp 50 million (US$5,000) each, while enterprises can sponsor candidates with up to Rp 350 million, or US$35,000 (paragraph 83-3). While these limits are high compared to developed democracies (the US allows for individual donations of US$2,300 for each candidate per election),[7] they are prohibitively low for the socioeconomic context of contemporary Indonesia. Given the small number of affluent citizens who are able and willing to make

5 For example, the subsidies received by PDI-P in 2005 were only enough to pay for 1% of its officially reported campaign costs in the 2004 elections.

6 Indonesia has currently more than 470 districts and municipalities, and 33 provinces. This number is likely to rise over the next few years.

7 Overall, political donors in the US can spend a total of US$108,200 to parties and candidates over a 2-year period.

campaign contributions, parties and candidates in Indonesia must raise large donations from an exclusive circle of sponsors. The limitations set by the law effectively obstruct this effort.

Similar to the income caps, the reporting obligations are tight and detailed – on paper, that is. Candidates in local elections have to set up official campaign accounts, and are personally responsible for their use. Nominees are not permitted to accept money from foreign groups or governments, or from domestic state enterprises, local administrations and unidentified sources. Every donation above Rp 2.5 million (US$250) needs to be reported to the local election commission, stating the amount and the name of the sponsor (paragraph 83-5). These reports have to be submitted one day before the campaign period begins, and the electoral commission is expected to publish them in the media. Three days after voting day, candidates are obliged to inform the commission of their expenditures during the campaign. However, no limits for campaign spending have been fixed, raising the question of what exactly it is that the commission is supposed to check or verify. According to the law, the commission has to forward the reports to public accountants, who are required to audit the submissions within 15 days. Subsequently, the reports are returned to the commission and made available to the public (paragraph 84-5). While these reporting regulations appear strict, the catalogue of sanctions attached to them is all but unenforceable and thus of a largely normative nature. Whoever receives campaign donations above the stated limit is threatened with jail terms between 4 and 24 months, and a fine between Rp 200 million (US$20,000) and Rp 1 billion, or US$100,000 (paragraph 116-6). The law also defines sanctions for accepting money from unlawful sources, and for making false statements in the reports. However, the regulations only scrutinize the formal accuracy of the submitted reports, suggesting that donations not listed in the official campaign account are legally irrelevant. In other words, as long as candidates are smart enough to keep their reports within the framework of the law, they don't have to fear legal consequences.

Local campaign financing: the reality on the ground

Since 2004, Indonesia has witnessed a huge increase in the cost of political activity. Previously, party leaders had to focus on only one parliamentary election every five years, with most top public officials subsequently selected through indirect votes in national and local legislatures. This electoral mechanism had kept costs relatively low; in fact, parties could raise additional income by demanding hefty fees from individuals interested in executive positions. After 2004, however, the expenditure of political parties and their nominees for electoral campaigns grew exponentially. The introduction of direct presidential elections in that year added two new national ballots to Indonesia's electoral cycle, stretching already tight party budgets.[8] More importantly, however, Indonesia launched direct local elections for governors, regents and mayors in June 2005, resulting in more than 500 polls over a five-year period.[9] Besides their overwhelming frequency, the direct nature of these elections has also created new costs: parties now have to conduct expensive opinion surveys in order to identify their nominees for the elections, flushing hundreds of billions of rupiah into the pockets of pollsters, political consultants and strategic advisors (Mietzner 2009a). Since the mobilization of party networks has often been insufficient to win personality-based elections, the nominees and their parties also have had to invest much more money into media campaigns than was previously the case. While parties typically have tried to shift these costs onto their candidates (even asking them for extra money in exchange for the nominations), many local party branches have found it difficult to stay financially afloat. Accordingly, parties and candidates have become dependent on external donations. Some of these contributions have been made to the official campaign accounts; most of them, however, have circumvented all legal channels.

Estimates of the campaign costs for local elections in Indonesia vary greatly, and concrete figures are hard to come by. However, it has been widely accepted that candidates need to spend around Rp 10 billion (US$1 million) to run professional campaigns in medium-sized districts, and around Rp 100 billion (US$10 million) to have a realistic chance of winning a governorship in an average province (Rinakit 2005). For key provinces with large populations such as West, East and Central Java, these figures are significantly higher. When the cost structure of such campaigns is analysed in detail, the steep price tag attached to political candidature immediately becomes apparent. In the run-up to the gubernatorial elections of Jakarta in 2007, for example, a campaign consultant estimated that each candidate would have to spend Rp 60 billion (US$6 million) on advertising campaigns just to increase their name recognition and 'electability'.[10] In addition, candidates in crucial provinces often pay Rp 20 to 40 billion (US$2 to 4 million) to large parties that nominate them, while smaller parties can ask for 5 to 10 billion (US$500,000 to 1 million).[11] For polling and consultancy services, nominees have to fork out another Rp 5 to 10 billion (US$500,000 to 1 million) for high-quality organizations with foreign-educated staffers, or a little less for more low-profile

8 Based on the electoral laws, the presidential elections require a second round if no candidate reaches more than 50% of the votes in the first round.

9 The change was introduced through Law 32 on Local Government, which was passed in September 2004.

10 'Opening for Jakarta governor: only the wealthy need apply', *The Jakarta Post* 12-6-2007.

11 Interview with a candidate in the 2007 gubernatorial elections in Jakarta, 23-9-2007.

groups.[12] Accordingly, it is perfectly possible for gubernatorial nominees to reach the 100-billion mark before they can even begin building up an electoral machine, handing out goodies to the electorate or paying for entertainment events at mass rallies. This, and the hiring of witnesses for each of the polling stations, can add another Rp 10 to 20 billion (US$1 to 2 million) to the bill. In the governor's election of South Sulawesi in November 2007, for instance, the number of polling booths was more than 12,000, and witnesses were generally paid Rp 100,000 to 150,000 (US$10 to 15) per person. Golkar's candidate prepared three witnesses for each station, and thus allocated Rp 5.2 billion (US$520,000) for their 'pocket money' alone.[13]

These exorbitant costs often stand in sharp contrast to the officially reported incomes and expenditures of nominees. In the gubernatorial elections in West Java of April 2008, for example, the three pairs of candidates submitted grossly understated financial reports – as did almost all of their colleagues across Indonesia. The incumbent governor Danny Setiawan (who eventually lost the elections) reported official campaign donations of Rp 16.39 billion (US$1.6 million), of which he claimed to have spent only 12.65 billion (US$1.3 million). The biggest chunk of the donated funds allegedly came from the private sector (7.95 billion), while the largest item on his expenditure list was the overhead cost for Golkar offices in the province (4.83 billion). The winners of the elections, Achmad Heryawan and his running mate Dede Yusuf, reported only Rp 3.23 billion (US$323,000) in donations, and Rp 2.9 billion (US$290,000) in costs.[14] The third team of candidates, led by former army general Agum Gumelar, was apparently so bitter over its defeat that it initially did not submit a financial report – following the example of many other electoral losers in Indonesia's local elections who see no point in disclosing their finances after being defeated at the ballot box. Only after the electoral commission sent Agum a friendly reminder did the retired officer comply. However, the figures suggest that he did not take the reporting task very seriously: he reported almost exactly the same amount of donations as Danny Setiawan, Rp 16.38 billion. Danny's and Agum's numbers are not only curious because of their 'coincidental' similarity, however. They also raise suspicions because both camps had earlier announced much higher investments into their campaigns. Danny's nominating party, Golkar, had stated in March that it had made Rp 30 billion (US$3 million) available for its candidate, while the Indonesia Democratic Party of Struggle (Partai Demokrasi Indonesia – Perjuangan, PDI-P) and the United Development Party (Partai

[12] The most frequently used professional pollster has been Denny J.A.'s Lingkaran Survei Indonesia (LSI, Indonesian Survey Cycle), which has even posted advertisements in newspapers to offer their services to local politicians across Indonesia. For the background of this group, see Mietzner 2009a.

[13] 'Sebar 36 Ribu Saksi, Uang Saku 5.2 Milyar', *Harian Berita Makassar* 3-7-2007.

[14] 'Laporan Aman Tak Lengkap', *Pikiran Rakyat* 15-4-2008.

Persatuan Pembangunan, PPP), which stood behind Agum, said they were close to raising 90 billion (US$9 million).[15] Even the Prosperous Justice Party (Partai Keadilan Sejahtera, PKS), which nominated Heryawan and Yusuf, acknowledged to have allocated Rp 25 billion (US$2.5 million) for the campaign – a far cry from the 3.23 billion later reported.[16]

None of these discrepancies have been clarified by the West Java electoral commission, the police, the state auditing board or prosecutors. However, such indifference towards obvious violations has been the rule rather than the exception in national and local elections in Indonesia. In the 2004 and 2009 national elections, critical NGOs identified a large number of fictitious donors, often tracing them back to non-existing addresses, or to poor villagers who allegedly had made donations worth hundreds of millions of rupiah (Badoh 2005; Indonesia Corruption Watch 2009). These 'phantom donors' appeared in the lists of all presidential candidates, including Megawati Soekarnoputri and Susilo Bambang Yudhoyono, and one party chairman admitted that 'all our financial reports were lies, nothing but lies'.[17] Despite indisputable evidence of blatant transgressions, no measures were taken.[18] Similarly, there were no legal implications for parties and candidates who failed to submit financial reports at all – in 2004, that were around half of all electoral contestants. Against this background, it comes as no surprise that 'investigations' into possible campaign financing violations in the local elections were equally lax. To be sure, that was not for a lack of cases. In the capital, the former head of Jakarta's PDI-P branch reported the winner of the election, Fauzi Bowo, to the electoral commission for claiming that the party had donated Rp 7 billion (US$700,000) to him, whereas PDI-P felt that it had never made such a payment.[19] In the West Java district of Sumedang, an official of the state auditing board suspected in April 2008 that 'tens of billions of rupiah' had been diverted from the district budget to finance campaign activities.[20] Needless to say, these complaints have not led to meaningful legal examinations of the incriminated funds. Since the direct local elections began in 2005, not a single case of campaign financing violations has ever been brought to court, and it is difficult to imagine that this will change in the near future.

The reasons for this 'mismatch between legal logic and everyday practice' – a phrase coined by John McCarthy in this volume to describe a similar phe-

15 'Parties prepare for W. Java governor race', *The Jakarta Post* 6-3-2008.

16 'Parties prepare for W. Java governor race', *The Jakarta Post* 6-3-2008.

17 Interview with a party chairman, Jakarta, 19-1-2008.

18 The authorities even refrained from investigating Amien Rais – one of the presidential candidates in 2004 – after he publicly admitted to having received hundreds of millions of rupiah from the corrupt former Minister of Maritime Affairs, Rokhmin Dahuri. In July 2007, Dahuri – who had established large off-budget accounts in his department – was convicted of embezzlement and sentenced to seven years imprisonment.

19 'Dana Kampanye Fiktif Fauzi-Prijanto Dilaporkan ke KPUD', Detik.com 4-10-2007.

20 'Kampanye Diduga Didanai APBD', *Pikiran Rakyat* 4-4-2008.

nomenon in Indonesia's natural resource management – are manifold. To begin with, an all-out persecution of violators would simply be impractical. It is no exaggeration to say that if all offences were to be consistently investigated and brought to trial, each and every governor, regent or mayor would lose his or her position. Political fundraising outside of the official campaign accounts has become so institutionalized in Indonesia that its legal prosecution would unseat much of the political elite. Confronted with the choice of paralyzing government on the one hand and turning a blind eye to a collectively tolerated practice on the other, state authorities have clearly opted for the latter. Secondly, there is a well-founded fear that losers of elections could exploit accusations of campaign financing transgressions to challenge the results of many local ballots, and that a precedence case could trigger an uncontrollable wave of lawsuits. In fact, one of the reasons for the stabilization of local governance after 2004 has been the tendency of the courts to throw out complaints by defeated candidates against the legitimacy of electoral outcomes, allowing incumbents to rule relatively undisturbed for five years.[21] This move has marginalized political operators who – before the introduction of direct local elections in 2004 – had regularly extorted local government heads with threats of impeachment by their respective legislatures (Malley 2003). Against this background, law enforces apparently are concerned that investigating political financing cases could throw Indonesia back into the instability so prevalent before 2004. Third, many citizens seem happy to stomach campaign financing infringements as long as the moneys are raised from private sources, and not from government budgets. Even NGOs have shown much greater tolerance towards illicit party donations from tycoons than towards attempts by electoral contestants to access state funds for their purposes.

To be sure, the reluctance of investigators to focus on campaign financing cases is also related to the tight patronage networks cultivated by both the providers and recipients of political donations. In most local elections, the main donors of the contestants are powerful contractors who hope that their client will reward them with government projects should he or she win the ballot. In many cases, such contractors have personally joined the campaign teams of their candidates (*tim sukses*), handing out money to voters or signing checks to cover electoral expenses. In their paper on Aceh's local elections, Samuel Clark and Blair Palmer (2008:14) have even described the contractors as a new 'economic class [which is] dependent on securing contracts and

21 In most cases, the legal complaints filed by electoral losers have been based on personal frustration and disappointment rather than on strong factual evidence of manipulations. In the vast majority of the lawsuits, the judges found it easy to dismiss them because no concrete examples of systematic distortions were presented in court. There have been some instances, however, in which judges did annul election results, often leading to a legal quagmire and political paralysis in the area concerned – Depok, Lampung and North Maluku being the most prominent examples.

exploitation licenses through political connections with both the local and national governments.' In some Acehnese regencies, contractors 'ran as vice-Bupati candidates, presumably providing the financial backing for the more well-known figure who ran as Bupati' (Clark and Palmer 2008:33). In other small Indonesian towns or rural districts, the picture is similar: contractors have forged highly effective relationships not only with their protégées in the political elite, but also with police officers, prosecutors, judges, journalists and NGO figures (Hidayat 2007). Consequently, authorities are hesitant to initiate legal proceedings against influential contractors and other political donors – who are often personal friends, golf partners or relatives. The only motivation for prosecutors to take on campaign funding violations would be significant public pressure, but this is almost non-existent in Jakarta and even less compelling in Indonesia's regions. The remarkable 'licitness of illegal activities' in Indonesia, identified by Aspinall and Van Klinken in their introduction, thus seems to be an important element in the area of political financing as well.

If the elite can so openly ignore existing laws and regulations, however, it appears curious that it has not tried to abolish them. Initially, it was in the interest of the post-Suharto elite to have a strict campaign financing regime in place in order to reduce Golkar's financial advantage, but this rationale is no longer relevant today. Given their almost unlimited power over legislation and executive orders, the leaders of political parties could have easily opted to lift the limits on the amount of donations, do away with reporting requirements and retract the threat of sanctions. There is very little pressure from society to maintain the existing regulatory framework, so there must be other explanations. Certainly, the ambition to meet international standards in campaign financing does play a role, as does the desire of the elite to create the impression of a sophisticated legal system operating within a modern, Weberian state. But the formulation of unenforceable stipulations is motivated by more than just the party leaders' wish to decorate their illicit fundraising with a façade of legality. Instead, many politicians view the existing legal directives as a blueprint for an ideal political system that Indonesia should aspire to achieve in the future. In the meantime, however, they argue that Indonesia's current economic and social conditions require pragmatism, improvisation and flexibility to deal with the challenges of transition. Defence Minister Juwono Sudarsono, a professor of political science, has been one of the main proponents of this view: 'It is simply unrealistic to expect that Indonesia with its current levels of economic development can adhere strictly to the same standards of transparency and good governance as consolidated democracies do. It will take time. But we will get there.'[22] Many party leaders agree. For them, it seems, the present laws reflect the rigorous

22 Interview with Juwono Sudarsono, Jakarta, 1-5-2007.

party financing system Indonesia should practise in the times ahead – when it can afford to do so.

Illicit campaign financing: political consequences and implications

Whatever its reasons, there is no doubt that the inability of the Indonesian state to uphold campaign financing regulations has negative consequences for the transparency of the democratic process. With most of the campaign donations made outside of official channels, voters are denied the opportunity to inform themselves about the origins of the candidates' financial resources. Even more importantly, they are unable to judge if electoral winners subsequently issue policies or reward contracts that benefit their financial sponsors. Given the high costs of campaigns, and the failure of most parties to pay for them, it is evident that new incumbents frequently take office with significant amounts of debt. While in office, they hence need to recoup their own investments and repay their sponsors, either through favours or cash.[23] Ironically, while prosecutors have largely refrained from investigating cases related to campaign financing transgressions, they have launched hundreds of investigations into corrupt practices by incumbent governors, regents, mayors and legislators. Roughly 10% of all top local government officials and parliamentarians are under legal investigation at any given time, with many convicted and sent to prison. However, surprisingly few investigators have examined the link between campaign debts and corruption while in office, despite the obvious circumstance that candidates who took up large credits to finance their election urgently require quick, regular and uncontrolled access to cash after their inauguration.

While Indonesia generally has made significant progress in its ongoing process of democratic consolidation (Mietzner 2009b), its current campaign financing practices stand in sharp contrast to more developed democracies. In most Western states, strict reporting stipulations serve as control mechanisms against corrupt deals between office holders and entrepreneurs, and senior politicians often have to resign when their violations of financing laws are exposed to the public (Hopkin 2004). This is not to say that these countries find it easy to sustain credible campaign financing regimes. In fact, cartelistic

[23] As electoral winners have the opportunity to regain and – in the long term – multiply their investment, losing candidates often face commercial, personal and political decline. While not making national headlines, the fate of some defeated nominees has occasionally become the focus of local newspaper stories. Often these articles tell of divorces, bankruptcies, arrests and even suicide attempts. The very divergent paths for electoral winners and losers highlight the fact that most nominees risk their personal wealth to gain office, which arguably explains why some incumbents irrationally plunder the state coffers without any caution or anticipation of legal consequences. See 'Gagal jadi bupati, coba bunuh diri', *Kompas* 5-8-2008.

political elites in Europe and the United States have spent much of their time and energy on creating legal loopholes through which they can continue raising funds in a non-transparent manner (West 2000). In the US, for example, many candidates bypass the US$2,300-limit for donations by entrusting much of their campaigning to formally non-partisan 'civil society groups', which are not subject to funding ceilings. With this, a huge portion of *de facto* campaign funds is never scrutinized, and corporations can contribute significantly more than the legal limits allow. Nevertheless, the campaign funding system in most Western countries is constantly debated and changed, while Indonesia seems still far away from developing a mechanism that would offer the electorate at least partial insights into the financial affairs of their parties and electoral nominees.

Some authors have suggested that public campaign financing may be the best way to interrupt the vicious cycle of exploding campaign costs, lobbyist interests and political corruption. Indeed, in 75% of all liberal democracies, the state is providing subsidies to political parties and nominees (Van Biezen and Kopecky 2007). This provision makes political actors less dependent on external sponsors, gives not-so-affluent nominees a chance to compete, and allows the state to impose stricter oversight over the monetary affairs of politicians. But while public financing can increase the electoral chances of monetarily disadvantaged candidates and parties, the system certainly has its drawbacks as well. To begin with, public subsidies tend to increase the dependence of political actors on the state, isolating party leaders from society and encouraging them to suspend organizationally important fundraising activities. Secondly, state funding can sometimes inflate the costs of political campaigning and thus lead to more, not less corruption after the election. Critics of public subsidies to candidates have argued that monies provided by the state simply add to the budgets of all contestants, forcing them to raise even more money externally if they want to beat their rivals.[24] Finally, Indonesian sceptics have maintained that when the country had a fairly generous system of public party financing in place between 2001 and 2005, the level of corruption in legislative and executive institutions was not lower than before or after that period.[25] Consequently, when state funding for parties was cut by 90% in 2005, the Indonesian public overwhelmingly approved.

The opponents of public subsidies to political actors have also plausibly argued that although the current campaign financing system is deeply flawed, it has not substantially distorted the outcome of electoral contests, particularly at the local level. In other words, candidates with large deposits

24 I am grateful to Ross McLeod for pointing this out to me.

25 Between 2001 and 2005, national, provincial and district-level boards of parties received Rp 1,000 (US$0.10) per vote obtained in the 1999 elections. This was substantially more than under the current system, which allocates Rp 21 million (US$2,100) per seat.

of (illegal) donations haven't really had a much better chance of winning elections than those who have run their campaigns on smaller budgets. To be sure, no electoral contestant can organize a competitive campaign without deep pockets. The costs of securing a nomination, posting advertisements in the media, and building up an effective campaign machine are substantial, and often prohibitively so. Nevertheless, there have been many candidates whose political track records were considerably better than those of their opponents, and thus had to spend less money. Their popularity was typically based on long attachment with the electoral area they ran in, their favourable coverage by the press, or their intense interaction with key society groups (Vel 2005). By contrast, candidates with weak roots in local communities or negative reputations had to expend significantly more cash to overcome their disadvantages. While it is difficult to extrapolate general patterns from the more than 500 local elections held since June 2005, there is evidence to suggest that nominees with positive images and less money are more likely to win than unpopular candidates with big budgets. One indication for this is the high number of incumbency defeats in local ballots, which currently stands at around 40%.[26] Incumbents usually control the largest campaign funds, but they also tend to struggle with disastrous reputations as a result of the corrupt or incompetent nature of their administrations. The gubernatorial election in West Java in April 2008 was one such example: there, a cashed-up incumbent finished only third, losing to a modestly funded PKS politician with a reputation for having high ethical standards.

It seems, therefore, that the impact of illegal campaign financing on the competitiveness and fairness of local elections has not been as severe as some observers have suggested. Without doubt, there are numerous examples of nominees who have used their oligarchic connections to illicitly raise huge war chests and bulldozer the competition (like in the gubernatorial elections in Jakarta and Banten). But there are an equally significant number of cases in which such mafiaesque patrons were trounced by capable technocrats or society leaders who enjoyed the genuine support of the electorate (Mietzner 2009c). While even truly popular nominees need money to fund their campaigns (and presumably raise much of it outside of official channels too), the results of local elections are not dependent on the financial superiority of the candidates alone. For instance, Michael Buehler (2007) has shown that local leaders who introduce themselves to grassroots voters over a longer period of time and show concern for their daily problems tend to command greater electoral support than those who quickly distribute large amounts of money without cultivating long-term relationships to voters. Attending weddings, circumcisions, funerals, religious holiday celebrations and other social events

26 'Golkar evaluasi calon incumbent', *Detik.com* 19-4-2008.

can have a much larger effect on the electability of nominees than rushed campaigns by wealthy but aloof elite figures.[27] In addition, bureaucrats who have established a reputation for delivering good public services and leading non-excessive private lives appear to be better positioned in elections than those who mismanaged their portfolios while filling their own pockets. Thus despite the damaging effect of illegal campaign financing on Indonesia's attempts to fight corruption and establish a more transparent political system, it has not led to significant distortions of electoral outcomes at the local level.[28]

Conclusion: campaign financing, local elections and the 'preliminary' state in Indonesia

This chapter has shown that Indonesian politicians habitually violate existing campaign financing regulations, with law enforcers and society openly tolerating the transgressions. Using the direct local elections for governors, regents and mayors as a case study, the analysis has outlined the legal framework, practice and political repercussions of Indonesia's campaign financing regime as well as its regular avoidance. On paper, the law defines clear limits for campaign contributions, requires candidates to establish official accounts, and sets deadlines for the submission of reports to state authorities. Contrary to claims of some observers, the legal regulations even include a catalogue of sanctions, ranging from fines to jail terms. However, the stipulations of the law are not enforced, and the 'transparency' with which they are circumvented suggests that neither politicians nor the state and society have a particular interest in their implementation. The chapter has offered several interpretations for this phenomenon. First of all, there is a widespread perception that a consistent enforcement of campaign financing laws would lead to the collapse of local governance in Indonesia as there is hardly any elected official who has not violated the law in one form or another. Against this background, prosecutors have apparently tried hard to avoid a precedence case that could open the floodgates for a wave of lawsuits by losers of elections. Equally important in this regard is the indifference or even 'social approval' offered by the public, which seems to care little about the violation

27 Obviously, intensive and sustained social networking requires funds as well, with political leaders expected to bring gifts and donations to every event they attend. But such costs are much lower than those of blitz media campaigns aimed to boost name recognition in a short period of time.

28 As indicated earlier, Indonesia's courts have generally issued very sensible verdicts whenever they felt that an election was manipulated through the financial superiority of the winning candidate. For example, the Constitutional Court in December 2008 overturned the result of the East Java gubernatorial election, in which the initially victorious former provincial secretary had offered village heads financial rewards if they achieved certain electoral benchmarks for him. The judges were satisfied that these efforts had distorted the elections in three districts, and consequently ordered a re-vote in two and a re-count in one district.

of campaign financing laws as long as politicians take the money from the private sector, and don't demand more funds from the state. By contrast, civil society groups and the press routinely express outrage whenever politicians propose to increase the level of public funding for parties, which would allow them to reduce their dependence on external donors.

The main problems created by Indonesia's deficient campaign financing system are post-election rent-seeking, corruption and collusion. In order to address these issues, Indonesia has two major options. First, Indonesia could follow the 'liberal' tradition of the United States and impose strict limits and transparency regulations on external donations. In the 2008 US elections, Barack Obama demonstrated that the transparent collection of small contributions from a large number of voters can make campaigns not only financially superior, but can also lead to the electoral mobilization of previously indifferent constituencies. Unfortunately, it appears unrealistic to expect that Indonesia will be able to successfully implement such a system in the next two decades – its middle class would have to grow at a much faster pace than it does today and voters would have to get used to the idea of giving donations to politicians rather than receiving money from them. Accordingly, Indonesia will probably have to be content with taking small steps towards increasing transparency. One such step was the decision by the national electoral commission to require political donors in the 2009 elections to submit their tax file number if their contribution exceeded Rp 20 million (US$2,000). This reform was designed to replace the old and unworkable system that asked donors only to attach photocopies of their identity cards, which in Indonesia are notoriously easy to fake or manipulate. Unsurprisingly, however, the reform was not fully implemented. While some contributors complied with the new rules, most donors still feared identification and therefore refused to reveal their tax file number. Although civil society groups published the names of many violators, no significant action was taken against them (Indonesia Corruption Watch 2009).

Beyond this 'liberal' solution of better transparency and accountability, the second option for Indonesia would be to revive its system of public funding, which has been virtually suspended since 2005. But despite the obvious advantages of this 'European' model (Donnelly, Fine and Miller 1999), it has few supporters in Indonesia. Ultimately, public pressure to reform campaign financing regulations is weak, and one important reason for this has been outlined above: while the failure to enforce campaign regulations has obstructed both Indonesia's democratic consolidation and its anti-corruption drive, it has not reduced the competitiveness of local ballots. Financially less privileged candidates have regularly toppled affluent incumbents, reducing – in the eyes of the public – the urgency to rebuild the campaign financing system from scratch.

In theoretical terms, the analysis of Indonesia's campaign financing practices has highlighted both the systemic and the pragmatic dimension of the relationship between state and illegality in Indonesia. Funding of political activity is one of the many areas in which the Indonesian state is aware but tolerant of illegal actions – not only because they are part of the state's inherent logic, but because they underpin a system that, in Aspinall and Van Klinken's words, 'gets lots of things done'. While flawed, many Indonesians see the current system of political financing as preferable to one funded by the state and subject to higher standards of transparency. Moreover, the strict prosecution of violators of campaign financing laws would have very impractical consequences, with much of Indonesia's government possibly collapsing. Despite the collective agreement that the campaign financing laws are unenforceable, however, there have been few demands to simply replace them with more 'realistic' laws. In fact, the catalogue of fines and sanctions has been expanded significantly over the years. But this discrepancy between utilitarian pragmatism and formal adherence to unachievable ideals of Weberian state control go well beyond the ordinary gap between rhetoric and action. More importantly, it reflects the essential self-perception of the post-Suharto state and its political elite. The nucleus of this self-perception is the acknowledgment that Indonesia is a work in progress, a still deficient version of the Indonesia it wants to be. In this sense, many of the legal regulations Indonesia has adopted since 1998 are reflections of its normative goals rather than of its belief that they can be successfully enforced. Hence the campaign financing laws mirror the political funding system Indonesia wishes to have, or expects to have in the future. However, even though many Indonesian politicians genuinely believe in this 'utopian' version of the state, it also provides the political class with a welcome pretext for its transgressions. The conceptualization of the state as a transitional entity allows the elite to use it as an arena to compete for power with all available (including illegal) means, while at the same time upholding the state's idealized image of a positivist, neutral regulator that could materialize in a fully consolidated Indonesian democracy.

GERRY VAN KLINKEN AND EDWARD ASPINALL

Building relations

Corruption, competition and cooperation in the construction industry

Building things has been the essence of development in Indonesia, at least since the oil boom began in the mid-1970s. Indeed, the word *pembangunan*, a central trope of the New Order regime, means both 'development' and 'building' (Heryanto 1988). But the very large construction industry is plagued by poor standards and corruption. It is widely known that money is routinely skimmed off construction contracts to pay off tendering committees, public works bureaucrats and other officials with influence over the allocation of public construction contracts, reducing the quality of the material and work. Construction contractors are an important part of the politico-business elite, especially in the regions, and it is often their political connections rather than their construction expertise that lands them the most lucrative construction contracts.

The approach in the recent wave of expert reports by multilateral agencies is to view problems of corruption and standards in the industry as public policy issues amenable to improved regulation. Beginning with a set of 'international best practice' norms, they develop sophisticated indices showing where Indonesian institutions fall short, and conclude with policy recommendations. But this normative approach lacks explanatory power. The present chapter aims to explain rather than prescribe. It seeks to account for the resilience of corrupt practices by viewing the construction industry ethnographically, namely as a set of social actors who strategize to promote their interests.[1]

In the 1980s and 1990s, multilateral agency reports on the sector traced its problems to developmental issues such as a shortage of technical skills, organization, capitalization and legal protection (Kaming et al. 1997; Kirmani 1988; World Bank 1984). Over the last decade, the emphasis has suddenly shifted to the issue of corruption (Kenny 2007; Pranoto 2005). A World Bank study on the public procurement system (mostly construction) argued:

1 Some work along these lines already exists. Most focus on the informality of construction at the bottom end of the market, for example, Van der Erve 1989; Hermanto et al. 1983; Sannen 1986; Thung Ju Lan 1989.

'[T]he public procurement system in Indonesia does not function well. It is not market driven, has been prone to misuse and abuse, and reduces value for money for public funds' (World Bank 2001:1). Not surprisingly, reform of public procurement has been a major target of post-Suharto reforms.

Part of the sudden shift in emphasis was externally driven. A broad ideological shift took place in Washington after the end of the Cold War. More or less sanguine behavioural analyses influential in the 1960s saw corruption as good or bad depending on context (Leff 1964; Scott 1969). But in the 1990s the language became pathological. World Bank president James Wolfensohn in 1996 spoke of corruption as a 'cancer'. He and other influential voices in international agencies began to portray corruption as, in the words of another senior World Bank official, 'a great obstacle to economic and social development'. They depicted corruption as a distortion in the orderly functioning of markets, caused mainly by excessive government interference and regulation, which increased opportunities for public officials to extract resources from market players. In keeping with the neo-liberal mood of the times, corruption was thus seen as something that could be corrected by the right policy settings, including by rolling back the responsibilities of the state in the economy. The ideological shift resonated in Indonesia among liberal-oriented sections of the growing middle classes, which made opposition to corrupt favouritism central to the agenda of the movement that ended Suharto's New Order regime in 1998. Responding to pressures from both international agencies and large segments of public opinion, post-Suharto governments have introduced anti-corruption measures of varying effectiveness, including in the area of government procurement.

However, since the collapse of the regime in 1998, it has been all too obvious that patterns of corruption and predatory behaviour that grew and consolidated under the New Order have persisted into the new era of democratic and decentralized politics. Neo-patrimonial networks linking politics with business have been both resilient and adaptable, especially at the local level. Observers have noted the important place that the construction sector occupies in the corrupt nexus between business and politics, especially in provincial areas (Clark and Palmer 2008; Sulaiman and Van Klinken 2007). In the regions, construction is often a dominant part of local economies, construction projects are a major focus of collusive and predatory behaviour, and *kontraktor* (contractors) are often prominent not only in business but also in politics. Provincial and district parliaments are full of contractors who live on building projects they themselves decide on. Contractors are prominent in the campaign teams for directly elected district heads and governors.

Thus Indonesian contractors are now the bad guys in two relatively new agendas: one international, focused on making government procurement more competitive; the other domestic, focused on making government more accountable. This chapter will show that they have not been very responsive to either agenda so far. Our question will be: how can we explain this resistance? We do so by combining detailed case study research one of us (Aspinall) has done in the province of Aceh, with broader national and historical research conducted by the other (Van Klinken).

Corruption in the government-funded construction sector is a matter of worldwide concern. In China, for example, one author refers to the sector as a 'quasi-criminal domain' in which widespread official corruption leads to shoddy building standards and fatal building collapses (Ding 2001:180). In Japan, corruption in the construction industry is a lynchpin connecting the worlds of business and politics. The country has been described as a construction state (*doken kokka*) in which 'money flows through the system guided by the bureaucrats to benefit those who form part of the privileged national grid of politicians, bureaucrats, and business people' (McCormack 1996). A study of 'everyday corruption' in West Africa describes a world of public procurement and construction based on 'a triangle composed of corrupting contractors, corruptor officers and intermediaries, [giving] rise to real chains of complicities' (Blundo 2006:260).

Government-funded construction is a site of predation in part because discretionary spending is vulnerable to corruption in every type of economy. It becomes especially vulnerable when there are few other sources of cash for provincial middle classes in an underdeveloped, otherwise agrarian and trade-based economy. In such societies, construction can become a major driver of a corrupted political process. According to business perceptions measured in a 15-country survey by Transparency International, construction is the most corrupt industry, exceeding even the arms industry and oil and gas (Stansbury 2005:36). A large international survey of company-state interactions in 22 transition countries (Business Environment and Enterprise Performance Survey, BEEPS) reported that:

> It appears that construction firms in the sample think it is more common to pay bribes in their industry than do firms in other industries, that firms like theirs spend a larger percentage of revenues on bribes, and they bribe more frequently to get licenses, deal with taxes and get contracts. [...] It appears (unsurprisingly) that private construction firms where the state is the largest customer are likely to report particularly high corruption in their industry. These results are highly statistically significant (Kenny 2006:14-5).

Kenny reports a common estimate that 5-20% of construction costs are being lost to bribe payments, with the average reported payoff for a government construction contract being around 7% in a range of transition countries. For government construction work in Indonesia in 2004 this would correspond to a range of US$0.3-1.4 billion, with the 7% figure equalling US$0.5 billion. Indonesian politicians quote much higher losses than this.[2] Indeed, bribes are not the only problem. A poorly constructed or sited project, for example, may result in economic losses many times greater than the bribes.

The problems in the construction sector have long made it the object of reforms. In Indonesia, as the sector became increasingly linked to the twin problems of corruption and the collusive provincial politics after *reformasi*, these reforms moved closer to the centre of the Indonesian good governance agenda. The first presidential instruction governing procurement was issued in 1979, and since then there have been improved presidential instructions in 1980 (twice), 1984 (twice), 1988, 1994, 2000, and finally 2003 (Keppres no. 80/2003). The first law on construction was implemented in 1999 (UU no. 18/1999).[3] All the regulations have striven to balance two competing demands: on the one hand, to ensure efficient use of state funds by improving competitiveness, and on the other hand, to ensure social equity and employment creation and to nurture an indigenous, and state-dependent, business class. The former goal led over the years to the gradual professionalization of technical qualification criteria, tendering procedures, contract provisions, and the like. The latter goal led to such protective measures as reserving smaller contracts for 'weaker' groups on the grounds that they were indigenous, small-and-medium, or local.

The tension between the free market and the protectionist impulses in the regulatory framework reflects not simply official 'lack of capacity' but a political struggle. Big Indonesian and international companies have a comparative advantage in the free market. They support the reforms that promote competitiveness. Smaller provincial operators know they cannot survive without protection, so they argue that the government has a responsibility to protect the weaker players. In their world, profits are not made by lone entrepreneurs fighting for market supremacy, but by well-connected people who know how to build political alliances to keep out rivals. If we want to know more about this political struggle, however, the otherwise highly informative public policy documents only take us so far.

2 Vice President Jusuf Kalla told an Indonesian business conference in 2006 that the introduction of open tendering for public works projects would save the state budget 30-50% a year, though he presumably meant that at least some of this saving would be made by the effects of competition (Gajah Kusumo, 'Tender terbuka hemat nilai proyek hingga 50%', *Bisnis Indonesia* 4-8-2006).

3 A convenient summary of the history of regulation is in footnote 3 of World Bank 2001. Most of the current laws and regulations, as well as more detailed implementing regulations, are available at a website of the Public Works Department (http://www.pu.go.id/bapekin/produk/produk_statuter.html, accessed 8-12-2008). Technical evaluation of the procurement system is in chapter 6 of World Bank 2007.

Why construction?

We begin by distilling some of the central facts about the construction industry readily available in the multilateral agency reports, which are nothing if not well-stocked with figures. Worldwide, the construction industry contributes about 5% in value-added to the GDP of middle income countries like Indonesia, and capital formation in construction makes up about 10% of GDP. These percentages tend to rise as an economy develops (Kirmani 1988:141). Combined government and private infrastructure investment in Indonesia ran at 5 to 6% of GDP before the 1997 crisis, but fell to below 2% in 2000. Since then it has slowly recovered (World Bank 2007:75), and by 2006 it had reached 7.5% or US$24 billion (Wongso 2007). The building sector employs 4.5 million workers, or almost 5% of the Indonesian workforce. But over 60% of them are unskilled or semi-skilled.[4] The high-tech end of the industry is dominated by oil and gas facilities, highways and other large projects built by private global companies such as Bechtel, Brown and Root, McDermott, and Leighton, as well as by large Indonesian companies such as Trans Bakrie and majority state-owned construction companies like PT Adhi Karya Tbk and PT Wijaya Karya Tbk.

The much more pervasive lower end of the industry is engaged in building infrastructure such as roads, irrigation systems, water supply, local power stations, telecommunication networks, hospitals, clinics, offices, shops, and housing. Collectively, this sector is very large: about one quarter of all construction in Indonesia involves building bridges and roads.[5] A large proportion of this lower end is government-funded. The World Bank (2007:79) estimates that actually expended government infrastructure investment (not counting operation and maintenance) in 2004 amounted to Rp 62 trillion (approximately US$6.8 billion). This amount has increased considerably since then. Decentralization means that over half of this government money is now spent by provincial and especially district governments. According to the 2003 Asia Foundation Rapid Decentralization Appraisal (Satriyo et al. 2003:25-6), local governments spend most of their development funds on building basic facilities in the areas of transportation (24.7% of development budget), housing and settlement (7.46%), regional development and settlement (7.31%), and natural resources and irrigation (3.50%). Little of it is spent on education and culture. It is estimated that 80% of building contractors depend entirely on government work (World Bank 2001:21), and out in the provinces this could be even higher.

The construction sector is of central importance to Indonesia's economic growth. It is also a major and growing employer. As we will see, however, the peculiar characteristics of the industry make it a regulator's nightmare.

4 'Dep. PU, Depnakertrans, dan LPJKN tingkatkan tenaga kerja konstruksi', *Business News* 9-1-2008.

5 Indonesian Bureau of Statistics figures at http://www.bps.go.id/sector/construct/table2.shtml (accessed 14-5-2008, archived at www.archive.org).

Here we focus not on the grand corruption practised by the big few,[6] but on illegality in the dense web of relationships between government officials and building contractors in the provinces.

A history of corporatism

The construction industry in Indonesia inherits a history of massive infrastructure work developed by the Dutch in the late nineteenth and early twentieth centuries. Built with taxes on agriculture, the roads and railways initially had mainly an imperial purpose, but later the emergence of a developmental aim led to the construction of extensive irrigation works.[7] The grand phase of infrastructure development came to an end around 1930 and did not resume for another half century. The worldwide economic depression, the predatory Japanese occupation, the national war of liberation, and the political and economic chaos of the first two decades of independence, left infrastructure in ruins. Furthermore, with independence came democracy. When construction work resumed, the new government had to take account of domestic politics. Previously disadvantaged groups demanded that business wealth be redistributed as a matter of justice. A brief history of the construction industry illustrates a growing conflict between protectionists and free-marketeers.

Unlike the unfailingly apolitical multilateral agency reports, Indonesian construction contractors have written their own history in openly political terms (Gapensi 2004). This history describes how aspiring Indonesian entrants to the building sector relied less on their technical skills than on their political leverage to gain advantage over economically stronger European and ethnic Chinese rivals. When Indonesia became independent there were only a few indigenous contractors. Most were very small, graduates of trade schools in the 1930s. Their best hope was to lobby for government work on the basis of their indigenous, nationalist credentials. In January 1959, city-level associations in the three biggest Javanese cities of Jakarta, Surabaya and Bandung joined together in the All-Indonesia Association of National Construction Implementers (Gabungan Pelaksana Konstruksi Nasional Seluruh Indonesia, Gapensi). Six months later the organization's first chairperson, Dipokusumo, became Minister of Public Works.[8] It was the end of party politics and the beginning of Guided Democracy. The new minister recognized Gapensi as the sole organization for building contractors, and

6 Such as Bechtel's controversial role in the construction of the Freeport mine in Papua (Perlez and Bonner 2005).

7 Mrazek 2002; Ravesteijn and Kop 2008.

8 Pekerjaan Umum, or PU, was successor to the colonial era Civic Public Works, or Burgerlijke Openbare Werken, BOW.

eliminated their Dutch rivals by nationalising all Dutch construction businesses, as part of the broader process of nationalization then underway. By its own rather honest 2004 account, Gapensi was somewhat thuggish especially out in the provinces, but its members now found themselves partnering with experienced engineers in the nationalized companies.[9] However, monopoly access to the government was difficult to achieve in the ramshackle state that was Indonesia in the late Sukarno years. Many non-affiliated local contractors continued to win work from local military commanders, government departments, banks, and other state agencies. Rival groups of contractors emerged, and political shifts favoured now one, now another. By 1961 Djuanda, the powerful coordinating minister in charge of the Economic and Development Council (Dewan Ekonomi dan Pembangunan), himself an engineer, insisted on another umbrella organization for building contractors, Consultative Body for Private National Entrepreneurs (Badan Musyawarah Pengusaha Nasional Swasta, Bamunas) and Gapensi was asked to join that. The Minister for Funds and Forces (!) asked them to help raise 'revolutionary' funds for the government by buying shares in development banks. Their reward was juicy construction plums in the newly Indonesian province of Irian Jaya in 1963, and in Jakarta (such as the Asian Games stadium at Senayan and the giant Conefo – Conference of the New Emerging Forces – facility that later became the national parliament house).[10]

From that time on, construction contractors were increasingly integrated into the state via formal corporatist organizations. A key construction industry broker in the militarist corporatism that began to crystallize in the 1960s and 1970s was the indigenous entrepreneur Edi Kowara Adiwinata (1919-1996). He had grown wealthy during the national revolution.[11] Close

9 Some of these nationalized construction companies still exist and are among the giants of the construction scene today. PT Adhi Karya was apparently formerly Associatie, PT Hutama Karya was Hollandse Beton, PT Waskita Karya was Volker Stevin, and PT Nindya Karya was Nedam (Van der Erve 1993:141).

10 The innocuous-sounding term 'national' deployed by Gapensi actually meant, in effect, non-Chinese, while ethnic Chinese were described as 'foreign' even if they had been born in Indonesia. Gapensi contractors for decades continued to pressure their ethnic Chinese rivals by deploying racist propaganda against them. The supposedly anti-social, anti-national character traits of the Chinese were constantly cited as a good reason to exclude them from government contracts. On Gapensi's urging, the President issued decrees in the mid-1990s (Keppres no. 16/1994 and no. 24/1995) giving special protection to small contractors on the grounds of expanding employment opportunities. These decrees were also thinly-veiled anti-Chinese measures (Gapensi 2004:65; Thung Ju Lan 1989).

11 Starting work in the Dutch state company BPM that ran the Cepu oil field in East Java just before the Second World War, Kowara got a break when the Japanese placed him in charge of the state oil company working the Indramayu field in West Java. He used his own company to do the construction work required. At the end of the war, under the cover of a revolutionary militia he commanded called Laskar Minyak Divisi III that was later integrated into the Siliwangi Division, he simply seized the oil company for himself (*Tempo*, Apa dan Siapa, http://www.pdat.co.id/hg/apasiapa/html/E/ads,20030617-15,E.html, 2003, accessed 4-4-2009; Aditjondro 1998; George J. Aditjondro, 'Kisah sukses yayasan-yayasan Suharto (bagian I)', Apakabar mailing list, 19-8-1997 (http://www.library.ohiou.edu/indopubs/1997/08/19/0008.html, accessed 4-4-2009).

connections with the military helped him survive the transition to the New Order. His son Indra Rukmana married Tutut Hardijanti, the daughter of retired general President Suharto, his golfing buddy. He expanded into livestock feed, life insurance, machine parts, Coca Cola bottling, coconut oil processing, rubber plantations, and a steel factory. His family became one of the three wealthiest indigenous entrepreneurial families of the New Order, alongside the Suharto and Djojohadikusumo families. Starting as the Jakarta chapter chairperson of Gapensi in 1959, he served on the national board of all its various incarnations throughout the 1960s and 1970s.

Unfortunately for domestic contractors, the New Order also threatened to reopen the doors to their foreign capitalist rivals. In 1966 a new team of powerful technocrats – Radius Prawiro, Ali Wardhana, and Wijoyo Nitisastro – met the contractors to explain that Indonesia was changing from a 'national economy' to a 'liberal economy'. There would be no more megaprojects for the moment, and 'foreigners' would be allowed to compete for construction work. The president dissolved Bamunas in 1967. However, the protectionists had the last laugh. Ten years later, after many organizational permutations, Gapensi emerged stronger than ever. Together with two other associations – one for big construction firms based in Jakarta (Asosiasi Kontraktor Indonesia, AKI), and one for construction consultants (Ikatan Nasional Konsultan Indonesia, Inkindo)[12] – it set up a Joint Secretariat in the office of Public Works Minister Radinal Mochtar in 1977. Five months later it was awarded a big contract to build cheap government housing for soldiers. Edi Kowara had already begun in 1974 to help Gapensi set up an intimate collaboration at provincial level with the Indonesian Chamber of Commerce (Kamar Dagang Indonesia, Kadin). Most Kadin provincial chapters were apparently run by Gapensi people. For 20 years from the mid-1980s, the Gapensi-Kadin link in Jakarta ran through Agus G. Kartasasmita, a Gapensi office-holder from 1983 and its chairperson continually from 1992 to 2008. Kartasasmita had been brought in to the organization by 1950s-era Public Works minister and engineer, Prof. Roosseno Soerjohadikoesoemo, known at the time as 'Mr Concrete Indonesia' (Bapak Beton Indonesia).[13] He always held a Kadin deputy chair for construction and real estate (Gapensi 2004:53). The Kartasasmita family grew wealthy under the New Order. Kadin became the only association of Indonesian entrepreneurs to be recognized in law (UU no. 1/1987) and this gave it a strong though not exclusive place in the Indonesian state's corporatist scheme.

12 AKI is Asosiasi Kontraktor Indonesia, Indonesian Association of Contractors; Inkindo is Ikatan Nasional Konsultan Indonesia, National Union of Indonesian Consultants.

13 Budianta 2008:195-202. He was re-elected to a (strictly speaking illegal) fourth term in 2004 ('BPD Gapensi gugat ketua umum terpilih', *Suara Merdeka* 23-4-2005).

The 1980s were the golden era for the corporatist construction sector. Flush with oil money, the New Order was firmly in the saddle, and the government's Five Year Development Plans, called Repelita, were the contractors' lifeline. In 1986, the Public Works Minister decreed that only members of AKI, Gapensi and Inkindo would be permitted to do construction work for the department. The Interior Minister sent a similarly worded letter to all provincial governors in 1987.[14] Together, the department of public works and the interior ministry, under which were located the regional governments, were the two most lucrative sources of government construction work. These rulings led to a large influx of under-qualified local construction contractors into Gapensi, where they were graded according to their financial and technical capacities. Membership was open to private companies as well as those controlled by state-owned enterprises and cooperatives. It grew steadily – membership stood at 21,000 in 1987, reached 38,000 by 1993, and 41,000 by 2000. The great bulk of membership always consisted of the least qualified small operators (Gapensi 2004:121-44).

We can gain a glimpse of the intertwining of Gapensi, Kadin, Golkar and local government from the provincial executives list that Gapensi published on the internet in 2000.[15] The chairman of Gapensi in Aceh, to take one random example, was Lukman C.M. This man served at the same time as deputy chairman of the provincial chapter of Kadin. He was also on the provincial executive of Golkar as the link with private business.[16] His first deputy chairperson in Gapensi was Armen Desky, who was at the same time a member for Golkar in the newly democratic national parliament (Dewan Perwakilan Rakyat, DPR). Armen Desky cut short his parliamentary career in 2002 when he was elected chief (*bupati*) in his home district of Southeast Aceh. There he immediately faced controversy over a local airport whose construction, evidently to be paid by the European Union, was delayed.[17] Another example from the Gapensi list is the oil-rich province of Riau. Chairing Gapensi here was the building contractor Rusli Zainal. He was at the same time district chief of Indragiri Hilir. Three years later he was elected governor of Riau. His own party Golkar at first failed to support him in this bitterly fought contest because it had made a deal with the then-governing party PDI-P. But newspapers reported that the outcome improved for Zainal after large

14 Surat Keputusan Mentri no. 187/KPTS/1986 of 24 April (p.64-5); Surat Edaran Menteri no. 230/766/Bangda of 13 April 1987 (p.69).

15 Gapensi's website www.gapensi.or.id for the year 2000 is archived on www.archive.org (accessed 19-6-2003).

16 'Firmandez ketua kadinda NAD', *Serambi Indonesia* 10-7-2003; Daftar nama personalia DPP Golkar, masa Bhakti 1993-1998 (www.golkar.or.id, archived for the year 1998 on www.archive.org, accessed 6-2-2003).

17 'Anggota dewan perwakilan rakyat Republik Indonesia, periode 1999-2004', *detik.com* 23-9-1999; 'Rp 50 M bantuan MEE diduga dilego UML', *Waspada* 18-4-2002.

amounts of money changed hands.[18] Sparser electronic news archives for the late New Order period make it difficult to be certain, but our experience leads us to think that, apart from the greater political uncertainties after 1998, the picture was much the same throughout the 1990s. In sum, the construction sector was organized along classic New Order corporatist lines. Corporatism has been defined as 'a pattern of state-society relations in which the state plays the leading role in structuring and regulating interest groups, organizing them along functional rather than class lines (in order to minimize both collaboration and conflict), and typically granting official recognition to only one representative body in any given sector' (MacIntyre 1991:1).

International pressure on Indonesia to liberalize the construction sector grew during the New Order. It was exercised through the International Federation of Asian and Western Pacific Contractors' Associations (IFAWPCA). Edi Kowara himself was big enough to play along and thus earn the chance of working with big international corporations at the top end of the market. In 1969 he initiated the association of large contractors called AKI specifically to join IFAWPCA. But Gapensi's large number of provincial members were not ready to compete on international terms. AKI agreed with Gapensi that it would confine itself to Jakarta, where its members would compete with international firms for international and domestic work, but it would not form provincial branches. The understanding was that Gapensi members would do the smaller domestic government work, especially in the regions outside Jakarta (Gapensi 2004:56-7).

Bribes were routine in the corporatist system in the provinces. They were known as 'wild retributions' (*pungutan liar* or *pungli*), but were quite institutionalized. Gapensi members did not like paying them, but they also saw them as a normal part of doing business, and they complained rarely. In 1996, as the New Order was beginning to fray, some did complain. A Gapensi bulletin in East Java reported that *pungli* amounted to 20-30% of the value of projects, and in some districts it reached 35%. The largest amount, up to 10% of the project value, went to the government project leader (*pimpinan proyek* or *pimpro*), which could be the departmental head, the district secretary, or even the mayor or district chief. The *pimpro* would visit the contractor at home to make sure he got his share. The cashier at the State Treasury Office (Kantor Perbendaharaan Negara, KPN) got an 'envelope' as well. Smaller payments went to other relevant officials in the public works department, the offices of the governor, district head or city mayor, and to relevant legislators. Visiting officials needed to have their trips paid and be entertained. Other people called on the contractor to make 'social contributions' to various causes.

18 'Zainal, champion of Riau development', *The Jakarta Post* 30-10-2003; 'Buntut pemilihan Gubernur Riau dugaan politik uang mulai terungkap', *Kompas* 6-11-2003.

Towards the end, thank-you gifts were made for the final handover and for a smooth report from the government's internal audit agency.

> [F]or a road construction project of one kilometre, for example, when the supervision team came to visit just before the work was handed over to the owner, the team filled an entire bus, there were up to 30 supervisors. 'From the section chief up, from the provincial down to the district level, they would all be there. As oriental people how could we refuse to provide accommodation, transport, food,' he [the Gapensi report author Somingan] said. Pocket money for the supervisors was normally Rp 200,000 per person [at that time US$40], Somingan added. ...Far from paying only to be allowed to join the tender, Somingan said, even just to know that there is a project at all, the contractor has to prepare grease money for the individual bureaucrat in the government office owning the project.[19]

The contractor knew these costs would occur and recouped them by marking up the project cost above market prices as well as by cutting corners on construction materials. We shall see that this system remains essentially unchanged even after the recent reforms.

Reforms

Regulatory reform has picked up pace since 1998, but change on the ground has been less impressive. The multilateral agency reports acknowledge this, as the following paragraphs will show, but they explain it in terms of institutional 'weakness'. Our own ethnographic work, on the contrary, sees remarkably successful organizational assertiveness rather than failure. An explanation of the resilience to reform must start by recognizing these realities, not by ignoring them. Like the reforms that had come before them, the 2003 Presidential Decree (Keppres no. 80/2003 on 'Guidelines for the Implementation of Government Procurement of Goods and Services') sought to enforce more competitive and transparent tendering procedures, while at the same time protecting smaller businesses. It addressed serious deficiencies in the system and promoted international 'best practice' principles of procurement: transparency, open and fair competition, economy and efficiency. It came after a period of both public and private pressure by major international agencies for reform to Indonesia's public procurement (see especially World Bank 2001, 2003:31-9). The World Bank (2003:31) explained its context as follows:

[19] 'Pungutan terbesar 'fee pimpro'', *Kompas* 14-4-1997.

> Looking ahead to the emergence of an Asian Free Trade Zone and the implementation of future WTO provisions that would require member states to allow access to government procurement for companies from Indonesia's trading partners, it well behoves Indonesia to develop a world class public procurement system rather than one that has a poor global reputation for encouraging corruption.

The decree set tight tendering standards for large projects, relaxing them for smaller ones (the cut-off limits have shifted downwards over time). It graded contractors according to their technical and financial capacities, allowing only the larger ones to take on big jobs, while reserving smaller jobs for smaller companies. Tendering committees now also had to be certified.

The implementation of these and other rules is another matter, however. A 2007 UN study measuring Indonesian public procurement practices by a set of OECD 'benchmarks' still gave the country poor marks on every indicator. For example Indonesia scored only 33.3% on the 'functionality of procurement market' (PCDC 2007). One problem is that the budget process actually stimulates corruption in the government building sector. Budget discussions involve many different departments and legislators, making them so drawn out that, every year, 50% of total capital expenditure is spent in the final quarter (World Bank 2007:98). This results in the routine use of a regulation permitting tenders for certain government contracts to be bypassed under 'emergency' conditions. Budget discussions often focus on specific project inputs – parliamentarians taking a particularly close interest – rather than broader program outputs (World Bank 2007:100-1).

Auxiliary institutions also remain 'weak'. Abuses should be picked up by the various government audit agencies (World Bank 2007:96). But low staffing levels, overlapping responsibilities, and corruption in the auditing bodies themselves mean that little is uncovered. The mess of contradictory regulations in a decentralized environment (World Bank 2001:1, 2007:103) is another reason why reforms are difficult to implement. A unifying National Procurement Office, to be located in the national development agency Bappenas, is still under construction. Administrative oversight is particularly anemic at the provincial and district levels. A World Bank report (2007:126) concluded: 'Overall, public financial management systems at the sub-national level are weak and risks of corruption are very high'.

In our view, contradictory, overlapping regulatory institutions are the sedimentation of political struggles within the state. On the one hand, the state budget is balanced centrally, so the pressure for reform comes mainly from Jakarta, especially from particular state agencies more committed to economic reform and, from further afield, from the international political economy and the neo-liberal currents and agencies that populate it. Since the 1998 economic crisis and political *reformasi*, governments in Jakarta have more frequently sought the technical advice of multilateral agencies on governance techniques. Local governments, on the other hand, derive nearly all their income from the centre and thus experience pressure to economize and regularize mainly as an external force. Internally, their need for local political support encourages collusive behaviour. In the following section we look at some actual examples of such struggles.

How the system works: the view from Aceh

Here we examine the construction sector from below, not as a set of institutions open to technocratic tinkering but as a set of social actors strategizing to promote their interests. Our field experience and reading of press reports indicate that the post-1998 regulatory reforms have so far had little impact on the informal practices that underpin construction contracting at the grassroots. Outsiders to the system still make the same complaints, reporting familiar types of abusive practices. Particularly out in the provinces, the system represents an informalized version of the New Order corporatist one described above. The corporatist organizations have lost the dominant position they once maintained, but they still act as important venues through which influence and information is traded. More importantly, the informal and collusive practices that underpinned the old corporatist system remain intact. From the individual contractor's point of view, success is all about the double strategy of building cooperation with allies and keeping out rivals.[20]

Aceh does not seem like a typical Indonesian province. Its long-running armed separatist revolt, the resulting military operations, and the terrible December 2004 tsunami created a degree of disruption not experienced elsewhere in Indonesia. The combination of a peace accord in 2005, tsunami disaster relief, and regional autonomy brought about an unparalleled flood of reconstruction money. However, the way this money was disbursed to local construction contractors – full of what the World Bank (2001:2) likes to call 'non-economic influence on public procurement' – looked much like that in any other province, only more extreme. Many of the former combatants of Free Aceh Movement (Gerakan Aceh Merdeka, GAM) rapidly transformed themselves into construction contractors, showing how easily political influence and coercive muscle power can be leveraged into business success in the sector. Aceh's construction industry thus turns out to be a rather useful window on that in the rest of Indonesia.

Construction takes up a large part of Aceh's post-tsunami economy.

20 The analysis of contracting in Aceh is partly derived from Aspinall (2009), and a more detailed discussion of the situation described here may be found in that publication. We thank the journal *Indonesia* for permission to re-use this material.

According to the head of the Aceh branch of the Institute for the Development of Construction Services (Lembaga Pengembangan Jasa Konstruksi, LPJK), Nova Iriansyah, in 2007 alone the total money circulating in Aceh from the national budget (APBN), regional budgets (APBD) and the post-tsunami Reconstruction and Rehabilitation Agency (BRR) was approximately Rp 30 trillion, of which about Rp 12 trillion (approx US$1.2 billion), or 40%, was allocated to construction activities.[21] Little wonder that the number of players is considerable. According to one experienced Department of Public Works official, there are about 5,000 contractors in Aceh.[22] The website of the LPJK puts the total at 3,800.[23] Construction contracting, however, is a steeply hierarchical world, and less than one percent of Acehnese contractors are in the highest grades and so entitled to bid for the largest contracts. According to the same informant, locals win only 30-40% of the big contracts, with the remainder typically being won by big companies from Jakarta (often state-owned enterprises known as BUMN) or by foreign construction companies cooperating with Indonesian firms. At the lower levels of the scale, contracting is virtually an Acehnese-only affair.

Most of the attention of corruption watchers in the construction industry has focused on the tendering process. But in fact illicit payments are routine at every turn, from conception to completion of a contract, as some lists have shown.[24] In theory the whole process is open and transparent. In reality, it is an open secret in Aceh – as in other parts of Indonesia – that it is shot through with manipulation. The central dynamic is between those bidding for contracts, the contractors, and those offering them. The latter constitute a large network of public officials that includes, at its core, the tendering committee (*panitia pelelangan*) that assesses the bids and awards the contracts, the bureau heads (*kepala dinas*) and officials who appoint them and, ultimately, the local government head – the district chief (*bupati*), mayor or governor – who is at the apex of the system. It also includes budget officials and parliamentarians who can influence local government budgets. Payment of fees and the trading of political influence are virtually ever-present ingredients. At the same time, because of the highly political nature of the contracting world, virtually any actor with political influence is able to claim a stake in it.

The process begins with the budget proposals for construction that go

21 '60 persen dana rekonstruksi Aceh mengalir ke luar', *Serambi* 13-4-2007. Of this money, Nova Iriansyah estimated that about 60% ended up leaving Aceh because contracts were won by outside contractors, or because of the need to purchase material and employ consultants and labour from outside the province.

22 Confidential interview, Lhokseumawe, 23-8-2008.

23 http://www.lpjk.org/modules/statistik/badan_usaha/2008/propinsi_golongan.php (accessed 4-4-2009). This is with a breakdown of 3,189 categorized as small, 597 as medium and 14 as large contractors.

24 One list occurs in a 2004 report by the Habibie Center, which described local governments' handling of development projects as a massive effort to divert public wealth into private pockets (The Habibie Center, 'Desentralisasi korupsi melalui otonomi daerah', *Tempo Interaktif*, 4 November 2004, http://www.tempointeraktif.com/hg/narasi/2004/11/04/nrs,20041104-01,id.html, accessed 4-4-2009).

into the draft provincial and district budgets (APBD). It continues through the local parliamentary discussion process, which, as noted above, tends to revolve around individual projects rather than aiming at a broad policy level. Legislators in the Regional People's Representative Councils (Dewan Perwakilan Rakyat Daerah, DPRD), at both the provincial and district or city (*kabupaten/kota)* levels, help executive officials set the regional development budget and spending priorities. They have leverage over the executive. Obstreperous legislators can make life difficult for local government heads and *kepala dinas*: they can alter budget allocations and so block favoured programs, they can delay budgets and other legislation, or launch investigations into government mismanagement. One way the executive tries to buy off legislators is by awarding projects to favoured contractors. Thus, Acehnese legislatures – as in other parts of Indonesia – have attracted large numbers of people with backgrounds as contractors. For example, after the 2004 election, 20 of the 25 newly elected South Aceh DPRD members – 80% – turned out to be contractors.[25] One of Aceh's largest contractors estimated that about 20% of all DPRD members in Aceh have a contracting background; a Department of Public Works staff member said he thought it was more like 60-70%.[26]

Executive government officials themselves often favour contractors of their own: sometimes they are relatives, more often their political backers and financiers. Such people can be assured a steady stream of construction contracts. Other persons able to stake a claim are from the police and military. During the conflict years in Aceh, it was widely known that the military (TNI, Tentara Nasional Indonesia) extracted massive rents from all manner of legal and illegal business in the province (McCulloch 2005). Since the 2005 peace agreement, the police are now more prominent in business, at least according to the daily gossip in the coffee shops where contractors, government officials and former combatants gather to swap stories and strike deals. Some contractors and government officials interviewed for this research mentioned cases where police were able to claim projects for themselves by launching corruption investigations at a suspect government agency, with the investigations being ended once new projects were directed their way. All players know that it is important to keep on side all actors with the power to punish. (Judges and, especially, prosecutors fall into the same category.)

For every departmental planning and tendering meeting the contractor pays compulsory 'fees' and 'commissions'. There are more players than contracts to go around. In order to keep everyone happy, the government will often break down large projects into smaller ones, in the name of creating employment and protecting small and medium enterprises. Next comes the pre-

25 '80% anggota DPRD Aceh Selatan didominasi kontraktor', *Waspada* 4-9-2004.

26 Confidential interviews, East Aceh and Lhokseumawe, 25 and 28-8-2008.

qualification and qualification for tender participants, which involves payments to the contractors association and the local government department for permits. This results in a lucrative trade in forged business permits (Sertifikat Badan Usaha, SBU). When, at last, it is time to actually award a contract, it is possible to do so without a tender (direct appointment, *penunjukan langsung*) only for very small contracts, or in the case of an 'emergency'. Both rules create loopholes for abuse. Large projects are sometimes split up into smaller ones that each fall below the limit. And a common emergency is the looming end of the budget year, when money must be spent quickly, as noted above.

Tendering is a key moment in the process. Tenders are announced publicly in newspapers. The tendering committee (*panitia pelelangan*), whose members must be properly certified public servants, rank the bidding companies on the basis of price and quality. In practice, collusion is the rule at this tendering stage. Sometimes the strongest participant pays the others to agree on one winner while compensating the losers. For instance, a group of companies might bid for the same project and end on the tendering short list, then all but one will withdraw, with the winner either making payments to the others or striking an agreement that they will take turns in future. In some provinces, the agreement is known as *arisan*, in reference to a popular neighbourhood social gathering where participants contribute a small sum each week and give a 'prize' to an agreed member at every meeting. The losers in the tender are promised 'withdrawal money' (*uang mundur*). The phrase used for this in Aceh is 'accompanying the bride/groom' (*intat linto: antar pengantin)*. Another technique to prevent an open tender is for a big player to put forward several of his private companies, their ownership thinly disguised through relatives, as 'competitors' in the same tender. These are known as 'flag companies' (*perusahaan bendera*) because they have nothing but their flag – usually not even an office, let alone equipment. They might all put in exactly the same tender and allow the tender committee to decide between them. Another common technique is the lending and borrowing of companies to allow poorly qualified constructors to bid for projects at a higher grade. Most of these techniques comply with the letter of the law. No one complains.

The primary axis of collusion, however, is between the contractors bidding for projects and the government officials in charge of awarding them. Winning contractors routinely pay fees to those on the *panitia pelelangan* or to their superiors or associates. These fees are often called *jatah pimpro* (the project leaders' 'share': *pimpro*, or *pimpinan proyek* was the term used in the past for the officials in charge of commissioning and overseeing projects). Various anti-corruption NGO activists, businesspeople and junior bureaucrats interviewed in Aceh made estimates of the amount that is usually paid by the winning bidder as *jatah pimpro.* Most fell in the vicinity of 5-10% of the project cost. Usually this money is paid by the winning company via an intermediary. Part of that money is 'deposited higher up' (*disetor ke atas*), that is, the receiving officials make payments to their superiors, who in turn pass part of it up the chain. Some ends up with the *kepala dinas*, some is passed higher to the regional government head. In exchange for such fees, the officials' superiors provide those lower down with political support and assist their promotion through the hierarchy.[27] Bureaucrats involved directly in awarding contracts can also secure their positions by granting other favours to their superiors, notably by directing contracts to their relatives or associates.

Although it is accepted wisdom in Aceh that direct payment of *jatah pimpro* occurs in most tendering process, few of the informants who were directly involved in deciding on or bidding for tenders and who were interviewed for this research admitted directly that this was how the system works. Instead, they typically described a looser set of exchange relations, using terms like lobbying (*melobi*) and building relations (*membangun relasi*). Big contractors typically said that being able to 'mix with all kinds of people', having wide social relations (*pergaulan luas*) and being able to 'bridge all sides' are keys to their success. In short, this is a world where to be successful a contractor must invest not only funds, but also considerable time and energy in getting to know all manner of bureaucratic and business players who might one day be useful, and distributing petty and informal favours to them. To the extent that most contractors admit making direct payments to officials, they typically talk about paying for entertainment or travel.

One successful contractor on Aceh's east coast explained the system in very direct language:

> We don't give *jatah pimpro*. There's no rule of that sort. But in reality it's not so much different. Instead it's lobbying. It just depends on how clever we are at making promises to him, that's all. You have to have insiders, people in the tendering committee or among the *kepala dinas*. You approach the people in the committee. As the Batak people say: 'to know someone is to love him, if you don't yet know them, you won't yet love them'. You have to know them. The key is you have to know the character of the people there. For example, if one likes girls on a Saturday night, then we'll take him to Medan on Saturday night. We'll take him to a hotel and give him a woman so that tomorrow he'll love us. If he likes entertainment, we'll give him entertainment. If another one likes fighting cocks, I'll go out and buy him a big rooster in a cage and bring it round to his house on a Sunday. If another likes to eat venison, we go and find venison and bring it to him. The key is that we must be able to read the character of other people. He won't

27 Two *bupati* interviewed for this research – former separatist fighters with no previous experience in government – explained that they were puzzled early on in their terms when *kepala dinas* began to make unexplained payments to them. They said they refused them. They presumed these monies were derived from project allocations in this way.

> ask for it: we need to be able ourselves to know what he likes. That's the general pattern. And how much does all this cost? Well if the project is 1 billion, then 100 million is pretty reasonable. That's not a written rule but, yes, it's about 10 %.[28]

Another big contractor was a little more philosophical:

> Actually there's no such thing as a set fee, say 10% of the contract cost. That's not how it works. Instead, if they [that is, government officials] have a meeting, then we have to support them, if they want to go to Jakarta, then we support them. The philosophy of the entrepreneur is we have to be close to the government leaders. There must be synergy.

One expression of this synergy is that contractors in Aceh, as in other parts of Indonesia, often play an important role in supporting candidates for executive office in direct election (*pilkada)* campaigns, often as members of their 'success teams' (*tim sukses*). Contractors fund district head or legislative election campaigns in the expectation of rewards to follow. Samuel Clark and Blair Palmer (2008:27) in their study of Aceh's 2006 *pilkada* note the prevalence in *tim sukses* of 'contractors and businessmen, people who were already enmeshed in neo-patrimonial networks with government figures, and used to pragmatic deal-making'. The *tim sukses* members expend their own financial resources in building networks and distributing material incentives down to the village level to build support for their candidate, with the hope 'that their assistance would be repaid by political or material favors' (Clark and Palmer 2008:28).

Once a contract is awarded there is no guarantee it will actually be filled by the company that won it. In fact, a well-established system exists in Aceh for 'borrowing' companies during the bidding process and the sale of contracts that follows. Sometimes, small contractors will 'borrow' a higher grade company to make a bid for a contract for which they would not be qualified to bid directly. At other times, the process is reversed and a well-established contractor with expertise, equipment and capital, but lacking the political access required to win, will purchase a contract that has been won by a better-connected, but less capable, contractor. This happened a lot in Aceh after GAM-affiliated candidates won a series of elections for local government heads from December 2006. Suddenly, with GAM members dominating local governments, former GAM fighters began to win many construction contracts, but they often lacked the capacity to do the work properly. As a result, many of them simply sold these contracts on to others, usually for a fee of about 6 to 15% of the contract value.

Once construction work finally starts, regular payments are made to all the officials concerned. Especially important in the system established under

[28] Confidential interview, 26-8-2008.

Keppres no. 80/2003, which aims to reduce corruption in government procurement, is the role of supervisory consultants (*konsultan supervisi* or *konsultan pengawas*). These are employed to check on the progress of a project and ensure it is running on time and in accordance with project specifications. The government agency commissioning a project will pay each instalment to the contractor only after receiving positive reports from the *konsultan supervisi*. Such consultants are typically paid 10% of the project cost to perform this task, and in large projects these roles are also awarded by tender. However, according to one local leader of an anti-corruption group, such consultants' reports are '80% lies', because the consultants receive side-payments from the contractor working the project.

Because so many fees and commissions are pulled out of the project cost at every stage, very few projects are completed well. To pay for all the fees, contractors skimp on material and equipment. Sometimes the project does not need to go any further than the paper stage to make money for those involved. The media regularly expose so-called 'fictive projects', which are completed only on paper but paid for with real money.

In sum, despite Keppres no. 80/2003, the world of contracting is still one in which a great variety of actors from the executive government, security and law enforcement agencies, the legislature and business are bound together by tight webs of mutual dependence, exchange of resources and of favours, and of the potential threats they represent to each other. This, in short, is the world of 'building relations', *membangun relasi*, where rivalries and competition are suppressed in order to build the wide networks of influence and familiarity that are the key to business success.

That success brings rewards. The system we have described makes the contractors prestigious members of provincial society. One Acehnese observer described their social status perceptively:

> Most contractors I know look rich, especially the young ones. They have a nice car, at least a 'Sabang' [second-hand luxury car imported through Aceh's free port Sabang]. Big house. They wear the latest fashion brands. Travelling to Medan or Jakarta, or these days even to Malaysia and Singapore, is nothing out of the ordinary for them. No surprise that many people admire the *kontraktor*. Older contractors adopt a simpler lifestyle, often just wearing an old T-shirt and sandals, even if they travel by plane overseas. Many girls love contractors. Potential mothers-in-law dream of getting a contractor for their daughter. A friend of mine complained because he lost the 'beautiful flower' he wanted to a contractor. 'Capital shortfall!', he said. Lots of people are proud to introduce themselves as a contractor, the family of a contractor, the friend or even just the neighbour of a contractor.[29]

29 Saiful Mahdi, 'Kontraktor', Aceh Institute, http://id.acehinstitute.org/index.php?option=com_content&view=article&id=326:kontraktor&catid=25:kolom-oase (accessed 29-11-2008).

Exclusion and violence in the contracting industry

The discussion in the preceding section suggests that political influence and corruption in the sector are peaceable, cooperative affairs. But competition for contracts produces losers as well as winners. Contractors say their system is based on 'building relations', but equally important is the exclusion of rivals, whether by means of gaining and defending privileged access to sources of government contracts, the 'manipulation of information' (Blundo 2006:238) (such as by tailoring bids to supposedly confidential information about tenders) or, sometimes, by executive fiat or violent intimidation.

The Aceh situation also illustrates this exclusionary and coercive side of contracting well. After the 2005 peace deal, former GAM combatants flooded into the construction industry, and their particular skills brought them dramatic success. Former GAM fighters did well not because they were skilled as contractors, but because they had privileged political access, especially after their allies won local government elections in December 2006, and because they deployed violence and intimidation against both officials who awarded contracts and rivals who competed with them (see Aspinall 2009 for more details). There have been numerous reports of former fighters threatening violence against officials responsible for awarding tenders, or kidnapping or beating them or rival contractors. GAM actors often violently threatened other contractors in order to force them to withdraw bids from tenders that they themselves were interested in. More importantly, the GAM network continued to control what they call 'access to the field' *(akses ke lapangan)* through much of Aceh, with a network of former fighters present in most villages. These men were willing and able to take action against any economic activities in their villages that were not authorized by local GAM leaders – for example, by attacking or threatening staff, burning or otherwise destroying equipment, or by stealing material. The result is that any construction entrepreneur who wants to carry out work in areas where GAM is strong is required to offer sub-contracting work to local GAM leaders, employ local GAM men, or simply pay fees to the network. As a result of such methods, what on the surface passes as respectable contracting activity by former GAM fighters often involves little more than extortion and stand-over tactics, through which the movement extracts money.

We have less data on violence, extortion and intimidation in other provinces, but exclusion has long been a central dynamic in the contracting industry. During the New Order, exclusion was legislated by the state, which gave Gapensi members a monopoly on government contracts in the provinces. Gapensi used this monopoly to keep out foreign capitalists and ethnic Chinese rivals. Internal discipline was strong because ejection from Gapensi was a career-killer. One of the more important innovations in the 1999 law on construction (UU no. 18/1999) was therefore to break the Gapensi monopoly.

The 1999 law provided for a 'forum' for the industry that took over some of the certificatory roles previously assigned to Gapensi, and allowed 'one or more' contractors' associations to be represented on this forum. The forum was the LPJK.[30] Its task is to professionalize the sector through research, training, and (most interestingly) accreditation. Initially LPJK awarded Gapensi the sole right to accredit contractors. But alternative contractors associations began to emerge from late 2000, such as Gapeksindo, Aspekindo, Gabpeknas, and Gapeknas.[31] The new entrants successfully challenged the Gapensi monopoly on certification, and managed to persuade the national parliament to allow every association to certify its own members.[32] The result has been a free-for-all. Increased local authority over construction budgets also meant each new organization had to persuade district and provincial governments it was acceptable to do business with them too.[33] Formal organizational pluralism is now a fact in every province. Nevertheless, by 2003 a new, less formal, corporatism had begun to re-emerge in the form of provincial 'forums' of contractors' associations. And LPJK membership statistics for its members organizations show that Gapensi remains the biggest organization in most provinces.[34] The only exceptions are Southeast Sulawesi and the new province of West Papua, where Gapeksindo dominates.

In the interim, the breakdown of monopoly on information caused severe distress to those who had done well out of the old system. In South Sulawesi, matters came to a head with a murder in the island district of Selayar, near Makassar, on 18 July 2001. The rival association was the Association of National Construction Entrepreneurs (Gabungan Pengusaha Konstruksi Nasional, Gapeknas). One of the Gapeknas board members in Selayar was Chiwang, and its chairman was Chiwang's brother-in-law Hasrun. Chiwang's father Alwi Hasan was a Golkar member of the district parliament – a rather typical combination in the construction business. It was the time of year when tenders are called, and the Selayar district chief was about to decide on up to Rp 12 billion (US$1.2 million) worth of projects including road improvements, schools and

30 http://www.lpjk.org.

31 Gapeksindo is Gabungan Perusahaan Konstruksi Nasional Indonesia, or Indonesian National Association of Construction Companies; Aspekindo is Asosiasi Pengusaha Konstruksi Indonesia, or Indonesian Association of Construction Entrepreneurs; Gabpeknas is Gabungan Perusahaan Kontraktor Nasional, or National Association of Contracting Companies; Gapeknas is Gabungan Perusahaan Kontraktor Nasional Indonesia, or Indonesian National Association of Contractor Companies.

32 'Sertifikasi perusahaan konstruksi terusik friksi', *Bisnis Indonesia* 28-2-2001.

33 For example, Gapeknas demonstratively visited the Yogyakarta local parliament late in 2000 to complain about the Gapensi 'monopoly' on gatekeeping construction contracts. Gapeksindo led a protest delegation to the local parliament in Garut, West Java, in mid-2006 to complain about being excluded from tendering for a road project ('Gapeknas berantas monopoli Gapensi', *Bernas* 5-12-2000; 'Asosiasi perusahaan minta bantuan DPRD', *Pikiran Rakyat* 22-6-2006).

34 http://www.lpjk.org/modules/statistik/badan_usaha/2008/asosiasi_golongan_propinsi.php (accessed 4-4-2009).

mosques. The Selayar branch of Gapensi, led by H. Anwar Ali, had repeatedly warned the district chief not to allow Gapeknas members to tender, since they were not in possession of a business permit. When the district head signaled he was about to do so anyway, the Gapensi chairperson placed an advertisement in the local newspaper threatening to take the district head to court for breaking the rules. Seeing the advertisement, Chiwang, his father and about 20 thugs went to the district Public Works office and threatened to blow it up with molotov cocktails unless they were allowed to tender. They then called by the Gapensi office and issued threats. The next day Chiwang and his father, who was wearing his parliamentary uniform, returned to the Gapensi office armed with knives. A shouting match ensued, followed by a frenzied attack that left Anwar Ali dead with 27 stab wounds to his body. By the end of the day hundreds of men had gathered at their respective Gapensi and Gapeknas offices. They were about equally matched and ready for war. The police took several days to calm the situation, while the district head threatened to stop all project work unless the two sides agreed to lay aside their differences.[35]

This example of violence in the construction industry is extreme but it is not unique, as the Aceh example also illustrates. In other provinces of Indonesia, rumours of violence and intimidation often swirl around the construction industry, and *preman*, or small-time thugs, typically play a role in running protecting rackets in the industry and, often, in working construction projects themselves.[36] The direct use of violence is only the most obvious form of exclusion in an industry where rivals are more often kept out by the assiduous construction of intimidate relationships of mutual benefit between businesspeople and politicians, relationships that yield privileged access to the most business opportunities and which therefore must be jealously guarded.

Conclusions

The neo-liberal fantasy of competition, in which there is a perfect market of entrepreneurial individuals who participate and succeed only according to their technical abilities, cannot be easily enforced in Indonesian provincial towns. There, emerging indigenous middle classes have made getting rich by

35 'Pembunuhan: rebutan proyek berbuntut maut', *Tempo* 30 July-5 August 2001; 'Diduga dibunuh anggota DPRD setempat: ketua Gapensi Sulawesi Selatan tewas dibunuh', *Tempo Interaktif* 19-7-2001; 'Gapensi-Gapeknas kisruh, proyek di Selayar ditunda', *Kompas* 21-7-2001.

36 For example, the Central Java branch of Gapensi described the behaviour of rival contractors associations in 2001 thus: 'These 'cowboys' terrorize anyone who don't do as they say'. Exclusionary tendering practices for a multi-million dollar project led to a riot between Bugis and Dayak in the small town of Nunukan, East Kalimantan, in July 2007 (Charles Siahaan, 'Antaretnis bersitegang di Nunukan', www.kabarindonesia.com, posted 8-7-2007 (accessed 7-12-2007); 'Cuplikan Munas Khusus Gapensi: problem kontraktor tiada berujung', *Suara Kontraktor* , no date (2001), http://www.suarakontraktor.com/lip_beton.asp (accessed 16-6-2003).

political means into an art form since the national revolution of 1945. The techniques they have developed – some of them are analysed in the present chapter – are part of their wider provincial struggles to seize state funding (known by economists as political transfer rents, see Khan 2000). Achieving political control not only gives them access to state budgets, it also allows them to keep out rivals. At the same time, in order to secure political dominance, they need to redistribute money and business opportunities to supporters, allies and, to varying degrees, potential rivals. In the construction sector they have done this by different means down the years. During the New Order years, state-dominated corporatist organizations were a principal arena through which redistribution took place. Since the collapse of the New Order, a much messier system of 'building relations' has evolved, in which contractors and political decision-makers are connected by intricate webs of influence and exchange. In both periods, there was still plenty of competition between rival contractors, but this was never competition in which decisions were made on the basis of 'rational' market considerations of efficiency and pricing. Instead, political connections and payments were always the key to success.

The provincial building contractors now must wage a defensive struggle. The technocrats who threatened to open the doors to foreign competition in 1966 have come to haunt them again after the reforms of 1999. In the long run they may prevail. In the meantime, the mess of contradictory regulations in the construction sector reflects slowly shifting trench warfare between provincial interests and stronger players in the centre and overseas, who push their agenda under the cover of anti-corruption regulations. The international pro-market agenda, increasingly being adopted by the government in Jakarta also in relation to the building industry, plays into a long-running social tension between what we may call a provincial intermediate class, consisting of an intermeshed amalgam of private entrepreneurs and public government officials, and metropolitan big business. Metropolitan actors, or at least some of them, are also more interested in satisfying pressures for reform imposed by multilateral agencies that ultimately determine the government's international credit rating. The larger construction companies based in Jakarta are relatively open to reform because they have superior skills and technology and would be able to compete in more open markets.

The provincial business and political class, by contrast, is interested above all in redistribution along clientelist lines and in buying political stability. It is access to state budgets which determines business success, ensuring that there is no clear boundary between the private world of business and the public world of the government official. In part, this is because provincial actors neither pay nor collect taxes, but only spend them.

The kind of networking provincial business players in Indonesia do, with each other and with government, is typical of smaller entrepreneurs all over the world, from India to Italy (Rutten and Upadhya 1997:13-43). Consider, for example, the following scene:

> The waiting rooms of town halls are thus crawling with a multitudinous microcosm composed of subcontractors, artisans and canvassers seeking to see the mayor, his assistants or the technicians of urban planning, in the hope of obtaining a small construction contract or an order for supplies. For these small contractors, the simple fact of walking the corridors, reminding the authorities of their existence and 'showing oneself' represents the chance of being called one day or, failing that, of meeting big contractors likely to give them a subcontract (Blundo 2006:239).

This description is from West Africa, but it is striking how it perfectly captures the atmosphere in government offices in provincial and small-town Indonesia. Visit almost any Indonesian district head's offices today and you will find a similar diverse mixture of small-time operators, milling around in an atmosphere steeped in ambition, obsequiousness and anxiety. This is the social world of the construction contractor. Across the developing world, construction is a major earner for small-town dwellers who have risen above agriculture and petty trade. Almost everywhere, gaining privileged access to local government is the path to success.

In Indonesia's building industry, corruption is thus part of a clientelistic system that has been in operation for a long time, and that is woven into the very fabric of social and political life in the regions. The agenda against it has been motivated by a neo-liberal push to reduce government powers. In fact clientelism has some advantages. It keeps wheels turning, ensures a degree of redistribution to small and medium entrepreneurs (albeit at the cost of efficiency), and it thus helps ensure political stability. Unbridled competition without the institutions to underpin it can increase uncertainty and instability by encouraging violent informal enforcement practices, as has happened in China and Russia (Ding 2001; Volkov 2002). It could even undermine existing institutional arrangements for guaranteeing property rights and personal security (Beeson 2001). If the globalizing anti-corruption agenda does prevail, it is by no means certain that Indonesia's construction industry would look as benign as the agenda's ideologues portray it. Instead of a better deal for average provincial contractors, it might spell their displacement by big and mainly foreign building companies.

Perhaps a more likely scenario than the wholesale dismantling of the existing clientelistic system, however, is the more familiar one of adaptation. Recent work on clientelism suggests precisely this outcome. Piattoni (2001) observed that democratization in Europe caused a reversal of the bureaucratic professionalization established in the nineteenth century era of modern state formation. Kitschelt and Wilkinson (2007) write that new forms of clientelism emerge out of the interaction of democratic competitiveness and economic development. Roniger (2004), in a review of recent literature, points out that the post-authoritarian transition in Brazil caused a 'reclientelization' of business and politics. In fact, adaptation is the result we have so far seen in Indonesia. Democratic change and attempts to overhaul government procurement have far from eliminated clientelism in the system. The relatively centralized corporatist system for the allocation of construction contracts that developed during the New Order regime has been eroded. A new shell of open bidding for, and competitive assessment of, construction contracts has been put in place. Yet the real world of construction contracting is no less clientelistic (though it is perhaps slightly more chaotic) than that which it replaced.

J. DANANG WIDOYOKO

The education sector

The fragmentation and adaptability of corruption

One sector of Indonesian life where corruption arouses surprisingly little passion is education. While few Indonesians would deny that corruption is present throughout the education system, there have been relatively few high-profile and spectacular cases in the sector. Many people view corruption in education, particularly at the school level, as being petty, unavoidable and perhaps even morally acceptable. They see it as an understandable response by low-status public servants and teachers to supplement their miserable incomes. Moreover, a large amount of corruption in the sector simply passes under the radar of the public: it either takes place behind the closed doors of bureaucrats and politicians, or it takes the form of various education fees and charges that school children and their parents routinely pay without even realizing they are illegal.

It is the contention of this article that corruption in Indonesia's education system is both pervasive and fundamentally political in character. A number of cases of high-level corruption in the sector reveal a pattern of collusion between senior bureaucrats and politicians that resembles in form and style corruption in other sectors of government. Meanwhile, surveys and detailed case investigations carried out by my organization, Indonesia Corruption Watch (ICW), suggest that petty corruption at the school level, in the form of illegal fees and charges, is ubiquitous and closely related to the structure of corruption in the national education bureaucracy. Corruption in schools exists because local authorities and bureaucrats permit it, do not punish it, even require it (Widoyoko et al. 2007; Widoyoko 2007).

The chapter, therefore, has several aims, and it makes several key arguments. The first aim is to explain the structural context that shapes corruption in Indonesia's education sector. Here, following the work of Michael Johnston, I argue that the general pattern of corruption in Indonesia is typical of a highly fragmented polity with a weak civil society. In particular, corruption in Indonesia since the collapse of Suharto's New Order regime in 1998 has undergone a process of decentralization that follows the broader rearrangement of the political structure. Instead of corruption occurring within a single, unified and centralized 'franchise system' (see McLeod in this volume), it has proliferated in an uncoordinated fashion around the new power centres that have emerged. The education sector is an example of this phenomenon. Education sector reforms have decentralized power and control over budgets both to the regions and to schools. As a result, the regional bureaucracy and the schools have become much more important foci of corrupt activity than in the past.

A second aim is to explain the structure of corruption in the sector itself. Here I argue that corruption is visible at four different levels. In the first and upper level the typical pattern involves collaboration between senior bureaucrats and politicians, with the former providing corrupt payments from the education budget or from project funds in order to secure political or personal support. At the second level, in the regional education bureaucracies, local government officials and bureaucrats are the key actors. As in the first level, a key mode of corruption involves collaboration between government officials and private business in the manipulation of tenders and project funds, though local bureaucrats also treat school principals and teachers, and school budgets, as important targets of predation. Finally, the third and fourth levels of corruption, involving school principals and teachers respectively, are both located in the schools themselves, and to a large degree involve the extraction of illegal levies from parents. It is these bottom two layers of corruption that have become more prominent as a result of Indonesia's recent political and education sector reforms.

A third and final aim is to scrutinize attempts to reform the education system and eliminate corruption from it, to evaluate their successes and failures and to suggest ways forward. Here it is noted that strategies so far pursued have been based on a public sector reform approach and have thus involved manipulating the internal rules and mechanisms used by the education bureaucracy (such as by making transfers of payments of school funds directly to schools rather than to local education bureaucrats). However, these initiatives fail to consider the broader context and the political structures within which education sector corruption takes place. As a result, corruption in the sector has shown an amoeba-like ability to adapt to the new reforms, demonstrating that a more fundamentally political approach involving empowerment of societal participation in the sector is required.

The fragmentation of corruption and its effects

In contextualizing corruption in Indonesia's education system, it is helpful to draw on the analysis and framework presented by Michael Johnston in his research on corruption and politics, and the typology of corruption.

Corruption is frequently understood in narrow terms, usually focusing on bribery and actions that cause the state financial loss. This understanding is reflected in the corruption perception indexes that so dominate public discourse on corruption in Indonesia. A narrow understanding of corruption means that strategies that are used to reduce and prevent corruption often differ little from one state to another. However, there are many factors and actors to be considered in corruption. Johnston (1997) proposes a typology in which he groups corruption into four syndromes, each based on a distinctive balance between state and societal, or private, interests (see Table 1). He does this by comparing the strength of elite interests (he focuses on both economic and political elites, and measures their influence in terms of their control of centres of political power and economic resources) to those of civil society.

Thus, in conditions where the ruling political elite is weak and where societal participation is high, such as in most Western liberal states, corruption takes the form of 'interest group bidding', in which powerful interest groups are able to influence and even enforce their will on state elites and so extract corrupt favours from them. The next category is 'elite hegemony' which is marked by both a powerful elite and high participation by society. In such circumstances political competition is limited and corruption predominantly takes the form of incumbent elites selling political access and directing the profits to themselves and their cronies. In conditions of elite hegemony, the border between the state and private interests is blurred, and collaboration between political elites and interest groups produces systemic and legal corruption. Examples include Japan under the Liberal Democratic Party, or Hong Kong before the formation of its Independent Commission Against Corruption.

More relevant to our own discussion is a system of corruption dominated by a patronage machine, which is how Johnston categorized Indonesia under Suharto. Patronage machine systems are characterized by a powerful elite and a weak society, in which interest groups can exercise little influence on the state. In such systems, corruption is centred in the patronage machines that infuse the state: in Suharto's Indonesia they were based around Suharto and the presidential palace. Yet this system also has implications for stability:

> The machine leadership profits, politically and economically, from the status quo; it is in business for the long term, and will dole out patronage with a goal of maintaining its dominance rather than of looting the state. This is not to imply that the corruption involved is not serious, or that it does not do economic and social damage. Machine-style corruption diverts wealth into the hands of the few, levies a 'political tax' on business, investment, and many ordinary jobs, and maintains the poor in a state of political dependency. (Johnston 1997:18-9.)

In such circumstances, the ruler or his circle can also control corruption if necessary. In Indonesia, if particular sites or varieties of corruption threatened the broader interests of Suharto and his cronies, he took action to curb it and order law enforcement. One widely known example was the privatization of the customs office in the mid-1980s which occurred when corruption there and poor law enforcement against smuggling threatened the economy. The famous 'mysterious killings' that occurred in the 1980s, and for which Suharto himself claimed credit, can also be seen as a tool to control crime rates when they were seen as threatening the economy (MacIntyre 2003; Duncan and McLeod 2007). With very high rates of corruption, but corruption that was centralized and controlled, Indonesia then enjoyed high rates of economic growth and was even considered in some quarters to be a successful development model.

> Although the Soeharto franchise imposed net 'private taxes' on the outsider firms, it still provided sufficient in the way of the institutions needed for reasonably good economic performance, because it was in its own interest to do so. On occasion when elements of the franchise became too greedy, Soeharto stepped in to bring them back into line. (Duncan and McLeod 2007:78; see also McLeod 2000.)

After the fall of Suharto, political power fragmented, giving rise to new power centres. At the national level, power was no longer so exclusively concentrated in the hands of the president. Parliament became much more influential and state reforms also created new auxiliary institutions, such as the Constitutional Court and the Corruption Eradication Commission (Komisi Pemberantasan Korupsi, KPK) that have become very influential. Equally importantly, the government's decentralization policy distributed power to the regions. Local executive government leaders – governors, mayors and district heads (*bupati*) – enjoy greater independence, as do local legislatures. The national government can no longer guarantee easy implementation of national policy as it could under Suharto. This, of course, also applies to anti-corruption policy: so we see that although President Susilo Bambang Yudhoyono has made eradication of corruption a priority in his administration, he has been unable to ensure that all government units and departments comply. At the same time, societal interest groups remain relatively weakly organized and find it difficult to control the government. In short, Indonesia has become what Johnston (2000:21) would categorize as a system of '"fragmented clientelism" in which elites are poorly institutionalized and economic opportunities are scarce; political entrepreneurs build personal followings by promising material rewards, but find it difficult to "deliver"'.

In a fragmented clientelistic polity, according to Johnston (2000:21) 'a corruption spiral is a real possibility' because politicians' followers are poorly disciplined and 'leaders must compete with other factions by promising ever-larger spoils.' Fragmented power in Indonesia has thus created mushrooming corruption throughout the country. Virtually all public officials now have greater authority and thus new opportunities to engage in corrupt activity. At the same time, members of the political elite generally feel more insecure than they did in the Suharto era, because of the much greater competition for power. The motives of corruption are thus not only self-enrichment, but also maintaining access to power and resources, by building political coalitions up into the state, down into society and even horizontally, to potential rivals. As a result, it is not only state officials and government leaders who can engage in corruption in Indonesia; corruption is often shared with outsiders, even members of the political opposition. To reduce internal opposition and threats from within the state, meanwhile, ruling elites share the proceeds of corruption with their staff in the bureaucracy, or at least tacitly give them permission to engage in petty corruption. This permission reduces instability within the institution headed by the official concerned. Finally, all this corruption flourishes in a system of fragmented clientelism such as contemporary Indonesia because society and organized interest groups remain insufficiently powerful to prevent it.

Table 1. Regime types and patterns of corruption

<table>
<tr><td colspan="4">Elite</td></tr>
<tr><td colspan="2"></td><td>Weak</td><td>Strong</td></tr>
<tr><td rowspan="2">Civil society</td><td>Strong</td><td>Interest group bidding

Strong private interests, accessible elites; economic competition, interest groups use wealth to seek influence; corruption is largely individual and non-systemic.</td><td>Elite hegemony

Entrenched elites exchange scarce political access for wealth.</td></tr>
<tr><td>Weak</td><td>Fragmented clientelism

Fragmented and politically insecure elites build personal followings that are poorly disciplined, unstable; mafias, violence and intimidation may be linked to corruption.</td><td>Patronage machines

Strong elites control participation and limit competition via patronage and capitalize upon followers' poverty; political monopolies; parties are hierarchical and tightly-controlled and extend power into state and society.</td></tr>
</table>

Modified from Johnston 1997.

Indonesia's system of fragmented clientelism has been highly consequential for Indonesia's education sector during the Reformasi period, especially since decentralization. It has generated a pattern of fragmented corruption in the sector. Before analyzing that pattern in detail, it is necessary to understand the new policy and institutional framework.

A policy of decentralization has been pursued in education. In the tertiary sector, it has led to the transformation of universities into state-owned legal entities (Badan Hukum Milik Negara, BHMN) which can request much higher tuition fees from students than previously, meaning that some high-demand courses in elite universities have become unaffordable even for comfortable middle class families. In the elementary and secondary schools (the main focus of this article), decentralization has taken the form of the introduction of a new system of school-based management (Manajemen Berbasis Sekolah, MBS). With this system, unlike in the past when all authority was concentrated with the bureaucrats in the Ministry of Education, school principals together with school committees, which consist of representatives of parents and the community, have the authority to formulate school budgets, design curriculum and handle school management in its entirety. At the city and district level, the MBS policy also promotes the establishment of local education councils that give recommendations regarding education to the local/city government (Irawan et al. 2004).

The MBS policy was thus intended to encourage societal participation in the education sector, particularly in school management. In part, the model was inspired by successful international experiences. Fung (2003), for example, has described how participatory school management in Chicago through the vehicle of Local School Councils (LSCs) has been widely seen as a successful model of grassroots participation in governance to rival the famous Porto Alegre participatory budgeting process.[1] In Chicago, the LSCs are elected every two years, and each consists of six parents, two community representatives, two teachers, the principal and an additional non-voting student. LSCs enjoy substantial powers and responsibilities, such as in hiring and firing principal, spending discretionary funds, and developing and implementing strategic plans for school improvement in areas including curriculum, physical design and administrative operation (Fung 2003:111). Fung does not pay particular attention to the problem of corruption; however, it is easy to surmise that the level of scrutiny of school affairs envisaged by LSC system would provide a mechanism for parents and community members to closely monitor, and reject, wasteful or unnecessary spending in the school budget.[2]

1 On the Porto Alegre participatory budgeting experience see Baiocchi 2003.

2 Currently my organization, ICW is working on participatory budgeting at the school level in Garut and Tangerang. Our experience is that during budget meetings, parents reject irrelevant school levies, automatically reducing the amount of money to be paid by parents.

The school-based management policy in Indonesia is seen by its supporters as a measure to return schools to community control, after the New Order years when schools were viewed as being dependent upon the government, thus killing their creativity and initiative. The policy is envisaged as a means to revive schools as an 'instrument for the community to achieve its interests', as Bejo Sudjanto, the Rector of the Jakarta State University has put it (Irawan et al. 2004:50). One focus of the policy is the school budget, which supporters of the policy view as being an important instrument of participatory governance. The idea is that the school budget would be subject to the scrutiny of parents and the broader community via the school committees. Clearly stating all school revenues and expenditures, and providing information about school programs, finances and sources of funds, the idea is that the budget would become the tool whereby community members would ensure that schools serve community needs, and not be used for other purposes, including corruption.

Unfortunately, the systemic character of corruption has made the policy of decentralization of school management to local committees fail in achieving its goal of eliminating corruption. Instead, corruption in education is now carried out 'in a new way, via school-based management. The chief actor in this new model of corruption is the school principal, assisted by the school committee and the education bureaucracy' (Purwanto 2008). As we shall see, corruption in the school is still not the only form of corruption in the education sector, but it remains virtually ubiquitous. The school-based management policy has clearly not worked as intended. One of the problems is that the members of school committees generally lack adequate capacity: most of them do not have the skills or experience to challenge school principals on budget formulation, and they generally lack sufficient information about school expenditures, income, curriculum and special projects to be able to form a clear picture of what might be wasteful expenditure or illegal charges. The result is that school principals dominate policy formulation and budgeting at the school level. Parents often even lack access to school budget documents. This imbalance in power relations often results in the school committee simply endorsing, and therefore providing a legal basis to, the various payments arranged by the principal in the budget. Very often, therefore, instead of improving societal participation, the new system legitimates corrupt practices in the school. Without better skills on the part of committee members, the participatory governance envisaged by the school-based management approach is unlikely to be meaningful. Furthermore, despite the policy, corrupt practices at the school level remain linked to the interests and intervention of the bureaucracy. To a large degree, local education authorities (specifically, the district and city offices of the Ministry of National Education) still control schools. Unlike the LSCs in Chicago that decentralize power right down to parents, the Indonesian policy of decentralization of education, despite being called school-based management, in some crucial regards stops at the level of the local bureaucracy. The power to hire and fire principals, and to approve school budgets, remains in the hands of local education authorities. Overall, the new school committees have become something like a fashion accessory in Indonesia's new education system: beautiful to look at, but not performing a meaningful function, and certainly not bringing about basic change in the way that the system is run.

The pervasiveness of corruption in education

Most Indonesians perceive corruption in the education sector as being relatively inconsequential, and as involving mainly petty corruption by low-level public servants and school teachers. Moreover, everybody knows that the salaries of teachers and junior public servants are relatively low. Many ordinary citizens are relatively forgiving of small-scale corruption by such people, viewing it as an understandable attempt to generate extra income by people in difficult personal economic circumstances. This situation then makes the education sector appear not to be as corrupt as many other government institutions, a picture confirmed by various corruption perception surveys (for example, ADB 2002, Simanjuntak and Akbarsyah 2008). The low ranking of the education sector in these surveys, it should be noted, partly reflects the backgrounds of the respondents: most such corruption perception surveys poll investors and businesspeople, who understandably highlight institutions whose corruption impinges most directly upon their own business affairs. Nevertheless, there does seem to be a wider public perception that corruption in the education sector is not especially serious.

As we shall see, the public perception is not entirely accurate. Corruption is as pervasive in education as in most other sectors of government. But the perception also does contain an element of truth. Certainly, the education sector is not mostly a site of the grand corruption that has so scandalized Indonesian public opinion over the last decade. In contrast, for example, to corruption in the banking sector, which has seen episodes like the Bank Indonesia Liquidity Support (Bantuan Likuiditas Bank Indonesia) scandal that nearly caused the collapse of the entire Indonesian economy, most corruption in education gives rise to only relatively minor state losses. Moreover, corruption in education relatively rarely involves prominent public officials or politicians (though, as we shall see, there are exceptions). More frequently it involves only school principals, teachers and low-ranking public servants.

Although corruption in education does not cause huge state losses and rarely involves elite politicians and businesspeople, it also has special characteristics of its own. Instead of involving theft of state money, corruption in education typically involves taking money directly from the pockets of ordinary citizens. Most commonly this happens when parents of schoolchildren are charged all kinds of irregular and unauthorized fees for their children's education. This kind of corruption, therefore, affects ordinary people very directly. Unfortunately, however, citizens are often not aware that money is being extorted from them to provide a public service that is theirs by right. A general lack of transparency and accountability at the school level make many parents think that the numerous levies they must pay are not corruption but obligatory charges for services. This lack of civic awareness about people's rights as citizens in turn creates opportunities and incentives to act corruptly.

The 'citizen report card survey' conducted in 2005 by Indonesia Corruption Watch shows that many parents share a perception that the government is not obliged to fully pay for their children's education (ICW 2005). The survey was conducted in three cities: Jakarta, Garut and Solo, with 1500 parents as respondents. Many of those surveyed agreed that parents should contribute to education costs, some even believed that it was the obligation of parents to fully pay for their children's education (Irawan 2006:40). In fact, the fourth amendment to the Constitution, passed in 2002, stipulates that every citizen should receive a basic education and that the government has the obligation to provide it (Article 31). Law no. 20/2003 on the National Education System states 'National and regional governments have the obligation to provide good education services and facilities, with a guarantee of good quality, and without any discrimination to all citizens' (Article 11(1)). Article 11(2) adds that 'National and regional government have to guarantee the availability of a budget for the education of every citizen aged between 7 and 14 years'.

Based on cases that have come to the attention of Indonesia Corruption Watch and research conducted by our teams in the field down the years, it is clear that corruption in education is systematic and embedded in every level of the education bureaucracy's structure. Virtually every actor who has authority in the structure abuses that authority by acting corruptly. Thus, the so-called petty corruption that is the most visible form of abuse exists because principals order it or at least give their permission for it to go ahead. The principals then use some of the money that is paid by parents to pay bribes, disguised as transportation fees or other payments, to the school supervisors from the local education authority (*dinas pendidikan*). As a reward for such payments, the local education authority will prioritize the schools run by the most 'generous' principals for projects, and also protect such principals from investigations or parents' complaints. ICW and parents associations have had experiences of filing reports on corrupt principals, who are then backed up by the local education office, rather than being punished. If public complaints increase dramatically, the office tends at most to transfer the principal to another school, where he or she will again engage in corrupt practices.

As well as this school-level corruption that involves direct interaction with parents, there is also less visible corruption in the education system, including in the higher echelons of the education bureaucracy and leaching into the world of national politics. As a major function of the government involving large sums of money (the Department of Education gets a budget allocation that surpasses that of other government departments) education is as vulnerable to corruption as other parts of government. Much of the education budget goes on costs, such as teachers' salaries, that are relatively free of manipulation (though even here bureaucrats sometimes invent phantom (*fiktif*) teachers or public servants to enable money for salaries to also be diverted). However, the government also provides funds for purchasing materials (school books for example), constructing school buildings and other projects, all of which are vulnerable.

By analyzing corruption cases that have come to light over the last decade, I have formulated a typology of corruption in the education sector summarized in Table 2. It can be seen here that only at the lower levels does corruption involve direct extraction of fees from parents, at the higher levels corrupt actors directly access government funds, or engage in manipulative behaviour to attract payments from private companies. Despite the differences, however, there is a common pattern: at each level government functionaries access whatever sources of funds they exercise direct authority over (money from parents at the school level, money for major national projects in the central ministry) and use those funds both for their own consumption and to buy political support and protection from more powerful players in the education hierarchy. Thus, teachers transfer money to principals, principals transfer money to local education authorities, and so it goes on, right up the chain to the senior ministry officials who make payments to national politicians to buy their support.

The first layer of corruption

The first layer of corruption involves high-level public officials at the Ministry of National Education. The motives of corruption at this level in the post-Suharto period, besides self-enrichment and the enrichment of cronies, include buying political protection by giving education projects to politicians or their allies. In particular, unless senior bureaucrats 'share' their corrupt activities with politicians, especially by making projects available for parliamentarians to distribute to their constituents and supporters, there is a likelihood that parliament will oppose, frustrate, delay or under-fund every education policy. This is how and why legislators have become such prominent participants in corruption in the new system of 'fragmented clientelism': legislatures at

Table 2. Varieties of corruption in education

Layer of corruption	Actors	Mode of operation
First layer	Ministry of National Education officials	▪ 'Tendering' education projects for local government or allocating projects without proper procedures to crony contractors. ▪ 'Buying' political support by giving vouchers to politician.
Second layer	Local education authority officials	▪ 'Tendering' government or donor-funded projects to schools. The schools that provide the highest bid in bribes will win the project. ▪ 'Tendering' principal's position to teachers.
Third layer	Principals and school committee members	▪ Double budgeting. The principals request money from parents for activities that have been funded by the government. ▪ Using school funds for non-educational activities, such as 'coordination fees' to be paid to bureaucrats and the police.
Fourth layer	Teachers	▪ Teachers use their authority to collect additional payments from students, for photocopying, examinations and so on.

Source: Irawan et al. 2004; Aditjondro 2002.

every level have the potential to be veto-players in all manner of government policy and budgets.

There are several examples of this first layer of corruption. One was a well-publicized scandal in a book procurement project funded by the World Bank. ICW publicly revealed details of this case in 2000. The case began in the final years of the Suharto government, with a Book Reading Development Project (BRDP) launched in 1995 by the Department of National Education. The aim of the project was to provide books to junior high schools. The total cost of the project was US$132.5 million, funded by a World Bank loan. It was planned that the project would be implemented in four phases between 1996 and 2000 but public complaints about corruption resulted in the fourth phase being cancelled and the project being closed on 31 December 2001, after it had disbursed only US$53.23 million.

The project involved Regional Offices of the Department of Education organizing book procurement by tender, although the books they purchased were from a list already recommended by the central office of the Department. According to the investigations by ICW, at least 19% of the budget was distributed corruptly to various actors. Ten percent went to local project leader (*pimpro*), 5% to the Directorate General of Basic and Intermediary Education (Ditjen Dikdasmen), 1% to World Bank staff, 1% to the book centre (Pusat Perbukuan) of the Ministry of Education, 1% to the State Treasury Office (Kantor Perbendaharaan Kas Negara) and 1% to other parties. Furthermore, every publisher that won a contract had to purchase paper from PT Pinasti, which charged 20% more than normal market prices.[3]

Because of the massive publicity in the national and international media that this scandal generated, the World Bank sent staff from INT, its Department of Institutional Integrity, a section based in Washington DC with authority to investigate corruption in World Bank projects. In 2004, the Bank acknowledged that corruption had occurred in the project. In response, it published a black list of publishers and persons who were not allowed to receive further World Bank projects for durations of between two and fifteen years. The list included top Indonesian publishing companies such as Grasindo, owned by the Gramedia Group, the publisher of Indonesia's leading newspaper *Kompas*, as well as Mizan, Erlangga and Kanisius.[4]

Corruption in the book project occurred, or at least began, in the final years of the Suharto regime and, typical of the pattern of corruption in that period, the chief beneficiaries of the Suharto 'patronage machine' were located in the state bureaucracy. A more recent case of national-level collusion involves a national education voucher project (Irawan 2007). This scandal

3 ICW report to Dennis de Tray, The World Bank Representative at Jakarta, September 1998.

4 The complete list can be seen at: http://web.worldbank.org/WBSITE/EXTERNAL/NEWS/0,,contentMDK:20262893~menuPK:34464~pagePK:64003015~piPK:64003012~theSitePK:4607,00.html (accessed 7-9-2010).

demonstrates that in recent years the pattern of patronage distribution has become increasingly fragmented.

In this scandal, the Ministry of National Education distributed vouchers to schools through politicians and other prominent figures. The so-called vouchers were in effect a block grant mechanism for private schools. Schools that received vouchers could submit proposals for the sum of the voucher – often up to hundreds of millions of rupiah – for financial support from the Ministry to build new class rooms or libraries, or to renovate school property. The case attracted media attention when the speaker of Indonesia's parliament (Dewan Perwakilan Rakyat, DPR), Agung Laksono, was exposed as distributing vouchers to schools. According to Bambang Sudibyo, the Minister of National Education, Agung Laksono was chosen not because he was speaker of the DPR but because he was the leader of Kosgoro, a mass organization related to the Golkar Party that owned around 600 schools (*Kompas* 19-10-2006). Then it was revealed that several other senior politicians, notably DPR members who served on the DPR's education commission, were doing the same thing. The MPs did not benefit by receiving money from these vouchers for their personal use, but they benefited politically, because they could determine where to distribute them. Instead of giving vouchers to the schools that needed them most, politicians distributed them to schools linked to their own constituents, as part of their attempts to construct their own patronage networks and expand or solidify their political influence. Investigations by ICW thus found that vouchers mostly went to schools that were linked closely to the individual politicians, their political parties or the socio-religious organizations with which they were affiliated. In particular, a large number of vouchers went to schools run by Muhammadiyah, the large modernist Islamic organization that runs many health and education services. It so happened that the Minister came from the National Mandate Party (Partai Amanat Nasional, PAN), a party that was established and previously led by Amien Rais, the former national leader of Muhammadiyah and which was still rooted in the Muhammadiyah milieu. Presumably, the minister needed to satisfy his own constituents in PAN and Muhammadiyah, and used the distribution of vouchers to do so. But other MPs also distributed vouchers to their own constituents, as the example of Agung Laksono and his distribution of vouchers to Golkar-linked Kosgoro schools demonstrates. In turn, by distributing these vouchers through politicians, rather than directly through the education bureaucracy, senior officials at the Ministry of National Education were buying good relationships with MPs and other politicians, with the aim of reducing criticisms of the Ministry's policies and securing their fast approval by parliament. In this way, the distribution of the vouchers was also creating a conflict of interest for MPs: receiving vouchers undermined their independence and meant they were less likely to objectively monitor the performance of the Ministry. From the politicians' point of view, however, the key motivation was that the vouchers were a convenient means to build their support bases and buy political support, precisely what we would expect in a system of 'fragmented clientelism'.

The second layer of corruption

In the second layer, corruption involves local education authorities, most importantly the education bureau (*dinas pendidikan*) offices at the district level. Substantial authority over the education sector, including authority over how to spend the education budget, was transferred to this level of government by Indonesia's post-1999 decentralization reforms.

One example of corruption at this level concerns book procurement, which had caused such a scandal in 2000 at the national level. As part of decentralization, the authority to procure school books was transferred to local governments, along with the other responsibilities in education and other sectors of government. Now, the Ministry of National Education in Jakarta only devises a list of recommended texts. However, this decentralized procurement system was not accompanied by a comprehensive corruption prevention policy, with the result that not only the authority to make decisions about procurement was decentralized, but so too were the opportunities to benefit corruptly from procurement. In several recent corruption cases to attract outside attention, local government officials have marked up book prices, particularly in cooperation with PT Balai Pustaka, a state-owned publishing enterprise. In some cases, local governments pay more for books than the price they are available for on the open market, despite being ordered in bulk. Book publishers often aggressively lobby local governments and pay bribes to local officials to ensure that they win tenders to provide books. With the bribes to officials being paid for from the money allocated to do the work, the result is often that very poor quality books are produced, or simply that less books are purchased than they would be if normal market prices were paid. Some local governments, for example in the province of Bengkulu, even procured books that were not on the list of recommended books, and which thus could not be used when they reached the schools. In several districts, the district heads (*bupati*) as well as members of local legislative councils and heads of education bureaus have been charged with corruption in book procurement scandals.[5]

Another example of corruption at this level involves the School Improvement Grant Project (SIGP), a multi-donor project managed by the World Bank. The project provided grants to 8,000 schools in about 130 districts, at a total cost

5 For details, see Sugiyanti 2008.

of about US$60 million (Baines 2004:2). This project is generally depicted as a good governance success story because it involved direct transfers of money to school accounts, a measure that was specifically designed to reduce corruption and respond most effectively to school-level needs (Baines 2004; Hallak and Poisson 2007). The rationale was that distributing money directly to schools would minimize opportunities for intervention by the bureaucracy and, therefore, corrupt manipulation by it. ICW conducted investigations into the program in 2003-2006 and showed that, indeed, there was no corruption in the program in terms of theft of state money. Probably 100% of the money distributed by the program went directly to the targeted schools, a considerable achievement. Nevertheless, the bureaucracy still played an important role. In particular, the local bureaucracy, namely the education bureaus at the district and sub-district levels, nominated which schools needed the grant. This gave local bureaucrats crucial power that they could abuse and they did so by inducing school principals to pay bribes, typically of around 10% of the total grant the school would receive, as a 'down payment' for being picked as a project recipient. This variety of corruption does not involve stealing state or donor money. An auditor would not find evidence of embezzlement in the project implementation. This is because the principals will have paid their bribe even before receiving the money from the grant, money which is then spent on school improvement as intended. To pay the bribe, however, the principals raised the money from other sources, such as fees charged to parents.

More generally, it is well-known among teachers that being appointed as a principal is a costly exercise. Teachers who want to be promoted as a principal have to bribe Education Bureau officials. The cost varies with the type and location of the school: to be a principal of a senior high school in a city is much more expensive than becoming the principal of a village elementary school. This situation then creates a cycle of corruption because the principal has to recoup his or her 'investment' by charging various fees in the school.

Another mode of corruption involving the local-level bureaucracy was revealed by investigations carried out by ICW and the Civil Society Working Group (Kelompok Kerja Masyarakat Sipil, KKMS) in the district of Lombok Tengah. In this instance, in order to deal with the 'problem' that block grant money was transferred directly to the school, local education bureau officials ordered the principals to hand the school account books to the local bureaucracy, which would then manage the accounts itself. By controlling school accounts in this way, the local bureaucracy could take part of the money they contained for their own purposes. The principals had little choice but to accept this irregular way of doing things because, if they refused, they would receive no future projects and might suffer other repercussions.[6]

6 Interview with Syamsudin Sirah and Ade Irawan, 2-5 November 2006.

Such examples show how difficult it is to eradicate corruption, even by quite radical technical adjustments and good governance programs. Even transferring money directly to school accounts, with the purpose of cutting out the influence of a swathe of the middle bureaucracy, does not eradicate corruption. Instead, it only shifts the target of corruption and does not affect the underlying distribution of power within and over the school from which corruption flows. Principals, themselves the dominant player at the school level, remain accountable basically only to the local government authorities. Even with their new power to control school accounts and receive money directly, any principal who refuses to make corrupt payments to local government officials will suffer adverse consequences. His or her school might not receive future grants or government projects. The bureaucracy can also punish recalcitrant principals by transferring them to schools located far away from their homes, potentially causing great personal inconvenience and additional transport, accommodation and other expenses. Moreover, the SIGP example demonstrates another change in the mode of corruption in the education sector. In this case, principals and officials did not take money directly from the state budget but instead obtained it from parents. According to the current anti-corruption law in Indonesia, such activity is not categorized as corruption. The anti-corruption law defines corrupt practices as involving theft of public money or bribery, not extortion from ordinary citizens. This limits the law enforcement options at the third and fourth levels of corruption, to which our attention turns now.

The third and fourth layers

In order to measure corruption at the school level, in 2006 ICW conducted citizen report card surveys about school finances and accountability in public elementary schools in several cities and districts (Jakarta, Tangerang, Padang, Garut, Manado, Bau-Bau, Central Lombok, and West Sumba). Respondents were more than 8,000 parents of public elementary school children (ICW 2007).

The extent of corruption at the school level can be seen from the enormous range of illegal levies that parents are charged. Although a number of local governments have declared that education services at the elementary and secondary school level are entirely free, in reality even public education is never free. Parents of children at public schools are generally not charged tuition fees – it is true – but instead they have to pay various charges for uniforms, books, building costs, renovations, furniture, photocopying of teaching materials and even such basic materials as chalk. Students are often charged compulsory religious donations and even for purposes such as farewell parties for school principals or the weddings of their teachers. ICW's surveys have identified at least 37 categories of such illegal levies for elementary school students in Jakarta alone (Irawan et al. 2004).

These various levies are illegal because the government already provides support through the national and local government budgets, block grants and school operational support transfers to cover costs for text books, new student registration, examinations, photocopying and the like. Likewise, parents should not be required to pay for construction or renovation of school buildings because these are also covered by national and local government budgets. Arguably, a few of the fees are in a legal grey area, such as those for photocopying, books and a few other expenses. In Jakarta, however, the Education Bureau announced to the public that there would be no entrance fees, school building fees or even charges for standard text books because all of those items had been covered by the local government budget (Elisabeth 2006). But parents regularly report that fees for such items are still charged in schools. Such fees seem legal to parents because they are directly administered by the school. There are even almost comical examples: such as when schools hold class competitions to clean up the school, requiring parents to purchase detergent, paint, brooms and other cleaning implements, even though the budget for purchasing items is already provided by the government. The levies thus involve another mode of corruption: double budgeting. The school requests money from parents for activities that actually have been paid for by the government. The excess money can then be used for the personal needs of the principal and teachers, for other more 'strategic' purposes, such as paying transportation fees or per diems for the school supervisor, or bribes to Education Bureau officials and other threatening actors.[7]

Teachers are the lowest link in the corruption chain in the school since various fees are announced or levied by teachers in the class. Teachers also can make profits themselves by levying their own fees for various activities, such as photocopying, buying particular books or sports. Of course the amount of money they collect is typically very small, because they exercise authority only over a small number of students and are limited by whatever subject or subjects it is that they happen to teach. Their motivations are typically more about basic economic survival because their salaries are small, so they view petty corruption as a way to supplement their income.

This pattern of school-level corruption reveals another feature of contemporary corruption in Indonesia: its adaptability. Post-decentralization changes in the way funds were disbursed in the education sector involved a new policy of making direct payments to school accounts. In particular, School

7 In the post-Suharto period, many journalists and NGO activists also target public servants for extortion, threatening not to expose them for misdemeanours in exchange for payment; schools are an attractive target for such extortion, not only because of their relative weakness, at the bottom of the bureaucratic feeding chain, but also because of new policies that transfer funds directly to school accounts.

Operational Assistance (Bantuan Operasional Sekolah, BOS) education subsidies are intended to cover all schools' operational costs and are transferred directly from the national ministry to school accounts. The amount of BOS subsidies payments received per school varies according to the number of students enrolled: the larger the school, the bigger the BOS transfer. At the same time, local governments also provide certain additional subsidies (thus, the Jakarta city government provides Education Operational Assistance (Bantuan Operasional Pendidikan, BOP) payments that are also transferred directly to school accounts. Transferring funds directly to school accounts was intended, in part, to cut a long corruption chain in the bureaucracy. The assumption behind the introduction of direct transfers was that schools were separable from the bureaucracy, and that reducing the bureaucracy's authority and discretionary power over school budgets, and therefore its capacity for abuse, would help to eliminate, or at least minimize corruption in the sector. However, as already indicated, our survey results show that much of the corruption that does occur now happens not by stealing state money, but by requesting parents to pay money. This is a clear adaptation in the pattern of corruption that has occurred since the post-Suharto reforms.

Another reason for the proliferation of illegal levies at school is lack of accountability. Schools rarely provide adequate financial reports to parents about how their money is spent. Again, this is a topic on which ICW has conducted extensive research, with a survey of 8,265 parents of school children. When asked about the various additional levies they were charged, a majority of parents responded that information was not available from the school about how these charges were used (the figures ranged from almost 35% of respondents saying that such information was available for how fees for farewell parties were used, down to 8% availability of information for sports class fees). Clearly, one very basic problem of accountability at the school level is the absence of adequate financial reports for parents (for the full data, see ICW 2007).

Another source of the lack of accountability at the school level is parents' generally poor levels of participation in school decision making. According to the school-based management system, school budgets are together formulated by principals and school committees. The system also supposedly provides for participatory planning of the budget and for evaluation by parents of its implementation.[8] However, to actively participate in school budgeting, parents have to be well-informed, not only about the substance but also about the procedures. The ICW survey of 8,265 parents thus checked whether parents were informed about school budgeting. One survey question asked parents if they knew about or had been invited to attend school committee

8 The relevant regulation is Keputusan Menteri Pendidikan Nasional (Kepmendiknas) no. 044/U/2002 Komite Sekolah dan Dewan Pendidikan (Minister of National Education Decree no. 044/U/2002 on School committees and Education Councils).

meetings to discuss the school budget: 78.4% respondents answered in the negative. Lacking access to such information, parents are obviously unable to actively participate in decisions on levies and charges, or to monitor how the school's budget is spent. Instead, principals are left to formulate and manage the budgets by themselves. Although formally speaking, school committees are powerful bodies, with bargaining power at least equivalent to that of school principals, because of the lack of skills, information, and knowledge about school management and other aspects of education on the part of their members and other parents, the committees are almost always dominated by the principal. Despite all the talk about participatory school governance in post-Reformasi Indonesia, in reality there is rarely extensive societal participation in school affairs, providing an environment in which corruption can flourish.

Critiquing the corruption eradication strategy

Anti-corruption and good governance programs in Indonesia over the last decade have often translated into attempts to improve public sector management, for instance by reforming the system of public finances. In this respect, the dominant response to corruption in Indonesia follows an approach that is promoted by many international financial and development agencies. For example, in their analysis of corruption in secondary and tertiary education systems around the world, published by the International Institute for Educational Planning, Hallak and Poisson (2007:22) recommend anti-corruption solutions like improving management skills, accounting, monitoring and auditing in the sector, indicating how they view corruption as essentially a product of poor public sector management.

In fact, if Indonesia's experience since 1998 has taught us anything, it is that corruption is not merely a product of poor management systems and skills, easily amenable to technical solutions. Instead, it is inherently political: it flows from the abuse of political power and from patterns of competition and cooperation among political actors, and is a part of how power relations are structured in society. A more satisfactory explanation for corruption can thus be found in Johnston's work (1997) that links different syndromes of corruption to relations between political elites and civil society, and finds that corruption becomes more systematic when the former are more powerful than the latter. The inherently political character of corruption helps to explain why technical solutions in the sphere of public sector management, such as those tried in Indonesia's education system, are not enough to eradicate corruption. In Indonesia, the decentralization of management in the education system was supposed to transfer ownership of schools directly to society, by establishing school committees at the school level and education councils at the district level. But actually ownership was not fully transferred. Decentralization through the school-based management system transferred authority over school management only to principals. Moreover, authority to hire and fire principals remains in the hands of local government education offices, as does the power to approve school budgets. Both the new authority enjoyed by principals, and the authority that local education bureaucrats exercise over principals, have become new sources of corruption. Domination by the bureaucracy also makes the schools themselves cash cows and forces the principals to act corruptly themselves, and permits teachers to do the same, in order to finance the expenditures of the school.

Here the contrast with Chicago's LSC experience is instructive. In that case, decentralization involved genuine transfer of school management to school committees and, according to Fung (2003), these LSCs worked as local-level democratic institutions that effectively encouraged direct participation from the community. It did this by transferring real authority to the LSCs, including authority to hire and fire principals and authority to make strategic decisions for the school ranging from curriculum design to formulation of school budgets. In Indonesia, by contrast, as a consequence of the 'incomplete decentralization' and weak power of school committees, policy formulation and budgetary management at the school level remain dominated by school principals and, to make matters worse, principals are still positioned as part of the education bureaucracy. The resulting proliferation of illegal levies and other forms of corruption at the school level seems to perfectly exemplify the proposition that corruption flourishes in the absence of strong societal participation.

Another useful analysis of anti-corruption strategies, that leads us toward a similar conclusion, is offered by Emil Bolongaita and Vinay Bhargava (2004). To develop an effective strategy, they argue, program designers should consider three factors: the level of state capture by corrupt interests, the extent of petty corruption and the quality of governance. For the Indonesian context, where there is simultaneously high state capture, pervasive petty corruption and poor quality of governance, an effective anti-corruption program cannot rely solely on the state apparatus, because it will be easily subverted. In such a context, Bolongaita and Bhargava (2004:37) argue that effective anti-corruption reforms should be found and nurtured outside the state. Civil society and the private sector can be mobilized to foster external demand for change. Following this logic, attempts to curb corruption in the education sector are best anchored in groups outside the state, such as school committees and independent teachers' association, and empowering the school committees with greater authority would be a logical (and relatively easy) first step.

Another important strategy for reducing corruption is law enforcement and effective punishment of wrong-doers. Huther and Shah (2000) suggest that law enforcement is likely to have a relatively high impact in poor governance conditions. In Indonesia's education sector, however, there is typically only weak law enforcement with respect to corruption and penalties therefore have little deterrence value. An example is the SIGP project. Public servants revealed to be corrupt in this program were only punished by being transferred to similar positions in other offices or schools. Police and prosecutors never followed up complaints from parents about embezzlement of schools funds.[9] At a much higher level, there was also no meaningful punishment in the scandal in the World Bank-funded book procurement project. The World Bank only sanctioned companies and individuals from the private sector, by black-banning them. Ministry of National Education and other public officials involved in the case were not punished. On the contrary, the World Bank and other donors still disburse large sums of money in the form of loans and grants through the Ministry which remains controlled by those involved in corruption. Of course, anti-corruption strategies cannot rely on law enforcement as their main solution: the simple fact is that there are not enough prisons in Indonesia to hold the huge numbers of people who are involved in what is a pervasive and systematic phenomenon. It would take decades to even prosecute all persons involved in corruption. But law enforcement is necessary, at least in exemplary cases, to show the public and the whole bureaucracy that corrupt practices are not tolerated as they were in the past. Law enforcement, in other words, should act as a 'shock therapy' that is then followed up by more substantial bureaucratic reform.[10]

In theory, law enforcement focusing on corruption at the school level should be relatively easy. Petty corruption in schools is small-scale when compared to corruption in banking, infrastructure, procurement and other sectors. Prosecuting corruption in schools therefore should not meet the political obstacles and sabotage caused by entrenched judicial corruption that often occurs in other cases. Instead, law enforcement at the school level faces a different obstacle caused by the prevailing narrow definition of corruption as involving only state losses. Law enforcement agencies define corruption as theft of state money, but in schools, as we have seen, corruption frequently involves taking money from parents rather than from the state. According to Indonesian anti-corruption law, this sort of fraud is not categorized as corruption. Furthermore, petty corruption at the school level is often

[9] Interviews with Ade Irawan and activists of the Education Coalition (Koalisi Pendidikan) which often provided assistance for parents to submit complaints regarding misuse of school funds.

[10] One relevant example is the recent high-profile (and large-scale) corruption in the central bank, Bank Indonesia. The KPK oversaw some dramatic prosecutions in the case, and then worked with the bank to reform its internal regulations (for example, those concerning overseas travel by family members of bank officials) in a way that reduced possibilities of corruption: 'KPK-BI rampungkan kajian aturan yang picu koruptif', *Media Indonesia* 9-5-2008.

missed in audits by the Indonesian Supreme Audit Agency (Badan Pemeriksa Keuangan, BPK), because BPK usually only examines the use of state funds, while fees paid by parents are not administered as a non-tax state revenue.

Conclusion

This study of the education sector has demonstrated how Indonesia, as a fragmented polity with a weak civil society, has become a place where corruption is all-pervasive and systematic. Petty corruption at the school level is part of a larger structure of corruption in the education bureaucracy. Corruption at the school level would not be allowed without permission from school supervisors in the local education authorities. In turn, corruption is entrenched even at the most senior levels of the bureaucracy where it is used, among other things, to buy political support and protection and to build political constituencies. In short, corruption is systematic and involves the top-level bureaucracy right down to the principals and teachers in the schools.

In such a context, it is worth considering briefly some of the consequences of corruption in the education system, not so far highlighted in this article. Corruption in the system has many deleterious effects. One major impact is on the quality of education itself because of all its ill effects on the standards of teaching materials, books and other facilities provided to students. Another impact is the cultivation of a culture of corruption among children, and the negative consequences this has for the future. Even young children are surprisingly aware of the extent of corruption in their schools. The KPK, Attorney General's Office and some international donors have promoted anti-corruption education programs for school students. However laudable the goals, it is possible that the effect of such programs is instead to drive home lessons about hypocrisy, when students know that the very people teaching them anti-corruption values are themselves directly implicated in the practice.

Another important lesson to be drawn from our discussion concerns the adaptability of corruption. During the Reformasi period there have been serious attempts to address some of the deficiencies in the education sector and to reduce corruption in it. In particular, international donors' good governance recipes have involved transferring money directly into school accounts and decentralizing management of the education system to the regions and to schools. These strategies had their roots in the 1997 economic crisis, after which donors (especially the World Bank) introduced a 'social safety net' policy by which money was transferred directly to poor people, a policy that donors judged to be successful. In education, the rationale has been to by-pass large segments of the intermediate bureaucracy, providing money instead to its ultimate users, and removing discretion over school accounts from middle-level bureaucrats, and thus eliminating their ability to abuse those funds.

Unfortunately, the strategy has not worked well because it does not concentrate upon the root sources of corruption in education which, it has been argued here, flow from the structures of political power in both state and society. The anti-corruption strategy in the sector has only changed how money is transferred between the bureaucracy and schools, it has not replaced the existing corrupt structure in the education bureaucracy. The structure of accountability mechanisms still flows from top to bottom in the system, binding the schools to the education bureaucracy. The power to fire and hire principals is in the hands of local education authorities, making principals directly accountable to bureaucrats. To be appointed as principals, teachers must pay bribes; to maintain their positions, principals also have to provide regular payments to local bureaucrats. This dynamic has encouraged the proliferation of fees and levies directed at parents and made money raised from parents a crucial site of corruption, displacing state funds as the source drawn upon by corrupt actors at the school level when buying the political protection and support they need in the bureaucracy.

On the societal side of the equation, while Indonesian reform has made a good start by creating and empowering school committees, it has not gone far enough. For anti-corruption strategies to be effective, the authority to select principals would need to be transferred to school committees, making principals accountable to the community rather than to the education bureaucracy. Further powers for school committees to make vital decisions about school policy and spending would also help to eradicate corruption at the school level. Strengthening such societal mechanisms needs to be the starting point of anti-corruption programs in a system like that of Indonesia where civil society weakness is one of the crucial ingredients that helps corruption to flourish. Public sector reform and narrow goals of 'good governance' will not be enough. Experiences in the education sector show that without deeper changes in the political structures that motivate and sustain corruption, public sector reform will only make corrupt actors adapt their modes and methods.

SIMON BUTT AND TIM LINDSEY

Judicial mafia

The courts and state illegality in Indonesia

For decades, Indonesians have regarded the Indonesian judiciary as one of their nation's most corrupt institutions.[1] Surveys indicate that its reputation, ironically, has been for its propensity to act illegally, rather than its capacity to enforce the law, let alone deliver 'justice' (Asia Foundation and ACNielsen Indonesia 2001). Popular belief has it that most of Indonesia's judges and court officials are willing to accept, or even to extort, bribes from litigants to secure victory in their cases, with the Supreme Court seen as one of the most corrupt courts in the country. The Indonesian joke – which even judges tell – has the word *hakim* (judge) as short for *hubungi aku kalau ingin menang* (contact me if you want to win).[2]

It is also often said in Indonesia that corruption within the judiciary is systematic and institutionalized: illicit payments are filtered into patronage networks within which the recipient's superiors take percentages. For these reasons, the Indonesian justice system is often described as a 'mafia' (*mafia peradilan)* because most bribes are paid as part of a complex web of well-organized 'arrangements' involving a number of corrupt players, rather than just a few rogue individuals (Assegaf 2002:130). Even Supreme Court parking attendants are said to be involved.[3]

Senior Indonesian judges, including retired Supreme Court Chief Justices, have admitted that there is much in these popular perceptions that is accurate. Former Chief Justice Soerjono, for example, estimated that 50% of Indonesia's judges were corrupt (Pompe 2005:414), as did former Chief Justice Asikin Kusumaatmadja,[4] although well-regarded lawyers have claimed that the pro-

1 Research for this article was in part funded by AusAID through the Australia-Indonesia Governance Research Partnership (AIGRP), administered by the Crawford School at the Australian National University. We also thank Firmansyah Arifin of the National Law Reform Consortium (Konsorsium Reformasi Hukum Nasional).

2 See 'Mafia atau Mahkamah Agung?' *Tempo* 2 April 2000.

3 See 'Mafia atau Mahkamah Agung?' *Tempo* 2 April 2000.; ICW 2001:1.

4 See 'Courting corruption' *Inside Indonesia* 49 (January-March 1997), http://insideindonesia.org/content/view/892/29/ (accessed 12-11-2009).

portion of corrupt judges is closer to 90%.[5] Another former Supreme Court Justice – Adi Andojo – went even further in the mid-1990s, publicly naming other Supreme Court judges whom he accused of receiving massive bribes from litigants.[6] The situation, according to one lawyer, was so dire that an Indonesian court

> [...] shouldn't be called a house of justice [*kantor pengadilan*] but instead an auction house [*kantor lelang*]. An auction house for cases. [...] [T]he judge himself calls me or the prosecution calls me or a policeman calls me – they're the ones who ask me, 'Do you want your client to be helped or not? Does your client have enough for a donation or not?' So they're actively pursuing this. They're the producers and they're offering their wares [...] 'Do you have money or not? If you don't, I'll make an offer to your adversary.' Now when I get a telephone call like this, I'm no longer surprised [...] Now I feel that it is natural (Pemberton 1999:200).

In 2001, respected NGO Indonesia Corruption Watch (ICW) conducted dozens of interviews with judges, lawyers, court employees, prosecutors, litigants and police.[7] Many interviewees testified that bribery was very widespread and that they had either witnessed it or had participated in it. One interviewee even claimed '[...] while I have been an employee of the court there have been no cases which did not involve the payment of money'.[8] He concluded that 'if most people who take bribes go to hell, I think that no judges will be let in heaven'.

If even some of these perceptions are accurate (and determining this is a complex issue, which we discuss below), then the implications go much further, of course, than mere corruption within the judiciary. This is because the courts in post-Suharto democratic Indonesia are, in principle, the forum where intractable disputes between citizens and between citizens and the state should ultimately be resolved. They are also where the meaning of laws, the powers and functions of private and public institutions, and the nature and extent of rights should be determined. In other words, much of the power to define and shape the relationship between state and citizens is formally in the hands of the courts. In theory, the judiciary in Indonesia is thus necessarily a key arbiter of the post-Suharto *reformasi* process that has sought to roll

5 See 'Wawancara Trimoelja; Mahkamah Agung memang sudah bobrok', *Republika* 21-4-1996, www.republika.com (accessed 12-11-2009).

6 As discussed below in detail, these judges were, however, never convicted in relation to these allegations. See also 'Wawancara Adi Andojo; Akhirnya karir saya dan juga Mahkamah Agung tidak ternoda' Tempo 3 March 1997, www.tempointeraktif.com/ang/min/02/09/nas1.htm (accessed 12-11-2009).

7 On file with authors – we thank ICW for providing this material to us. Some of the interviews were later published in an ICW report entitled 'Opening the curtains on judicial corruption' (ICW 2001).

8 Interview with a judge conducted by Narullah from ICW on 26-7-2001 (in the possession of the authors).

back the overwhelming power of the authoritarian state built under Suharto's New Order and replace it with a more open, transparent system of governance in which individual rights have greater currency and the powers of the executive and the legislature are hemmed in by institutionalized democratic checks and balances (Lindsey 2002, 2004).

If, however, the courts are dysfunctional or lawless in themselves, then none of this can happen, or at least it cannot happen in a predictable, rational and fair fashion: a properly functioning judiciary is crucial to the maintenance of state legality. Governments everywhere push the boundaries of legality and it is often left to the judiciary to formally determine whether an act is illegal and, if so, to punish it. In some circumstances, governments may breach the law blatantly, deliberately and with some form of ulterior intent, such as to remove political rivals or dissidents, to secure personal benefits from public resources, or to cover up military human rights abuses. In other circumstances, however, the legality or otherwise of state action is far less clear-cut. Well-intentioned governments might test existing rules in an attempt to provide welfare benefits to citizens or improvements to governance systems by, for example, establishing a judicial watchdog or anti-corruption court to handle corruption cases more effectively (Fenwick 2008; Lindsey 2008); or upholding important socioeconomic human rights of the majority in the face of the competing human rights of a minority (Butt 2007b).

Regardless of the rationale for the government's illegality, if the judiciary fails to enforce the law against state officials, then there is little else to prevent the state acting illegally, save for 'shaming' through the media or academic critique. Such strategies can be risky if the state actor can wield political or physical power or threats. During the New Order period, for example, journalists were routinely threatened and publications shut down for criticizing the government. Even after the fall of Suharto, and with the general opening-up of the media and more permissive stance towards criticism of the state that followed, some critics have been met with threats of defamation litigation. Without an effective judiciary, the state can proceed largely unrestrained by law.

The dangers of judicial dysfunction for the weaker party in the state-citizen relationship are thus obvious. In this sense, illegality within the judiciary contributes to state illegality more generally. Real reform of the kind that might eventually rein in the broader patterns of Indonesian state illegality that persist from the New Order and earlier must therefore itself depend on a transformation of the judiciary that ends illegal practices and delivers a competent, transparent and predictable judicial system (Butt 2008; Goodpaster 2002; Lev 1978).

Accordingly, in this chapter we discuss a number of different types of judicial illegality and their prevalence, as well as their effect on different forms of broader 'state' illegality. Attention is also paid to various attempts at detecting and pursuing judicial illegality and how some members of the

Indonesian judiciary have persistently, strenuously and effectively resisted efforts to hold them accountable for this illegality.

Internal and external illegality

In analyzing the conduct of Indonesia's courts, we distinguish between two types of illegality. The first we call 'internal illegality', by which we mean illegal actions performed by judges when exercising their judicial functions. Judicial corruption and lack of judicial independence in decision making are prime examples of this type of illegality.

The second type we call 'external illegality' or 'authorizing or validating illegality'. This occurs when judges perpetuate or legitimize the illegality of the actions of parties to litigation by not enforcing or upholding the law. When these parties are governments or state officials, the judiciary contributes to 'state illegality' by, in effect, providing them with legal immunity for their illegal acts.

Of course, these two types of illegality are usually linked, because external illegality is typically preceded by internal illegality, such as when judges are bribed or succumb to government pressure, leading to a prearranged outcome in cases involving state officials. We distinguish between them, nonetheless, because we argue that while internal illegality has not significantly deceased overall, it is arguable that external illegality has declined since Suharto fell in 1998.

Defining illegality

We define 'illegal' for the purposes of this chapter to mean 'contrary to law'[9] and it is clear that when judges act corruptly – that is, when they decide a case in favour of one party in return for some form of personal or professional benefit to which they would otherwise not be entitled – they violate Indonesian law. Indonesia's 1999 Anti-corruption Law, amended in 2001, provides in Article 2(1) a very broad definition of what constitutes corruption, which includes

[9] 'Law' here means any type of written law, whether contained in the 1945 Constitution, statutes (*undang-undang*), government regulations (*peraturan pemerintah*), presidential regulations (*peraturan presiden*), regional regulations (*peraturan daerah*), or any other of the myriad types of executive-level regulations (*peraturan*) or decisions (*putusan*) (see Article 7(1) of Law no. 20/2004 on Making Laws for Indonesia's so-called 'hierarchy of laws'). 'Law' also includes Islamic law, to the extent that it has been incorporated into state-made law, through the 1991 *Kompilasi* of Islamic Law (issued by Presidential Decree in 1991), for example; and to the extent that it is applied in Indonesia's religious courts (Feener 2007; Hooker 2003, 2004, 2008; Lev 1973; Lindsey 2008; Lindsey and Hooker 2007). It also includes customary law (*adat*), where applicable (Davidson and Henley 2007; Hooker 1978). *Adat* may, in turn, also include elements derived from Islamic legal traditions.

any 'illegal' act that enriches the perpetrator or another, and which damages the finances of the state. Article 3 prohibits any person from, with the aim of enriching him or herself, another or a corporation, misusing their authority, opportunities, or means at their disposal because of the office they hold, in a way which could damage the state's finances or the economy. It is clear, too, that judges act illegally when they act with bias – that is, when they are influenced (whether by inducement or threat) – or choose by reason of personal prejudice, not to decide a case independently on its merits. Bribery and corruption would constitute such interference, as would government pressure. A raft of Indonesian laws make the requirement of independence unequivocally clear.[10]

Detecting judicial illegality: methodological challenges

As our definition of 'illegality' suggests, behaviour that is merely inappropriate or immoral is not 'illegal' unless that behaviour is also contrary to law. This has the important implication that judicial actions or decisions that are merely unpopular are not necessarily 'illegal', but this distinction is not often drawn in Indonesia, or at least is not often clearly drawn. In the media, and among lawyers and civil society observers, unpopular judicial decisions are commonly criticized, regardless of their legal merits, for not 'meeting the community's conception of justice' (*memenuhi rasa keadilan masyarakat*), a phrase borrowed from the Elucidation to Article 1(1) of the Judiciary Law. Such claims are often made without a considered analysis of the factors that the judges took into account in coming to their decision or of the legal reasoning they adopted. This is unsurprising, however, given that, as discussed below, most Indonesian courts do not provide easy access to their decisions.

It should be self-evident that whether 'illegality' has played a part in a judicial decision cannot be determined conclusively purely on the basis of the verdict or sentence in a case. Likewise, court staff (including judges) who may have acted illegally in the chain of events that led to the production of a decision are, of course, hardly likely to admit that. There also may well be reasonable legal explanations for decisions that appear to be undesirable by reference to the vague criterion of 'community standards'. These may not always be obvious, and judges may not necessarily disclose these explanations in their decisions. In respect of criminal cases, for example, prosecutorial standards in Indonesia are, in general, low, and prosecutors may simply fail to convincingly prove the allegations made in their indictments. Crucial witnesses or documents may be unavailable. Evidence that might be portrayed in

10 Article 24(1) of the Indonesian Constitution, for example, states that 'Judicial power is an independent power to maintain a system of courts with the objective of upholding law and justice.' The 2004 Judiciary Law (Law no. 4/2004) also requires judicial independence in a number of its provisions.

the media or elsewhere as indisputable may be brought into question at trial by judges and defence lawyers and, after examination pursuant to evidentiary rules, may be found to be of little or no weight or benefit in a formal sense. As in most jurisdictions, the testing of evidence is one of the main purposes of trial in Indonesia and that process can often lead to a conclusion that evidence is insufficient in a technical sense to ground a guilty verdict (in a criminal case) or a finding of liability (in a non-criminal case). As in many other countries, the subtleties of this process rarely survive media reports.

The laws that judges must apply might also be weak. Classic examples in the Indonesian context are Criminal Code (Kitab Undang-undang Hukum Pidana, KUHP) and Code of Criminal Procedure (Kitab Undang-undang Hukum Acara Pidana), both of which are criticized by Indonesian lawyers for being light on detail and desperately out-of-date, particularly in matters of evidence law (Butt 2008; Fitzpatrick 2008). A judge might, therefore, be acting entirely 'legally' to release an unpopular suspect given the weakness of these two statutes – indeed, a proper application of the law might require the judge to do so – but still find him or herself accused of 'illegality'. In the media, and in public perception, this sort of decision is likely to be portrayed as simple wrongdoing on the part of the judiciary.

Finally, a judicial decision might also employ weak legal arguments, as is, in fact, often the case in Indonesia, but this could be a result of judicial incompetence, rather than corruption. The two are not the same thing, even if they are often found together.

If detection of illegality by reference to case outcomes alone is unreliable, then by what means can illegality by detected? Unfortunately, particular aspects of 'judging' make both internal and external illegality very difficult to detect and prove. This is so in the legal systems of many countries, but the problem is particularly severe in the Indonesian context.

One potential source for detection is the judicial decision itself. It is often presumed that close scrutiny of judicial reasoning will reveal impropriety, if any occurred in the case. A key preliminary issue to be addressed in this regard is access to judicial decisions in Indonesia. It is, of course, impossible to analyse a decision without access to it. Although it would seem basic to any court's credibility that its judgments be freely available, this does not occur in contemporary Indonesia, feeding damaging speculation on the reasons for unpopular decisions.

So, for example, although several thousand decisions of Indonesia's Supreme Court, the Religious Courts (Pengadilan Agama) and the Constitutional Court (Mahkamah Konstitusi) are, at time of writing, available on their websites,[11]

[11] For Supreme Court decisions, see http://putusan.mahkamahagung.go.id/ (accessed 13-10-2010; for Constitutional Court decisions, see www.mahkamahkonstitusi.go.id (accessed 8-9-2010).

and are available through the AsianLII database,[12] this constitutes only a miniscule proportion of the total number of decisions handed down by Indonesian courts each year, around 3.5 million (Mahkamah Agung 2008). The vast majority of the Supreme Court's decisions are not published on these websites or elsewhere, and most of the millions of decisions of Indonesia's lower courts remain accessible only with great persistence, often involving a personal visit to the court in which the decision was handed down. The most obvious reasons for the lack of publication in Indonesia are budgetary and, as discussed below, unwillingness by judges to subject their decisions to scrutiny, particularly in controversial cases. Another reason is that these judgments have for decades been seen as valuable commodities by court staff, who can extract significant payments for their provision to desperate lawyers, litigants, researchers or journalists, and who thus have a vested interest in making decisions unavailable. It is therefore not unusual for parties who have a judgment entered against them to only discover this fact from the media. Some may, in fact, never receive a copy of the judgment (Butt 2008).

Another impediment to detecting judicial illegality is judicial discretion. Judicial discretion is a fundamental and unavoidable part of adjudication. It is exercised, most obviously, when judges decide whether the evidence presented is sufficient to indicate liability or guilt, but it comes into play in many other contexts in Indonesia, for example, when judges must choose between two or more laws that could be applied in a particular case, but which might lead to different outcomes.

The level of discretion judges exercise differs from place to place and from time to time. Logically, the more scope for judicial discretion, the more difficult illegality will be to detect. The more free judges are in their choice of law to apply, the evidence they will allow, their analysis, and, ultimately, their decision making, the easier it becomes to justify any decision they are inclined to make.

Indonesia's legal system provides judges with what is, by international standards, a relatively high degree of discretion and many opportunities to exercise it. This is partly because Indonesia's laws are, typically, generally worded and thus allow much judicial flexibility when applied to the facts of a given case. Broadly cast laws are a feature of many, if not most, countries in the world, although it is sometimes said that it is particularly prevalent in the European-derived 'Continental' civil law tradition,[13] which Indonesia follows. However, such laws can often make detecting illegality extremely difficult. Judges can simply declare that the facts that come before them do or do not fall within the scope of a particular provision without being forced to justify this conclusion in detail.

12 See www.asianlii.org (accessed 8-9-2010).

13 Dawson 1994; Glendon, Gordon and Osakwe 1985; Lasser 2004; Merryman 1984.

Detection difficulties are arguably aggravated in countries that do not require judges to provide decisions that contain a detailed and reasoned account of the evidence put forward in the case, the legal arguments made by all parties, the legal difficulties the case raised, and an analysis of the law applicable to the case (Lasser 2003, 2004). Because there are usually at least two sides to any legal dispute, each party often has a reasonable legal argument, particularly in cases that reach the appeal level in the higher courts. In many such cases, it can be easy for judges simply to choose the argument of the party he or she favours. This might require judges to do little more than regurgitate in the judgment the arguments of that party, perhaps simply claiming that the choice was a legitimate exercise of judicial discretion.

Finally, as in many other civil law countries, Indonesia has relatively few rules of evidence, and the admissibility of evidence is therefore largely a matter of judicial discretion. Although hearsay and opinion evidence are not formally admissible, Indonesian judges have otherwise very broad powers to admit or reject evidence. They can, for example, allow highly prejudicial evidence, even if it lacks significant probative value; and they can reject the most convincing evidence in general criminal cases merely on the basis that it is not a formal 'document' or 'testimony'.[14] Likewise, decisions as to the weight to be given to evidence are often reserved until judgment, allowing potentially inappropriate material full play during the hearing, such that findings about its worth in the judgment may come too late to remedy any prejudice already caused. Clearly, then, Indonesian judges have great discretion to accept or reject evidence that might determine innocence, guilt or liability.

Doctrinal issues raised by the guarantees of judicial independence can also compound difficulties in detecting judicial illegality. Judicial independence might appear to be a straightforward proposition: judges must be free to decide cases in accordance with their view of the law and the facts of the case before them; and they should not be pressured into making a decision in favour of one of the parties. If judges were not independent, litigants would have little faith in courts to resolve their disputes (Shapiro 1981:1, 7). Issues arise, however, in determining precisely how judicial independence should be achieved and how much independence judges require to adequately perform their adjudicative functions. One issue is whether judges should be immune from accountability measures such as performance and competence reviews because of fears that these measures might affect the way judges decide cases, thus opening the door to improper influence. Some judges claim that if they are subject to review by a non-judicial body, such as parliament

14 Butt 2008. This wide discretion exists largely because civil law tradition countries, such as Indonesia, have traditionally not employed juries (Merryman 1984). There is, therefore, no need to protect juries from prejudicial or defective evidence – a concern underlying much of the detailed evidence law often found in common law tradition countries.

or a judicial commission, they might be more likely to issue decisions of the kind that would be favoured by their reviewers. This is an argument that has long had much support among judges in developed democracies, and should be taken seriously. It is, however, open to exploitation by the unscrupulous. The Indonesian cases of Endin and the 'three judges', both discussed below, show that Indonesian judges have gone to extraordinary lengths to avoid scrutiny and that, typically, they have pointed to the doctrine of judicial independence when doing so (Aspandi 2002:101). By resorting to pleas of 'judicial independence', Indonesian judges have, for example, resisted a return to the early New Order practice of *eksaminasi* under which the superior of each judge periodically examined three criminal and three civil decisions handed down by that judge.[15]

For example, the Constitutional Court, in a case discussed below, used the principle of judicial independence to justify a decision disallowing scrutiny of judicial decisions by the Judicial Commission in an attempt to detect irregularities. It declared unconstitutional parts of the Judicial Commission Law that purported to allow the Commission to supervise performance of Indonesia's judges – including Constitutional Court judges – by analysing their decisions. This activity, the Court held, was best left to the formal appeals process, under which senior judges assessed the previous decisions of lower-court judges. According to the Court, having non-judicial officers performing this assessment compromised the constitutional requirement of judicial independence.

If Indonesian judicial decisions are difficult or sometimes even impossible to access and, even if one were to obtain them, unlikely to clearly reveal internal or external judicial legality, how then can judicial illegality be identified? The answer, we argue, is, somewhat unreliably, through admissions, anecdotes, estimations, perceptions and presumptions. These measures might provide an overall impression of the extent to which internal and external illegality occurs within the judiciary, but they are far from scientifically rigorous and are susceptible to being based largely simply on the outcome of cases – a danger we identified above. There are, however, usually no alternative methods by which judicial illegality can reliably be measured in contemporary Indonesia.

For these reasons, in asserting corruption and lack of judicial independence in this chapter, it is generally impossible to offer unequivocal data. Instead, we are forced to refer to statements made by senior judges, lawyers and others about the prevalence of corruption, and to public perceptions, often informed by experience, about illegality within the judiciary. Likewise, in discussing the courts' authorizing or legitimizing illegality, we have to focus on the impropriety of meetings between judges and government officials; and the former

15 Supreme Court Memo (*Surat Edaran*) no. 1/1967 on Examinations, Monthly Reports and Appeals Lists. See Aspandi (2002:80, 127) and Butt (2007a).

structural relationship between the Department of Justice and the Supreme Court that gave the Department a degree of authority over judges and, by all accounts, allowed the Department to interfere in cases. We do so, however, without resiling from our own critique of the limitations of this approach.

Internal illegality and corruption

At the start of this chapter we described the parlous reputation for pervasive corruption of the Indonesian judiciary, and, in particular, the general courts, led by the Supreme Court. The perception that the general courts are utterly rotten is only rarely displaced by shining examples of judicial integrity or excellence. It is usually accepted that the Religious Courts and the new Constitutional Court are relatively clean. Overall, however, there are now signs that internal illegality within the judiciary probably has not decreased and might even be on the rise. Complaints of corruption – particularly within the general courts and within the Supreme Court – are still very common. The majority of complaints lodged with Indonesia's National Ombudsman Commission, for example, relate solely to this issue (M. Crouch 2008:386).

Why these high corruption levels? In Indonesia, a combination of factors is at play. Low operational budgets and low judicial salaries have often been cited as factors forcing judges to seek additional sources of finance and income.[16] On the (highly questionable) presumption that increasing salaries will somehow reduce corruption, judicial salaries have been substantially increased in recent years.[17] The Supreme Court's budget has also recently been greatly expanded, although, so have its administrative responsibilities. Its budget increased drastically from Rp 79.5 billion in 2002, to Rp 153 billion in 2004,[18] and after the *satu atap* (one roof) reforms, discussed below, to Rp 1.2 trillion in 2005, Rp 2.2 trillion in 2006, and Rp 3 trillion in 2007.[19] This appears to be a significant increase, but in real terms it is arguably a reduction, given the vast expansion of the court's responsibilities and administrative burdens. With this budget, the Supreme Court must, for example, administer 67 appeal courts and 706 first instance courts, including paying for building infrastructure and the salaries of over 7,000 personnel (Mahkamah Agung 2008:i).

In any case, increased salaries, even combined with strong new corruption

16 World Bank 2004:83-5; *Menuju independensi* 1999:62; Dakolias and Thachuk 2000:398.

17 See 'ICW; Makin besar gaji hakim "gila-gilaan"', 23-7-2002, http://www.hukumonline.com/warta/2002/7/23 (accessed 8-9-2010).

18 See 'Kekuasaan kehakiman satu atap, anggaran MA membengkak', 4-9-2004, http://www.hukumonline.com/warta/2004/9/4 (accessed 8-9-2010).

19 See 'Permasalahan menahun, anggaran tak cukup', 27-4-2007, http://www.hukumonline.com/warta/2004/9/4 (accessed 8-9-2010).

laws, have apparently failed to reduce corruption. Judges are, of course, rational persons: corrupt ones are unlikely to change their behaviour unless it is in their best interests to be honest (Dakolias and Thachuk 2000:365, 398; World Bank 2004:vii). This might occur if detection is probable and sufficiently punitive sanctions are likely to be imposed for contravention of those laws. The Indonesian judiciary has, however, resisted the imposition of mechanisms designed to do just that, so it remains unlikely that an errant judge will be punished. This is an issue to which we return below, when we discuss the ill-fated Judicial Commission.

Perhaps the most prominent example of the contempt with which some Indonesian judges view efforts to bring them to account for their alleged illegalities is the Endin case, which occurred after the fall of Suharto in 1998 but before the *satu atap* reforms. We focus on this case because it is one of the few in which the decision is available to us and because it does, on its face and when read in the context of the circumstances surrounding the case, appear to demonstrate clearly both impropriety and the courts' determination to avoid outside scrutiny and detection of internal illegality.

Case study; The Endin and three judges cases

Endin admitted to bribing three Supreme Court judges on behalf of the plaintiff in an inheritance case, for whom he worked as a *calo*, or go-between.[20] He claimed to have paid Supreme Court judges Yahya Harahap Rp 96 million, and Marnis Kahar and Supraptini Sutarto Rp 50 million each. Subsequently, Endin's client won the case, but the defendant refused to comply with the decision and the district court failed to enforce the Supreme Court's decision. Such enforcement failures are common in Indonesia because of serious flaws in its regime for enforcement of judgments that expose that process to opportunities for corruption and political interference.[21]

Endin's client was, unsurprisingly, perplexed by her unenforceable victory. Frustrated, Endin claimed that he delivered a letter to the judges at their Supreme Court offices, in which he reminded the judges of the payment, and sought their assistance with the enforcement of their decision.

> In September and October, I, along with my friend, gave an amount of operational money to win case no. 560.K/Pdt/1997 to Mr Yahya Harahap, Ms Marnis Kahar and Ms Supraptini Sutarto [...] I requested that [the three judges] contact me to find a solution that is best for everyone.[22]

20 Case no 560.K/Pdt/1997.

21 For a detailed account of Indonesia's troubled record on enforcement of judicial decisions, see Butt 2008.

22 Endin defamation case (Central Jakarta District Court Decision no. 427/PID.B/2001/PN.JKT.PST), p. 18, copy on file with authors.

Obtaining no response, an apparently infuriated Endin reported the judges to the police, accusing them of accepting his bribes. In a deal struck with then Attorney General Marzuki Darusman and Adi Andojo Soetjipto, Head of the Joint Corruption Eradication Team (Tim Gabungan Pemberantasan Tindak Pidana Korupsi, TGPTPK) and a former well-respected Supreme Court Judge, Endin was assured that he would not be prosecuted for making the report.[23]

The Joint Team duly began preparing their cases against the judges. However, before the criminal case involving the judges as defendants could be heard, the judges reported Endin to the police, alleging that he had defamed them. Defamation proceedings began in the Central Jakarta District Court before the three judges were tried for bribery. In Indonesia, defamation is often dealt with by means of criminal law, and Endin was charged under several articles of the Criminal Code including Article 310(1). This Article provides that anyone who attacks the honour or good name of a person by accusing them of something, with the intent that it is to become publicly known, faces a maximum of nine months in prison for defamation. The Criminal Code does not make 'truth' a defence to defamation in all circumstances but, under Article 312, a court can permit the defendant to avoid punishment by proving the truth of the allegedly defamatory allegation if it is made against an official performing his or her official duties (Article 314(1)). If the defendant fails to prove the truth of the allegation, however, the maximum penalty increases from nine months to four years under Article 311.

Endin was convicted under both Article 310(1) and 311. As for the Article 310(1) charge, the Court considered Endin's letter and concluded that it accused the judges of accepting a bribe to 'fix' a case.[24] The Court found this allegation to be insulting and, therefore, defamatory.[25] The Court gave Endin the opportunity to attempt to prove the truth of his allegation under Article 311, but held that he failed to do so. The judges maintained throughout the trial that they had never met Endin and that they did not accept the bribes as alleged. The panel emphasized inconsistencies in Endin's version of events that cast doubt on his story.[26] In the end, Endin was convicted and sentenced to three months in jail, suspended for six months.

The Court's reasoning in its decision in this case was highly questionable, for two main reasons. First, the Court failed to consider Article 310(3) of the Criminal Code, which provides that no defamation occurs if the allegation is

[23] Lubis 2001. Declaration of Head of Tim Gabungan Pemberantasan Tindak Pidana Korupsi, 22-6-2000 (on file with authors).

[24] Endin defamation case, p. 19.

[25] Endin defamation case, p. 19.

[26] For example, Endin had claimed that he had given the judges Rp 50,000 notes, upon which was a picture of WR Supratman – the composer of the Indonesian national anthem. However, testimony from an expert from Bank Indonesia revealed that these notes circulated from 1-6-1999, which was, according to the evidence adduced at trial, well after Endin claimed to have bribed the judges in late 1998. Endin defamation case, pp. 20-1.

made in the public interest. Surely allegations of corruption within the highest level of the Indonesian judiciary are a matter of public interest? Second, Article 314(3) of the Criminal Code states that if criminal prosecution has begun of a person allegedly defamed, and the prosecution relates to the same matter that the person claims to be defamatory, then defamation proceedings should be stayed until a final decision has been issued in the criminal case relating to the matter alleged. In this case, this would mean that as the judges faced prosecution for corruption based on Endin's allegations, their defamation claims should be delayed until their own prosecution was complete, to ensure consistency in decisions. The Court, however, did not even consider this provision.

In the meantime, prosecution cases against the three judges were thrown out of court in pre-trial (*pra-peradilan*) proceedings.[27] The arguments presented by counsel for dismissing these cases, and which were accepted by the Court, were feeble in the extreme. They included that the Joint Team lacked jurisdiction to investigate the three judges because the Joint Team had not been formed at the time the alleged crime took place. As Assegaf (2002:138) points out, this was irrelevant, because the Joint Team was a taskforce within the Attorney General's Office made up largely of pre-existing prosecutors and police who coordinated the handling of particular corruption cases. It was thus not a new body with new powers exceeding those normally exercised by police and prosecutors.

Lawyers appearing for the judges also argued that the 1971 Corruption Law, under which they had been charged, could not be applied in this case.[28] They pointed to Article 44 of the 1999 Anti-Corruption Law which states that the 1971 Anti-Corruption Law 'is declared to be not in force (*dinyatakan tidak berlaku*)' with the coming-into-effect of the 1999 Law (which occurred on 16 August 1999). In this interpretation, Article 44 deemed the 1971 Anti-Corruption Law never to have existed. Some kind of specific 'transitional provision' is, they argued, customary when laws (particularly criminal laws) are changed in Indonesia and the 1971 Corruption Law contains one of these customary provisions.[29]

The act of bribery was alleged to have taken place in 1997, that is, before the 1999 Law came into effect. The judges, their lawyers argued, could therefore not be charged under the 1971 Law, given that the national legislature had revoked it by enacting the 1999 Law. They could not be charged under

27 Marnis Kahar and Supraptini Sutarto appeared together and Harahap separately.

28 See 'Kasus korupsi hakim agung; Terdakwa bisa dikenai UU No 3/1971 dan UU No 31/1999', *Kompas* 3-8-2001.

29 It states in Article 36 that it replaces Law no. 24/1960 for crimes committed after the 1971 Law came into force, but that alleged acts of corruption committed before 29-3-1971 (the date the 1971 Law came into force) would be prosecuted under the 1960 Law. The conspicuous absence of such a provision in Law no. 31/1999 – it simply declares Law no. 3/1971 invalid – appears to lend support to this argument.

the 1999 Law either, because to apply this to an act taking place before the Law's enactment would breach the Indonesian legal prohibition on retrospectivity.[30] This interpretation of Article 44 would give any person who had committed a corruption crime before 16 August 1999 de facto immunity from prosecution. The argument is unconvincing. Clearly, the legislature intended that the 1999 Law replace the 1971 Law, not to deem it never to have existed.

In any event, whether or not their claim had merit, it is strongly arguable that the Court lacked jurisdiction to hear the application made by the judges' lawyers at all. Article 77 of the Code of Criminal Procedure limits *pra-peradilan* proceedings narrowly to determining the legality of arrests, detentions or seizures (Fitzpatrick 2008:505-6). The focus of the judges' claim at this hearing was the jurisdiction of the Joint Team itself, an issue that would seem to fall well outside the ambit of Article 77. Despite this, the Court accepted the arguments of the judges' lawyers and dismissed the charges against their clients.

There was, of course, no legal reason to prevent prosecutors from revising and resubmitting their indictments; however, they did not (Assegaf 2002:138). Discussions with Andojo himself suggest that the Joint Team simply recognized that it could no longer prevail against what appeared to him to be an insuperable judicial – and, he claimed, political – conspiracy against it.

It seems he may have been right. Not content with having the case thrown out, the judges' legal representatives then filed a request with the Supreme Court to review the Government Regulation by which the Joint Team was established against the statute under which the Regulation was issued. In their application, they argued that Law no. 31/1999 (which declared that the Joint Team could be established to hear particular corruption cases) and Government Regulation no. 19/2000 on the Joint Team (which contains details about the Team's composition and functions) contradicted each other.

Several provisions of the Regulation, particularly Articles 6(2) and 18, seemed to indicate that the Team was permanent (*bersifat tetap*); yet Article 27 of the Law only stated that the Team 'could be established' (*dapat dibentuk*) 'in the event that corruption is discovered that is difficult to prove' pending creation of a later Corruption Eradication Commission (Komisi Pemberantasan Korupsi, KPK). This, they argued, indicated the Team was, in the words of the Court, 'impermanent, temporary, or incidental and facultative and causative'.

> [...] Article 18 of the [Regulation...] has eliminated and placed Article 43 [of the Law...] in a position as a 'etre en soi' (bein in its self), that is the Anti-Corruption Commission has become an 'item' which has been alienated so that

[30] Aspandi 2002:34-5. This principle is contained in the first provision (Article 1(1)) of Indonesia's Code of Criminal Procedure (Kitab Undang-Undang Hukum Acara Pidana, KUHAP). A prohibition on prosecution for an act occurring before a law was passed has also been introduced in Article 28I(1) of the 1945 Constitution.

> it has no power and even doesn't exist because the Commission is substituted to become the Joint Team.[31]

The Court's reasoning is nonsensical. Rather than just affirming that the Joint Team was indeed only a temporary stopgap measure until the Anti-Corruption Commission was established, the Court decided that it was necessary to invalidate the entire regulation. Lacking a legal basis, the Joint Team was forced to cease operating altogether and so the prospects of prosecuting the three judges ceased with it.

Perhaps most disturbing of all, the judge who chaired the Supreme Court panel appeared to have a serious conflict of interest. Justice Paulus E. Lotolong had previously been assigned by the Association of Indonesian Judges (Ikatan Hakim Indonesia, Ikahi) to 'accompany' the judges being investigated and, if necessary, to take any action as their legal advisor (Assegaf 2002:139). Surely his participation on the panel should have invalidated the Court's decision?[32]

We described earlier the very significant difficulties of detecting illegality in Indonesian court decisions, and those caveats remain valid. The Endin and three judges cases, however, are remarkable for an absence across them of clear and compelling reasons for the decisions reached, and for the strong suggestion of ulterior motives for those decisions arising from circumstances in which they were made. Read together, it is hard to resist the conclusion that these cases demonstrate the willingness of the Indonesian judiciary to conduct the most ruthless and aggressive institutional resistance to attempts to detect corruption in its ranks and hold its officers to account, regardless of the merits of accusations against individual judges, and despite what the law intends in such cases. This, in turn, suggests that the reason for the judiciary's fiercely revanchist response in these cases is most likely a wish to protect an institutionalized model of corruption that implicates most of its members.

On this view, the problem of internal illegality in Indonesia's judicial institutions in the form of corruption and resistance to efforts to detect and punish corruption is now primarily about advancing and defending the interests of the members of that institution, rather than being driven by any attachment, ideological or political, to any particular institution outside the judiciary – for example, the New Order, the state, the government, Pancasila or Reformasi.

This can be seen, we would argue, from the fact that at the same time that the judiciary has continued determinedly defending its own members from

[31] MA Decision no. 03 P/HUM/2000, which can be found on http://www.hukumonline.com (accessed 8-9-2010); mis-spelling in original.

[32] Article 220 of Indonesia's Criminal Code states that if a judge has a conflict of interest in a case, he should step down from the case. It does not, however, go so far as to state that the judges' continued involvement in hearing the case will invalidate any decision made in that case.

scrutiny, offering them de facto impunity, it has been prepared to withdraw that impunity from other state actors. In other words, while the role of the general courts in authorizing external illegality has declined (although it has not entirely disappeared), and although its independence from the government has been largely won, internal illegality in the sense of corruption has been largely undiminished, despite the immense pressure that has been brought to bear for judicial reform. To demonstrate this, we begin by describing briefly the practice of external illegality prior to Suharto's fall.

External illegality and government interference

The weakening of judicial institutions under Indonesia's first president, Sukarno, and their systematic degradation during Suharto's 32 years in power, has been well-documented.[33] The downfall of what had been a reasonably professional and independent judiciary in the 1950s, began with Sukarno's introduction of 'revolutionary law' (*hukum revolusi*). Under this approach, courts and judges were targeted for obstructing presidential and executive prerogative which, Sukarno claimed, needed to be strong and largely unconstrained so that the new state could realize the goals of the revolution. Sukarno's campaign against the legal system culminated in Law no. 19/1964 on Judicial Power. This statute explicitly rejected the *trias politika* (separation of powers), including the principle of judicial independence; stated that the courts were an instrument of the national revolution; and enabled the president to interfere in, and retrospectively alter, any decision of any Indonesian court for the sake of the 'ongoing revolution or national interests'.

Sukarno's policy was catastrophic for judicial independence and integrity, but the courts fared even worse under Suharto's New Order. Although the overt legal power of intervention under the rubric of revolutionary law was abandoned by Suharto, by the mid-1970s, the regime was, in any case, able to influence – even dictate – virtually any decision, and it consistently did so in cases in which it had any interest at all, even 'petty cases, in which [...] important Justice Department officials or the Supreme Court leadership defined an interest' (Pompe 2005:140).

The government achieved this influence by exercising bureaucratic control over individual judges and administrative control over the judiciary. Most of Indonesia's judges (like judges in many civil law countries), became civil servants and as such were formally required to support government policy. They could, in fact, even be disciplined for breaching civil service

33 See Butt 2008; Lev 1972, 1978; Lindsey 2000, 2001, 2002, 2004, 2007, 2008; Pompe 2005. The beginning of Suharto's rule is often traced to his actions on 1 October 1965.

regulations, which required adherence to the state ideology (Pancasila), the state and the government, and the prioritizing of the interests of the state over those of groups or individuals.[34]

As for administrative control, despite strenuous objections from many Indonesian lawyers and judges (Lev 1978), the Ministry of Justice wielded organizational, administrative and financial control over the lower general and administrative courts, under the so-called 'two roof' (*dua atap*) system.[35] This gave the Ministry ultimate control over matters critical to the functioning of the courts and to the personal well-being of judges, such as the allocation of budgets, promotions, transfers, and dismissal, although responsibility for the legal competence of judges was nominally retained by the Supreme Court.

In many other civil law countries, the government controls these administrative and organizational matters, with little apparent adverse effect on judicial independence (Wells 1994), at least where there are guidelines and protocols preventing government intrusion. However, government control has had a deleterious effect on judicial independence in some civil law countries, particularly countries still developing cultures of legal and judicial professionalism (see Hammergren 2001; Mattei 1997). In Indonesia it was regularly blamed for very low levels of judicial independence. Specifically, the government was said to commonly exploit judges' reliance upon it for continued employment, pay, promotion and transfer to ensure loyalty, particularly from the early to mid-1970s (Pompe 2005:125-9).

A system thus developed by which judicial promotions were very rarely based on merit; rather, they mostly were based on seniority, 'dedication to service', and 'demonstrated loyalty' (Supreme Court of Indonesia 2003:132). The Department's power to transfer was also a powerful weapon (*Menuju independensi* 1999:50). Indonesia has a broad range of living conditions – from major centres with world-class facilities and luxuries, particularly in Java, to more remote, underdeveloped – and, at times, even dangerous – locations. The prospect of five years in a major centre for 'toeing the line', instead of in a backwater as punishment for recalcitrance, was a strong incentive indeed.[36]

This non-merit promotion and transfer system that encouraged judicial acceptance of government interference is also responsible for other scourges that, at the time of writing, remain firmly part of the Indonesian judiciary. Continuing judicial education and the *eksaminasi* system, mentioned above,

34 See Government Regulation no. 30/1980 on Disciplining Civil Servants, Articles 2(a) and 2(b).

35 Law no. 14/1970 on the Judiciary, Article 11(1). The Defence and Security Ministry and the Religious Affairs Ministry had similar levels of control over, respectively, the military courts and religious courts.

36 Lembaga Kajian dan Advokasi untuk Independensi Peradilan (LeIP) points to one judge who served in Aceh for 11 years and to some judges who served for similar times in other 'hardship' provinces, and notes that other judges have been promoted and transferred to more comfortable locations (including the capital, Jakarta) far earlier than they would normally be (Supreme Court of Indonesia 2003:131).

were virtually abandoned during the 'two roof' period. After all, there was no need to maintain or improve judicial standards if the primary loyalty of judges was to the government rather than the law. In fact, forensic skill could be a positive disadvantage for a judge, as it might lead him or her to make politically unacceptable decisions. The accountability mechanism of *eksaminasi* was also not required, indeed, it became an embarrassment: the smaller the chances of detection of interference in judicial decision making (even accepting that detection would be difficult in any event), the better for the judiciary and government alike.

It must be acknowledged, however, that some judges (albeit clearly a minority) refused to succumb to these pressures, and continued to decide cases as they saw fit, and there were high-profile cases where the government was defeated in decisions at one level of appeal at least. One well-known example was the celebrated *Tempo* magazine case, where the government lost at first instance and at the first level of appeal, but ultimately succeeded in the Supreme Court (Millie 1999). This seems to indicate that the Department's control over judges, at least with respect to particular cases and particular times, was sufficient to generally ensure that it ultimately secured the outcomes it desired, but was not as absolute as is often presumed.

Unwinding external illegality

Within this 'two roofs' system, the New Order courts did not, for the most part, 'punish' illegal acts by state actors, including judges themselves, unless the executive directed them to do so. Rather, they generally operated to authorize or validate illegal acts of the state, with the politically influential enjoying virtual immunity from conviction. Much has been written about this process and for reasons of space the detail will not be rehearsed here. [37]

After the fall of Suharto, significant reforms were made to Indonesia's judicial system. One of the most important of these was, as mentioned, the transfer of the organizational, administrative and financial affairs of the lower courts to the Supreme Court – the so called 'one roof' (*satu atap*) reforms. These reforms take ultimate responsibility for the appointment, education, transfer, promotion and dismissal of judges away from the government. By forcing the government out of judicial career paths and the detail of court budgeting, these reforms constituted a radical reinvention of judicial administration in Indonesia.

Although to the knowledge of the authors no comprehensive or rigorous study has yet been able to measure how these reforms have, in fact, improved

[37] See, for example, Aspandi 2002; Butt 2008; Goodpaster 2002; Lev 1972, 1978; Lindsey 2000, 2008; Pompe 2005.

judicial independence, it is generally assumed in Indonesia that they have. Certainly it is now much rarer to hear allegations in the media and within Indonesian legal circles of government interference in cases in which it has an interest. And indeed, significant cases have emerged in which the government or state actors have been defeated. There is even evidence suggesting that private parties in disputes against the state might now be on such a level playing field that they are able to defeat the state by offering illicit payments to the judges hearing those cases (Butt 2008). If this is the case, then we speculate that illegality in the form of internal corruption might be filling some of the vacuum left by a decline of state-authorized illegality.

The apparently reduced levels of judicial authorization of external illegality cannot be attributed to *satu atap* reforms alone. The establishment of the Anti-Corruption Court (Pengadilan Tindak Pidana Korupsi, Tipikor) appears also to have made a significant contribution. This it has done by diverting some types of corruption cases involving state officials away from the general courts which would, in the past, have been the forum before which such matters would have been determined. The Anti-Corruption Court has, precisely as it intended, removed some potentially lucrative opportunities for corruption from corrupt judges. In doing so, and by increasing the possibility that general court judges themselves may one day appear before it as defendants, it also constitutes an implicit threat to the impunity of state actors and, in particular, of other judges.

The Anti-Corruption Court was established in 2003 to hear cases investigated and prosecuted by the Corruption Eradication Commission (Komisi Pemberantasan Korupsi, KPK). The KPK, made up of carefully selected seconded police and prosecutors, has been institutionally independent of Indonesia's ordinary law enforcement apparatus. It has the authority to investigate and prosecute cases of corruption that implicate law enforcement officers or government officials, involve a significant amount of the state's finances, or attract significant public concern (Articles 6(c) and 11 of the KPK Law). It can also take over corruption investigations from ordinary police and prosecutors if it determines that the case is not being handled expeditiously, if there are indications of corruption in the investigation or prosecution, or if the case is particularly complex or otherwise difficult (Article 9 of the KPK Law). Initially the KPK was criticized for choosing easy cases it could win, and for avoiding the 'big fish' corruption cases (Fenwick 2008), but in 2008 it began to dispel such criticisms, investigating corruption allegations against members of the national legislature (Dewan Perwakilan Rakyat, DPR), senior state officials involved in significant bank scandals, and even the father-in-law of President Susilo Bambang Yudhoyono's son.[38]

[38] Purba 2008; Kong and Ramayandi 2008. See 'Vonis Hamka dan Antony tidak seragam; Aliran dana BI', 7-1-2009, http://www.hukumonline.com/warta/2009/1/7 (accessed 8-9-2010), and 'Hamka divonis 3 tahun, Antony 4.5', *Kompas* 8-1-2009.

The Anti-Corruption Court had, at the time of writing, heard and decided around 100 cases that the KPK brought before it and had convicted the defendant in every case.[39] Although there are several differences between the Anti-Corruption Court and the general courts (Fenwick 2008), this 100% conviction rate is often credited to one in particular: the Anti-Corruption Court's use of non-career judges. Anti-Corruption Court hearings employ five-judge panels. Two judges are career judges, but three are non-career judges, giving the non-career (ad hoc) judges a majority if the court is split on whether to convict. These non-career judges are legal experts, such as academics, practitioners and retired judges and are considered less likely than career judges to be entwined in institutionalized corruption or to have divided loyalties. This appears to have been borne out in practice: several Anti-Corruption Court decisions have been split along ad hoc vs career lines (Fenwick 2008:414), with the majority ad hoc judges convicting the defendant and the minority career judges declaring that they would have acquitted or imposed a lower sentence.[40]

The contribution of the Anti-Corruption Court should not be overstated: at the time of writing it was still hearing far fewer corruption cases than the general courts (ICW 2008). However, presuming that it remains effective in the future – a matter to which we return below – and assuming also that it continues to have high-profile cases presented to it by the KPK, it seems reasonable to expect that the Court could continue to have a significant effect on the reduction of judicial validation of state illegality in the future, and may even come eventually to address internal illegality within the courts.

Obstacles on the road to reform; Internal illegality and resistance to scrutiny

As mentioned above, Indonesia's courts – particularly the Supreme Court – have strongly resisted attempts to hold them to account for misconduct, whether this be in the form of scrutiny of their decisions in particular cases (such as in the Endin case) or a more systematic mechanism to review their performance (such as a reintroduction of the *eksaminasi* system). The success of this resistance, it seems, allowed internal and external judicial illegality to continue virtually unchecked, at least until the *satu atap* reforms and the Anti-Corruption Court were introduced.

Now it seems Indonesia's new Constitutional Court, itself enjoying a reputation for internal integrity, strong commitment to the new democratic arrangements and apparent freedom from corruption, has supported the wider cause of judicial resistance to external scrutiny. This court, established

39 See 'Pengadilan umum; 'Kuburan' pemberantasan korupsi', Indonesia Corruption Watch, http://antikorupsi.org/docs/lathukum2008.pdf (accessed 12-11-2009).

40 Appeals from the Anti-Corruption Court are lodged with a High Court, and then with the Supreme Court, again with three ad hoc and two career judges on the panel (see Articles 59(2) and 60(2) of the KPK Law).

in 2003, is the first Indonesian court to have been formally granted powers of constitutional review. This enables it to review national statutes against the Constitution. This function is particularly important now that Indonesia's Constitution has been expanded to include an international-standard Bill of Rights in Chapter XA that closely tracks the Universal Declaration of Human Rights (UDHR). It is the Court's job to ensure that the legislature does not illegally intrude upon these rights when making law.

From its earliest days, the Court made it clear that it was independent and professional, that it intended to establish itself as a model judicial forum immune to bribery, and that it genuinely intended to uphold the Constitution (Butt 2007a, 2007b; Butt and Lindsey 2008). In recent years, however, the Court has handed down some problematic decisions grounded in weak legal argument that have undermined the efforts of the national legislature to increase judicial accountability and tackle corruption. To that extent they have, intentionally or not, contributed to obstructing efforts to reform the general courts. Two of these decisions – concerning, respectively, the Judicial Commission and the Anti-Corruption Court – deserve discussion, albeit briefly for reasons of space.

In the first decision,[41] Constitutional Court judges used the doctrine of judicial independence to make decisions that had the effect of protecting themselves and other judges from external scrutiny by the Judicial Commission.[42] The case was the final stage in a very public war between the Supreme Court and the Judicial Commission. The controversy began when Professor Bagir Manan, then Supreme Court Chief Justice, rejected a Judicial Commission request to investigate several Supreme Court judges (including himself) for alleged corruption in cases they had handled. In response, members of the Judicial Commission visited the President to demand a reselection or rigorous performance assessment of all 49 Supreme Court justices as the first stage of a comprehensive overhaul of the entire judiciary. This demand was leaked to the media, as was a list of allegedly 'problematic' or corrupt judges. In response, several Supreme Court judges reported then Judicial Commission Chairperson, Busyro Muqoddas, to the police for defamation. They also lodged an application with the Constitutional Court, arguing that the Judicial Commission's power to monitor the judiciary contradicted the doctrine of judicial independence mandated by the Constitution.

On their petition, the Constitutional Court reviewed Law no. 22/2004, the statute which established the Commission. This Law gave the Commission two primary functions: to propose judicial appointments to the Supreme Court and to supervise the performance and behaviour of Indonesia's judges.[43]

41 This section draws on Butt (2007a), in which this dispute is discussed in detail.

42 The creation of an Indonesian Judicial Commission was mandated by the third amendment to Indonesia's 1945 Constitution (see Article 24B of the Constitution).

43 Law no. 22/2004, Article 13.

However, the supervisory powers of the Commission were limited, presumably in the interests of judicial independence. If the Commission suspected a judge of acting improperly, it could propose that the judge be punished by written reprimand, suspension or dismissal. However, the Commission could take no further direct action – it could only send the proposed sanction and reasons for suggesting it to the Supreme or Constitutional Court leadership. The statute allowed the Commission to review the performance of judges, but the final decision on whether action would be taken lay with other judges.

The Court began its decision by excluding itself from Judicial Commission supervision, pointing to the principle of judicial independence contained in the Constitution, an issue neither party had asked it to rule on. The Court next found that judicial independence also prevented the Commission from supervising the Supreme Court's exercise of judicial powers. The nub of the Court's decision was as follows:

> [...] even though assessing the technical-judicial skills of judges by reading judicial decisions might assist the Judicial Commission to identify a breach of a code of conduct or ethics, reviewing judicial decisions might place unjustifiable pressure on the judges, thereby breaching judicial independence. Only the courts could review judicial decisions, and then only through the appeals process – not by evaluating and directly interfering with decisions or by influencing judges (Butt 2007a:192).

In December 2008, the DPR amended the Supreme Court Law (Law no. 3/2009), presumably in response to this decision. Article 11A of the Law gives power to the Supreme Court alone to recommend the removal of a judge to the president if that judge has been found guilty of a crime, neglects judicial duties for three months, has breached the judicial oath, or takes on additional unauthorized work. The Judicial Commission can propose removal for inappropriate behaviour (*perbuatan tercela*) or for a breach of the judicial code of ethics.[44] Judges, however, have a 'right to defend themselves' before a Judges' Honour Council (Majelis Kehormatan Hakim), comprising four Judicial Commission members and three Supreme Court judges. If the Council rejects the judge's defence, then it is to convey its recommendations to the Supreme Court and the Judicial Commission and, within 14 days the Supreme Court Chief Justice is to convey the recommendation to the President.

In the opinion of the authors, it is possible that these new provisions are vulnerable to constitutional challenge on grounds similar to those accepted by the Constitutional Court in the Judicial Commission case. The Judicial Commission members are in the majority on the Honour Council and, presuming that the Council votes by majority, the Judicial Commission appears

[44] At time of writing, a code of ethics had not been established.

to have the potential to hold sway over the Council. If such a constitutional challenge against the review process was brought, the Constitutional Court might view the Judge's Honour Council's inclusion of Judicial Commission members as a threat to judicial independence.

In the second case in which the Constitutional Court appears to have made decisions that have weakened efforts to reduce internal judicial illegality,[45] a number of people convicted by the Anti-Corruption Court petitioned the Constitutional Court to review several provisions of the statute by which the Anti-Corruption Court was established – the same statute that created the KPK.[46]

The Court accepted their arguments, holding on two grounds that the Anti-Corruption Court had been established unconstitutionally. The first constitutional fault arose from the fact that both the general courts and the Anti-Corruption Court have jurisdiction over corruption cases. Whether the Anti-Corruption Court heard and decided particular cases was entirely dependent on whether the KPK had chosen to investigate and prosecute those cases. If the KPK decided not to pursue a particular case, it would be handled in the ordinary way, that is, through the normal police, prosecutors and courts. This caused what the Constitutional Court referred to as 'dualism', which it saw as contradicting the constitutional principle of equality before the law. An underlying presumption in the Court's decision appeared, however, to be that defendants were far more likely to be convicted and sentenced if their case was heard in the Anti-Corruption Court rather than the general courts and that this was unfair. As for the second ground, the Court read into the Constitution a requirement that new judicial bodies be established by their own separate statute. The mere fact that the Anti-Corruption Court was established in the Anti-Corruption Commission (KPK) Law was, it held, enough to fall foul of this requirement.

Despite holding that the Anti-Corruption Court had been established unconstitutionally, the Court recognized the seriousness of Indonesia's corruption problem and decided not to disband the Anti-Corruption Court with immediate effect. Rather, it gave the DPR three years to enact a new specific-purpose Law to re-establish the Anti-Corruption Court. The DPR met this deadline in late 2009, at a time when the KPK was cutting a swathe through legislators, with DPR members facing serious corruption charges. It is therefore perhaps unsurprising that the statute the DPR enacted (Law no. 46/2009) may, in any case, render the KPK and the Anti-Corruption Court largely impotent. This is because the new Law appears to bring the ordinary general courts and prosecutors (and thus the problems described above that are so

45 Constitutional Court Decision no. 012-016-019/PUU-IV/2006.

46 Law no. 30/2002 on the Corruption Eradication Commission.

closely associated with them) back to the fore in corruption cases. It does this in two ways. First, the Law removes the requirement that ad hoc judges constitute a majority on judicial panels in the Anti-Corruption Court. This means that future decisions over which career and ad hoc judges split could now result in acquittals rather than convictions, given that historically career judges have been more favourable to the accused in corruption cases than have ad hoc judges. Second, the statue does not mention the KPK at all, referring instead only to general prosecutors. This has raised concerns that the statute may, in fact, have implicitly removed the KPK's prosecution function entirely.

Conclusion: A persistent mafia

Despite the existence of some special-purpose courts that enjoy relatively good reputations for integrity, judicial corruption (internal illegality) in Indonesia probably remains as strong as ever in the general courts, where it may even have increased. Certainly, the judiciary as an institution has so far been effective in resisting almost every effort to impose tighter scrutiny on it, and has been able to obstruct enhanced detection of illegality within the courts. Against this, however, although it continues to be extraordinarily difficult to convict senior members of the security forces, the judiciary's role under the New Order as source of validation for state (external) illegality at the behest of the elite has diminished significantly since the end of the New Order. This has occurred largely as a result of the reduction of direct government interference in the administration of the courts through the introduction of the 'one roof' system and the removal of some of the Court's control over corruption cases.

We would also argue, however, that pressure for change in the courts has been brought to bear by the freeing up of the media in the post-Suharto era and the parallel growth of assertive and capable civil society organizations, both of which continue to see monitoring of state institutions and public 'shaming' as legitimate levers for reform and have deliberately targeted the courts to this end.

In any case, despite some signs of shift away from the high-water mark of judicial illegality that marked the 1990s, the magnitude of the challenge facing proponents of judicial reform in Indonesia remains almost overwhelming. The reformers must somehow force the institutional development of a hitherto neglected and aggressively resistant institution, the Supreme Court and the general courts below it, at the same time as driving a massive cross-sectoral law reform agenda, most of which will ultimately end up before one or another of those same courts. To make matters worse, the advocates of reform must continue doing all this at a time of sweeping political transition, in the context of a developing and shaky economy facing a global economic crisis, with all the long-standing geographic, political and demographic complexities that have challenged every Indonesian government since independence in 1945.

It is therefore little wonder that the perceptions of Indonesia's judiciary as little more than a 'mafia' with which this chapter began are still widespread. It will likely be some time before they will change substantially.

Illegality and insecurity

GERBEN NOOTEBOOM

Out of wedlock

Migrant–police partnerships in East Kalimantan

In 2002, two Dutch inspection officers working on a joint Indonesian–Dutch operation against illegal trading in endangered species travelled to a large provincial capital in Indonesia. Shortly after arriving, they discovered that a brand new camera had been stolen from their luggage at the airport. In a meeting with the city police chief (*kapolres*), the Dutch officer complained about the incident. He said he had just bought the camera in Singapore for about €1,000. 'Hold on', said the police chief. 'Let's see what we can do.' The next morning, when the team met again, the camera lay undamaged on the chief's desk. 'It has been returned', the *kapolres* announced triumphantly. 'We know how to access their networks.'[1]

This incident illustrates how close the ties can be between police and criminal organizations in Indonesia. The police often know the thieves and pickpockets who are active in their district and can pinpoint the areas in which they operate. Sometimes they even know the pickpockets personally. To some extent, the police treat criminal practices as acceptable or legitimate. As one police officer put it, criminals are allowed to operate 'as long as they do not bother the people too much and do not target government officials, military officials and officers and their families'.[2] According to researchers at two Yogyakarta universities, pickpocketing gangs in most Javanese towns use the 'cupboard' method.[3] They store the wallets or mobile phones they steal in a special cupboard. If, after four days, no police officer, soldier or high-ranking official has claimed any of the stolen items, the cupboard is opened and the items are sold.

Other ties between the police and the underworld are more serious. Researchers and journalists have found evidence of direct involvement of police officers in criminal activities or even killings (Colombijn and

1 Personal communication with AIVD (Dutch General Intelligence and Security Service) officer, 2003 and 2008.

2 Personal communication with local police officer (polsek) in Samarinda, 2004.

3 Personal communication with Pujo Semedi (Gadjah Mada University, December 2005) and Argo Twikromo (Atma Jaya University, August 2008).

Lindblad 2002:19-20). Today, most reported cases of police illegality involve graft (Montlake 2008; Shari and Einhorn 1998), illegal logging (Casson and Obidzinski 2002), and fraud. Some of these stories are well-documented and are reported in the media. Some are exposed in corruption cases in the courtroom. Others stay hidden or remain the subject of rumours, such as the alleged police involvement in the 'mysterious shootings' (*penembakan misterius* or *petrus*) of the early 1980s (Schulte Nordholt 1991; Van der Kroef 1985).

However fragmentary the evidence from around Indonesia may be, it does suggest that police involvement in certain kinds of illegality is common enough to be considered systematic. Significant research into this phenomenon has been possible only in the last decade, since the separation of the police force from the armed forces in 1999. Previously, the police force had always been part of the military and the army had political clout. When the police became independent, they were made responsible for daily security tasks at the local level. This sparked a growing interest in their doings in scholarly journals and in reports from advocacy groups (for example, Amnesty International 2009). From what research has been done, it would appear that the police practices described in this chapter are commonplace in many parts of Indonesia. In the following chapter of this volume, for example, Ian Wilson explains the interaction between police officers and 'protection racketeers' in Jakarta. A report by the International Crisis Group illustrates how politicians and police officers in Bali and Lombok use local militias to levy taxes and keep immigrants off the islands (ICG 2003). The international NGO Global Witness (*Paying for protection* 2005) has revealed how Freeport pays government security forces to guard its massive copper and gold mine in Papua. Writing for the *The Jakarta Post*, Apriadi Gunawan provides a detailed account of forced prostitution in the Walet Complex in Bagan Batu, Riau, where the guards are local police officers. On behalf of bar owners, the police provide sex workers with written permission to ply their trade. The same article mentions other brothels in Jakarta and Surabaya where similar practices take place (Gunawan 2006). These are just a few of the many known examples of police involvement in illegal activity.

Such stories raise several questions: How are relationships between the Indonesian police and criminal actors structured? In which types of illegality do these relationships tend to occur? How are the activities legitimized? And how do these relationships affect both the actors involved and the functioning of the state?

These are complex questions. They are difficult to answer as well, for more reasons than one. Not only is police involvement in illegality typically veiled in secrecy, it also tends to be organized at a local level. The aim of this chapter is to provide some insight into the intricacies of state involvement in illegality in Indonesia. This will be achieved by presenting a local case study that lays bare hidden practices of police officers and entrepreneurs in East Kalimantan. It may well be that these practices are not restricted to East Kalimantan, but reflect general patterns of illegality in Indonesia as a whole.

This chapter focuses on Madurese migrant entrepreneurs in East Kalimantan and the relationships some of them have with police officers. The analysis presented here is based on the assumption that understanding local circumstances is the key to grasping the relationships between state and illegality in Indonesia. Hence, this chapter does not deal with the Indonesian police in general terms, but focuses instead on the relationship between poor people and the police in a local setting. It provides a view of state and illegality from the bottom up, by offering an account from the perspective of ordinary people's lives. In so doing, this chapter shows how essential illegality often is to poorer people's lives. Without illegality, life would be considerably more difficult for migrants.

This research is based on field work I conducted in East Kalimantan from August 2003 to March 2004, with follow-up visits in 2005, 2007 and 2008. This is a continuation of earlier work on social security, livelihood and risk-taking among Madurese in East Java.[4] In East Kalimantan, I had originally set out to study Madurese migrants and entrepreneurs and the strategies they employed to make a living under the threat of ethnic violence. Before long, however, I expanded my research focus to include illegal activities and the relationships between migrants and police. I realized that I could only understand the successes, failures, and security problems of Madurese migrant entrepreneurs in East Kalimantan if I had a clear picture of their involvement in underworld activities. As we shall see, my investigations led me to the conclusion that migrants benefit from illegal activities and from their relationships with the police, while police in the East Kalimantan capital of Samarinda have to permit a degree of criminality in order to keep crime under control.

Risky business

Becoming an entrepreneur is a risky business, especially for poorly educated immigrants of an ethnic group unpopular in the recipient society. Migrant entrepreneurs face numerous obstacles, including a lack of cash or credit, limited access to local information and support networks, and a general ignorance of – and exclusion from – local bureaucratic procedures. They may face discrimination and even threats of ethnic violence. Low-skilled migrants often find themselves excluded from the better paid jobs because these are distributed

4 Nooteboom 2003. Many villagers from this area migrate to East Kalimantan. Chapter 7 of my dissertation describes illegal activities organized by local government officials (village heads), police, army officers, criminals, and gamblers in East Java (Nooteboom 2003:231-4).

among more established groups. Immigrants are left with few options, aside from doing menial labour, taking up a trade, or going into business.

The disadvantage of being from an ethnic minority group is compensated somewhat by a relative advantage. The minority group's isolation from local society and its governing norms makes it easier for the group's members to engage in profitable, but illicit activities. Hans Dieter Evers (1990:11) describes the traders' dilemma,

> [...] of either being integrated into the moral economy of the host society, and consequently subjugated to the pressure of solidarity and sharing, or, on the other hand, of separating from the host society, facing discrimination but also being able to claim debts, to accumulate capital and to conduct business and trade successfully.

Elsewhere, Evers emphasizes how traders tend to minimize risk and maximize trust in inter-ethnic relationships by engaging in many kinds of trading and other relationships (Evers and Schrader 1994; Evers and Mehmet 1994:1). Such considerations may explain why large parts of many immigrant minority groups the world over are entrepreneurs (Raillon 1994) and why they often are successful, especially in the informal sector. The success of immigrant entrepreneurs seems to be the result of a combination of factors: their will (and need) to succeed, their strategic use of ethnic trading networks and inter-ethnic trust, their lack of assimilation, and their willingness to carry out any tasks – no matter how dirty, difficult or unacceptable to others in local society. The last of these factors explains why immigrant entrepreneurs are regularly reported to be involved in illegality.

This general impression also seems to apply to Madurese entrepreneurs in East Kalimantan. In Samarinda, the provincial capital, about 15% of Madurese migrants own a business or trade. Most of their businesses are small, but they provide jobs to about three-fourths of the estimated 15,000-20,000 Madurese in the city. Some of the migrants who arrived before the 1990s are now well-off and own land, houses, cars, transport businesses, recycling firms, construction companies, gambling dens and brothels. They earned their fortunes in the late 1980s and 1990s when the local economy experienced a logging and mining boom. A number of their businesses seem to occupy a grey area, combining perfectly legal trade with activities such as theft, fraud, illegal logging or land occupation, brothels and gambling dens. Many individual Madurese also work as security guards and assistants for ethnic Chinese businessmen who organize large-scale gambling operations at malls, discotheques and bars. However, widespread violence against Madurese in other parts of Kalimantan from 1997 to 2001 damaged the image and the self-confidence of Madurese migrants, making them less attractive as guards for others.[5] Some Madurese who formerly worked as security guards have started their own businesses; others have retreated into less risky business.

When considered against the backdrop of all illegal economic activity in Samarinda, the Madurese are small players. Very few of them were involved in the massive illegal logging operations of the late 1990s and early 2000s, for instance. Nor did they play a major role in recent cases of corruption linked to government projects, timber and plantation concessions, or the embezzlement of mining royalties.[6] Although people in Samarinda often brand the Madurese as a criminality-prone group, they are in fact no more involved in illegal activities than other ethnic groups such as the Buginese, Banjarese, Javanese, Torajanese, and Butonese.

According to one local, middle-ranking police officer, the Banjarese and Buginese are currently the most criminally active ethnic groups in Samarinda. Buginese gangs are dominant in protection rackets, the lucrative harbour and market areas, and large-scale illegal trading of all kinds, while Banjarese gangs tend to engage in petty crime such as burglary and pickpocketing. It appears the police look the other way, as long as the crimes committed remain petty and mobs punish some of the perpetrators themselves by public lynching.[7] In general, the Indonesian population tends not to trust the police and 'people feel that lynching makes the streets safer' (Colombijn 2002:302).

The relationships between small entrepreneurs, illegal activities and the police in Indonesia are the subject of a great deal of speculation but very little actual research. For my own study, I closely followed several East Madurese entrepreneurs and analysed their involvement in both legal and illegal activities. There are several types of illegal activity which the police accept and even benefit from. This does not apply to all crimes, however. There are categories of criminality which the police attempt to stamp out. Among Madurese themselves, there are different views on what is acceptable behaviour. Moreover, it appears that police officers often collaborate with the Madurese or even help them carry out some illegal activities. Before discussing these situations in detail, I will first elaborate on the research methodology I used and then sketch the background and structure of Madurese migration and entrepreneurship in East Kalimantan.

5 For analysis of anti-Madurese violence elsewhere in Kalimantan see Schiller and Garang 2002; Davidson and Kammen 2002; Peluso 2006; Peluso and Harwell 2001; Van Klinken 2002. I have discussed the loss of self-esteem and its impact elsewhere: De Jonge and Nooteboom 2006; Nooteboom 2005.

6 For illegal logging in East Kalimantan, see Casson and Obidzinski 2002.

7 In his discussion of public lynching across the country, Freek Colombijn (2002) describes several mob lynchings which occur while the police stand idly by. He concludes: 'The response of the police to mob justice is in general half-hearted [...] After the fact, however, the police accept the lynching as it is. They never try to investigate the matter' (Colombijn 2002:319). See also Welsh 2008.

Researching illegality

For obvious reasons, studying relationships between police and migrants in the context of illegality is not easy. By nature, illegality concerns covert activities, sensitive topics, uneasy relationships, distrust, and a shared interest in secrecy for all actors involved. Migrant groups and police networks are both difficult to gain access to. Information and locations are often blocked by gatekeepers – these may be gang leaders or even police officers – who tend to prohibit activities, deny access, or frustrate interviews and observations. Outsiders, including researchers, represent a potential threat. Silence is essential to the continuation of illegal activities.

Information on illegal activities is not limited to leaders though. Often there are many people who are aware of such activities and who possess crucial information about them. This is because the activities usually depend on social networks and may involve huge numbers of actors. These actors seldom know all the facts, but they are able to reveal part of the illegal practices they are involved in. There are anthropological research methods suitable for approaching such people, gaining access to their networks and gathering insights without directly mentioning illegality as a research theme.

The study of illegality in daily life requires an unobtrusive and indirect approach. I used a bottom-up method in which I gathered information about various economic activities by Madurese migrants in East Kalimantan, embedding it in a larger study on livelihood and social security styles.[8] By studying the migrants' livelihood activities, insecurities, and social networks, it proved feasible also to study their illegal activities and their relationships with police officers. This method provided access to the perspective of the Madurese migrants themselves, rather than that of police officers. In order to conduct this research, I had to develop close contacts with ordinary Madurese workers, migrants and entrepreneurs. Many were willing to tell me about their livelihood activities – including the less legal ones – and to show me around behind the scenes at markets, wedding ceremonies and bars, or take me to cockfights, illegal brothels, and gambling dens.

I studied Madurese settlers in three clearly demarcated clusters of economic activity: brick making, stone cutting, and vegetable growing. The first two sectors are dominated by Madurese from Bangkalan (West Madura) and Sampang (Central Madura) respectively. Most brick makers work on the outskirts of the city of Samarinda, while stone cutters can be found in the hills of Batu Putih and Batu Besaung, west and north of the city. In the vegetable growing area of Lempake, to the northeast of Samarinda, Madurese-speaking migrants from Malang (East Java) dominate.

8 For the wider study see Nooteboom 2008.

Within these clusters of economic activity, which were relatively homogeneous with respect to place, descent, social class, and ethnic identity, I observed a wide variety of ways in which people tried to make a living, interpreted ethnic violence, maintained contacts with other ethnic groups, and strove for business success and social advancement. My research comprised three phases with a progressively narrowing scope. In the first phase, I mapped out the various economic activities, locations and backgrounds of Madurese migrants. To conclude this phase, I selected three sectors dominated by Madurese. In the second phase, I conducted semi-structured interviews with questions on livelihood constitution, livelihood patterns, incomes, remittances, social security, perceptions of crisis and violence, relationships with state officials (including police officers) and inter-ethnic relationships. In the last phase, I revisited a dozen families on a weekly basis to conduct lengthy interviews and construct life histories; I again revisited some of these families in 2005, 2007 and 2008.

During the second phase, I became interested in the illegal activities people were involved in. I made further inquiries among brick makers and workers in the quarries and brothels and carried out participant observation of cockfights, gambling, and brick making activities. Although it was nearly impossible to interview police officers, officials from the State Intelligence Agency (Badan Intelijen Negara, BIN), or politicians, I managed to conduct a few informal interviews with such people without revealing the purpose of this study. It is mainly for this reason that this chapter adopts a bottom-up perspective on state and illegality, looking at interactions through the eyes of Madurese migrants.

The Madurese in Samarinda

Most Madurese in Samarinda are still economically unsuccessful and have not escaped poverty. They are poorly educated though famous for being hard workers. As a result, they are in demand in sectors where hard physical labour is required, such as transport and construction. Many porters at the harbour and the markets are Madurese, as are many road workers, builders, garbage collectors, stone cutters, and brick makers. Others work as security guards, carpenters, owners of repair shops and hairdressers. The banana trade and *sate* sector are dominated by Madurese, as well as most of the canteens at the main university campus. In general, Madurese migrants occupy the lower strata of East Kalimantan society.

It is widely claimed that Madurese migrants in Kalimantan tend to spatially isolate themselves from other groups (Peluso and Harwell 2001:103). In this, however, they do not differ from other ethnic groups who also prefer to live close together. In East Kalimantan, Madurese tend to settle in close proximity to each other, often in relation to their occupation or village of origin. In Samarinda, they live in old districts close to the harbour and the city markets. Clusters of brick makers from rural Bangkalan can be found on the outskirts of the city on otherwise unused lands. Temporary labourers who work in road construction and on building sites mostly originate from eastern Java and Sampang in Madura; they tend to live in barracks or deserted houses scattered throughout the city. Migrants who stay for long periods are more likely to live in mixed communities and interact with other ethnic groups such as the Javanese, Banjarese, Kutai Malay and Butonese. However, relationships between Madurese and Buginese, the second largest ethnic group in East Kalimantan, have long been tense. Traditionally, contacts with the indigenous Dayak are relatively cordial, although they became tense following violent attacks on Madurese by Dayak in West and Central Kalimantan.

During the colonial era, most Madurese in this province were employed as unskilled labourers on plantations and in the mining and oil industries around Balikpapan.[9] This situation remained basically unchanged until the late 1970s. From that time onwards, migrants have mainly been engaged in road construction, recycling (scrap metal and tires), small trade, brick making, logging, and the building and transportation sectors. Some have become very successful, acquiring heavy machinery and large trucks. A small number have also become involved in illegal activities.

Madurese in Samarinda live simply, save money to invest, marry young, and help each other. They also provide accommodation to newcomers – many of whom are relatives or people from their villages of origin – and help them to find jobs. They tend not to seek an education; the few Madurese in East Kalimantan who have graduated from university have difficulty finding suitable jobs. As a result, there are almost no Madurese in the government bureaucracy or higher ranks of the police in East Kalimantan. According to Hendro (2001:72), 'the majority can neither read nor write', with illiteracy rates of 40% to 50% for male workers and even higher percentages for women. Madurese parents often keep their children home from school and expect them to help the family make a living. Religious knowledge, though, is highly valued. In East Kalimantan, several Madurese *pesantren*, religious boarding schools, have been founded. Well-to-do Madurese often send their children to *pesantren* in Madura and Eastern Java. Some have made hajj.

The Madurese in East Kalimantan are not a homogenous group. They make a distinction between Madurese from Bangkalan, Sampang, Pamekasan and Sumenep. These groups speak different dialects, follow different re-

9 During the Japanese occupation an unknown number of forced labourers (*romusha*) were recruited from Madura to work on plantations and infrastructural projects in Kalimantan.

ligious leaders (*kiai*) and emphasize different cultural traits. For instance, Sumenep Madurese are said to be more refined than those from Pamakasan, whereas those from Sampang are generally perceived by others and themselves as being the least refined of all, as unreliable troublemakers.

According to many Dayak, Malay, Buginese and Banjarese sources, the Madurese have done little to adapt to their new social environment. Instead of accommodating other groups, they are said to look down on others. Their behaviour is routinely described as arrogant, short-tempered, boorishly masculine, rude, uncivilized, unfair, avaricious and vengeful. These are all characterizations and stereotypes that have been applied to the Madurese since colonial times. In times of crisis, such prejudices are infused with additional meaning because they are sometimes used to justify violence against the Madurese (De Jonge 1995). Many Madurese who were born in Kalimantan blame this negative image on newcomers, who they claim do not know how to behave, and on thugs (*preman*) who belong to criminal gangs involved in illegal logging, running brothels and gambling dens, and smuggling consumer goods. According to these more established Madurese, the newcomers cast a shadow over the whole Madurese community.

Relationships with police officers

Whenever a theft takes place in Samarinda, local Madurese are the usual suspects. This is just one effect of negative stereotyping. The negative image also makes it hard for Madurese to establish new businesses or to expand existing ones. However, their lowly status as a migrant underclass also puts them at an advantage in the sense that they have more room to manoeuvre in illegal sectors of the economy. To protect their position, many Madurese entrepreneurs maintain regular contacts with police officers, who protect their businesses and informally facilitate illegal activities.

For the police, such arrangements with marginalized Madurese entrepreneurs are also beneficial because this is how the police gain access to lucrative illegal activities. Moreover, the entrepreneurs are willing to do the 'dirty' jobs which the police cannot do themselves. Examples include running semi-legal stone quarries and excavations of clay for the brick industry, running brothels, organizing cockfights and other forms of gambling, running protection rackets, and even engaging in petty crime such as pickpocketing, organizing pyramid schemes, and stealing. For each activity, the participants need to pay regular premiums to the police officers who routinely visit them. These premiums can vary widely: 5-20% of the earnings for unlicensed brick, stone and transport businesses, over 50% for most illegal and criminal activities such as running brothels or organizing large-scale gambling. According to some

Madurese informants, police officers tend to keep quiet about their involvement in smaller-scale activities. They usually do not tell their colleagues for fear of putting their own profits in jeopardy.

Moreover, their position as members of a feared and reviled minority group makes Madurese ideal candidates to be hired by security personnel for dirty work involving intimidation and competition between political rivals or interest groups. Active involvement by Madurese in intimidation of business or political groups has declined in recent years. Many Madurese *preman* used to be involved in such activity in the 1980s and 1990s. However, the widespread violence against Madurese in West and Central Kalimantan that began in 1997 made them more politically vulnerable in East Kalimantan and diminished their role as henchmen, in gang conflicts and in protection rackets. Many Madurese are, however, still employed as security guards in gambling dens, bars, discotheques, and brothels. Good relationships with the police are essential to maintaining these positions; if relations with the police are poor, the Madurese are the first to be punished.

By not engaging directly in illegal activities, the police remain free of direct responsibility while enjoying the profits. The ordinary police officers who collect the proceeds from petty crime in turn pay part of these proceeds as tribute to their superiors within the police apparatus. The Madurese who engage in these mutually beneficial relationships with the police end up, by visibly participating in illegality, reinforcing the negative public image of the Madurese as a group.

Communal norms

Within their own community, the Madurese are relatively intolerant of illegal activity. On the contrary; most Madurese take pride in their community and are religiously orthodox. They clearly distinguish between licit and illicit behaviour in business. Drinking, prostitution, and gambling are considered unacceptable, for instance. Involving Madurese women in prostitution, no matter how bad their reputation may be, is perceived as shameful to the whole community and is severely punished.[10]

Crimes such as stealing and cheating customers (by not repaying debts or by supplying a lower quantity or quality of goods than paid for, for example) are considered less serious, as long as the aggrieved party is not Madurese

10 Remarkably, Madurese-speaking prostitutes from the island of Java, especially from the areas of Pasuruan, Lumayang, Besuki, Bondowoso, Jember and Sitobondo, are permitted to work in Madurese-run brothels in East Kalimantan. They are generally considered to be outsiders by members of the local Madurese community who come from the island of Madura. A quick survey among brothel owners indicates that these Madurese-speaking women from East Java comprise the largest ethnic group among prostitutes in Samarinda.

and nobody gets hurt. Many Madurese men retell stories of their own feats of cheating and stealing over and over again; this enhances their status as 'daredevils' and demonstrates strength and cleverness. Nevertheless, no matter how much money is earned from such activities, the profit is generally perceived as unclean or forbidden (*haram*) and cannot be used for religious purposes such as paying Islamic tax (*zakat*), donating funds for the building of mosques, or – according to some purists – spending on household needs. Many Madurese say such profits are hot money (*uang panas*), in other words: easy come, easy go. Some women told me they would not knowingly accept *haram* money from their husbands, even if they badly needed it for food and other basic needs. As a result, men often spend the money on clothes, food, or presents, and give their wives these goods rather than money.

At Idul Fitri, the festivities that follow Ramadan, I witnessed the youngest son of Hajji Yusuf visiting his father's home.[11] Members of the family had avoided talking about this son in most of my conversations with them, as he was a habitual gambler and working as a game organizer and security guard for a Chinese businessman in Balikpapan. I never got a complete picture of his activities because his father and brothers did not want to talk about him. During his visit, he offered his father some sorely-needed Rp 50,000 notes. But his father refused the money and ignored his son completely, which I thought was quite embarrassing for the son. Hajji Yusuf later told me he had not wanted to accept money that was probably earned through *haram* activities. Later still, when I was getting ready to leave, Yusuf's wife proudly showed me the money her son had given her. She had accepted it with gratitude. Hajji Yusuf will probably never know how his wife paid for food that month.

Illegality appears first and foremost to be men's business, but women often condone their husbands' activities and create a conducive environment. Wives are often prominent in money laundering, in sending profits to and investing in Madura, in managing the girls in the brothels, or in establishing legitimate businesses as a cover for illegality. They often remain silent when their husbands lose large sums of money gambling or from fines for illegal activities without police protection. The wives of men involved in illegality often secretly save gold or cash for difficult times, act as moneylenders to other Madurese, or invest in legitimate businesses such as local shops, trades, food stalls (*warung*), or trucks. Some of these wives buy cattle, land or houses in Madura. At the same time, women often try to coax their husbands away from criminal activities and sometimes play a crucial role in persuading them to go straight.

After achieving success illegally in their younger years, many men reach a turning point when they become older, typically in their mid-thirties or early

11 Hajji Yusuf is a close friend of Hajji Romli, who is introduced later in this chapter. Hajji Yusuf worked for Hajji Romli before they travelled to Mecca.

forties. They come to see the dirty and dangerous work they are involved in as emotionally exhausting or unsustainable. Gradually, or sometimes abruptly, men abandon their criminal activities and invest their money in legitimate business activities. This change often goes hand in hand with a turn towards religiousness, which is usually seen as a kind of repentance and is sometimes sealed by a pilgrimage to Mecca. Such a transformation is usually celebrated by Madurese friends and relatives, who do not view this as a sign of weakness or decline but as a move towards a better life. In a way, leading a 'life of sin' in youth is almost a precondition for becoming a real man and a genuine Muslim later. Most entrepreneurs pay a high price for their conversion, however. Their legitimate enterprises quickly lose customers and resources, and household income drops accordingly. A certain degree of illegality facilitates economic success. Therefore, good relations with the police are essential even to those who run a simple business.

Three life stories

For the remainder of this chapter, I will illustrate the structure of relationships between Madurese entrepreneurs and police based on three examples. I will discuss them in ascending order of intimacy with the police and with illegality. The three Madurese who I will refer to by the pseudonyms Sudi, Romli, and Tamim are all self-made men. We begin with 'Sudi', a brick maker who has no proper deed for the land he uses. He receives protection from a police officer in return for bricks or money. His good relations with the police, although costly, ensure the survival of his enterprise. They spare Sudi time-consuming red tape and legitimize his excavation of fertile topsoil. Moreover, his connections with the police protect him from competing land claims and hostility from his neighbours.

My next example is 'Romli', a trader and transporter of building materials who formerly made a living from smuggling, theft and extortion. After ceasing these activities under police pressure, Romli fell on hard times. With the help of his wife and brother-in-law, he succeeded in transforming himself from a feared gang leader into a respected community leader. Due to his close contacts with the police, he is often able to negotiate on behalf of Madurese who have been jailed for petty crimes. He can get their fines reduced or even secure their release from police custody. In return, Romli has to act as a police informant in cases of murder or ethnic violence.

My final example is 'Tagil', who offers us a glimpse into the double life led by many criminals in Indonesia. He is a gambling boss and pimp who runs his own illegal activities, but is also an instrument in the hands of the police force.

Seeking protection: Sudi

I met Sudi several times in 2003 and 2004. I observed him at his brick kiln, situated on a back road to Bayur. Whether he was taking a break, overseeing his employees, or firing bricks himself, he was always prepared to talk to me at length. He openly shared his life story with me. Sudi arrived in East Kalimantan from Madura in the mid-1980s. Within five years he had become a successful organizer of cockfights and other betting events. He was feared for his aggressiveness and bad temper. Many people saw him as one of the most daring young Madurese 'madmen' roaming Samarinda in the mid-1990s. 'Everyone was afraid of me', he told me during one of our conversations. 'I could beat anyone. Be it in fighting, drinking or motorbike racing, I always wanted to win. There were times when I had loads of money, but sometimes I lost large amounts and did not come home for days. In the end, I had run up a debt of Rp 26 million.' In one of our interviews I ventured to ask his wife, who did not take part in our conversation but listened closely to our every word, whether she had been angry about his behaviour or tried to prevent him from gambling. 'Angry? What do you think? Of course I was angry at him. But, you know, it was better to remain silent with this man. I had two young children. If you get mad with hot-headed people like him, they get even meaner and rougher. It's better to be careful.' Sudi nods. 'That's what I was like. When I came home late at night and my wife didn't open the door fast enough, I would kick it in.'

After a violent fight with Buginese thugs, one of whom was reportedly severely wounded or killed, Sudi ended up in a police cell.[12] One of his maternal uncles in East Kalimantan, Saïd, knew the right people in the police force and managed to bribe him free on condition that Sudi would never again engage in crime. Saïd demanded that Sudi give up his life of drinking, gambling, and consorting with prostitutes, and offered him a job as foreman in his brick making enterprise. Saïd's close ties with the police protected Sudi from the revenge of the Buginese men. This marked the start of a new kind of life for Sudi.

Nine years later, Saïd sold some of his possessions in Kalimantan and made a pilgrimage to Mecca. When he returned, he went bankrupt, due to his own overspending and embezzlement by his business partner. This meant Sudi was out of a job. He started to gamble again. Over the course of a few months he lost millions of rupiah. In the hope of changing his luck, he borrowed money from a friend and bought a cheap brick kiln in Bayur. The kiln had previously belonged to a Madurese who had been accused of

12 Sudi did not tell me exactly what happened to these Buginese men, whom he called 'wounded thugs'. I got some information about them from others, but the accounts were second hand and sometimes ambiguous. Some said one or more Buginese thugs had been killed, while others said some had been severely wounded but none killed.

theft and killed by an angry mob. To obtain clay, Sudi rented land from villagers with the help of a policeman, a friend of his uncle Saïd's. The policeman paid a few of the villagers money and ordered them to cease hostilities against Madurese. Around the same time that Sudi was producing his first bricks, it became clear that there were several land claims on the plot where the kiln was located and where Sudi obtained his clay. Villagers from two neighbouring villages claimed the plot was their communal land and protested the commercial excavation of the soil. Moreover, they did not want any Madurese living nearby.

Sudi called on the help of the policeman. The policeman visited the area often and word of his friendship with Sudi spread fast. Regular sightings of him at Sudi's kiln discouraged villagers from protesting. According to Sudi, the policeman also talked to the village elders. His relations with the neighbours have settled down. 'I even visited their mosque and donated 4,000 bricks for its renovation. But I do not fully trust them. I need my friend the police officer. He also helped me when some Buginese men were hunting for me in an attempt to reclaim a gambling debt. My friend [the police officer] brought them some of my money and told them to go away. They never returned.'

The policeman's protection comes at a price, however. From the beginning of their cooperation, the officer asked to be paid 5% of all the bricks Sudi produced. In Sudi's first year, when bricks were expensive and his production was still low, the policeman took 17,000 bricks whose total value was nearly Rp 6 million. 'Rumour had it he was building a house for himself.' Later, when the price of bricks fell, the police officer wanted to be paid Rp 500,000 for every 100,000 bricks produced. Currently, Sudi has a large business. He produces some 250,000-300,000 bricks per year and employs eight to ten people. Yet the cooperation continues. When the bricks are fired, about five or six times a year, the policeman visits Sudi and asks for payment. 'I do not know where he lives, but if he comes, I give him Rp 100,000 or more if he keeps on asking. He's actually poor', Sudi explains. 'He has to give most of his money to his superiors.'

In the course of my study of Madurese livelihoods in East Kalimantan, I encountered several enterprises such as Sudi's. The entrepreneurs I met got access to land or even land titles thanks to their close ties with the police. Some of them received direct police protection during land conflicts, hostilities or problems with creditors. In seven cases out of the 118 in my sample, entrepreneurs told me explicitly, and without being prompted, about their relationships with the police, including information about the payments they made and the percentages taken. In another five cases, businesspeople informed me about similar relationships, but in less detail.[13] Two-thirds of these

13 I could not inquire directly about relationships with the police in interviews I conducted. In some cases I thought discussing these relationships would be deemed inappropriate, and in some of my earlier interviews I had not yet begun to focus on this topic.

twelve cases were brick making enterprises. Most of the others were remote quarries where stones are cut for road construction.

Most quarry labourers are from Sampang and prefer, for one reason or another, to work in these remote locations. Some of them have fled from ethnic violence in West and Central Kalimantan, while others are migrants with dubious legal status because they lack local identity permits (Kartu Tenaga Kerja, KTP). Some have problems such as unpaid debts, criminal charges or accusations of extra-marital relationships hanging over their heads. Many told me they were working in such a remote place because they had received threats of revenge murder (*carok*). The quarries are located in largely uninhabited, hilly areas some 5-20 kilometres from the city. In the quarries, individual police officers provide protection in return for a percentage of the earnings for all truckloads of stone delivered. They come to visit every week and sometimes bring basic supplies such as drinking water, salt, soap or rice. In the quarries, policemen are paid commissions of up to 15% of the value of the stone produced. In general, this is higher than the percentages paid at the brick kilns. I did not hear of the police receiving any more than 5% in the brick industry. Percentages at the quarries are probably higher because people there are more vulnerable and the money covers personal as well as business protection.

It is money well spent. In Sudi's case, the premiums have protected the enterprise against legal claims by neighbouring villagers and ended his troubles with old enemies. Unlike earlier situations in which he paid police officers who turned out to be unreliable or incapable of helping out, this relationship has yielded results. It has ensured continued access to resources and the sustainability of the family business. Five to 15% is a small price to pay for success, certainly for a migrant. But premiums depend on the kind of business, the level of illegality, and the tolerance of higher-ranking police officers. Sometimes the police want more control and make greater demands.

Conflicting loyalties: Romli

Hajji Romli lives on one of the main roads connecting Samarinda to the hinterland of East Kalimantan. His white *peci* hat and grey beard make it difficult to guess his age. He stares intently with his black eyes. He speaks quickly and asks direct questions. He and his wife run a successful distribution centre stocked with building materials such as sand, bricks, stone, cement, and timber. Since 2006, he has also operated as a subcontractor for basic construction work in large building projects. On these projects, Romli delivers the supplies and carries out the groundwork, lays the foundations and sometimes completes the construction of brick walls, sewage systems and roads. Other subcontractors take care of the wood, iron and roof work and other refined tasks. Romli also tenders as the main contractor for smaller projects, such as public buildings, small roads and drainage systems. The trade and contracting business are basically his, but his wife organizes the transportation. She owns four trucks and an excavator. Romli usually uses two of these trucks for construction orders. 'I only take large orders such as houses, blocks or shops, otherwise I do not make a profit. If the work is big, I send for more labourers from Java and use trucks that belong to fellow Madurese businesses.'

As my research progressed, I slowly realized how important Romli was as an informal leader in the Madurese community and a broker in relations with the police. He negotiates bribes when Madurese are arrested for petty crimes or taken into custody after traffic accidents. He supports Madurese who occupy land claimed by others, and he mediates in property conflicts. He was also involved in peace negotiations during ethnic tensions in 2005 and 2007.[14] In return for his loyalty to East Kalimantan's elites, he has been granted excavation concessions in the rocky hills of Batu Besaung and is allowed to bid for construction projects. Whenever ethnic tensions arise in Samarinda and surroundings, Romli is called upon by the town mayor, members of the East Kalimantan parliament, the chief of police or a military commander to persuade the Madurese to refrain from violence. He is regarded as influential among the Madurese and loyal to the interests of the ruling elites who set great store by stability.[15] During our conversations, fellow Madurese were continuously visiting his house to ask for advice, borrow money, or discuss matters of political interest. The nearly constant beeping and ringing of his several cell phones illustrated the extent of his social network.

In the 1970s and 1980s, Romli was one of Samarinda's most notorious gang leaders and gamblers. His wife saved part of the profits and at the end of the 1980s she bought a truck to rent out and to use for the transport of construction materials. In those years, Romli was involved in petty theft as well as swindles that involved receiving payment for goods that were never delivered and loans that were never paid back. He also organized betting fraud on a large scale. However, he is quick to point out that he 'did not steal from our friends and fellow Madurese'. He is also said to have been involved in several killings of Buginese rivals, but he always skirted this issue in our discussions. The rumours about him added to his reputation for toughness.

[14] The 2005 negotiations, which were initiated by East Kalimantan's security forces, are briefly described in De Jonge and Nooteboom 2006:470-1. At the end of 2005 tensions rose between Dayak and Madurese in Samarinda due to the stabbing of the son of a Dayak *adat* leader and the deaths of two Madurese. Romli was invited to the security meetings and was able to calm Madurese groups who were calling for revenge. This increased his political influence and improved his contacts with high-ranking security officials.

[15] See De Jonge and Nooteboom 2006 and Van Klinken 2002 for a description of these elite interests in East Kalimantan.

To this day, Madurese enjoy a great deal of respect from their community if they killed Buginese gang leaders in those years. 'In the 1980s, it was not safe in Samarinda', Hajji Romli recalls quietly. But, as he explains, he reached a turning point.

> I lived a bad life and almost daily we had fights at the market. I was clever enough never to be caught and I had many friends in the police who informed me when activities were getting too hot. On a certain day, a high-ranking police officer came to my house and asked me to stop stealing and to help them fight criminality. If I rejected [their offer], I would be the first Madurese to be taken to prison, they said. I could not do anything but obey. Moreover, deep inside of me, I already knew the things I was doing were wrong. I longed to live a better life.

At this point, Romli stepped down as a gang leader and stopped stealing.

> I also did not fight anymore, but rather tried to prevent my people from gambling. [...] I was regularly asked by police officers to 'convert' certain hotheads and criminals who were fighting and causing trouble at the market. I had to turn them into hardworking people which I did by offering them jobs. The police would allow me to continue to organize gambling, but they asked for a cut of the profit.

Only after Romli made a pilgrimage to Mecca did he stop gambling. As Hajji Yusuf told me, Hajji Romli had persuaded him to go to Mecca. 'He even paid part of my way', Yusuf said. 'But we could not quit our habits at first. During the long wait at the airport, we continued gambling for money. Only after our return from the holy land did we stop gambling for money. Now we use penalties.'

In the meantime, his wife had purchased a second truck. Thanks to increasing demand for construction materials, the business expanded and Romli offered jobs to several former members of his gang. Not everyone accepted his decision to go straight. Many of his former followers continued their criminal activities, while others joined different gangs or started businesses of their own. But, said Romli, 'the majority remained loyal to me and after some time, I was able to persuade them to start working for me.' Eventually, the police caught most of the notorious thieves from his group. 'I was a good leader and paid the bribes needed to get them out of prison.' He smiles self-confidently when he says 'this was a good investment. They are now my most loyal workers [...] And, I made some good friends on the police force, which is important.'

Living dangerously: Tagil

Tagil's activities are far more dangerous than either Sudi's or Romli's. Tagil is a notorious gambler and a known *preman*, gang leader, cockfight organizer, and operator of a large bar and brothel in Damanhuri, a prostitution compound on the outskirts of Samarinda. Every season, 30 to 40 women and girls work in this brothel. Most of them come from mainland East Java and 40% to 60% of them speak Madurese. But none of them originate from the island of Madura itself, Tagil says. 'We would never permit a Madurese woman to do this. It would cause us shame. She would be killed.'

On Saturdays and Sundays, Tagil organizes cockfights. During these fights, 200-300 people place bets. Most of the gamblers are Madurese and Buginese, but Chinese, Banjarese, Javanese, Dayak, and Butonese also take part. The stakes are high. Chinese and Buginese gamblers in particular place large bets, but Madurese are also known to get involved in this risky level of gambling. On days like Christmas and New Year's, the stakes per fight can soar to the tens of millions of rupiah. However, many spectators also bet smaller amounts ranging from Rp 50,000 to Rp 500,000 on the same fight. The winning better on each fight pays 10% to Tagil, who in turn pays half of that amount to policemen secretly present in the arena and to higher-ranking police officers. Tagil also takes a cut of the Rp 5,000 entrance fee each spectator has to pay, and from other gambling activities run at the same location, such as Cap Ceki, card and dice games. He also takes a percentage of the concession fees collected from the dozens of ordinary vendors there. The concessions range from Rp 10,000 a day for a single cigarette seller, to Rp 50,000 for a fully equipped food stall offering a range of food and beverages.

With such high stakes, tempers often flare during the cockfights. Things can get so tense that Tagil's gang sometimes needs to restore order. If they are unable to do so, the undercover policemen in the crowd intervene by shooting into the air, arresting people or even randomly shooting some of the fighters in the leg or knee. Tagil then provides payment and mediation to free the arrested gamblers. The fees charged by the police in such a case depend on the status of the person taken into custody and the severity of the offence. Usually they range from Rp 5 million to Rp 15 million. Tagil maintains close ties with the policemen who attend his cockfights. They regularly visit each other's homes, or go out for dinner or drinks. Police officers are said to visit his brothel as well.

On one of my visits, Tagil told me how in the early 1980s he was being sought by the police for the murder of a competing Buginese gang member.

> I fled to Madura, to a place where they would never be able to find me. After a few years, a distant relative of mine succeeded, after making large payments,

> to have my name expunged from the police archives. The police officer at that time urged me to never commit murder again and asked if I wanted to help search for criminals who had fled to Java. That's what I did and I still sometimes do. I have become quite good at it. Last year, we chased down a lad in Malang who had raped a girl here and run away to Java.

But Tagil's situation was not as secure as he made it sound. 'The police are asking for more and more money all the time', he complained in confidence later, in 2004. 'The work is dangerous and I cannot do business with the new chief commissioner. I would prefer to retire and move to Java. But I am obliged to keep in touch with them. It's like an arranged marriage.' He hoped to be able to save enough money for a quiet retirement. He told me he was no longer welcome in his home village in Madura. 'They don't want to take my money there anymore. It's *haram*, they say, unclean.'

A few months after this conversation, in early 2005, Tagil was sent to prison by the new police chief, who accused him of verbally abusing the governor of East Kalimantan. At a meeting with high-ranking officials, Tagil had argued against the closure of the Damanhuri compound during Ramadan and accused the governor of being inconsistent because some other compounds were allowed to remain open. The governor took offence. Other people subsequently told me that Tagil's business had in fact been on the decline for some time, as he had been unable to pay adequate protection money to the police. The new chief of police demanded more money than Tagil was able or willing to pay. Remarkably, the Damanhuri compound did not close during Ramadan that year and Tagil continued to run his racket from his prison cell.

Three months later, Tagil was freed after paying large sums of money. Some people say that his freedom was bought by his uncles, successful entrepreneurs with close ties to the governor. The uncles told me they had merely helped Tagil a bit to succeed in business. 'This is just a family obligation', they said. By 2006, Tagil had gone to work for his uncles in their new business. They had just acquired a badly managed coal concession and started to excavate in areas contested by other claimants, with the backing of influential police officers and politicians. In 2008, Tagil and his uncles actively supported candidates for the provincial elections. One uncle expressed an ambition to enter politics himself. The fact that their business is risky and legally dubious does not prevent them from becoming involved in politics. On the contrary: it makes political ties and protection all the more important.

Conclusion: Out of wedlock

Madurese migrant entrepreneurs in East Kalimantan have to overcome numerous obstacles in making their businesses profitable. Brick makers face difficulties acquiring land rights and cheap firewood, transportation entrepreneurs have to contend with a great deal of red tape in obtaining transportation licences, and workers in stone quarries need protection against exploitative middlemen and insecure contracts. Moreover, Madurese migrants are not exactly the most favoured ethnic group in East Kalimantan and sometimes face discrimination and deep-seated hostility. This is not always unjustified, as some Madurese migrants are, or have been, involved in illegal and illicit activities such as cockfights, gambling, theft, gang warfare, and prostitution rackets. Madurese entrepreneurs and *preman* involved in such illegal activities consider it crucial to maintain good relationships with police officers, generally low-ranking ones, to guarantee protection and the continuity of their operations. They maintain close ties with police officers by way of regular visits and payments of either irregular sums or fixed shares of the profit their business generates.

Obviously, the relationships with Madurese migrants also benefit the police. Aside from generating additional income, these relationships offer the police access to a closed migrant community and help them control that community.[16] In case of increased ethnic tension or an unacceptable rise in crime, the police call on their contacts with entrepreneurs, preman and ethnic leaders who depend on the police for business success. These same contacts can now be used to help control the Madurese community and fight criminality. These individuals can provide the police with information or utilize their own networks to try to restore calm or curb the activities of particular people. In extreme cases, they may even detain members of the community and hand them over to the police.

These examples show how the interdependence of Madurese entrepreneurs and police officers not only provides direct financial and legal benefits to those involved, but may also serve a higher goal of maintaining security and stability in society. Ironically, this social control is only made possible by allowing criminality and instability to exist at controlled levels.

In the cases of Sudi, Romli and Tagil, it is difficult to pinpoint the exact demarcation line between legality and illegality. There is no need to do so. And it is precisely this grey area which offers Madurese entrepreneurs and the police financial and political room for manoeuvre. The police give migrants protection and in return both sides get a share of the profits generated by illegal activities. At the same time, the police do not tolerate any and all forms of criminality.

[16] The strategy is similar to one used by the army's special forces (Kopassus), which frequently recruit criminals to use in counter insurgency campaigns (Liem Soei Liong 2002:202).

On the contrary, they use their ties with gang leaders to help fight crime. They control the underworld through a combination of taxation and repression. At the same time, they also receive a steady flow of income from illegal activities.

Bribes, commissions and profits from illegal activities lower the transaction costs for disadvantaged groups who have no access to formal, legal economic activity or who lack knowledge of how the legitimate economy works. Without the payments and commissions, it would probably be much more difficult for Madurese to sustain their economic activities. At the same time, the police are also dependent on the entrepreneurs. Police officers in Indonesia are still underpaid, while the people in their social surroundings (friends, family members, neighbours and so on) expect them to maintain a comfortable standard of living and to offer financial help when it is needed. Police officers also face demands for contributions from their superiors on the police force. In short, there is a successful and mutually beneficial 'marriage' between entrepreneurs and the police. The intimacy of the marriage makes it unlikely that there will be a victory anytime soon in Indonesia's repeatedly proclaimed war on corruption.

The marriage is not based on love, however. Just as some marriages involve a certain amount of discretion or even feigned ignorance, the relationship between the police and Madurese businesspeople and criminals in East Kalimantan is equally paradoxical. The police in Samarinda need to turn a blind eye to a certain level of criminality in order to keep criminality in check. By permitting some forms of 'petty' crime such as pickpocketing, stealing, cheating, gambling and prostitution – activities which are detested by the community, but which can be kept within bounds by mob lynchings and public justice – they get access to information about the worst aspects of organized crime (such as killings, gang fights, gang rapes, and car theft) and even ethnic violence. They do this by mingling with networks of criminal groups and engaging in some aspects of their activity.

This world of petty criminality, in East Kalimantan at least, involves collaboration between police and small entrepreneurs and the regular payment of small fees (5-15% of turnover). The payments ensure the smooth operation of a system based on personal contacts that is an alternative to a properly functioning Weberian taxation and policing system. In this alternate system, the state needs to be involved in illegality in order to control criminality. In Indonesia, state officials have been relatively successful at this. From a citizen's perspective, it is a fairly safe country. In most Indonesian cities, people live without constant fear of being robbed, killed, or raped. And when justice falls short, the police leave the mob enough space to take revenge. A 5 to 15% premium is a much lower price for security than the taxes most people pay in countries with far less corruption. Clearly, illegality is not destructive per se; it can also help to sustain order in society.

IAN WILSON

Reconfiguring rackets

Racket regimes, protection and the state in post-New Order Jakarta

> Over and over again, effective nongovernmental specialists in violence have made alliances with governments, become parts of governments, taken over existing governments, or become governments of their own. (Tilly 2003:38.)

In Indonesia the nongovernmental 'specialists in violence' described by Charles Tilly have been a ubiquitous and conspicuous figure throughout both recent and more distant history albeit in a variety of regional variations and manifestations. This chapter will focus upon one particular manifestation, the racketeer, and attempt to chart the shifting nature of protection rackets in post-New Order Jakarta. It will argue that, in the decade since the end of the New Order regime, rackets operating under a variety of guises have reorganized and consolidated themselves in ways that make it increasingly difficult to disentangle the 'legal' from the 'illegal'. Going beyond criminality, these new configurations of rackets have become a fundamental currency of relations through which street-level power is exercised. As perpetual opportunists, predatory interests have sought to adapt rackets to the particular sociopolitical conditions in which they are immersed. These articulate and correlate to some of the defining features of the post-New Order political landscape and are useful in helping to identify the ways in which repressive forms of social order have been produced and reproduced within the constraints of formal institutional democracy and a market-driven economy.

A protection racket is, according to Vadim Volkov (2000a:491), 'an institutionalized relationship whereby tribute is collected on behalf of a criminal group that, in exchange, claims to offer physical protection from other such groups' or, some other form of external threat. Implicit in the relationship is the threat of violence, either from the external threat from which protection is offered or from the protector directly, both often being one and the same. Whether the protectee considers the ostensive protector either 'legitimate' or a racketeer is largely determined by the extent to which the claim of protection against an external threat is considered real. What sets the racket apart from other forms of organized crime is the particular kind of commodity it deals in. Whereas organized crime seeks to monopolize particular spheres of illegal activity, for example prostitution or drug trafficking, racketeers are concerned with the production, supply and monopolization of one particular commodity: protection (Varese 2001:4). In this respect organized racketeers are similar to another agency dealing in protection, the state.

While making an analogy between the state and a protection racket is simplistic at best, it does pose a number of intriguing questions and, as Gambetta (1996:2) notes, makes us reflect on some disturbing aspects of the state. Tilly (1985:171) provocatively suggested that in so far as the threats against which the state claims to protect its citizens are either imaginary, exaggerated or the product of its own activities, the state itself operates in a manner not dissimilar to that of racketeers. In so far as the state can be defined in Weberian terms, as a monopolistic control over the use of organized coercive force and taxation, what does the existence of non-state providers of protection tell us about the extent of state power and its effective presence at the local level? If both racketeers and the state deal in the same commodity, protection, and have a shared interest in selling its desirability, then what forms has the relationship between them taken? What strategies have racketeers used to try and establish legitimacy, and at what point, if any, is this legitimacy considered a substantive challenge to state authority? In part, racketeers count on the inefficiency of the state in providing protection, imposing their own taxes within the state's 'turf' but without the constraints of at least nominal adherence to rules and laws. This would suggest that from the perspective of the state, non-state providers of protection would at the very least be considered 'criminal', if not dangerous rivals requiring elimination. However, in Indonesia the relationship has been far more complex, in part a product of the ambiguous nature of protection as both a genuine commodity and as a strategy of domination. This chapter will ask, what was the relationship between the state and non-state providers of protection during the New Order, and what can the more recent consolidation of both criminal and non-state rackets tell us about the nature of the post-New Order state?

Racket and regimes in a comparative perspective

The concern with the monopolization of resource extraction, the use of violent coercive force, secretive hierarchical modes of organization and hostility towards organized labour are all elements that criminal rackets and violent entrepreneurship share with authoritarian regimes and repressive modes of government. In a comparative perspective it is perhaps then unsurprising that organized rackets have with few exceptions aligned themselves with authoritarian governments. In post-WWII Sicily for example, the role of the mafia has been described by Hess (1986:128) as 'a reactionary force [...] employed to resist change, to maintain privilege and to suppress attempts to redefine property relations and rights'. Similarly in Japan the Yakuza has been linked with ultra-nationalists within the military (Kaplan and Dubro 2003). Latin America is also replete with examples of drug lords joining forces with military dictatorships to fight left-wing rebels and suppress pro-democracy movements (Koonings and Kruijt 2004). The globalization of markets and the decline in state power have done little to alter this tendency. Louise Shelley (1999:25) described the resulting growth of transnational organized crime as 'a new form of non-state based authoritarianism'.

The criminologist Schulte-Bockholt has sought to theorize this relationship between regimes, organized crime and non-state providers of protection (Schulte-Bockholt 2006). According to this theory, a strong centralized state will generally endeavour to eliminate or co-opt alternate sources of protection. However during a 'crisis of hegemony', when elites believe their interests to be under threat, such as during a period of rapid sociopolitical upheaval or democratic transition, they will often seek to form alliances with organized criminal gangs in order to suppress counter-hegemonic forces (Schulte-Bockholt 2006:26). In these circumstances the interests of state elites and violent entrepreneurs dovetail. Elites require the localized coercive power and revenue extraction of organized crime, while for the groups themselves alignment with elite interests can further integration within the central structures of domination. Rather than being purely profit-orientated non-ideological groupings, as organized crime is often portrayed, it regularly adopts the ideological preferences of political elites in order to facilitate integration within them. From the perspective of political elites, organized crime, gangs, militias and mafia are all potentially useful partners, particularly when their own interests are contested.

This results in what Schulte-Bockholt (2006:35) refers to as 'protection racket regimes' which are 'formed by state and/or non-state elites in order to preserve their domination through the violent exclusion of large groups in society that experience conditions of substantial social disparities'. In these racket regimes, coercion replaces hegemony as the primary means to maintain political and social control, and is used to extract wealth from society irrespective of the opposition it creates (Schulte-Bockholt 2006:27). In order to consolidate power, elites incorporate potentially disruptive sub-hegemonic groups such as gangs within their networks of economic advantage. In doing so the dominant class is expanded across conventional class lines, becoming a 'structure of rackets rooted in a specific mode of production' (Schulte-Bockholt 2006:27). The degree to which organized crime and gangs are integrated into elite structures is determined by the needs of elites, who can always use state power whenever the services of organized crime are considered a threat or simply no longer needed (Schulte-Bockholt 2006:36). Non-state entrepreneurs in violence are rarely allowed to share political power as equal partners. There are however exceptions such as post-Soviet Russia or Bulgaria, where organized crime has successfully integrated itself within state institutions to the extent that it is almost impossible to disentangle 'criminal' and 'state' interests (Volkov 2000b:709). In the case of Indonesia, the New Order regime managed a complex network of rackets and institutionalized patterns of state-sanctioned illegality. Its unravelling after 1998 has resulted in a proliferation of what could be described as 'mini-racket regimes', territorially based forms of repressive socioeconomic order in which local entrepreneurs in violence, to varying degrees, 'corner the market' in protection.

The New Order racket state

During the New Order the institutionalization of local gangs, a process which had begun in the 1950s, was further intensified. Many gangs were at the forefront of the anti-communist pogroms that brought General Suharto to power in 1965. They were co-opted by arms of state, most significantly the military, and allowed to operate their own localized rackets largely undisturbed on the condition that most of the proceeds made their way into formal government structures. As Barker states, *preman*, a colloquial term for a thug or gangster, became a 'necessary component in the maintenance of state power and the collection of taxes'.[1] Lindsey (2001:291) proposes that in the low-wage economy of the New Order, where access to wealth by the urban poor was so tightly restricted, racketeering was for some a rational livelihood strategy for gaining access to wealth through illegal rents. In this respect the New Order manufactured the conditions that resulted after its demise in the reproduction of its own predatory racketeering, albeit on a more localized scale.

For these layers of rackets to function, *preman* also needed to be amenable to performing 'regime maintenance chores', including terrorizing dissidents and others who held the potential to disrupt established power relationships, and paying lip service to state ideology. To this end, *preman* groups often took

1 Barker 1999b:122. *Preman* is originally derived from the Dutch word *vrijman*, meaning 'free man', and was used during the colonial period to describe those who were exempt from forced labour. During the 1950s up until the early 1980s *preman* was used to refer to a military officer or soldier wearing civilian clothes. It was not until the late 1980s that it started to take on its current meaning of a thug or gangster. For a detailed genealogy of the term, see Ryter 1998.

on the appearance of nationalist and youth associations devoted to state-designated goals, or affiliated with state-created ones.[2] They acted as sub-franchises of state power, adopting nationwide organizational structures that mirrored those of the state. Ryter (1998:66) has described their structures as a system of local strongmen or *jago* 'where local bosses would be formally subordinate to the higher level 'manager' of the branch or sub-district but expect to retain significant local autonomy over revenues'. While the state could not completely co-opt *preman,* it did create the conditions whereby a *preman*'s strength was ultimately dependent upon their networks of political patronage: a metaphorical 'leash' that could be pulled when necessary. Without this patronage they were vulnerable to state sanction, but also to the wrath of the communities upon which they preyed. Organizations provided a necessary 'cover'. This also allowed the state to divide economic spoils, whilst still appearing to at least partially fulfil some of the demands placed upon the modern state, such as providing the conditions for economic prosperity and at least mediating problems of poverty and distress among the larger population.

The possibility that the cultivation of criminal networks by political elites and the military could result in the development of rival power bases as much as it could bolster state power was managed by Suharto by encouraging rivalries and power struggles between groups. In this way he avoided the kind of warlordism and 'bossism' found in the Philippines and Thailand (Sidel 1999:153). It was a recurrent but unrealized fear of the New Order that *preman* could form broader structural networks similar to the Yakuza or Sicilian mafia, which could coalesce into a significant challenge to its monopolization of resource extraction. Whenever such networks appeared possible the state intervened dramatically and brutally to reassert its power. This happened during the so-called 'mysterious shootings' (*penembakan misterius* or *petrus*) of the early 1980s, when the New Order state summarily executed around 10,000 alleged thugs, petty criminals and recidivists (Van der Kroef 1985). Hence the *preman* gangs served a dual political purpose that reflected the 'double-edged' nature of protection, as described by Charles Tilly (1985:170):

> The word 'protection' sounds two contrasting tones. One is comforting, the other ominous. With one tone 'protection' calls up images of the shelter against danger provided by a powerful friend, a large insurance company, or a sturdy roof. With the other, it evokes the racket in which a local strong man forces merchants to pay tribute in order to avoid damage – damage the strong man himself threatens to deliver. The difference, to be sure, is a matter of degree. [...] Which image the word 'protection' brings to mind depends mainly upon our assessment of the reality and externality of the threat.

2 The most prominent of these groups during the New Order were the nationalist youth organization Pemuda Pancasila and Pemuda Panca Marga, a paramilitary type organization for the children of army veterans. For a detailed account of Pemuda Pancasila see Ryter 1998.

Informally these networks were an integral part of the mechanisms of power, while formally they could be invoked as a threat from which society needed to be protected. As long as groups remained relatively atomized or firmly under the reign of military loyal to Suharto they were left for the most part undisturbed. But the relationship implied an inherently unstable balancing act that brought with it the danger that the state could itself be revealed as criminal and 'criminalized'.

The New Order's 'crisis of hegemony' seemed to be unending. For most of its 32 years of rule, the crisis was manufactured deliberately, a quintessential racket. As Tim Lindsey has argued, in order to justify its extra-legal 'order' the regime invoked a protracted state of 'imminent crisis', initially from the threat of communism and later from gangsters and thugs before finally it became almost spectral, such as in so-called 'organizations without form' (Organisasi Tanpa Bentuk, or OTB) (Lindsey 2001:296). The result was that the state became in this sense 'an enterprise that operated on the same basis as criminals' (Lindsey 2001:289). The state was criminal also in functional terms, as it used the same methods of extortion, racketeering, violence and secrecy as the *preman* gangs that it employed. Via state-backed subterfuge, including the use of *preman* as agents provocateurs to discredit opposition movements, the New Order sought to give the impression that without strict controls society would descend into chaos. The New Order's racket system was multi-layered and the relationship between its component parts complex. By the late 1980s this state-gang relationship has often been categorized as one of *beking* or 'backing', described by Lindsey (2006:32) as a 'delicate mechanism' whereby *preman* gangs became part of the grassroots structure of state power. It was in practice a privatization or franchising of state power, which allowed the state to distance itself from excesses conducted on its behalf, whilst making use of gangs as a mode of social control and rent extraction. For the gangs themselves, such arrangements were ultimately pragmatic. They opened up the opportunity for economic advantage and political advancement, and reduced the risk of becoming a target of state pogroms.

Unravelling rackets

Now facing a real rather than a manufactured crisis of hegemony due to the unpredictability of political fortunes in the post-New Order environment, political elites have increasingly turned to *preman* groups and other violent entrepreneurs to defend their economic and political interests. This has been exacerbated by the morphing of struggles for social power into more diffuse forms, such as party politics. The New Order normalized patterns of state-sanctioned illegality which have continued into the present. But a crucial difference is that elites and state agents no longer possess the same coercive means they once did. Even military figures infamous for their patronage of particular gangs have conceded that in the current political environment they are not capable of controlling them as they did previously.[3] The unravelling of central state power together with the fracturing of social power and the rise of new social forces has created an open, dynamic and unstable market in violent entrepreneurship and its central commodity of protection. As a result, *preman* and other violent entrepreneurs have increasingly been able to negotiate on their own terms, transforming from sub-hegemonic groups, rent-a-thugs and middle-men to significant political and social actors in their own right. Elite patronage, while 'useful', is no longer a necessity for survival.[4] The relationship of inter-dependence has in this respect tilted in favour of the *preman*, a process of 'inverse racketeering' whereby political elites have increasingly become clients rather than providers of protection.

By the same token however, the very nature of what is now a highly competitive unregulated market has meant that groups have been forced to take various measures to seek a competitive advantage. This has taken two general directions. The first has been the development of 'legitimations' for rackets. 'Protection' as an imposed form of exchange continues to exist in criminal rackets, informal security groups and localized territorial monopolies over violence, but has also surfaced on a variety of new 'frontiers of legitimacy' that reflect the decentralized environment, the emergence of identity politics and opening of markets. It is found in the exclusivist rights claims of ethnic groups and local communities, political constituencies and alliances in the context of electoral politics and regional autonomy, turf wars between state agencies and political parties and 'morality rackets' in the form of religious and 'law and order' vigilantism.

The other has been a product of the demands of the market for 'security' in lieu of an adequate degree of provision by the state. Gambetta (1996:3) has argued in his study of the Sicilian mafia that consumers of private protection do not necessarily consider themselves to be better off if protection is supplied by the 'legitimate' state. The corruption and inefficiency of the police is one of many factors making non-state sources of protection appear an effective and economic option. As one Jakarta saying goes, 'you lose a chicken and report it to the police, you end up losing a goat'. The economist Frederic Lane (1979:2) has proposed that on the 'frontiers of the state', where no one possesses an enduring monopoly over protection, merchants and other consumers of protection would avoid over-priced providers when they could obtain protection more cheaply elsewhere. When the state is ineffective or inefficient in sup-

3 Confidential interview with former TNI general, Jakarta, August 2006.

4 Interview with Jakarta gang leader, Jakarta, December 2007.

plying a sufficient degree of protection for business transactions, property rights and land tenure and so on, an opening emerges for other actors to fill the demand. In Indonesia, in so far as the market can be considered 'rational', it has shown that it has tended to favour those groups that are predictable, well-organized and 'reasonable' in the costs imposed. This has resulted in a fundamental shift in the protection relationship towards a contract between a 'provider' and their 'customer'.

These new providers supply protection both as an illegal service demanded by the illicit economy, as an imposed relationship of exchange (extortion), but also as a 'public good', one that is either 'necessary' or claimed as such.

Post-New Order Jakarta

As Robison and Hadiz (2004:31) have detailed, the fall of Suharto, while resulting in a collapse of centralized state power, did not result in its complete demise. Rather it 'open[ed] the door to a fresh round of struggles to reshape and redefine economics and politics'. The end of the New Order in 1998 was heralded as the beginning of a new more democratic and open phase in Indonesia's political history. Institutional reforms took place, most crucially the implementation of political decentralization and regional autonomy laws plus the hosting of multi-party elections. However the weak governments that followed Suharto's departure, the intensification of political rivalries coupled with the chaotic manner in which administrative decentralization measures have been implemented, all contributed to the disruption of patron-client linkages and established rackets but without the necessary strengthening of state institutions required to prevent their reconfiguration into new forms of rackets. Elements of the old regime have been able to successfully reinvent themselves and re-establish economic and political power relationships within the new formally democratic institutional arrangements and market economies (Robison and Hadiz 2004:10).

This has also applied to the lower levels of the New Order's structure of rackets, including its *preman* and political gangsters, who have emerged as major beneficiaries of reforms introduced to decentralize power in Indonesia, taking advantage of the inability of the post-New Order state to ensure security and the opportunities presented by electoral politics (Hadiz 2003a). This new system, which has given greater autonomy and power to regional and local government, has led to gangsters and violent entrepreneurs becoming a valuable form of political capital and influential power brokers, similar to their ancestors, the *jago* charismatic martial-arts strongmen of the colonial period.[5] In instances where the functional role of the state has been weak and the position of elites fragile, the local territorial power and coercive capacity of violent entrepreneurs has meant that elites themselves have become at times the object of rackets, forced to make political and economic concessions in order to secure the backing and muscle needed for consolidating power. The implications of this for understanding *preman* rackets are that rather than operating solely as the appendages or foot soldiers of elites, or as a criminal sub-class, they have in some instances successfully reconfigured themselves in line with the changed political format in ways that have seen them emerge as increasingly important and even 'legitimate' political actors.

We can loosely categorize *preman* and violent entrepreneurs and the modes of legitimation for rackets they employ into three types, namely: 1) vigilantism, the offering of 'protection' against crime and a variety of detrimental effects of rapid social change; 2) new forms of identity politics in localized territorial struggles over power and resources; and 3) a product and cause of the emergent market in security, protection and coercive force. As Schulte-Bockholt (2006:35) has argued, the specific composition and strength of groups which come to dominate a particular racket will determine both its nature and the way it conducts itself. While the categories presented for classifying rackets and their modes of legitimation have general applicability for the whole of Indonesia, the specifics of the examples given below remain of course most applicable to their geographic setting, Jakarta.

Vigilantism

If we accept Ray Abraham's proposition that vigilantism exists on the frontiers of state power, we can demarcate such frontiers in conventional terms along geographical fringes and peripheral zones, but also in more abstract 'frontiers of legitimacy' where the state is judged not only in technocratic terms of functioning institutions but by its ability to articulate and enforce a moral and social order and ideas of normative justice that are accepted by significant sections of society (Abrahams 1998:9).

Community Vigilance

A case of the opening up of such a 'frontier' can be found in the *preman* politics in the Central Jakarta district of Tanah Abang. Throughout the 1990s

5 The *jago* has been a reoccurring figure in popular culture and legend, often portrayed as a kind of Robin Hood. For the role of *jago* during the colonial period, see Schulte Nordholt 1991.

Tanah Abang's streets and markets were controlled by a gang of largely East Timorese youths led by a wiry *preman* known as Hercules. Brutal in its extraction of protection dues from vendors and local business, Hercules's gang was able to withstand the enmity of the local community and rival gangs due to the patronage of military figures such as Special Forces commander Prabowo Subianto and General Zaki Anwar, whom Hercules had befriended during his time as a military operations assistant in East Timor. However by late 1997 and early 1998 Hercules's difficulties in mobilizing support for the pro-integration cause and the subsequent withdrawal of his patrons' backing left his gang exposed.[6] It didn't take long before an alliance of rival gangs formed, named Family of Tanah Abang Association (Ikatan Keluarga Tanah Abang, IKBT), to challenge his protection regime.

Within a few weeks of the emergence of the IKBT, Hercules's gang was violently expelled from Tanah Abang.[7] The district was no stranger to *preman* gang wars. However, this new crop of gangsters packaged themselves not as rivals but as representatives of the 'community' determined to rid the area of the '*preman* problem'.[8] Straddling the end of the New Order regime in May 1998, the takeover signalled a shift towards a new mode of organization for *preman* in Tanah Abang, the community vigilante, who invoked images of the charismatic and honour-bound *jago* martial-arts strongman of popular legend. With its own rich folklore of *jago* strongmen and *silat* martial arts masters, this means of representation for the new *preman* regime struck a cord with many long-term Tanah Abang residents, as did the IKBT's strong stance against gambling, drugs and prostitution.[9] Local government was happy to portray the formation of a local community vigilance group as the empowerment of local communities to self-police in lieu of the under-resourced and discredited police.[10] The mayor of Central Jakarta, Abdul Kahfi, made the

6 The gang had regularly held pro-government rallies and harassed pro-independence East Timorese activists. However, tensions emerged in 1996 after Tanah Abang police shot dead Manuel Soares, a member of Hercules's gang, ostensibly after he resisted arrest over a minor criminal offence. Convinced this was due to his reluctance to take part in pro-integration activities, Hercules's second-in-command Duartes Freitas issued a press release stating it was a politically motivated killing. Freitas then joined with left-wing activists from the student-based Peoples Democratic Party (Partai Rakyat Demokratik, or PRD) in a demonstration protesting Soares's death at the national parliament.

7 An anecdotal account of the expulsion written by a member of Hercules' gang can be found at: Indonesia-L mailing list, MateBean, 'Tergusurnya eksistensi orang Timtim dari Jakarta', http://www.library.ohiou.edu/indopubs/1997/12/16/0036.html (accessed 10-3-2009). After his expulsion Hercules continued to operate both legitimate and illegal businesses in Jakarta as well as Indramayu. More recently he returned to his native East Timor, where he signed an agreement with the government to build a hotel and swimming pool in Dili.

8 Interview with Bang Ucu, IKBT chairman, Jakarta, 15-6-2005.

9 This stance is rumoured to have brought the IKBT into conflict with the police, some of whom profited from the lucrative drug trade operating in Kampung Bali, a neighbourhood of Tanah Abang. The IKBT only succeeded in removing the drug dealers after gaining the support of marines affiliated to the New Order period nationalist youth organization the Pemuda Panca Marga. Confidential interview, Jakarta, December 2007.

10 Interview with Tanah Abang government official, Jakarta, June 2006.

takeover official when he recruited 48 *preman* drawn from each of the two main gangs comprising the IKBT into a 'District Civil Defence Unit' (*keamanan distrik*, or *matrik*) that was authorized to patrol the Tanah Abang markets and extract regular 'official' protection fees from vendors.[11]

Tensions within the IKBT over distribution of turf as well as resistance from transport workers to the new fees led to the alliance fracturing after several months, leading to ongoing rounds of gang conflict.[12] However, the paradigm of gang-state relations had shifted to one in which gangs, in the guise of community organizations, were recognized by government, and by significant sections of the community, as legitimate 'community partners'. Despite the failure of the IKBT to consolidate control over Tanah Abang, Jakarta Governor Sutiyoso heralded the organization as a success story, a community-driven initiative to deal with the problem of *preman* that should be emulated throughout the capital. He invited IKBT's chairman Bang Ucu and other IKBT leaders to advise him on how to best tackle the problem of *preman* in Jakarta.[13] The New Order logic of fighting 'crime' with criminals continued, but this time the initiative came from *preman* themselves. *Preman* no longer required state backing to survive, whereas the weakened post-New Order state needed the territorial power of the *preman* if it was to regain a modicum of control over Jakarta's streets.

Identity rackets

As in the case of Hercules, the withdrawal of patronage left many previously 'invulnerable' gangs open to challenges from rivals. Post-1998, close association with the discredited regime had become a political and operational liability. The Pemuda Pancasila for example, a New Order period nationalist youth organization who enjoyed significant patronage from the military and political elites and dominated protection rackets and illegal rents throughout the 1980s and early 1990s, found themselves in direct competition with new formations of *preman* who gradually began to gain ascendancy in Jakarta's streets. In contrast to their predecessors who had pledged undying loyalty to nation, state and Golkar, the new guard of *preman*, such as the IKBT, took on distinctly 'local' identities, developing territorial power framed in terms of local cultural idioms and ethnicized identities. Faced with the fragmentation of *beking* arrangements, many *preman* networks started to reconfigure themselves away from dependency upon vertical patronage patterns linked

11 'Preman Tanah Abang aktif lagi', *Kompas* 28-8-2000.

12 'Minivan drivers go on strike over illegal levy', *The Jakarta Post* 27-6-2000.

13 'IKBT tangani program percontohan pembinaan preman', *Kompas* 11-5-2001. Consultation with IKBT affiliates has been continued by Sutiyoso's replacement as governor, former vice-governor Fauzi Bowo.

to national elites, and towards embeddedness in the domain over which they ruled, the *kampung*. With the weakening of centralized power, assertions of place-based distinctiveness became the new grounds for 'securing rights to territories and resources' (Elmhirst 2001:292).

Abidin Kusno (2004:2384) has described how in post-1998 Jakarta the 'loosening' of power at the centre has resulted in a proliferation of civil groups formed around identities that 'are all linked by a sense that the nation-state no longer commands any power to protect and rule, or, at best, the political elites only safeguard their own interests'. This sense that political elites had little concern with improving the conditions of the general populace has, according to Kusno, encouraged these citizens groups, often violently, 'to act on their own, creating a condition in which everyone safeguards his or her own space, often without regard for the public'. The streets of the capital became a zone of contestation between a complex mix of interests: the poor and middle-classes, the city administration, developers and business. The Indonesian NGO Yappika documented the spread of this 'us vs. them' mentality, identifying 135 instances of communal and inter-neighbourhood violence in Jakarta from March 2001 to March 2002 alone (Fitri 2004:10). While the high level of conflict of this particular period has not extended into the present, it nonetheless set in motion dynamics that contributed to the emergence of a new crop of local gangs and rackets. Localism has become a new pole for contesting the territorial boundaries of these aggressive forms of 'spatial power'.

The rise of the Betawi

From mid-2000 till early 2001, inter-gang rivalries intensified in East Jakarta between largely ethnic Madurese and Betawi-based gangs.[14] These tensions came to a head in the semi-industrial district of Cakung in 2001, resulting in several days of intermittent street fighting and the torching of several houses of Madurese. The incident became the catalyst for a new 'ethnic' *preman* organization.[15] On 29 July 2001 the Betawi Brotherhood Forum (Forum Betawi Rempug, FBR) declared itself at a ceremony at the group's headquarters in a religious school in Pengillingan, Cakung. The FBR was led by Fadloli el-Muhir, a religious scholar with long-standing links to elements of the former New Order regime, such as the former Jakarta military commander and later governor of the Indonesian capital, Lieutenant General Sutiyoso. A leaflet distributed by the FBR in Cakung at the time further incited hostility towards Madurese and other 'outsiders'.

14 'Murder suspects gang members', *The Jakarta Post* 29-3-2001.

15 For more on the construction of ethnicity within the FBR see Brown and Wilson 2007.

> Oh children of Betawi, it is the responsibility of all sons of the land to create peace, tranquillity and beauty in the Betawi land which has become the capital of Indonesia. Forgiving, compromising, not vengeful and always seeking consensus, this is the character of the Betawi. But starting from now, let us rise up and unite as Betawi to oppose the migrants who are arrogant, conceited, selfish, vengeful and disrespectful of the indigenous Betawi. We are sick of cruelty and barbarity, one drop of Betawi blood must be answered with an ocean of blood. Starting from now, let us make the Betawi champions (*jawara*) and respected ones (*juragan*) in Betawi land.[16]

The battle was no longer one between warring gangs, but between self-proclaimed representatives of the disenfranchized indigenous community of the nation's capital, who sought to reclaim the rights, land and jobs 'stolen' from them by migrants such as the Madurese. In the space of six months over a dozen new 'Betawi' groups emerged, each claiming exclusive rights for control over the informal economy in the neighbourhoods in which they were based, as well as jobs and 'taxes' from local business on the pretext of 'empowering' the Betawi.[17] Publicly endorsing the FBR's identification of '*preman*' and other 'troublemakers' as migrant outsiders, Governor Sutiyoso, by then a tough retired major-general, sought to establish alliances with Jakarta's Betawi *preman* and to harness them to the task of reconsolidating his security-orientated approach to governing the city. Sutiyoso was quick to recognize the utilitarian value of gangs citing an 'indigenous' Jakarta identity. Enamoured by this initial support, the FBR, Forkabi and others enthusiastically and independently harassed and assaulted critics of the governor, including NGOs such as the Urban Poor Consortium.[18]

The FBR's appeals to 'the oppressed' struck a cord not just with local *preman* looking for a new organizational cover for their racketeering, but a broader spectrum of the unemployed and those scraping a living in the informal street economy, in particular *ojek* motorcycle taxi drivers. With this membership base, the FBR rapidly expanded to become by far the largest Betawi organization in Jakarta.[19] According to chairman Fadloli Muhir, Jakarta's rapid development had left the Betawi dispossessed and marginalized. Unlike other regions where local autonomy and decentralization has

16 Extract from a reproduction of a leaflet distributed by the FBR in Cakung in 2001.

17 These included Forkabi, Forum Betawi Rempug, Gerakan Ketahanan Betawi and Ikatan Keluarga Betawi.

18 'NGOs accuse Sutiyoso of rent-a-thug-methods', *The Jakarta Post* 23-3-2002. Sutiyoso was later to withdraw this support due to the FBR's 'unruly' nature. Vice-governor Fauzi Bowo was later to do the same prior to the elections for governor in 2007, which he won. Up until this time the FBR had been enthusiastic supporters of Bowo due to his Betawi heritage. Bowo was advised that public hostility towards the FBR could result in a voter backlash if he was seen as courting the group. The FBR subsequently switched their support to rival candidate Adang Daradjatun.

19 Its current membership is estimated to be around 60,000.

seen indigenous populations gain seats in power and an improved standard of living, this had not been the case in the nation's capital.[20] FBR's answer to this, has been an aggressive form of ethnic chauvinism, holding to the belief that it is only through predatory behaviour that one will get ahead in society. In order to achieve their vision of a Jakarta dominated by Betawi strongmen, the FBR has used a number of tactics and strategies. These traverse the line between legal and illegal, ranging from classic extortion and stand-over tactics, to political lobbying, legitimate business ventures and entrepreneurial initiatives.[21]

As one member argued, 'If the government fulfilled its obligations and provided us with work, and satisfied our basic needs then there would be no reason for FBR to exist. As it stands, if we don't stand up and fight for what is rightfully ours, we will end up with nothing.'[22] In the context of a myriad of gangs contesting territory, the reinvention of Jakarta as an ethnic homeland for the Betawi has served an important function in legitimating localized rackets, thus cementing a role for themselves as political brokers.

Morality racketeering

In his examination of the market in private protection in post-Soviet Russia, Federico Varese (2001:7) has stated that the greater the realm of activities defined as illegal by the state, the higher the demand will be for mafia services. If for example alcohol or pornographic materials are outlawed, this will create a demand for the protection offered by organized crime. This has to an extent also been the case in post-New Order Jakarta. For example, public order laws outlawing street-side vending have opened opportunities for street gangs, who operate in this domain as a form of informal 'governance', to cooperate with the authorities in forced evictions, but also in some instances to protect communities from over-zealous public order officials.[23] A far more pervasive phenomenon however, has been the proliferation of groups offering protection from more abstract 'moral threats' identified generally as vice (*maksiat*). Rather than seeking to fill the illegal demand for protection created by government prohibitions, these 'morality racketeers' play a kind of wedge politics, on the one hand publicly denouncing the dangers believed to be posed to society by bars, clubs, gambling dens and prostitution, while privately benefiting materially from their existence. In the past protec-

20 Interview with Fadloli el-Muhir, Jakarta, 3-8-2005.

21 For more detail on the FBR's activities, see Wilson 2006, and Brown and Wilson 2007.

22 Interview with FBR member, Jakarta, 14-6-2006.

23 Public order laws such as Jakarta Regional Law no. 11/1988, recently revised in Law no. 8/2007, allows for the arrest and removal of those considered to be creating a public disturbance.

tion of these kinds of illicit activities was the exclusive domain of *preman*. Structurally the relationship remains the same; however the dynamics have been inverted. Instead of profiting from protecting 'vice', *preman* now profit from ostensibly combating it.

Defenders of the Faith

The best-publicized of these morality racketeers has been the Defenders of Islam Front (Front Pembela Islam, FPI).[24] The FPI was established in 1998, as part of the Pam Swakarsa civil defence force. Consisting of a rag-tag collection of thugs, unemployed youth and Islamic militants supportive of Suharto's presidential replacement, B.J Habibie, the Pam Swakarsa were the brainchild of military chief General Wiranto and General Kivlan Zein. Intended to bolster the over-stretched police force and help counter widespread opposition to the Habibie presidency, as a political strategy the Pam Swakarsa was a failure and it was disbanded in late 1998.[25] The FPI outlasted the Pam Swakarsa, and has over the past ten years made a name for itself as a self-proclaimed defender of public morality from a variety of social ills. It has focused its activities on night venues that it accuses of breaching operating hours during the fasting month of Ramadan. By the end of 2001 the FPI found that many of its more generous financial backers were no longer prepared to subsidize its activities, due to what one former patron described as its increasing 'recalcitrance' as well as the perceived political liability of its well-publicized links to radical Islam.[26] This increased pressure upon members to find other sources of income, most commonly in the form of pay-offs and protection fees from the targets of its anti-vice raids.[27] While not openly condoned by the group's leadership, such practices are recognized as common-place. For many preman seeking new organizational affiliations, the FPI offers not only rent-seeking opportunities but also the possibility of personal redemption, making it an attractive option.

The FPI uses a particular 'procedural method' for choosing the targets of its anti-vice raids.[28] Once a potential target has been identified, the FPI investigates the strength of the interests attached to it, that is, military, rival *preman* groups and so on. If they consider these interests to be politically weak, they then register a formal complaint with the police requesting that the venue

24 For more on the FPI's background see Wilson 2008.

25 The street presence of the Pam Swakarsa further provoked an already tense political situation, resulting in violent clashes with student demonstrators and locals that left fatalities on both sides. 'Jika preman dan bambu rucing ikut bermain', *Gatra* 21-11-1998, p.73.

26 Confidential interview, Jakarta, August 2005.

27 Interview with senior FPI member, Jakarta , 16-8-2005.

28 Interview with Alawi Usman, head of the FPI's 'investigations division', Jakarta, 15-8-2005.

or activity be shut down on the grounds that it threatens public morality, or that is in breach of government regulations. Police almost never act on these complaints, but it gives them the opportunity to forewarn businesses on the FPI's list, which can then pay for police protection, find an alternate source of protection from the market of suppliers, or make the FPI an offer.[29] This police complicity in the racket may also explain the frequent absence or late arrival of the police at FPI raids despite prior warning.

The vocal support of the FPI, FBR and similar groups for increased state regulation of morality issues, such as through the controversial anti-pornography bill, has often been portrayed as an ideological battle between militant Islam and liberal social forces.[30] However advocates of religious conservatism such as the FPI are well aware of the tangible opportunities these campaigns can create for them. Increased levels of regulation over behaviour require increased policing in order to enforce the regulations. Violations of these regulations generate income for those enforcing them as those who seek to avoid them pay up. With the authorities lacking the human resources, and in some instances the political will, to police such laws, increased opportunities arise for 'civil' morality vigilantes to extract rent and protection dues, while at the same achieving a degree of 'legitimacy'.

As in the classic protection racket, Islamic and ethnic *preman* first create a threat, for example a 'moral crisis' or 'heresy', which they are themselves strategically placed to resolve. By eschewing the staples of organized crime and *preman* such as protecting prostitution, gambling and drug trafficking, the new breed of 'moral' gangsters strategically position themselves as a moral vanguard, a 'defender' of the community and the faith from a variety of threats. No longer are they seen as the source of trouble but as its solution.

The market in protection

Increasing crime rates, rampant unemployment, poorly enforced government regulations and the inefficiency and continued corruption of the police have all been factors increasing the demand for non-state forms of protection. While vigilantism surfaced as a 'community'-based response to this demand, a thriving and highly competitive market in private protection services has also emerged. This ranges from local level gangs, private security companies, off-duty police and military to international security firms with branches in Jakarta. Former and serving members of the police or military run many of

29 This information derived from confidential interviews with several bar owners in Jakarta who have been the object of FPI raids.

30 Despite threats of non-compliance from provincial governments such as Bali and West Papua, a modified version of the bill was passed into law on 31-10-2008.

these smaller local companies, such as the marines-operated company PT. Bass (Masaaki 2006). Aside from protecting client's assets, these security agencies also offer services such as personal bodyguards, debt collection and asset repossession, land acquisition brokering, 'community mediation', and the intimidation of a client's business rivals. Several security industry associations have been established, the largest of which is the Indonesian Security Manager Association (AMSI) which currently has 300 affiliate companies. However, it accounts for only a small percentage of the overall number of security providers, the majority of whom operate almost entirely outside any regulatory framework (Robison, Wilson and Meliala 2008). Formally, regulation of this sector is the responsibility of the police, who issue licences for registered companies and are required to monitor their activities and personnel. In practice however the actual level of police supervision is at best minimal. The prevailing shaping force has been the demands of the market itself.

The inevitability that a business will be approached by a protection agency of some description has resulted in many entrepreneurs pre-emptively seeking out those with a reputation for being reliable and efficient.[31] This has impacted upon the way in which protection groups market themselves. They recognize the importance of 'professionalizing' their services in order to attract clients. Some groups have made a transition from street gang and racketeer to more tightly organized protection organization, in order to carve a niche in this growing protection 'industry'. This has entailed a range of organizational strategies: tightening membership criteria, more rigorous physical and mental training regimes, and the introduction of 'procedural guidelines' and 'rules of engagement' for 'conflict resolution', alongside regularized fees for the services offered to clients. In a competitive but unregulated market, groups need to justify their coercive presence at the local level, and also 'deliver' on promises to reduce petty crime, lest clients seek protection elsewhere. In simple economic terms, there has been recognition that extortion and crude racketeering is not a viable long-term strategy in the face of a myriad of rival providers. At the same time, territorialism still dominates the industry, defined either geographically or via sectors, and groups often negotiate agreements regarding the demarcation of boundaries.

[31] An unpublished survey of small businesses conducted by the author in Tanah Abang in 2007 suggested that protection can cost anywhere between 5% and 20% of total profits. As a general rule, the bigger the business the fewer problems they have with protection groups. Big business, including the corporate sector, is better able to protect itself and many have created their own security services.

Protection franchises

One example of a successful security company is Putra Perkasa, run by Abraham Lunggana. A former Tanah Abang gang leader, Lunggana was deputy of the IKBT and head of the Jakarta branch of the Pemuda Panca Marga. In recent years he has become chairman of the Central Jakarta branch of the Islamic United Development Party (Partai Persatuan Pembangunan, PPP), and in 2008 he secured the deputy leadership of an umbrella organization for Betawi social and cultural associations known as the Badan Musyawarah Betawi (Bamus).[32] Much of the conflict that occurs between rival providers of protection emerges due to perceived breaches of territorial domains. For example, the presence of a security company in an area dominated by a gang that has no stake in that company is often considered a provocation warranting reprisal. In order to negotiate this territorialism, Lunggana has developed a franchise-like system he refers to as 'environmental investment'.[33] A potential client for his security services, such as a department store, is asked to identify (in consultation with community leaders) who are the local youths or *preman* they consider to be reliable. Putra Perkasa then approaches these youths, offering them formal employment, training and a uniform. The promise of a regular fixed income is usually enough to convince them to join.[34] In this way the company integrates local gangs within its business franchise, increasing its ability to secure contracts whilst maintaining community and client confidence and a 'professional' standard of service. This technique neutralizes the threats of local gangs while expanding the sphere of influence of the business. This franchising system has proven highly successful for Lunggana. His company has secured contracts in major shopping malls in Central Jakarta, as well as control of lucrative parking areas in and around southern Jakarta as well as the Taman Ismail Marzuki arts centre.

The police

If the fragmented state is no longer the racket regime it was during the New Order, then what has been its relationship with racketeers' post-1998? At the street level, the main interface between state power and the informal power of *preman* racketeers has been the police. Individual and territorial relationships

32 Lunggana was also a campaign manager in the successful 2007 bid for the governorship of Jakarta by former vice-governor and head of Bamus, Fauzi Bowo. He has since been appointed the deputy head of Bamus.

33 Interview with Abraham Lunggana, Jakarta, 6-12-2007.

34 Recruits undergo intensive training and are supervised for several months. Breaches of company policy result in immediate expulsion, and franchise branches are required to regularly submit detailed activity reports and audits.

between police and *preman* racketeers range from collusion, cooperation and mutual expediency to, in some instances, overtly hostile competition. The form the relationship takes is highly dependent upon local conditions such as the relative size, strength and political connections of local groups and the immediate resources available to the police. In one district of South Jakarta for example, the local branch of the FBR is a major financial contributor to the upkeep of the under-resourced local police station, providing drinking water and even stationery. According to FBR members, in return the police turn a blind eye to occasional 'excesses' on the part of the group and allow them to manage many day-to-day policing tasks such as the apprehension of petty criminals.[35] While this example is in some respects an extreme one, it does nonetheless point to the extent to which racketeers and the police establish 'pragmatic' working relationships, in which *preman* can hold the upper hand. As one police officer explained, 'as there are no clear rules for engagement we have to adopt an informal and conciliatory approach. The reality in the field is that these groups exist and exercise authority, so the police, like it or not, need to engage with them.'[36]

Not all police however are comfortable with this kind of mutual co-existence. Junior police officers at the Indonesian Institute of Police Science (Perguruan Tinggi Ilmu Kepolisian, PTIK) for example, expressed frustration at what they perceived as the 'double-bind' in which they were caught in relation to *preman* racketeers. On the one hand they experience immense pressure from the public to uphold the law and tackle crime, while on the other they are constrained politically by their own links with certain groups and elites, by the ambiguity of the law and by limited resources.[37] As one officer quipped, 'Our job (of tackling *preman* groups) would be far easier if parliament didn't keep interfering. On the one hand politicians will condemn these groups, but then use them or give them overt support.'[38]

At a governmental level, the primary response from the Jakarta administration to public concern over the prevalence of racketeering, extortion and street crime has been a series of high-profile 'anti-*preman*' campaigns. The first of these campaigns was held in 2001, and they have been subsequently repeated in 2004, 2005 and 2008. The initiative of former governor Sutiyoso, the campaigns were initially limited to Jakarta but by 2004 were national in scope and coordinated directly by the National Chief of Police. As with the *petrus* pogroms of the 1980s, the campaigns have largely avoided targeting established organizations, instead focusing upon mass arrests of those identi-

35 Interview with FBR member, Jakarta, August 2007. These excesses have included hospitalizing burglary suspects and truck drivers who refused to pay parking fees imposed by the group.

36 Interview, Jakarta, 3-9-2007.

37 Interview, Jakarta, 12-11-2007.

38 Interview, Jakarta, 12-11-2007.

fied as '*preman*'.[39] Ambiguity in the operational definition of who constitutes a '*preman*', which in itself is not a criminal offence, has allowed the authorities to be highly discretionary in whom they have targeted. Identifiable patterns have emerged. *Preman* and racketeers with links to established organizations and political parties, including the FBR, have been largely left untouched, whilst illegal traffic wardens (*pak ogah*), small street gangs along with others identified as 'undesirables' such as beggars, street kids, buskers and sex workers have been arrested en masse.[40]

Subsequently many street *preman* joined groups such as the FBR in order to gain what is perceived to be 'invulnerability' from the law. During the 2005 campaign for example, membership of the FBR increased by 200%.[41] Hence one effect of the campaigns has been to aid in the consolidation of territorial control of established groups by, temporarily at least, rounding up small fry competitors for protection dues and creating the imperative for them to amalgamate with larger groups, many of whom already have some kind of negotiated established working relationship with the police.[42] Whether this has been a deliberate strategy on the part of the authorities is debatable. Regardless of intent, it does indicate the limits of the power of the state and also shows the extent to which the 'legitimations' used by protection groups have been successful. During the most recent campaign, at a meeting with the vice governor, the head of the FBR, Fadloli Muhir, offered to 'take in' arrested *preman* in order to 'empower' them, in effect expanding the membership and territorial reach of his own group.[43] It is also notable that throughout these campaigns public complaints of extortion and corruption on the part of the police have increased threefold, suggesting that some police at least have used the campaigns as an opportunity to reclaim sources of illegal rent extraction taken from them by street level racketeers.[44] While the fragmented state and its agents appear not to possess the capacity or political will to curtail racketeer groups or comprehensively to regulate the market in protection, the anti-*preman* campaigns have shown that some of the more unruly players can be absorbed into more 'stable' formations.

39 In the most recent campaign, begun in November 2008, police attempted to answer criticisms that the campaign only targeted 'small fry' *preman* by arresting Hercules on assault charges. As a gangster with a high media profile but whose actual power and influence is now limited, Hercules was the perfect scapegoat for the police.

40 'Puluhan preman di kawasan Jakpus digaruk', *Liputan6.com*, 1-12-2008, http://www.liputan6.com/hukrim/?id=169065 (accessed 24-10-2008).

41 Interview with Nahrowi, FBR public relations official, December 2005, Jakarta,

42 One *preman* interviewed was arrested in both the 2001 and 2005 campaigns. In each case he was released with a warning to 'watch his step' after being detained for 48 hours.

43 'Tokoh Betawi minta pemerintah Jakarta bina preman', *Tempo Interaktif*, 13-11-2008, http://www.tempointeraktif.com/hg/jakarta/2008/11/13/brk,20081113-145730,id.html (accessed 10-3-2009).

44 'Number of thugs down, number of bad cops up', *The Jakarta Post* 19-9-2005.

Conclusion: The consolidation of rackets

In modern democratic states formal legitimacy is ostensibly established via consensual democratic processes such as elections, and the provision of basic services such as health, education and the maintenance of law and order. However, it is a particular heritage of the New Order that 'legitimacy' in the use of force has been produced as a 'racket effect'. The state has presented itself as the lesser of evils in relation to imminent, imaginary or actual threats posed by 'others': rival gangs, crime, ethnic and religious minorities, corrupt authorities, or more abstract 'spectral' threats such as 'moral decay' and 'sin'. The examples described previously point to an expansion, consolidation and diversification of racket relationships, with the state operating as, at best, a kind of 'meta-manager'.

The logic of power articulated during the New Order, of consolidating repressive forms of social order through the invocation of threats, has been retranslated in the context of a decentralized political environment and shaped by the market economy. In the perspective of post-colonial Southeast Asian states, Carl Trocki (1998), John Sidel (1999) and others have identified a correlation between the consolidation of gangsters and post-authoritarian transitions towards institutional democracy. As Volkov (2002) has shown in his study of violent entrepreneurs in post-Soviet Russia, in an under-regulated informal market economy organized crime groups, vigilantes and those trading in protection thrive and can become a significant shaping force. In the case of Russia, these forces have become increasingly domesticated under President Putin as he reconsolidated centralized state power. The possibility of a similar domestication or co-option in Indonesia appears unlikely due to the continued fragmentation and disorganization of post-New Order elites. What seems more likely for the foreseeable future is a continuation of current patterns, whereby state agents such as the police engage in largely symbolic campaigns aimed at containment of unruly groups in order to appease public concerns, whilst informally cooperating with larger and better organized groups. The double-edged sword of protection, as a public good and a public nuisance, will continue for some time.

JUN HONNA

Orchestrating transnational crime

Security sector politics as a Trojan horse for anti-reformists

Indonesia is widely regarded as a hotbed of transnational crime in Southeast Asia. Criminal rings involving illegal logging, human trafficking, illicit drugs, arms smuggling, and sea piracy have developed cross-border networks rooted in Indonesia's underground economy. These crimes quickly emerged as major concerns for post-Suharto governments, posing serious threats to both the national economy and human security. For example, timber smuggling and illegal logging cost Indonesia an estimated US$4 billion in revenues annually, approximately five times the yearly budget for the Ministry of Health (Setiono and Husein 2005:4; EIA/Telapak 2007:3). Illegal fishing has also increased and cost between US$2 and 3 billion annually in state losses.[1] An estimated 100,000 Indonesian women and children are trafficked every year, according to UNICEF (2006:4), but the police handle less than 200 cases annually (Yuwono et al. 2005:19). The abrupt increase of the illicit drug trade also poses a national threat, as the government estimates that the country's drug trade is now worth almost US$4 billion a year, and that as many as 4 million people use illegal drugs.[2] Violence at sea also became more conspicuous after 1997, as reflected in the number of piracy incidents and armed robberies in Indonesian waters – from 47 in 1997 to 119 in 2000 – and in the Straits of Malacca, from zero in 1997 to 75 in 2000 (ICC International Maritime Bureau 2006:5).

Though these developments in some respects reflect a global trend in criminal activity facilitated by the sophistication of information and communication technology, Indonesia's outlaws have benefited greatly from domestic political changes since the fall of Suharto in 1998. They have successfully identified and exploited the new opportunities of democracy and decentralization to increase their power and influence in legitimate arenas to further their illicit economic activities, often involving transnational crime networks. The rela-

1 See 'RI forms new courts to fight illegal fishing', *The Jakarta Post* 18-10-2007, and Fegan 2003.

2 'Empat juta penduduk Indonesia pencandu narkoba', *Sinar Harapan* 7-6-2006.

tionship between the state and criminal activity is becoming a more complex issue in the age of globalism when the illegal cross-border flow of human beings, goods, and money exceeds the capacity of state surveillance and control. Criminal actors are also empowering themselves by teaming up with foreign counterparts regardless of differences in political ideology and regime.

The scholarship on transnational crime has long been dominated by international relations, criminal investigation and defence-security experts. This is understandable as research on 'transnational crime' has become key to 'new' security or 'non-traditional' security analysis in the post-Cold War era.[3] Their works have contributed to identifying the nature of the threat, related security risks, and the state's lack of adequate institutions and policies to deal with transnational crime.[4] Nevertheless, these studies tend to overlook domestic political analysis and do not elucidate the local dynamics necessary to contextualizing the 'global threat' of transnational crime. This is where area studies remains crucial in order to enrich the analysis of cross-border crime and – perhaps more importantly – to highlight the potential unintended consequences generated by the spread of criminal activity and state response(s) thereto. It is important to emphasize that anti-crime countermeasures are not produced in a political black box – they are the product of politics and shaped by existing agendas and competition for resources among different actors and institutions. From this perspective, this chapter examines the nexus between security sector politics and expanding transnational crime in Indonesia. We first look at how cross-border crime has flourished after the collapse of Suharto's authoritarian regime in the context of democratic security reform and political decentralization. Then we examine how security-sector actors have seized this opportunity by shaping the discourse over countermeasures in order to advance institutional interests. The politics of security and institutional competition is evident in the 'campaigns against transnational crime' waged by the police, army and navy, examined below.

Security sector reform and the criminalized turf battle

Democratization after the fall of Suharto has caused significant changes in the dynamics of crime and law enforcement. Most prominent among these is the escalating rivalry between the military and police after the former's retreat from its long-standing domestic security role in 1999. This rivalry has undermined state control over the criminal underworld and created space for the extension of transnational crime activities.

3 In the development of these discussions, the Copenhagen Peace Research Institute played an influential role by building a school of thought in security studies. Buzan 1991 and Lipschutz 1995 represent the school.

4 Some major studies focusing on Southeast Asia include: McFarlane and McLennan 1996; Emmers 2002; Caballero-Anthony, Emmers, and Acharya 2006.

During the Suharto presidency (1967-1998),[5] the armed forces consisted of four services, including the police. The army was responsible for internal security, relying on a territorial command system with ten army divisions based around the archipelago and extending down to the village level where it maintained politico-security surveillance. This military network of surveillance and repression was developed to implement the orders of the army chief down to the village level. The police worked under the army in handling internal security, supporting its repressive operations against citizens and assuming responsibility for law enforcement. Suharto's Indonesia established a military authoritarian polity in which the army played a twin role in national defence and politics. This role was formally known as the 'dual function', or *dwifungsi*, of the military.

The fall of Suharto in May 1998 created political space for questioning the relevance of *dwifungsi*. Emboldened civilian leaders in both parliament and civil society criticized past atrocities committed by the military and demanded military reform to professionalize the armed services and to democratize civil-military relations. The military leadership responded to these pressures by formulating a vision of military reform. One of the first proposals was the separation of the national police from the military in April 1999. The armed forces returned to the pre-Suharto era organization of three services – army, navy and air force. This functional separation was inevitably accompanied by the redefinition of responsibilities between the police and the military. In an attempt to professionalize the security services, the military (Tentara Nasional Indonesia, TNI) was assigned responsibility for national 'defence' and the police given the role of maintaining domestic 'security' and 'order'. It was expected that the new role-definition would lead the military to professionalize its capacities regarding external defence matters.

However, the reform generated dissatisfaction among TNI officers. Given the elimination of posts related to political affairs within the TNI and the shifting of domestic security functions to the police, military officers found gaining promotion more competitive and difficult. These frustrations fanned distrust of, and resentment against, the police. The relationship worsened due to a growing turf war between the two institutions over the conduct of business activities, such as protection rackets. Before the separation of the police, it was an open secret that the military largely dominated 'security services' for private companies – including those operating brothels, gambling dens and night clubs.[6] The criminal underworld also viewed the military as the sole hegemon controlling the constellation of criminal forces during the

5 Although some date his rule from decisive acts in March 1966 and even October 1965, he was appointed acting president on 12 March 1967.

6 For details of these operations, see Human Rights Watch 2006.

New Order.[7] The transfer of domestic security duties from the military to the police inevitably reduced lucrative opportunities for the military as the newly independent police muscled in on these services. The impact on the TNI was devastating, particularly for local army commands which had relied heavily on revenue from such unofficial business activities to provide for their troops' 'welfare'. As business income dried up significantly after the 1997-1998 economic crisis, police encroachment on army turf after 1999 constituted a serious threat for an institution that is expected to raise its own funds to make up for inadequate budgetary support. Frustration within the TNI boiled over, leading to outright conflicts in various places around the archipelago.

In 2001, for example, the tension between military and police units in the East Java town of Madiun escalated into a violent clash marked by pitched gun battles. TNI soldiers ran amok, attacking the Madiun police station, killing two citizens and wounding several policemen. The army chief-of-staff at that time, General Endriartono Sutarto, admitted that the soldiers involved in the clash had been involved with illegal businesses in the area, referring to brothels, gambling dens and the drug trade.[8] He also claimed that the frequency of TNI-police clashes dramatically increased by 300% in the period after the separation of the two organizations. Due to these turf wars and the financial losses caused by the shifting of domestic security to the police and the overall economic crisis, the military developed closer ties with criminal groups involved with the lucrative smuggling of goods and people. For the police, it was important to crack down on criminals linked with soldiers both in order to expand its turf and to demonstrate to the public that it was able to manage security and order. The turf battles between the army and police led to similar mayhem in cities such as Maumere (Flores) and Binjai (North Sumatra) in 2002.[9] In response, top leaders of the TNI and police pledged to tighten discipline over local personnel in the field, but this did not stop the clashes. At least six serious melees between the TNI and police occurred in 2007.

From the police perspective, these conflicts were triggered by 'the jealousy of TNI which has no more authority to dictate to society but is still preoccupied with the old thinking'.[10] Clearly, the rivalry, suspicion, resentment and hostility between the two institutions is now deep-rooted, hampering post-Suharto governments' efforts to establish an effective mechanism for controlling criminal activities in the archipelago.[11] Importantly, the logic of

7 On the New Order management of criminal activities, see Siegel 1998 and Barker 1998.

8 'Army chief says Madiun victims shot by police', *The Jakarta Post* 20-9-2001.

9 For details, see *Current data* 2003.

10 Interviews with police officers in Police Headquarters, July 2007.

11 This is by no means to generalize local TNI–police relations in the archipelago. In some areas, we see the development of 'peaceful' and perhaps even entrepreneurial turf-sharing between the two institutions. I thank David Jansen in making this point. See his analysis on Yogyakarta (Jansen 2008). See also Baker 2008.

turf battles – which was triggered by the separation of the police from the military – focused both the TNI and police on cultivating the sources of fund-raising. Under these circumstances, criminal enterprises easily found patrons either in the military or the police. For example, in Riau Province, criminal groups have relied on the police in operating big gambling dens while collaborating with TNI in the business of illegal logging.[12] By consolidating such patronage ties, criminal groups quickly developed business networks around the country and some actively sought cross-border ties.

Localizing power, capitalizing crime

In addition to the security sector infighting, political decentralization in the post-Suharto era facilitated the flourishing of transnational crime. The decentralization legislation (passed in 1999) was implemented in 2001, involving the transfer of control over local economic resources from the central administration to local governments, providing them with wide discretion in making use of these resources. As a result, the competition for tapping these resources intensified among local power elites, a development characterized as 'predatory decentralization' (Hadiz 2007).

In fact, as competition intensified among local political elites for concessions and graft, political engineering of 'mass movements' became a popular means of lobbying. Since government projects – such as land-use planning, large-scale construction, and community development – were promoted in tandem with the implementation of regional autonomy, local political elites learned to orchestrate and mobilize 'local residents' to pressure their governments to ensure that these projects came under their control. Astute politicians organized various types of 'resident groups' so that they were prepared to pounce on any opportunity to shake down the government. Responding to this surging demand for their services, local hoodlums (*preman*) started to play a decisive organizing role in mobilizing people to take to the streets as required.

During the Suharto era, the two most infamous semi-official *preman* groups, Pemuda Pancasila and Pemuda Panca Marga, enjoyed privileges as the designated providers of state-sponsored civilian protest and violence throughout the archipelago. The collapse of the New Order, however, ended their privileged status, as democracy liberalized this sector and sparked fierce competition from other service providers eager to cash in on the bonanza of democracy.[13]

12 In fact, 147 policemen, including 6 high-ranking officers, were suspected of involvement with Riau's gambling ring. 'Officers questioned over Riau gambling operation', *The Jakarta Globe* 2-12-2008. There are hundreds of illegal sawmills in Riau and many have military support. 'Masih ada militer di hutan', WAHLI 25-6-2007, http://www.walhi.or.id/ kampanye/hutan/shk/070625_militer_htn_cu (accessed 6-5-2008; archived at www.archive.org).

13 About this, see Ian Wilson's study in this book, and Ryter 2005.

Diversification of underworld power has been a discernible consequence of democratization, most notably involving a growing number of local ethnic identity groups, political party-affiliated youth organizations, and religious vigilantes, oddly mirroring the rapid growth of civil society NGOs in the early 1990s. Since the economic crisis in 1997-1998, which boosted the number of unemployed youth, the recruitment of *preman* members has become easy and less costly. The proliferation of such organizations coincided with the increasing reliance of local power elites on mass mobilization as an effective weapon in their competition for concessions. Thus, cooperation between local elites and *preman* has become extensive and 'normal' as politicians have tapped the coercive power of 'popular' protests to muscle in on the government's economic resources. This trend has effectively blurred the boundary between political and criminal societies as the mutual dependency allows the latter's penetration into the legitimate political process, bolstering the criminalization of local politics in many places.

In Medan, a city dubbed as gang city (*kota preman*), local political authorities have developed a close relationship with the Youth Work Institute (Ikatan Pemuda Karya, IPK), whose leader is referred to as the 'real' mayor of the city (Hadiz 2003b). In West Kalimantan, a Malaysian Chinese timber boss has extended his influence among gangsters in the borderland community, and local political elites have weak incentives, and capacity, to eliminate such informal power (Wadley and Eilenberg 2006). In East Java, the local gambling king has strengthened relations with politically well-connected Madurese *preman* groups (Honna 2006). In Jakarta, many of the capital's gambling dens and brothels are operated by various criminal agencies and different *preman* networks provide similar protection rackets for them.[14] This phenomenon has become so ubiquitous that Henk Schulte Nordholt (2002) suggests that post-Suharto Indonesia is becoming a '*preman* state'.

In this manner, the growing presence and power of criminal networks is rooted in the government's failure (or its incapacity, or indifference) to manage security in the context of democratization and rapid decentralization. Conveniently overlooking the local roots of this problem, however, the government has fingered 'transnational crime' as the culprit, aiming to synchronize the problem with a 'global' paradigm of securitizing cross-border organized crime orchestrated by the post-9/11 Western security community. For the US and its allies, the nexus between terrorism and transnational crime is explained in terms of drug money financing terrorists, the undocumented cross-border movement of people providing cover for terrorist operations, arms smuggling facilitating terrorist logistics, and money laundering by

14 Among others, Madurese, Timorese, Ambonese and Betawi groups are known to be powerful in Jakarta's preman sector. Regarding the Betawi *preman* and its links with the Jakarta government, see Wilson 2006.

criminal syndicates being exploited by terrorist financiers (Shelley 2002; Makarenko 2003; Picarelli 2006). It is this discourse that has encouraged the Western security community to emphasize transnational crime as a top security priority along with counter-terrorism. Drawing on this logic, several new 'global wars' were declared on drugs, trafficking of persons, illegal logging, and other crimes linked to transnational non-state actors.

In Indonesia, where the risk of terrorist attacks and criminal penetration of the legitimate economy is relatively high, it is not difficult for the government to focus attention on transnational crime and emphasize the 'limitations' of individual countries to deal with the threats posed by 'transnational actors'. Given that Indonesia shares porous and extensive borders with other countries and clearly lacks the state capacity to conduct nation-wide border surveillance, the logic of this argument appears persuasive. Here, the emphasis on 'transnationality' effectively obscures local roots and the question of extensive domestic politico-criminal collusion is transformed into a 'capacity deficit', which in turn provides a pretext for inviting international cooperation for bolstering relevant security capabilities. Thus, the rhetoric of the transnational crime threat enables the state to repackage the domestic problem of criminal penetration into state institutions as a capacity deficit issue that fits with the foreign policy agenda of promoting international cooperation. I argue that state security actors intentionally repackage the problem to exploit global concerns in order to promote their conservative institutional agendas. The three different cases of dealing with transnational crime examined below shed light on this institutional sleight of hand.

BNN and the 'war on drugs'

It was during the Megawati administration (2001-2003) that Indonesia explicitly declared a war on drugs. In March 2002, the president strengthened national anti-drug operations by establishing the National Narcotics Board (Badan Narkotika Nasional, BNN), a successor to the existing National Narcotics Coordinating Board (Badan Koordinasi Narkotika Nasional, BKNN), established in 2000.[15] Following this, Megawati instructed all government agencies down to the village level to take necessary measures to tackle the problem of illegal drugs.[16] With these initiatives, the war on drugs

15 During the Suharto regime, the drug problem was handled by the State Intelligence Coordinating Board (Bakin) which was traditionally headed by a military man. When responsibility was transferred to BKNN in 2000, police officers dominated the new organization. Since then, the police chief simultaneously occupies the head of BKNN or BNN. Again, this issue is related to the turf battle between the military and police.

16 The presidential instruction is Inpres no. 3/2002 Tentang Penanggulangan Penyalahgunaan dan Peredaran Gelap Narkoba.

(perang melawan narkoba) was launched in 2002. It nearly coincided with the seizure of a very large illicit drug laboratory in Tangerang, Banten, in April 2002. This laboratory which produced 150,000 ecstasy tablets per day was the largest drug factory ever discovered in Indonesia.[17] The surprising scale of production convinced the international community of the fact that Indonesia was no longer a mere transit country for illicit drug trafficking, but had emerged as a source of the regional narcotics trade.

Demonstrating the government's anti-drug commitment, BNN immediately prepared a 'war plan' to combat drug crime and announced its goal of 'a drug-free Indonesia in 2015'. In its 16-page document, the BNN emphasized that Chinese and West African drug syndicates were key players in the growing domestic production and distribution of illicit drugs – China as the source of precursor chemicals used for the production of synthetic drugs, such as ecstasy, and Nigerian crime enterprises as the smuggler of heroin and cocaine in Indonesia. The BNN also highlighted the sharp increase in drug abuse among youth, citing a survey that indicated 55% of respondents from 64 high schools used drugs. In laying out its action plan, the BNN stressed major difficulties and constraints: porous borders in the world's largest archipelagic country that render it vulnerable to drug smuggling; an ongoing economic crises since 1997 that led to budget cutbacks for programs targeting drug trafficking and abuse; and the weak capacity of BNN in terms of human resources, budget and equipment. These arguments effectively led BNN to conclude that 'a drug-free Indonesia in 2015' could be achieved only if these constraints are addressed. To this end, it recommended that: 1) BNN's capacity – manpower, budget, equipment – should be increased; 2) international cooperation in the field of law enforcement should be enhanced since the crimes were transnational, and; 3) programs for treatment and rehabilitation (T and R) of drug users should be urgently developed.[18]

In this way, BNN transformed Indonesia's 'traditional' problem of border-control into a very 'fundable' global problem involving organized drug trafficking requiring extensive international assistance. BNN underscored the need for promoting international cooperation, institutional capacity building, and victim protection at the grassroots level. These countermeasures are no doubt important and widely recognized as such by the international law enforcement community, but BNN deliberately obscures one vital 'domestic' cause of rapid drug proliferation during the post-Suharto era – that is, the collusion between the criminal syndicates and legitimate political actors and institutions. In the first year of BNN's campaign, it was announced that the cases of drug abuse in 2003 increased by 21% from the previous

17 'Digerebek, pabrik ekstasi terbesar di Indonesia', *Sinar Harapan* 8-4-2002. According to BNN, US DEA (Drug Enforcement Administration) identified the laboratory as the world's largest (Badan Narkotika Nasional 2003).

18 All citations in this paragraph are from Badan Narkotika Nasional 2003:5-6, 14-5.

year. Ansyaad Mbai, the Vice-Director of BNN, declared that drug abuse had reached epidemic proportions, but BNN was hamstrung due to limited human resources, and an inadequate budget and equipment to combat the transnational crime of illicit drug trafficking.[19] Having aroused public anxieties, he announced that BNN would establish provincial branches (Badan Narkotika Propinsi, BNP) throughout the archipelago to wage the 'war on drugs' by promoting Preventing and Combating Illicit Drug Trafficking and Abuse (Pencegahan dan Pemberantasan Penyalahgunaan dan Peredaran Gelap Narkoba, P4GN).[20] Then, in 2004 when the budget for the P4GN dropped to Rp 105 billion from Rp 150 billion in 2003, BNN started to prioritize activities that directly affected potential drug users and victims. Both Da'i Bachtiar (Director of BNN) and Makbul Padmanegara (Vice-Director of BNN) stressed that the anti-drug campaign should have a positive impact on the younger generation, and required the full cooperation of the public.[21] These shifts in strategy illustrate how BNN and its patron – the police – pursued institutional interests in waging the 'war on drugs'. The establishment of BNP and the extension of grassroots community activities both contribute to larger budget allocations while evading institutional responsibility and accountability regarding the politics-crime nexus. BNN focused on the symptoms rather than the cause of the problem.

To maintain institutional interests, the rhetoric of war requires constant escalation. Coinciding with the international day for the anti-drug campaign led by United Nations Office on Drugs and Crime (UNODC) on 26 June 2005, BNN set its national agenda, 'Improving the P4GN Implementation with High Commitment and Clear Actions', in order to socialize BNN's campaign both at the national and local levels.[22] When General Sutanto was installed as the new police chief and BNN director under the government of Susilo Bambang Yudhoyono in July 2005, he gathered all regional police chiefs, instructing them to make a contract with him for eradicating illicit drugs and gambling dens in their regions.[23] Nonetheless, the P4GN program in 2005 hardly changed in its combating (*pemberantasan*) initiatives. In its annual report, BNN explained that it had conducted seven activities to improve law enforcement capacity for combating illicit drugs – namely, hosting an international law enforcement meeting; providing a training course for the Lao police; conducting a joint seminar with the chemical industry; cooperating with

19 'Kejahatan narkoba meningkat 21,66 persen selama 2003', *Tempointeraktif* 6-1-2004.

20 'BNN siapkan strategi bebas narkoba', *Kompas* 7-1-2004.

21 'Police war on drugs taken to grassroots', *The Jakarta Post* 9-7-2004; 'BNN lancarkan peran melawan narkoba', 24-9-2004, available at BNN website, http://www.bnn.go.id/konten.php?nama= KegiatanCegah&op=detail_kegiatan_cegah&id=23&mn=2&smn=f (accessed 12-09-2010).

22 Badan Narkotika Nasional, 'Pedoman Peringatan Hari Internasional Melawan Penyalahgunaan dan Peredaran Gelap Narkoba', 26-6-2005.

23 'Kontrak kerja kapolda se-Indonesia: Berantas judi seminggu', *Bali Post* 12-7-2005.

UNODC to develop computer-based training; spreading information about drug-related laws; destroying drug materials; and distributing operational equipment such as portable x-ray machines to BNN teams (Badan Narkotika Nasional 2006:23-4).

There is no denying that these activities bolstered BNN's international cooperation and investigative capacity, but it is telling that there were no efforts targeting the domestic politics-crime nexus. As drug abuse continued to rise under the Yudhoyono administration, critics expressed doubts about the approach taken by BNN and the police. At the end of 2005, however, BNN persisted in emphasizing that the eradication of illicit drugs was a serious challenge because it involved transnational crime among other complex factors and consequences (Badan Narkotika Nasional 2005). Perhaps trying to boost the six-years-old anti-drugs campaign, and to gain popular support, Yudhoyono underlined the need for escalating the war on drugs in 2008 on international anti-drug day by insisting that the current P4GN – which had two main pillars, that is, prevention and eradication – would be upgraded with an additional three pillars. The new pillars were 'therapy and rehabilitation', 'alternative development' and 'research and information'.[24] The expanded P4GN now emphasizes the 'protection' approach and victim care, making the 'war' more like a social campaign aimed at 'saving the youth of the next generation'.

It is widely believed that the fundamental problem of Indonesia's illicit drug trafficking is corruption in the law enforcement sector which allows large scale criminal enterprises to operate hand-in-hand with corrupt officers. Adrianus Meliala, a prominent criminologist, openly criticizes 'the police, who are supposed to fight drug crime, are drug dealers and consumers'.[25] These allegations raise few eyebrows among those familiar with how the police work and certainly resonate with public perceptions. In 1999, 2nd Lieutenant Agus Isrok – a son of army chief of staff General Subagyo – was arrested with packs of '*shabu-shabu*' (methamphetamine), and 7,000 ecstasy pills at Manggabesar, Jakarta's notorious nightspot district. Isrok was a member of the elite military commando unit Kopassus often deployed in secret operations, indicating that the police did not have a monopoly on drug dealing.[26] This incident was followed by the establishment of BKNN in 2000 and its operations resulted in the arrests of 398 police personnel, mostly low-ranking officers, in the same year.[27] Even after this 'shock therapy', the army-police gun battles in Madiun (East Java) in 2001 and in Binjai (North Sumatra)

24 'SBY: Tingkatkan perang terhadap narkoba', *Berita Sore* 23-6-2008.

25 'From ecstasy to agony: Indonesia's war on drugs', *Asia Times* 26-11-1999. The general public also shares this perception as seen in *The Jakarta Post*'s special coverage, 'Drug dealers are untouchable', *The Jakarta Post* 16-1-2003 and 'Police rely on money from drug dealers', The Jakarta Post 17-1-2003.

26 'Setelah Agus Isrok digaruk operasi narkotik', *Tempo* 16-8-1999.

27 'Citra Bhayangkara ternoda Nila', *Gatra* 3-7-2008.

in 2002 both involved conflicts over the illicit drug business.[28] Sutanto's strong anti-drug commitment since 2005 was welcomed at large. However, the public still believes that the police are deeply involved in the drug business; an opinion survey conducted by Institute for Social and Economic Research, Education and Information (Lembaga Penelitian, Pendidikan dan Penerangan Ekonomi dan Sosial, LP3ES) revealed that more than 40% of 600 respondents believe the police are the main 'backers' of drug trafficking.[29] There are even plausible allegations that drug trafficking networks exist within the regional police command in East Java, and probably elsewhere.[30]

To sum up, the post-Suharto 'war on drugs' exhibits three interesting features. First, the government has repeatedly expressed its commitment to eradicate illicit drugs by promoting international cooperation. Such 'diplomacy' is always highlighted in the documents of anti-drug campaigns, and it effectively constructs an image of the government trying to combat domestic repercussions of 'global' crimes. The problem of illicit drug trafficking in Indonesia is typically tied to drug syndicates originating in the Netherlands, China and Nigeria.[31] This emphasis portrays Indonesia as a 'victim' of transnational organized crime. Stoking the sense of victimization no doubt helps the government to whip up nationalism against external criminal actors, bolster budgets and gain public support for both a crackdown and more extensive international cooperation.

Second, it is also notable that the war on drugs emphasizes the significance of targeting the alleged 'root cause' of the problem – in this instance community unawareness of the drug menace. BNN usually argues that transnational criminal groups target the country's less-educated social strata. In fact, this is the largest market for illicit drugs and there is a tendency for targeting young users with cheap synthetic narcotics. Underlining 'unawareness' and targeting of the poor constitutes a significant element in the framing of the transnational crime threat. This helps mobilize public support for the war on drugs as a facet of the larger 'war on poverty'. It is in this context that policies such as 'grassroots socialization' and 'alternative development' are emphasized as long-term viable approaches to protect citizens from the alleged dangers of transnational crime. This 'root-cause discourse' effectively legitimizes government allocation of its resources for community development projects in the name of combating crime while obscuring the key role played by security professionals in the drug trade.

28 Regarding the Madiun incident, see 'Perseteruan saudara tua dan saudara muda', *Tempo* 24-9-2001. On Binjai's case, see Roosa 2003.

29 'Survei: Hampir separuh polisi jadi beking bandar narkoba', *Koran Tempo* 7-12-2007.

30 About the allegation, see 'Karena narkoba, rusak reputasinya', *Gatra* 19-6-2008.

31 According to Sri Soegiarto, Deputy Director of BNN, Jewish syndicates are also recently active in Indonesia. Interview 4-7-2007.

Third, it is also remarkable that Indonesia's war on drugs highlights the point that drug smuggling in the age of globalism cannot be controlled effectively by a government that only provides a minimum budget for law enforcement agencies. The war campaigns constantly draw attention to the lack of manpower, knowledge, instruments and finance to conduct effective anti-crime operations. Against this backdrop, foreign 'stakeholders' who share concerns about the growing threat of transnational crime – such as the US and UNODC – are eager to cooperate with BNN to improve its capacity in crime prevention and enforcement. Here, the agenda of 'capacity building' is described as the key to improve performance in the war on drugs. This discourse fits seamlessly with the agenda of the police and BNN, reflecting the fruits of their lobbying.

There is no denying that issues like capacity building, root causes and foreign-organized crime are important in understanding the problems surrounding transnational crime. However, Indonesia's 'war' suggests that these issues serve to conceal the vital core of the problem – the growing criminal influence in political and security sectors. The rhetoric of transnational crime effectively contributes to the construction of a discourse that neglects the political pollution while emphasizing alleged global threats, diplomatic policies and socioeconomic agendas.

Army and the 'war on terrorism'

The discourse about the transnational crime threat has also aided the army in promoting policies to preserve institutional interests, survive turf battles and emasculate pressures for reform. In particular, the 'war on terrorism' provides a golden opportunity to achieve these existing agendas and has been instrumentalized accordingly. As discussed above, the army has seen the rise of the police in terms of a turf battle over domestic security roles and business opportunities. After formally transferring the role of internal security to the police, the army has been particularly concerned about growing pressure to reform its territorial command structure, a holdover from the authoritarian past. In this sense, reclaiming a role in internal security would be a welcome lifeline, enabling the army to maintain its command structure with only cosmetic changes. For many army officers, the elimination of the territorial command structure is unacceptable. They believe that Indonesia – a multi-ethnic nation spread over a large archipelago – may fall apart without the firm grip of the army, and also fear, perhaps even more, that such a reform would inevitably lead to institutional downsizing. To stave off this threat, fanning fears about the role of transnational actors to generate domestic instability can be a viable strategy. The war on terrorism created such an institutional opportunity to regain lost ground and deflect pressures to reform.

Particularly since 9/11, the army started to disseminate a discourse which insisted that national defence and internal security are actually inseparable because many of the non-traditional security threats are situated in a 'grey zone' between defence and security. The 'theory' then asserts that Indonesia's geopolitical circumstances require the army to defend the nation from domestic penetration by external threats and thus domestic security should be an integral part of 'defence' operations. From this standpoint, the army began to criticize the Defence Law enacted in 2002. They problematized article 7 of the law, which stated that the role of the military was to respond to military threats, but assigned non-military threats to other government institutions. In the eyes of army officers, this law ignores the 'grey zone' and does not reflect the reality of defence-security linkages.[32] A window of opportunity to become more assertive came following the October 2002 terrorist bombing in Bali. This tragedy revealed Indonesia's vulnerable security situation, and the army quickly responded by revitalizing the activity of *babinsa* – the village level unit in the territorial command – ostensibly to detect possible terrorist movements. Since the police organization did not reach the village level, the army was confident that *babinsa* in the army network could restore the legitimacy of military surveillance at the local level and the military's role in domestic security. In the aftermath of the Bali bombing, Indonesia's political community was reticent about questioning the army tactic to re-deploy territorial command resources for counter-terrorism operations.

Subsequently in March 2003, when the military published its first post-Suharto Defence White Book, the army-orchestrated 'grey zone' theory was more explicitly articulated in terms of defence-security syncretism. The army stressed that the primary concerns of Indonesia's 'defence' sector had shifted from 'traditional' threats – that is, conventional military attacks by foreign countries – to 'non-traditional' ones such as terrorism, piracy, illegal migrants, separatist movements and armed rebellions (Departemen Pertahanan 2003). In order to respond to these new threats, it was argued, the military needs to strengthen its capacity and role in military operations other than warfare (Operasi Militer Selain Perang, OMSP) in which the demarcation between defence and security is irrelevant. Since then, the army has intensified internal socialization about the legitimacy of defence-security syncretism by producing a set of guidelines for OMSP (Markas Besar TNI 2003). This effort peaked in 2004 when the long-awaited Military Law – replacing the old one of 1982 that legalized *dwifungsi* – was enacted. The army lobby successfully put an article in the new law to address OMSP as TNI's basic duty.[33] For the army, this legal basis was significant to fortify the grey zone theory, assert its

32 Interview with Lieutenant General Djaja Suparman, Inspector General of the TNI, 9-1-2005.

33 The new TNI law is UU no. 34/2004 tentang Tentara Nasional Indonesia. OMSP is described in the article 7(2).

legitimate role in security affairs, and to maintain the utility of the territorial command structure.

The OMSP discourse was further consolidated under the Yudhoyono government. In July 2005, Yudhoyono claimed that Indonesia's national integrity was seriously threatened by transnational crime, such as drugs and other illegal trade, and instructed both the police and the military to boost their law enforcement operations.[34] This construction of a fiction (that is, cross-border crimes threaten national integrity) was repeatedly reiterated by other political and military elites, including the governor of Lemhanas, the national defence think-tank, who acknowledged rivalry between the military and the police, but suggested that the military had a legitimate role to play since the police cannot handle transnational crime on its own.[35] The military commander, General Djoko Santoso, similarly stressed that acts of terrorism, both global and regional, constantly pose serious threats to Indonesia. The TNI, he continues, is committed to combat the terrorist threat, as specified in the Military Law.[36]

In this manner, the army skilfully neutralized pressure to limit its role to external defence by incorporating transnational crime – including terrorism – into the scope of non-traditional security issues that support the 'defence' agenda in the context of 'grey zone' theory. Although the army's efforts to undo the separation of security and defence partly embraces its long-standing self-image as the sole guardian of the nation, it also reflects institutional resistance to reform targeting the territorial command structure. As discussed above, the territorial commands are vital for the army to promote fundraising, generate economic and promotion opportunities, and maintain the size of a force that is the largest – and thus most powerful and prestigious – within the military. The army discourse concerning transnational crime and terrorism contributes to this strategy of resisting reform.

The navy and transnational crime at sea

The navy has also developed its own interpretation of the transnational crime threat in creating a pretext for regaining its supremacy vis-à-vis the police in the field of maritime law enforcement.[37] Warning that regional criminal rings operate in Indonesian waters without facing serious state interference, the international community has pressured the government to strengthen its law

34 'Presiden: Kejahatan transnasional rugikan Indonesia', *KapanLagi.com* 18-7-2005.

35 'Muladi: Masih ada kompetisi TNI-Polri soal keamanan nasional', *AntaraNews* 13-5-2008; 'Pemerintah perkuat koordinasi TNI-Polri', *Suara Merdeka* 29-7-2008.

36 'Panglima TNI: Teroris mula tebar ancaman', *Kompas* 29-11-2008.

37 For a detailed discussion in this section, see Honna 2008.

enforcement capacity to combat transnational crime at sea. Donor countries, such as the US, Australia, Japan, and ASEAN members have made commitments to promote regional and bilateral cooperation to fight cross-border maritime crime. It is in this arena that the role of the navy as a stakeholder in maritime security has been neutralized vis-à-vis 'civilian' law enforcement agencies that can institutionally promote closer cooperation with other countries and operate in a less threatening manner compared to the armed forces.

Clearly the navy faced several obstacles in promoting international cooperation against transnational crime. First, the navy has been the subject of a US ban on military aid since 1999.[38] This US sanction effectively helped the police to gain greater assistance from Washington in developing capacity to deal with maritime security related to terrorism and crime. With this cooperation in progress, the navy was left behind the water police (Polair) which enjoyed various offers of grants, including the provision of patrol vessels and training, under the US International Criminal Investigative Training Assistance Program (ICITAP).

Second, it has gradually become common practice for the regional security community to build up civilian coast guard agencies both in order to deal professionally with maritime crime in the sovereign territory and to promote regional cooperation between these agencies.[39] The navy's warships are not suitable for handling transnational crime; instead, smaller, speedier patrol boats are most appropriate for the mission and cost far less to purchase, run and maintain. In recognition of the rising threat of crime at sea, the Philippines established its coast guard in 1998 and Malaysia did so in 2004. Clearly, the navy found itself out of the loop in the region's newly emerging maritime strategic environment.

Third, there was a new priority for port security in the wake of 9/11. The US strongly demanded the international community, in the name of the global war on terrorism, to review the existing International Ship and Port Facility Security (ISPS) Code, resulting in the adoption of an amended version by the International Maritime Organization (IMO) in December 2002, and its implementation in July 2004. The amended ISPS Code had two key revisions: 1) all countries which signed the 1974 International Convention for the Safety of Life at Sea (SOLAS) – including Indonesia – are obliged to provide appropriate security measures in their ports; and 2) these countries are allowed to formally exercise control over foreign ships in their territorial waters, including the denial of port entry. These revisions came as a big shock for the shipping industry in Indonesia since the country's maritime waters were identified

[38] The ban was to protest human rights abuses by TNI in East Timor. This ban was mostly lifted in 2005 under the Bush administration which saw Indonesia as a partner in its 'war on terrorism'.

[39] About this trend, see Bateman 2003.

as a 'black spot', or dangerous zone, in the international community,[40] and therefore ships from Indonesia to the US could be stopped and denied access in accordance with the amended ISPS Code (Supit 2004:13-4). For Indonesia's maritime industry, it became apparent that Indonesia's weak governance at sea could prove a huge economic liability. The improvement of port security soon became a major concern for the government in dealing with the new security regime at sea, but the agenda of strengthening law enforcement in the ports was not a navy matter. Again, the navy was left bobbing in the wake of new developments in maritime security.

Having assessed the changing strategic environment in the age of transnational crime, and the limits of the navy to deal with it, the Yudhoyono government issued a presidential decree in 2005 to transfer the authority of the Maritime Security Coordinating Body (Badan Koordinasi Keamanan Laut Republik Indonesia, Bakorkamla) from TNI headquarters to the Coordinating Ministry of Political, Legal and Security Affairs. The new Bakorkamla is charged with formulating national maritime policy and coordinating the activities of 12 maritime-related institutions, including the navy and Polair.

When the idea of a new Bakorkamla first emerged in 2004, it was the navy that expressed the strongest resistance, fearing the possible loss of maritime authority and business interests that it has enjoyed.[41] Significantly, however, the navy quickly recognized that its resistance would not change the situation, because – unlike the army – it had no strong political resources to shape the direction of government discourse. Thus, how to take the initiative in developing Bakorkamla soon dominated the agenda of the navy's top echelons. They found an answer in proposing the establishment of the Sea and Coast Guard of Indonesia (SCGI). In December 2006, the navy headquarters submitted its initial plan to establish SCGI as Indonesia's contribution to regional maritime security cooperation.[42]

According to Vice Admiral Tedjo Edhy Purdijatno, 'it is difficult for the navy to fully respond to the changing demands of maritime security, therefore we encourage Bakorkamla to take further steps to build our Coast Guard and streamline the inefficient structure of maritime authority today'.[43] According to the navy proposal, many democratic countries have professional civilian paramilitary organizations called coast guards that conduct maritime law

40 See, for example, 'Indonesia piracy black spot as attacks rise', *Lloyd's List* 7-11-2000, p.18.

41 Like other services, the navy established its own foundation and corporations, and both controlled various enterprises involving shipping, resorts, oil refineries, real-estate, cocoa plantations, maritime electronics and telecommunications, transportation, fisheries, construction, and timber. For details, see Widoyoko et al. 2003:120. The navy's involvement in illegal business is typified by its protection of smuggling rings, most notoriously in the case of illegal logging. See, for example, EIA/Telapak 2005.

42 The official document is Markas Besar Angkatan Laut 2006.

43 Interview, 24-8-2007. Tedjo Edhy Purdijatno was Director-General of Defense Planning at the Defence Ministry. In 2008, he was promoted to the navy chief-of-staff.

enforcement activities. Responsibility for Indonesia's coast guard function is unclear because of overlapping authority and legal responsibilities spread across 12 institutions related to maritime governance. To meet global expectations, the proposal argues, it is time to streamline maritime authority and establish a unified representative in the global community of coast guards (Markas Besar Angkatan Laut 2006:11). The navy insists that the new coast guard, or SCGI, should be given a clear legal status as a maritime law enforcement agency, and that it be placed under the Ministry of Transportation in order to comply with international standards. With this new organization, the navy is proposing to rationalize the overlapping functions of other related agencies, including the navy itself. In this way, the navy, which was originally very reluctant to reorganize maritime security management, has now become the prime mover in reform and reorganization.

What were the calculations behind this shifting attitude? First, the new organization can absorb some of the officers in the top-heavy navy. 'The navy will be more professional if SCGI is established and staffed with our friends', according to one navy officer.[44] It is expected that the transfer of high-level officers may encourage the promotion of younger generation officers within the navy. In addition, if SCGI recruits personnel from the navy – like the coast guards of the Philippines and Malaysia – it may contribute to confidence building between the two institutions and nurture respect for each other's jurisdictions. In the cases of the Philippines and Malaysia, many naval officers wished to move to the new agencies, motivated by higher salary and the relatively 'clean' image enjoyed by the coast guards.

Second, emphasising the global trend of international coast guard cooperation is a very effective way for the navy to neutralize the role of the police in maritime security. With the creation of SCGI, the navy expects donor countries to provide both financial and technical assistance to develop its capacity to combat transnational crime, which in turn may help constrain the ascendancy of the police in security sector governance. If a significant number of SCGI personnel is drawn from among former navy officers (as expected), the navy-SCGI alliance may overwhelm the presence of Polair. In May 2008, a new Shipping Law (UU no. 17/2008) was enacted with the powerful lobbying of the maritime industry and the navy. The new law's Chapter 17 is about the establishment of SCGI and the new organization is directly under the President. Although the details of the plan are not clear yet, it is basically in line with the navy's proposal.[45]

In this manner the discourse of transnational crime threat (at sea) has provided a rationale for the navy to insist on the need for 'harmonizing'

44 Interview with Col. Desi A. Mamahit, Assistant of Operation to the Western Fleet Commander, 16-12-2007.

45 Interview with former navy chief-of-staff, General Bernard Kent Sondakh, 8-10-2008.

Indonesia's security structure with 'global standards', a clever tactic aimed at promoting navy interests. In promoting the establishment of SCGI, the navy expects to have significant influence over and within this new civilian institution, seeing an opportunity to build a 'second navy' that may effectively undermine the role of the police in maritime security governance. Significantly, this navy agenda perfectly fits with the institutional interests of the TNI as a whole.

Conclusion

One cannot neglect the problem of transnational crime in discussing the relationship between the state and crime in the globalizing world. It is particularly so since 2000 when leaders from 154 counties gathered in Palermo, Italy, in order to sign a new UN Convention against Transnational Organized Crime. It was a watershed in the post-Cold War global security agenda, in a sense that national leaders jointly identified transnational crime as a 'security' threat. Various 'wars' have been conducted around the globe to fight against the alleged threats – including illicit drugs, terrorism, sea piracy, and human trafficking. The international community has supported and promoted these 'fight against' projects by providing 'weak states' with financial support, capacity-building assistance, and joint training programs. Realist political scientists may argue that the state advances such international cooperation as a rational policy to enhance its ability to control anti-social forces in the sovereign territory. The constructivist school of thought may stress that the 'shared value' – that is, the threat posed by trans-border, non-state criminal actors – plays an important role in harmonizing security designs of the states in the region. These views are well-embedded in the current trend of international assistance programs sponsored by donor countries and major aid institutions aimed at 'combating common enemies together.'

What we have discussed in this chapter provides a critical view on these trends. The threat of transnational crime is undoubtedly real, but its image can be constructed arbitrarily by the state as it typically dominates intelligence regarding criminal activities and can curb transparency and avoid accountability in the name of state and diplomatic secrecy. This creates political space to manipulate the interpretation and discourse of transnational crime. Those engaged in power politics exploit this open space, and construct scenarios to promote varied and often long-standing agendas. For BNN, inventing a root cause of drug trafficking that avoids the messy and dangerous nexus of drug syndicates and state actors helped accelerate the expansion of budget and institutional capacity; an important mission for the police to establish a 'second police'. For the army, the discourse over transnational crime served as a pretext for legitimizing OMSP which in turn helped resurrect its internal security role and preserve the territorial command structure. For the navy, it was able to preserve its influence vis-à-vis the police in maritime law enforcement activities by skilfully insisting on the need for establishing a civilian coast guard to deal with transnational crime at sea. In all these cases, there seems to be a common political strategy of instrumentalizing the threat of transnational crime. With this strategy, these three institutions were able to deflect criticism, reclaim ground lost during the democratization movement, and articulate this revanchism in the legitimizing vernacular of 'global wars'. In this sense these security actors are hijacking transnational crime as a Trojan horse to regain power, build budgets, strengthen institutions and undermine reform pressures.

As we noted at the outset, a notable development in the post-Suharto polity is the deepening criminalization of the legitimate political and security sector triggered by the police-military rivalry and political decentralization. This is the very factor which has sustained the growing industry of cross-border illegal businesses in Indonesia. Thus, any anti-crime countermeasures which fail to target the core factor may facilitate unintended consequences, most seriously the empowerment of anti-reform agendas. To prevent the international community being a blind enabler of the Trojan horse, it is crucial to understand the dynamics of power politics and the possible impact of introducing counter-crime cooperation programs on the constellation of power relations among domestic stakeholders. This is perhaps the most important contribution that area studies can make – opening the black box of domestic politics – to infuse global agendas with an understanding and appreciation for sobering local realities. Here lies the raison d'être of area studies in the borderless world.

Abbreviations

AIVD	Algemene Inlichtingen- en Veiligheidsdienst (General Information and Security Service)
AKI	Asosiasi Kontraktor Indonesia (Indonesian Association of Contractors)
AMSI	Asosiasi Manager Security Indonesia (Indonesian Security Managers Association)
ANRC	Australia Netherlands Research Collaboration
APBD	Anggaran Pendapatan dan Belanja Daerah (Indonesian Provincial and District Budget)
Aspekindo	Asosiasi Pengusaha Konstruksi Indonesia (Indonesian Association of Construction Entrepreneurs)
Babinsa	Bintara Pembina Desa (non-commissioned officer for village guidance, lowest level unit in territorial command)
BAKIN	Badan Koordinasi Intelijen Negara (National Intelligence Coordinating Agency)
Bakorkamla	Badan Koordinasi Keamanan Laut (Maritime Security Coordinating Agency)
Bamus Betawi	Badan Musyawarah Betawi (Betawi Community Consultation Agency)
BEEPS	Business Environment and Enterprise Performance Survey
BHMN	Badan Hukum Milik Negara (state-owned legal entity)
BIN	Badan Intelijen Negara (National Intelligence Agency)
BKNN	Badan Koordinasi Narkotika Nasional (National Narcotics Coordinating Board)
BNN	Badan Narkotika Nasional (National Narcotics Board)
BNP2TKI	Badan Nasional Penempatan dan Perlindungan Tenaga Kerja Indonesia (National Agency for the Placement and Protection of Indonesian Migrant Workers)
BOW	Burgerlijke Openbare Werken (Civic Public Works)
BPKRI	Badan Pemeriksa Kuangan Republik Indonesia (Indonesia Supreme Audit Board)
BRDP	Book Reading Development Project

BRIMOB	Brigade Mobil (Police Mobile Brigade)
Bulog	Badan Urusan Logistik (Logistics Agency, government-owned company which deals with food distribution and price control)
BUMN	Badan Usaha Milik Negara (state-owned enterprise)
CIFOR	Centre for International Forestry Research
DEA	Drug Enforcement Administration
DFID	Department for International Development [United Kingdom]
DPR	Dewan Perwakilan Rakyat (People's Representative Council, Indonesia's parliament)
DPRD	Dewan Perwakilan Rakyat Daerah (Regional People's Representative Councils)
FBR	Forum Betawi Rempug (Betawi Brotherhood Forum)
FPI	Front Pembela Islam (Defenders of Islam Front)
Gabpeknas	Gabungan Perusahaan Kontraktor Nasional (National Association of Contracting Companies)
GAM	Gerakan Aceh Merdeka (Free Aceh Movement)
Gapeksindo	Gabungan Perusahaan Konstruksi Nasional Indonesia (Indonesian National Association of Construction Companies)
Gapensi	Gabungan Pelaksana Konstruksi Nasional Seluruh Indonesia (All Indonesia Association of National Construction Implementers)
IBRA	Indonesian Bank Reconstruction Agency
ICG	International Crisis Group
ICITAP	International Criminal Investigative Training Assistance Program
ICW	Indonesia Corruption Watch
Ikahi	Ikatan Hakim Indonesia (Association of Indonesian Judges)
IKBT	Ikatan Keluarga Besar Tanah Abang (Tanah Abang Greater Family Association)
IMO	International Maritime Organization
INFID	International NGO Forum on Indonesian Development
Inkindo	Ikatan Nasional Konsultan Indonesia (National Union of Indonesian Consultants)
INT	Department of Institutional Integrity [World Bank]
IPK	Ikatan Pemuda Karya (Youth Work Institute)
ISPS Code	International Ship and Port Facility Security Code
JK	Jusuf Kalla
Kadin	Kamar Dagang dan Industri Indonesia (Indonesian Chamber of Commerce)
kapolres	Kepala Kepolisian Resor (district or city police chief)
KRHN	Konsorsium Reformasi Hukum Nasional (National Law Reform Consortium)
KKMS	Kelompok Kerja Masyarakat Sipil (Civil Society Working Group)

KKN	Korupsi, Kolusi dan Nepotisme (Corruption, Collusion and Nepotism)
KPK	Komisi Pemberantasan Korupsi (Corruption Eradication Commission)
KPN	Kantor Perbendaharaan Negara (State Treasury Office)
KTKLN	Kartu Tenaga Kerja Luar Negeri (overseas employment card)
KTP	Kartu Tanda Penduduk (personal identity card)
KTP musiman	seasonal identity card [valid for 6 months]
KUHAP	Kitab Undang-Undang Acara Hukum Pidana (Code of Criminal Procedure)
LeIP	Lembaga Kajian dan Advokasi untuk Independensi Peradilan (Institute for Research and Advocacy for the Independence of the Courts)
LP3ES	Lembaga Penelitian Pendidikan dan Penerangan Ekonomi dan Sosial (Institute for Social and Economic Research, Education and Information)
LPJK	Lembaga Pengembangan Jasa Konstruksi (Institute for the Development of Construction Services)
LSC	Local School Council
MBS	Manajemen Berbasis Sekolah (school-based management)
MPR	Majelis Permusyawaratan Rakyat (People's Consultative Assembly), supreme decision-making body comprising members of parliament and regional, military and community representatives
NIE	New Institutional Economics
OECD	Organization for Economic Cooperation and Development
OMSP	Operasi Militer Selain Perang (Military Operations other than War)
OTB	Organisasi Tanpa Bentuk (organization without form)
P4GN	Pencegahan dan Pemberantasan Penyalahgunaan dan Peredaran Gelap Narkoba (Preventing and Combating Illicit Drug Trafficking and Abuse)
Pam Swakarsa	Pasukan Pengamanan Swakarsa (Voluntary Security Guards)
paspor TKI	Paspor Tenaga Kerja Indonesia (labour migration passport)
PCDC	Procurement Capacity Development Centre [UN]
PDI-P	Partai Demokrasi Indonesia – Perjuangan (Indonesia Democratic Party of Struggle), party led by Megawati Sukarnoputri
PPM	Pemuda Panca Marga (New Order nationalist youth organization; semi-official *preman* group)
Petrus	Penembakan Misterius ('mysterious shootings', phrase coined during anti-crime killings in 1983)
pilkada	pemilihan kepala daerah (direct election of chiefs of regions)

pimpro	pimpinan proyek (project overseer); local project leader
PKB	Partai Kebangkitan Bangsa (National Awakening Party)
PKS	Partai Keadilan Sejahtera (Prosperous Justice Party)
Polair	Polisi Air (water police)
polsek	Kepolisian Sektor (sub-district police)
PRD	Partai Rakyat Demokratik (People's Democratic Party, student-based)
PTIK	Perguruan Tinggi Ilmu Kepolisian (Institute of Police Science)
PU	Pekerjaan Umum (Public Works)
SBU	Sertifikat Badan Usaha (business permit)
SBY	Susilo Bambang Yudhoyono
SCGI	Sea and Coast Guard of Indonesia
SIGP	School Improvement Grant Project
SIP	Surat Izin Pengerahan (migrant worker placement licence, held by Pelaksana Penempatan TKI or migrant worker placement agency)
SOEs	State-owned enterprises
SOLAS	International Convention for the Safety of Life at Sea [1974]
TGPTPK	Tim Gabungan Pemberantasan Tindak Pidana Korupsi (Joint Corruption Eradication Team)
TNI	Tentara Nasional Indonesia (Indonesian military)
UDHR	Universal Declaration of Human Rights
UNCED	United Nations Conference on Environment and Development
UNDP	United Nations Development Program
UNICEF	United Nations Children's Emergency Fund
UNODC	United Nations Office on Drugs and Crime
UNPAN	United Nations Public Administration Network
USAID	United States Agency for International Development
VOC	Verenigde Oost-Indische Compagnie (Dutch East India Company)
WTO	World Trade Organization

Glossary

beking	backing
bupati	district chief
carok	murder by knifing (Madura)
demang	colonial native district chief outside Java
Dewan Ekonomi dan Pembangunan	Economic and Development Council
dinas pendidikan	education bureau
disetor ke atas	deposited higher up
dwifungsi	the army's 'dual function' (military and sociopolitical) in New Order Indonesia
fiktif	phantom or fictitious
hakim	judge
haram	unclean, forbidden
hukum revolusi	revolutionary law
Idul Fitri	celebrations to mark the end of the fasting month (Ramadan)
jatah pimpro	project overseer fee
jawara	champions (Betawi, Banten)
juragan	small business boss (Betawi)
kabupaten	district
kantor lelang	auction house
kantor pengadilan	office of the justice department
Kantor Perbendaharaan Kas Negara	State Treasury Office
kepala dinas	bureau head
kiai	religious leader
konsultan pengawas/supervisi	supervisory consultants
kota	city
kota preman	gang city
Mahkamah Konstitusi	Constitutional Court
Majelis Kehormatan Hakim	Judges Honour Council
maksiat	vice, 'moral threat'
melobi	lobbying
membangunan relasi	build relations

pak ogah	illegal traffic wardens
Pancasila	The five guiding principles of the Indonesian state: belief in one supreme God; just and civilized humanity; national unity; democracy led by wisdom and prudence through consultation and representation; social justice
panitia pelelangan	tendering committee
pemberantasan	combating
pengadilan agama	religious court
penunjukan langsung	direct appointment
perang melawan narkoba	war on drugs
perbuatan tercela	inappropriate behaviour
pergaulan luas	having wide social relations
perusahaan bendera	'flag' company with nothing but its logo
preman	thug, gangster
polisi gadungan	fake police
pusat perbukuan	book centre
reformasi	reform
tim sukses	success team
uang mundur	'withdrawal money'
uang panas	hot money
zakat	Islamic tax

Bibliography

Abdul Rahman, Noorashikin

2003 *Negotiating power; A case study of Indonesian foreign domestic workers in Singapore*. PhD thesis, Curtin University of Technology, Victoria.

Abraham, Itty and Willem van Schendel

2005 'Introduction; The making of illicitness', in: Willem van Schendel and Itty Abraham (eds), *Illicit flows and criminal things; States, borders, and the other side of globalization*, pp. 1-37. Bloomington: Indiana University Press.

Abrahams, Ray

1998 *Vigilant citizens; Vigilantism and the state*. Cambridge: Polity Press.

Abrams, Philip

1988 'Notes on the difficulty of studying the state', *Journal of Historical Sociology* 1-1:58-89.

Acemoglu, Daron R. and James A. Robinson

2006 *Economic origins of dictatorship and democracy*. Cambridge: Cambridge University Press.

ADB

2002 *Country governance assessment report Republic Indonesia, draft report*. Jakarta: Asian Development Bank.

Aditjondro, George J.

1998 'Chips off the old block: Suharto's corrupt children', *Green Left Weekly* 305, 11 February.

2002 'Bukan persoalan telur dan ayam; Membangun kerangka holistik bagi gerakan anti-korupsi di Indonesia', *Wacana* 2-4:17-30. [Yogyakarta: Insist Press.]

2006 *Korupsi kepresidenan – Reproduksi oligarki berkaki tiga; Istana, tangsi dan partai penguasa*. Yogyakarta: LKiS.

2009 'Jejak rekam para capres', *Indonesia Media Online* (30 March). http://www.indonesiamedia.com/2009/4/MID/berta/jejak.html (accessed 5-4-2009).

Afiff, Suraya, Noer Fauzi, Gillian Hart, Lungisile Ntsebeza and Nancy Peluso

2005 *Refining agrarian power; Resurgent agrarian movements in West Java, Indonesia*. Berkeley, CA: Center for Southeast Asia Studies, University of California. http://escholarship.org/uc/item/7rf2p49g (accessed 11-3-2010).

Allan, T.R.S.

1998 'Rule of law (Rechtsstaat)', in: Edward Craig (ed.), *Routledge encyclopedia of philosophy*. London: Routledge. http://www.rep.routledge.com/article/T022 (accessed 29-4-2009).

Amnesty International
2009 *Unfinished business; Police accountability in Indonesia*. London: Amnesty International.

Anderson, Benedict R.O'G.
1972 'The idea of power in Javanese culture', in: Claire Holt (ed.), *Culture and politics in Indonesia*, pp. 1-69. Ithaca, NY: Cornell University Press.
1983 'Old state, new society; Indonesia's New Order in comparative historical perspective', *Journal of Asian Studies* 42-3:477-96.
2001 (ed.) *Violence and the state in Suharto's Indonesia*. Ithaca, NY: Southeast Asia Program, Cornell University.

Arthur, John A. and Otwin Marenin
1995 'Explaining crime in developing countries; The need for a case study approach', *Crime, Law and Social Change* 23:191-214.

Asia Foundation and ACNielsen Indonesia
2001 *Survey report on citizen's perceptions of the Indonesian justice sector; Preliminary findings and recommendations*. [Jakarta]: The Asia Foundation and ACNielsen.

Aspandi, Ali
2002 *Menggugat sistem hukum peradilan Indonesia yang penuh ketidakpastian*. Surabaya: Lembaga Kajian Strategis Hukum Indonesia dan Lutfansah Mediatama.

Aspinall, Edward
2005 *Opposing Suharto; Compromise, resistance, and regime change in Indonesia*. Stanford, CA: Stanford University Press.
2009 'Combatants to contractors; The political economy of peace in Aceh', *Indonesia* 87:1-34.

Assegaf, Ibrahim
2002 'Legends of the fall; An institutional analysis of Indonesian law enforcement agencies combating corruption', in: Tim Lindsey and Howard Dick (eds), *Corruption in Asia; Rethinking the governance paradigm*, pp. 127-46. Leichhardt, NSW: Federation Press.

Athukorala, Prema-Chandra
2006 'International labour migration in East Asia; Trends, patterns and policy issues', *Asian-Pacific Economic Literature* 20-5:18-39.

Backman, Michael
1999 *Asian eclipse; Exposing the dark side of business in Asia*. Singapore: Wiley.

Badan Narkotika Nasional
2003 'Strategic concept to combat the drug menace in pursuit of a drug free Indonesia – 2015'. Paper, March.
2005 'Press release tahunan ketua Badan Narkotika Nasional'. Paper, December.
2006 'Laporan pelaksanaan kegiatan Kalakhar BNN tahun 2005'. Paper, February.

Badan Pemeriksa Keuangan Republik Indonesia
2006 *Hasil pemeriksaan atas pengelolaan dana pembinaan dan penyelenggaraan penempatan tenaga kerja Indonesia dan pelaksanaan penempatan tenaga kerja Indonesia ke luar negeri tahun anggaran 2004 dan 2005 pada Ditjen Pembinaan dan Penempatan Tenaga Kerja Luar Negeri, Dinas Tenaga Kerja, Balai Pelayanan dan Penempatan Tenaga Kerja Indonesia serta instansi terkait lainnya di Jakarta, Surabaya, Pekanbaru dan Batam.* Jakarta: Badan Pemeriksa Keuangan Republik Indonesia.

Badoh, Ibrahim Fahmy
2005 'Manipulasi dana kampanye dan politik uang pemilu; Deskripsi dan evaluasi untuk perbaikan pasal-pasal dana politik dan paket undang-undang politik'. Jakarta: Indonesia Corruption Watch. [Position Paper, Political Finance.]

Baines, Stephen
2004 'Controlling corruption; Lessons from the School Improvement Grants Program in Indonesia'. Jakarta: RTI International. https://register.rti.org/EducationFinance/background/Accountability/Baines_%20Lessons%20learned%20from%20SIGP.pdf (accessed 5-4-2009).

Baiocchi, Gianpaolo
2003 'Participation, activism, and politics; The Porto Alegre experiment', in: Archon Fung and Erik Olin Wright (eds), *Deepening democracy; Institutional innovations in empowered participatory governance*, pp. 45-76. London: Verso.

Baker, Jacqui
2008 'A sibling rivalry', *Inside Indonesia* 93 (August-October). http://www.insideindonesia.org/content/view/1106/47/ (accessed 28-3-2010).

Barfield, Thomas J.
1989 *The perilous frontier; Nomadic empires and China.* Cambridge, MA: Blackwell.

Barker, Joshua
1998 'The state of fear; Controlling the criminal contagion in Suharto's New Order', *Indonesia* 66:7-42.
1999a *The tatoo and the fingerprint; Crime and security in an Indonesian city.* PhD thesis, Cornell University, Ithaca, NY.
1999b 'Surveillance and territoriality in Bandung', in: Vicente Rafael (ed.), *Figures of criminality in Indonesia, the Philippines and colonial Vietnam*, pp. 95-127. Ithaca, NY: Cornell University.

Barr, Christopher M.
1998 'Bob Hasan, the rise of Apkindo, and the shifting dynamics of control in Indonesia's timber sector', *Indonesia* 65:1-36.

Basri, Faisal
2005 *Analisis ekonomi Faisal Basri; Kita harus berubah!* Jakarta: Kompas.

Bateman, Sam
2003 *Coast guards; New forces for regional order and security.* Washington, DC.: East-West Center. [Asia Pacific Issues 65.]

Bates, Robert H.
2008 'Probing the sources of political order', in: Stathis N. Kalyvas, Ian Shapiro and Tarek Masoud (eds), *Order, conflict, and violence*, pp. 17-42. Cambridge: Cambridge University Press.
Bayuni, Endy M.
2005 'Tactical fund; No receipts, no questions asked', *The Jakarta Post*, 16 May.
Beeson, Mark
2001 'Globalization, governance, and the political-economy of public policy reform in East Asia', *Governance; An International Journal of Policy and Administration* 14-4:481-502.
Benda-Beckmann, Franz von
1989 'Scapegoat and magic charm; Law in development theory and practice', *Journal of Legal Pluralism* 28:129-48.
Benda-Beckmann, Franz von and Keebet von Benda-Beckmann
1980 'Rechtspraak; Traditionele en westerse waarden in historisch perspektief', in: R.N.J. Kamerling (ed.), *Indonesië toen en nu*, pp. 127-45. Amsterdam: Intermediair.
Biezen, Ingrid van and Petr Kopecky
2007 'The state and the parties; Public funding, public regulation and rent-seeking in contemporary democracies', *Party Politics* 13-2:235-54.
Biografi Prof. Dr. Sumitro
2009 'Biografi Prof. Dr. Sumitro Djojohadikusumo: Begawan ekonomi Indonesia', *Ensiklopedi Tokoh Indonesia*. http://tokohindonesia.com/ensiklopedi/s/sumitro-djojohadikusumo/index.shtml (accessed 1-4-2009).
Blundo, Giorgio
2006 'An ordered corruption? The social world of public procurement', in: Giorgio Blundo and Jean-Pierre Olivier de Sardan (eds), *Everyday corruption and the state; Citizens and public officials in Africa*, pp. 225-62. London: Zed.
Blundo, Giorgio and Jean-Pierre Olivier de Sardan
2006 'Introduction; Why should we study everyday corruption and how should we go about it?', in: Giorgio Blundo, Jean-Pierre Olivier de Sardan, N. Bako Arifari and M. Tidjani Alou (eds), *Everyday corruption and the state; Citizens and public officials in Africa*, pp. 3-14. London: Zed.
Bolongaita, Emil and Vinay Bhargava (eds)
2004 *Challenging corruption in Asia*. Washington, DC: The World Bank.
Bourchier, David
1990 'Crime, law and state authority in Indonesia', in: Arief Budiman (ed.), *State and civil society in Indonesia*, pp. 177-214. Clayton, Victoria: Monash University Centre of Southeast Asian Studies.
Bowen, Roger
2003 *Japan's dysfunctional democracy; The Liberal Democratic Party and structural corruption*. Armonk, NJ: M.E. Sharpe.
Brown, David and Ian Douglas Wilson
2007 'Ethnicized violence in Indonesia; Where criminals and fanatics meet', *Nationalism and Ethnic Politics* 13-3:367-403.

Buchanan, James M. and Gordon Tullock
1962 *The calculus of consent; Logical foundations of constitutional democracy*. Ann Arbor: University of Michigan Press.
Buchanan, James M., Robert D. Tollison and Gordon Tullock (eds)
1980 *Toward a theory of the rent-seeking society*. College Station: Texas A&M University Press.
Budianta, C.A. Eka
2008 *Cakrawala Roosseno*. Jakarta: Yayasan Obor Indonesia.
Buehler, Michael
2007 'Local elite reconfiguration in post-New Order Indonesia; An analysis of the 2005 elections of district government heads', *Review of Indonesian and Malaysian Affairs* 41-1:119-47.
Butt, Simon
2007a 'The Constitutional Court's decision in the dispute between the Supreme Court and the Judicial Commission; Banishing judicial accountability?', in: Ross H. McLeod and Andrew MacIntyre (eds), *Indonesia; Democracy and the promise of good governance*, pp. 178-200. Singapore: Institute of Southeast Asian Studies. [Indonesia Update Series.]
2007b *Judicial review in Indonesia; Between civil law and accountability? A study of Constitutional Court decisions 2003-2005*. PhD thesis, University of Melbourne.
2008 'Surat sakti; The decline of the authority of judicial decisions in Indonesia', in: Tim Lindsey (ed.), *Indonesia; Law and society*, pp. 346-62. Second edition. Leichhardt, NSW: Federation Press.
Butt, Simon and Tim Lindsey
2008 ' Economic reform when the Constitution matters; Indonesia's Constitutional Court and Article 33', *Bulletin of Indonesian Economic Studies* 44-2:239-62.
Buzan, Barry
1991 *People, states and fear; An agenda for security studies in the post-Cold War era*. Boulder: Lynne Rienner.
Caballero-Anthony, Mely, Ralf Emmers and Amitav Acharya (eds)
2006 *Non-traditional security in Asia; Dilemmas in securitization*. Hampshire: Ashgate Publishing Limited.
Casson, Anne and Krystof Obidzinski
2002 'From New Order to regional autonomy; Shifting dynamics of 'illegal' logging in Kalimantan, Indonesia', *World Development* 30:2133-51.
Cassutto, Is.
1927 *Het adatstrafrecht in den Nederlandsch-Indischen archipel*. Semarang: Van Dorp. [First edition 1924.]
Choi, Nankyung
2005 *Local elections and democracy in Indonesia; The case of the Riau archipelago*. Singapore: Institute of Defence and Strategic Studies. [Working Paper 91.]
Chua, Christian
2008 *Chinese big business in Indonesia; The state of capital*. London: Routledge.

Clark, David H. and Mayling Oey-Gardiner
1991 'How Indonesian lecturers have adjusted to civil service compensation', *Bulletin of Indonesian Economic Studies* 27-3:129-41.

Clark, Samuel and Blair Palmer
2008 *Peaceful pilkada, dubious democracy; Understanding Aceh's post-conflict elections and their implications*. Jakarta: World Bank. [Indonesian Social Development Paper 11.]

Cleaver, Frances and Tom Franks
2003 *How institutions elude design; River basin management and sustainable livelihoods*. Bradford, UK: Alternative Water Forum, Bradford Centre for International Development, Bradford University. [Research Paper 12.] http://www.brad.ac.uk/acad/bcid/research/papers/ResearchPaper12Cleaver-Franks.pdf (accessed 5-11-2009).

Collier, Paul
2007 *The bottom billion; Why the poorest countries are failing and what can be done about it*. Oxford: Oxford University Press.

Colombijn, Freek
2002 'Maling, maling! The lynching of petty criminals', in: Freek Colombijn and Thomas Lindblad (eds), *Roots of violence in Indonesia; Contemporary violence in historical perspective*, pp. 299-329. Leiden: KITLV Press. [Verhandelingen 194.]

Colombijn, Freek and Thomas Lindblad
2002 'Introduction', in: Freek Colombijn and Thomas Lindblad (eds), *Roots of violence in Indonesia; Contemporary violence in historical perspective*, pp. 1-31. Leiden: KITLV Press. [Verhandelingen 194.]

Cribb, Robert
1984 'Elections in Jakarta', *Asian Survey* 24:655-64.
1988 'Opium and the Indonesian revolution', *Modern Asian Studies* 22:701-22.
1990 (ed.) *The Indonesian killings of 1965-1966; Studies from Java and Bali*. Clayton, Victoria: Monash University Centre of Southeast Asian Studies.
1991 *Gangsters and revolutionaries; The Jakarta people's militia and the Indonesian revolution, 1945-1949*. Sydney: Allen and Unwin.
2009 'Introduction; Parapolitics, shadow governance and criminal sovereignty', in: Tim Lindsey and Eric Wilson (eds), *Government of the shadows; Parapolitics and criminal sovereignty*, pp. 1-9. London: Pluto Press.

Crook, Richard C. and Peter Houtzager
2001 'Making law matter; Rules, rights and security in the lives of the poor', *IDS Bulletin* 32-1:1-7.

Crouch, Harold
1975 'Generals and business in Indonesia', *Pacific Affairs* 48:519-40.
1978 *The army and politics in Indonesia*. Ithaca, NY: Cornell University Press.
1979 'Patrimonialism and military rule in Indonesia', *World Politics* 31-4:571-87.

Crouch, Melissa
2008 'Indonesia's national and local Ombudsman reforms; Salvaging a failed experiment?', in: Tim Lindsey (ed.), *Indonesia; Law and society*, pp. 382-405. Second edition. Leichhardt, NSW: Federation Press.

Current data
2003 'Current data on the Indonesian military elite', *Indonesia* 75:9-60.
Daftar calon
2006 *Daftar calon pemberangkatan calon TKI tahun 2006*. Tanjung Pinang: DTKKS-TP. [Dinas Tenaga Kerja dan Kesejahteraan Sosial Pemerintah Kota Tanjung Pinang.]
Daftar kedatangan
2006a *Daftar kedatangan dan keberangkatan TKI-B deportasi dan keluarganya kota Tanjung Pinang bulan Januari-September 2006*. Tanjung Pinang: Pemkot. [Satuan Tugas Tim Pemulangan Tenaga Kerja Indonesia Bermasalah (TKI-B) dan Keluarganya dari Negeri Malaysia Kota Tanjung Pinang.]
2006b *Daftar kedatangan dan keberangkatan TKI-B deportasi dan keluarganya kota Tanjung Pinang bulan Oktober 2006*. Tanjung Pinang: Pemkot. [Satuan Tugas Tim Pemulangan Tenaga Kerja Indonesia Bermasalah (TKI-B) dan Keluarganya dari Negeri Malaysia Kota Tanjung Pinang.]
2006c *Daftar kedatangan dan keberangkatan TKI-B deportasi dan keluarganya kota Tanjung Pinang bulan November-Desember 2006*. Tanjung Pinang Pemkot. [Satuan Tugas Tim Pemulangan Tenaga Kerja Indonesia Bermasalah (TKI-B) dan Keluarganya dari Negeri Malaysia Kota Tanjung Pinang.]
Daftar PJTKI
2006 *Daftar PJTKI yang memohon surat rekomendasi bebas fiskal luar negeri (BFLN) Tahun 2006*. Tanjung Pinang: DTKKS-TP.[Kepala Dinas Tenaga Kerja dan Kesejahteraan Sosial Kota Tanjungpinang.]
Dakolias, Maria and Kim Thachuk
2000 'Attacking corruption in the judiciary; A critical process in judicial reform', *Wisconsin International Law Journal* 18-2:353-406.
Davidson, Jamie S. and David Henley (eds)
2007 *The revival of tradition in Indonesian politics; The deployment of adat from colonialism to indigenism*. London: Routledge. [Routledge Contemporary Southeast Asia Series.]
Davidson, Jamie S. and Douglas Kammen
2002 'Indonesia's unknown war and the lineages of violence in West Kalimantan', *Indonesia* 73:53-87.
Dawson, John P.
1994 *The oracles of the law*. New York: Legal Classics Library. [Thomas M. Cooley Lectures.]
Day, Tony
2002 *Fluid iron; State formation in Southeast Asia*. Honolulu: University of Hawai'i Press.
Departemen Kehutanan
2008 *Statistik kehutanan Indonesia 2007*. Jakarta: Departemen Kehutanan.
Departemen Pertahanan
2003 *Mempertahankan tanah air memasuki abad 21*. Jakarta: Departemen Pertahanan.
Deventer, C.Th. van
1899 'Een eereschuld', *De Gids* 63-3:205-57.

DFID
2007 'Tackling illegal logging in Indonesia'. London: Department for International Development (DFID). http://www.dfid.gov.uk/casestudies/files/asia/indonesia-illegal-logging.asp (accessed 13-3-2009).

Dick, Howard
1993 'A fresh approach to Southeast Asian history', in: John Butcher and Howard Dick (eds), *The rise and fall of revenue farming; Business elites and the emergence of the modern state in Southeast Asia*, pp. 3-18. London: Macmillan.
2002 'Corruption and good governance; The new frontier of social engineering', in: Tim Lindsey and Howard Dick (eds), *Corruption in Asia; Rethinking the governance paradigm*, pp. 71-86. Leichhardt, NSW: Federation Press.
2008 'The new shipping law (2008); Deregulation or re-regulation?', *Bulletin of Indonesian Economic Studies* 44-3:381-404.

Ding, X.L.
2001 'The quasi-criminalization of a business sector in China; Deconstructing the construction-sector syndrome', *Crime, Law and Social Change* 35:177-201.

Donnelly, David, Janice Fine and Ellen S. Miller
1999 *Money and politics; Financing our elections democratically*. Boston: Beacon Press.

Duncan, Ron and Ross H. McLeod
2007 'The state and the market in democratic Indonesia', in: Ross H. McLeod and Andrew MacIntyre (eds), *Indonesia; Democracy and the promise of good governance*, pp. 73-92. Singapore: Institute of Southeast Asian Studies. [Indonesia Update Series.]

EIA /Telapak
2005 'The last frontier; Illegal logging in Papua and China's massive timber theft'. *Environmental Investigation Agency*. http://www.eia-international.org/files/reports93-1.pdf (accessed 15-9-2010).
2007 'The thousand-headed snake; Forest crimes, corruption and injustice in Indonesia'. *Environmental Investigation Agency*. http://www.eia-international.org/files/reports135-1.pdf (accessed 15-9-2010).

Eilenberg, Michael
2008 'Claiming authority at the edges of the state; Regional autonomy and local politics in the West Kalimantan borderlands', *University of Sydney Indonesian Studies Working Paper 7*. http://sydney.edu.au/arts/indonesian/docs/USYD-IS_Eilenberg_WestKalimantan.pdf (accessed 15-9-2010).

Elisabeth, Stevani
2006 'Sekolah Negeri dilarang pungut biaya PSB', *Sinar Harapan*, 16 May.

Elmhirst, Rebecca
2001 'Resource struggles and the politics of place in North Lampung, Indonesia', *Singapore Journal of Tropical Geography* 21-3:284-306.

Emmers, Ralf
2002 *Non-traditional security in the Asia-Pacific; The dynamics of securitization*. Singapore: Eastern University Press.

Emmerson, Donald K. (ed.)
1999 *Indonesia beyond Suharto; Polity, economy, society, transition*. Armonk, NY: Sharpe.

Erman, Erwiza
2007 'Deregulation of the tin trade and creation of a local shadow state; A Bangka case study', in: Henk Schulte Nordholt and Gerry van Klinken (eds), *Renegotiating boundaries; Local politics in Post-Suharto Indonesia*, pp. 177-201. Leiden: KITLV Press. [Verhandelingen 238.]

Erve, Hubertus Jacobus van der
1989 'The diversity of work relationships in the construction sector of Semarang', in: Paul van Gelder and Joep Bijlmer (eds), *About fringes, margins and lucky dips; The informal sector in Third-World countries; recent developments in research and policy*, pp. 91-111. Amsterdam: Free University Press.
1993 *De kleinschalige bouwnijverheid in Semarang; Een studie naar bedrijvigheid en werkgelegenheid in de bouwsektor*. PhD thesis, Vrije Universiteit Amsterdam, Amsterdam.

Evans, Peter
1995 *Embedded autonomy; States and industrial transformation*. Princeton, NJ: Princeton University Press.

Evers, Hans-Dieter
1990 *Trading minorities in Southeast Asia; A critical summary of research findings*. Bielefeld: Sociology of Development Research Center. [Working Papers 139.]

Evers, Hans-Dieter and Heiko Schrader
1994 *The moral economy of trade; Ethnicity and developing markets*. London: Routledge.

Evers, Hans-Dieter and Ozay Mehmet
1994 'The management of risk; Informal trade in Indonesia', *World Development* 22-1:1-9.

Feener, R. Michael
2007 *Muslim legal thought in modern Indonesia*. Cambridge: Cambridge University Press.

Fegan, Brian
2003 'Plundering the sea; Regulating trawling companies is difficult when the navy is in business with them', *Inside Indonesia* 73 (January-March). http://www.insideindonesia.org/index.php/component/content/339?task=view (accessed 10-5-2010).

Feith, Herbert
1967 'The politics of economic decline', in: T.K. Tan (ed.), *Sukarno's guided Indonesia*, pp. 46-57. Brisbane: Jacaranda Press.

Fenwick, Stuart
2008 'Measuring up? Indonesia's Anti-Corruption Commission and the new corruption agenda', in: Tim Lindsey (ed.), *Indonesia; Law and society*, pp. 406-29. Second edition. Leichhardt, NSW: Federation Press.

Ferrell, Jeff and Mark S. Hamm (eds)
1998 *Ethnography at the edge; Crime, deviance and field research*. Boston: Northeastern University Press.

Fitri, Fransisca (ed.)
2004 *Peta konflik Jakarta; Warga, mahasiswa, preman, suku, negara dan warga*. Jakarta: Aliansi Masyarakat Sipil Untuk Demokrasi (YAPPIKA).
Fitzpatrick, Daniel
2008 'Culture, ideology and human rights; The case of Indonesia's code of criminal procedure', in: Tim Lindsey (ed.), *Indonesia; Law and society*, pp. 499-514. Second edition. Leichhardt, NSW: Federation Press.
Ford, Michele
2001 'Indonesian women as export commodity; Notes from Tanjung Pinang', *Labour and Management in Development Journal* 2-5:1-9.
2006 'After Nunukan; The regulation of Indonesian migration to Malaysia', in: Amarjit Kaur and Ian Metcalfe (eds), *Mobility, labour migration and border controls in Asia*, pp. 228-47. Basingstoke and New York: Palgrave Macmillan.
2007 'Advocacy responses to irregular labour migration in ASEAN; The cases of Malaysia and Thailand'. [Unpublished report prepared for Migrant Forum in Asia and the South East Asian Committee for Advocacy.]
Fox, Jonathan
1994 'The difficult transition from clientelism to citizenship; Lessons from Mexico', *World Politics* 46-2:151-84.
France, Anatole
1905 *The red lily [Le lys rouge]*. Paris: Mazarin. [Original edition 1894.]
Freud, Sigmund
1991 *The interpretation of dreams*. Harmondsworth: Penguin.
Fung, Archon
2003 'Deliberative democracy, Chicago style; Grass-roots governance in policing and public education', in: Archon Fung and Erik O. Wright (eds), *Deepening democracy; Institutional innovations in empowered participatory governance*, pp. 111-43. London: Verso.
Galtung, Fredrik
2006 'Measuring the immeasurable; boundaries and functions of (macro) corruption indices', in: Fredrik Galtung and Charles Sampford (eds), *Measuring corruption*, pp. 101-30. Aldersgate: Ashgate.
Gambetta, Diego
1996 *The Sicilian mafia; The business of private protection*. London: Harvard University Press.
Gapensi
2004 *Sejarah Gapensi*. Jakarta: Badan Pimpinan Pusat Gabungan Pelaksana Konstruksi Nasional Indonesia. [Second edition.]
Glendon, Mary Ann, Michael Gordon and Christopher Osakwe
1985 *Comparative legal traditions; Text, materials, and cases on the civil law, common law, and socialist law traditions, with special reference to French, West German, English and Soviet law*. St Paul, Minn.: West.
Goodpaster, Gary
2002 'Reflections on corruption in Indonesia', in: Tim Lindsey and Howard Dick (eds), *Corruption in Asia; Rethinking the governance paradigm*, pp. 87-106. Leichhardt, NSW: Federation Press.

Government of Malaysia
2007 'Analysis of labour force in Malaysia'. http://www.statistics.gov.my/eng/images/stories/files/otherlinks/finding_report_LFS_english.pdf (accessed 13-3-2009).
Gray, Clive
1979 'Civil service compensation in Indonesia', *Bulletin of Indonesian Economic Studies* 15-1:85-113.
Grewcock, Mike
2003 'Irregular migration, identity and the state; The challenge for criminology', *Current Issues in Criminal Justice* 15-2:114-35.
Griffiths, Anne
2002 'Legal pluralism', in: Reza Banaker and Max Travers (eds), *An introduction to law and social theory*, pp. 289-310. Portland, Oregon: Hart Publishing.
Gunawan, Apriadi
2006 'Teen escapes life of prostitution', *The Jakarta Post*, 23 May.
Gupta, Akhil
1995 'Blurred boundaries; The discourse of corruption, the culture of politics, and the imagined state', *American Ethnologist* 22-2:375-402.
Hadiz, Vedi
2003a 'Local power; Decentralisation and political reorganisation in Indonesia'. Paper, Conference on Globalisation, Conflict and Political Regimes in East and Southeast Asia, Asia Research Centre, Murdoch University, Western Australia, 15 August.
2003b 'Power and politics in North Sumatra; The uncompleted *reformasi*', in: Edward Aspinall and Greg Fealy (eds), *Local power and politics in Indonesia; Decentralization and democratization*, pp. 119-31. Singapore: ISEAS.
2007 'The localization of power in Southeast Asia', *Democratization* 14-5:873-92.
Hallak, Jaques and Muriel Poisson
2007 *Corrupt school, corrupt universities; What can be done?* Paris: International Institute for Educational Planning.
Hamim, Anis
2003 'The impact of corruption on trafficking', in: Ruth Rosenberg (ed.), *Trafficking of women and children in Indonesia*, pp. 145-7. Jakarta: International Catholic Migration Commission and the American Center for International Labor Solidarity.
Hammergren, Linn
2001 'The judicial career in Latin America; An overview of theory and experience'. *The World Bank*. http://siteresources.worldbank.org/INTLAWJUSTINST/Resources/Jcareer.pdf (accessed 12-11-2009).
Haris, Syamsuddin
2007 *Konflik presiden-DPR dan dilema transisi demokrasi di Indonesia*. Jakarta: Grafiti.
Harriss-White, Barbara
2003 *India working; Essays on society and economy*. Cambridge: Cambridge University Press.

Heine-Geldern, Robert
1956 *Conceptions of state and kingship in Southeast Asia*. Ithaca, NY: Department of Asian Studies. Cornell University. [Revised version of an article published in *The Far Eastern Quarterly*, vol. 2, pp. 15-30, November 1942.]
Hendro, Suroyo Sudagung
2001 *Mengurai pertikaian etnis; Migrasi swakarsa etnis Madura ke Kalimantan Barat*. Jakarta: Institut Studi Arus Informasi.
Hermanto, Elia, Tjuk Kuswartojo and Heinz Kull
1983 *Peningkatan sektor informal bidang konstruksi dalam perkembangan kota di Jakarta - Indonesia*. Bandung: Pusat Studi Lingkungan Hidup (PSLH), Institut Teknologi Bandung.
Heryani, Erna and Chris Grant
2004 'Land administration in Indonesia'. *International Federation of Surveyors*. http://www.fig.net/pub/jakarta/papers/ps_04/ps_04_3_heryani_grant.pdf (accessed 28-3-2010).
Heryanto, Ariel
1988 'The "development" of development', *Indonesia* 46:1-24.
Hess, Henner
1986 'The traditional Sicilian mafia; Organized crime and repressive crime', in: Robert J. Kelly (ed.), *Organized crime; A global perspective*, pp. 113-34. New Jersey: Rowman and Littlefield.
Heyman, Josiah McConnell (ed.)
1999 *States and illegal practices*. Oxford: Berg.
Hidayat, Syarif
2007 '"Shadow State"? Business and politics in the province of Banten', in: Henk Schulte Nordholt and Gerry van Klinken (eds), *Renegotiating boundaries; Local politics in post-Suharto Indonesia*, pp. 203-24. Leiden: KITLV Press. [Verhandelingen 238.]
Higley, John and Michael Burton
2006 *Elite foundations of liberal democracy*. Lanham, MD/London: Rowman and Littlefield.
Higley, John, Jan Pakulski and Wlodzimierz Wesolowski (eds)
1998 *Postcommunist elites and democracy in Eastern Europe*. New York: St. Martin's Press.
Honna, Jun
2006 'Local civil-military relations during the first phase of democratic transition, 1998-2004; A comparison of West, Central and East Java', *Indonesia* 82:75-96.
2008 'Instrumentalizing pressures, reinventing mission; The Indonesian navy battles for turf in the age of reformasi', *Indonesia* 86:63-80.
Hooker, M. Barry
1978 *Adat law in modern Indonesia*. Kuala Lumpur: Oxford University Press.
2003 *Indonesian Islam; Social change through contemporary fatawa*. Crows Nest, NSW: Asian Studies Association of Australia in association with Allen and Unwin and the University of Hawai'i Press.
2004 'Perspectives on shari'a and the state; The Indonesian debates', in: Virginia Hooker and Amin Saikal (eds), *Islamic perspectives on the new millennium*, pp. 199-220. Singapore: ISEAS.

2008 *Indonesian syariah; Defining a national school of Islamic law.* Singapore: Institute for Southeast Asian Studies.

Hopkin, Jonathan

2004 'The problem with party finance; Theoretical perspectives on the funding of political parties', *Party Politics* 10-6:627-51.

Horstmann, Alexander and Reed L. Wadley

2006 *Centering the margin; Agency and narrative in Southeast Asian borderlands.* Oxford/New York: Berghahn.

Hugo, Graeme

2005 'The new international migration in Asia; Challenges for population research', *Asian Population Studies* 1-1:93-120.

Human Rights Watch

2004 *Help wanted; Abuses against female migrant domestic workers in Indonesia and Malaysia.* New York: Human Rights Watch.

2005 *Always on call; Abuse and exploitation of child domestic workers in Indonesia.* New York: Human Rights Watch.

2006 *Too high a price; The human rights cost of the Indonesian military's economic activities.* New York: Human Rights Watch.

Huther, Jeff and Anwar Shah

2000 *Anti-corruption policies and programs; A framework for evaluation.* Washington, DC: World Bank. [World Bank Policy Research Working Paper Series 2501.] http://www.thaigoodgovernance.org/upload/content/300/anti-corruption%20policies%20and%20programs.pdf (accessed 28-03-2010).

ICC International Maritime Bureau

2006 'Piracy and armed robbery against ships; Annual report, 1 January-31 December 2005'. London: ICC-IMB. [31 January.]

ICG (International Crisis Group)

2003 *The perils of private security in Indonesia; Guards and militias on Bali and Lombok.* Jakarta/Brussels: International Crisis Group. [Asia Report 67].

ICW (Indonesia Corruption Watch)

2001 *Menyingkap tabir mafia peradilan (hasil monitoring peradilan ICW).* Jakarta: Indonesia Corruption Watch.

2005 *Laporan dugaan korupsi SIGP.* Jakarta: Indonesia Corruption Watch.

2007 *Laporan Survey CRC 2006.* Jakarta: Indonesia Corruption Watch.

2008 *Pengadilan umum; 'Kuburan' pemberantasan korupsi.* Jakarta: Indonesia Corruption Watch. http://www.antikorupsi.org/docs/lathukum2008.pdf (accessed 14-9-2010).

2009 *Catatan atas laporan dana kampanye; Tim sukses pasangan Capres dan Cawapres Pilpres 2009.* Jakarta: Indonesia Corruption Watch.

Idrus, Nurul Ilmi

2008 '"Makkunrai Passimokolo"; Bugis migrant women workers in Malaysia', in: Michele Ford and Lyn Parker (eds), *Women and work in Indonesia,* pp. 155-72. London: Routledge.

IFES (International Foundation for Electoral Systems)

2004 'Campaign finance, regulation and public disclosure in the Republic of Indonesia; Reporting and public disclosure of financial activity of political parties and electoral participants'. Jakarta: IFES. [Unpublished paper.]

Indonesian migrant workers
2002 *Indonesian migrant workers; Systematic abuse at home and abroad; Indonesian country report to the UN Special Rapporteur on the Human Rights of Migrants, Kuala Lumpur, 2 June 2002*. [Jakarta]: National Commission on Violence Against Women.

Irawan, Ade
2006 *Desentralisasi bisnis buku pelajaran*. Jakarta: Indonesia Corruption Watch. [Public Accountability Review Paper.]
2007 *Voucher pendidikan, jalan lapang bagi KKN dan diskriminasi*. Jakarta: Indonesia Corruption Watch. [Public Accountability Review Paper.]

Irawan, Ade, Eriyanto, Luky Djani and Agus Sunaryanto
2004 *Mendagangkan sekolah*. Jakarta: Indonesia Corruption Watch.

Irawan, Ade, Agus Sunaryanto, Febri Hendry and Luky Djani
2006 *Buruk wajah pendidikan dasar*. Jakarta: Indonesia Corruption Watch.

Jackson, Karl D. and Lucian W. Pye (eds)
1978 *Political power and communications in Indonesia*. Berkeley, Calif.: University of California Press.

Jansen, David
2008 'Relations among security and law enforcement institutions in Indonesia', *Contemporary Southeast Asia* 30-3:429-54.

Jessop, Bob
2007 *State power; A strategic relational approach*. Cambridge: Polity Press.

Johnston, Michael
1997 'Public officials, private interests and sustainable democracy; When politics and corruption meet', in: Kimberley Ann Elliot (ed.), *Corruption and the global economy*, pp. 61-82. Washington, DC: Institute for International Economics.
2000 'Corruption and democratic consolidation'. Paper, Conference on Democracy and corruption, Shelby Cullom Davis Center for Historical Studies, Princeton University, 12 March 1999. [Revised June 2000.]
2005 *Syndromes of corruption; Wealth, power and democracy*. New York/Cambridge: Cambridge University Press.

Jones, Eric L.
2006 *Cultures merging; A historical and economic critique of culture*. Princeton, NJ: Princeton University Press.

Jonge, Huub de
1995 'Stereotypes of the Madurese', in: Kees van Dijk, Huub de Jonge and Ellen Touwen-Bouwsma (eds), *Across Madura Strait; The dynamics of an insular society*, pp. 7-25. Leiden: KITLV Press. [Proceedings 2.]

Jonge, Huub de and Gerben Nooteboom
2006 'Why the Madurese? Ethnic conflict in West and East Kalimantan compared', *Asian Journal of Social Science* 34-3:456-74.

Kaming, Peter F., Paul O. Olomolaiye, Gary D. Holt, and Frank C. Harris
1997 'Factors influencing construction time and cost overruns on high-rise projects in Indonesia', *Construction Management and Economics* 15:83-94.

Kaplan, David E. and Alec Dubro
2003 *Yakuza; Japan's criminal underworld*. Berkeley and Los Angeles, California: University of California Press.

Kaufmann, Daniel, Aart Kraay and Massimo Mastruzzi
2008 'Governance matters VII; Aggregate and individual governance indicators 1996-2007'. *World Bank*. http://papers.ssrn.com/sol3/papers.cfm?abstract_id=1148386## (accessed 15-9-2010).
Kaufmann, Daniel, Aart Kraay and Pablo Zoido-Lobaton
1999 'Governance matters VIII; Aggregate and individual governance indicators, 1996-2008'. *World Bank*. http://papers.ssrn.com/sol3/papers.cfm?abstract_id=1424591 (accessed 1-6-2010).
Kelly, Jamie
2005 'Transnational NGO involvement in the new age of migration; Building a framework for the protection of the human rights of undocumented economic migrants', *Michigan Journal of Public Affairs* 2:1-30.
Kenny, Charles
2006 *Measuring and reducing the impact of corruption in infrastructure*. Washington, DC: World Bank. [World Bank Policy Research Working Paper 4099.]
2007 *Construction, corruption, and developing countries*. Washington, DC: World Bank. [World Bank Policy Research Working Paper 4271.]
Khan, Mushtaq H.
2000 'Rents, efficiency and growth', in: Mushtaq H. Khan and Jomo Kwame Sundaram (eds), *Rents, rent-seeking and economic development; Theory and evidence in Asia*, pp. 21-69. Cambridge: Cambridge University Press.
King, Dwight Y.
2003 *Half-hearted reform; Electoral institutions and the struggle for democracy in Indonesia*. Westport, CT: Praeger.
Kirmani, Syed S.
1988 *The construction industry in development; Issues and options*. Washington, DC.: World Bank, Infrastructure and Urban Development Department. [Discussion Paper, Report INU-0010.]
Kitschelt, Herbert and Steven I. Wilkinson
2007 *Patrons, clients and policies*. Cambridge: Cambridge University Press.
Klinken, Gerry van
2002 'Indonesia's new ethnic elites', in: Henk Schulte Nordholt and Irwan Abdullah (eds), *Indonesia; In search of transition*, pp. 67-106. Yogyakarta: Pustaka Pelajar.
2007 *Communal violence and democratization in Indonesia; Small town wars*. London: Routledge.
2008 'Special issue; The state and illegality in Indonesia - introduction', *South East Asia Research* 16-2:157-63.
Klinken, Gerry van and Joshua Barker (eds)
2009 *State of authority; The state in society in Indonesia*. Ithaca, NY: Cornell University Press. [Southeast Asia Program Studies 50.]
Kong, Tao and Arief Ramayandi
2008 'Survey of recent developments', *Bulletin of Indonesian Economic Studies* 44-1:7-32.
Koonings, Kees and Dirk Kruijt (eds)
2004 *Armed actors; Organised violence and state failure in Latin America*. London: Zed.

Kristiansen, Stein and Muhid Ramli
2006 'Buying an income; The market for civil service positions in Indonesia', *Contemporary Southeast Asia* 28-2:207-33.
Kroef, Justus M. van der
1985 'Petrus'; Patterns of prophylactic murder in Indonesia', *Asian Survey* 25-7:745-59.
Krueger, Anne O.
1974 'The political economy of the rent-seeking society', *The American Economic Review* 64-3:291-303.
Kuhonta, Erik Martinez
2008 'Studying states in Southeast Asia', in: Erik Martinez Kuhonta, Dan Slater and Tuong Vu (eds), *Southeast Asia in political science; Theory, region, and qualitative analysis*, pp. 30-54. Stanford: Stanford University Press.
Kusno, Abidin
2004 'Whither nationalist urbanism? Public life in Governor Sutiyoso's Jakarta', *Urban Studies* 41-12:2377-94.
Kwik, Kian Gie
2003 'Kwik; Kebocoran dana juga terjadi dalam APBN', *Tempo*, 29 January. http://www.infoanda.com/linksfollow.php?lh=BgNaB1sFAFdX (accessed 1-4-2009).
Lambsdorff, Johan
2007 *The institutional economics of corruption and reform; Theory, evidence and policy*. Cambridge: Cambridge University Press.
Lane, Frederic C.
1979 *Profits from power; Readings in protection rent and violence-controlling enterprises*. Albany: State University of New York Press.
Lasser, Mitchel
2003 *Anticipating three models of judicial control, debate and legitimacy; The European Court of Justice, the Cour de cassation and the United States Supreme Court*. New York: New York University School of Law.
2004 *Judicial deliberations; A comparative analysis of judicial transparency and legitimacy*. Oxford: Oxford University Press.
Leff, Nathaniel H.
1964 'Economic development through bureaucratic corruption', *American Behavioral Scientist* 8-3:8-14.
Leith, Denise
2003 *The politics of power; Freeport in Suharto's Indonesia*. Honolulu: University of Hawai'i Press.
Lemos, Maria Carmen and Arun Agrawal
2006 'Environmental governance', *Annual Review of Environment and Resources* 31:297-325.
Lestari, Nina
2008 'Illegal mining in Indonesia', *Resource Management in Asia-Pacific News*, 22 June. http://rspas.anu.edu.au/blogs/rmap/2008/06/22/illegal-mining-in-indonesia (accessed 5-10-2009).

Lev, Daniel
1972 'Judicial institutions and legal culture in Indonesia', in: Claire Holt (ed.), *Culture and politics in Indonesia*, pp. 246-318. Ithaca, NY: Cornell University Press.
1973 *Islamic courts in Indonesia; A study in the political bases of legal institutions*. Berkeley, Calif.: University of California Press.
1978-79 'Judicial authority and the struggle for an Indonesian *rechtsstaat*', *Law and Society Review* 13:37-71.
1999 'Between state and society; Professional lawyers and reform in Indonesia', in: Tim Lindsey (ed.), *Indonesia; Law and society*, pp. 227-46. Second edition. Leichhardt, NSW: Federation Press.

Levi, Margaret
1990 *Of rule and revenue*. Cambridge: Cambridge University Press.

Leys, Colin
1965 'What is the problem about corruption?', *Journal of Modern African Studies* 3-2:215-30.

Liem Soei Liong
2002 'It's the military, stupid!', in: Freek Colombijn and Thomas Lindblad (eds), *Roots of violence in Indonesia; Contemporary violence in historical perspective*, pp. 197-225. Leiden: KITLV Press. [Verhandelingen 194.]

Lindsey, Tim
2000 'Black letter, black market and bad faith; Corruption and the failure of law reform', in: Chris Manning and Peter van Diermen (eds), *Indonesia in transition; Social aspects of reformasi and crisis*, pp. 278-92. Singapore: ISEAS.
2001 'The criminal state; *Premanisme* and the new Indonesia', in: Grayson Lloyd and Shannon Smith (eds), *Indonesia today; Challenges of history*, pp. 283-97. Singapore: ISEAS.
2002 'Indonesian constitutional reform; Muddling towards democracy', *Singapore Journal of International and Comparative Law* 6-1: 244-301.
2004 'Indonesia; Devaluing Asian values, rewriting rule of law', in: Randall Peerenboom (ed.), *Asian discourses of rule of law; Theories and implementation of rule of law in twelve Asian countries, France and the U.S.* pp. 286-323. London: RoutledgeCurzon.
2006 'From Soepomo to Prabowo; Law, violence and corruption in the preman state', in: Charles A. Coppel (ed.), *Violent conflicts in Indonesia; Analysis, representation, resolution*, pp. 19-36. London: Routledge.
2007 'Shari'a revival in Aceh', in Mark Cammack and Michael Feener (eds), *Islamic law in contemporary Indonesia; Ideas and institutions*, pp. 216-55. Cambridge, MA: Harvard Law School. [Harvard Series in Islamic Law 5.]
2008 (ed.) *Indonesia; Law and society*. Leichhardt, NSW: Federation Press.

Lindsey, Tim and Howard Dick (eds)
2002 *Corruption in Asia; Rethinking the governance paradigm*. Leichhardt, NSW: Federation Press.

Lindsey, Tim and M. Barry Hooker with Jeremy Kingsley and Ross Clarke
2007 *Law reform in developing and transitional states*. London/New York: Routledge.

Linnan, David K.
2008 'Indonesian law reform, or once more unto the breach; A brief institutional history', in: Tim Lindsey (ed.), *Indonesia; Law and society*, pp. 68-91. Second edition. Leichhardt, NSW: Federation Press.

Lipschutz, Ronnie D.
1995 *On security*. New York: Columbia University Press.

Loveard, Keith
1999 *Suharto; Indonesia's last sultan*. Singapore: Horizon Books.

Lubis, Todung Mulya
2001 'Kasus Endin; Sebuah perlawanan', *Tempo* 21 May.

Lund, Christian
2006 'Twilight institutions; Public authority and local politics in Africa', *Development and Change* 37-4:685-705. [Special issue.]

Lyons, Lenore and Michele Ford
2007 'Where internal and international migration intersect; Mobility and the formation of multi-ethnic communities in the Riau Islands transit zone', *International Journal on Multicultural Societies* 9-2:236-63.

McCarthy, John F.
2002 'Turning in circles; District governance, illegal logging, and environmental decline in Sumatra, Indonesia', *Society and Natural Resources* 15:867-86.
2004 'Changing to gray; Decentralization and the emergence of volatile socio-legal configurations in Central Kalimantan, Indonesia', *World Development* 32:1199-223.
2006 *The fourth circle; A political ecology of Sumatra's rainforest frontier*. Stanford, CA: Stanford University Press.
2007a 'The demonstration effect; Natural resources, ethnonationalism and the Aceh conflict', *Singapore Journal of Tropical Geography* 28:314-33.
2007b 'Sold down the river; Renegotiating public power over nature in Central Kalimantan', in: Henk Schulte Nordholt and Gerry van Klinken (eds), *Renegotiating boundaries; Local politics in post-Suharto Indonesia*, pp. 151-76. Leiden: KITLV Press. [Verhandelingen 238.]
2008 'Shifting resource entitlements and governance reform during the agrarian transition in Sumatra, Indonesia', *Journal of Legal Pluralism* 55:65-122.

McCarthy, John F. and Carol Warren
2008 'Communities, environments and local governance in reform era Indonesia', in: John F. McCarthy and Carol Warren (eds), *Community, environment and local governance in Indonesia*, pp. 1-26. London: Routledge.

McCarthy, Paul
2002 'Korupsi bantuan luar negeri; Kenaifan, kepuasan diri dan keterlibatan donor', in: Hamid Basyaib, Richard Holloway and Nono Anwar Makarim (eds), *Mencuri uang rakyat; 16 kajian korupsi di Indonesia*, pp. 33-89. Jakarta: Yayasan Aksara.

McCawley, Peter T.
1978 'Some consequences of the crash of Pertamina', *Journal of Southeast Asian Studies* 9-1:1-27.

McCormack, Gavan
1996 *Afterbubble; Fizz and concrete in Japan's political economy*. San Francisco: Japan Policy Research Institute, University of San Francisco Center for the Pacific Rim. [JPRI Working Paper 21.]

McCulloch, Lesley
2005 'Greed; The silent force of the conflict in Aceh', in: Damien Kingsbury (ed.), *Violence in between; Conflict and security in archipelagic Southeast Asia*, pp. 203-27. Clayton: Monash Asia Institute.

McFarlane, John and Karen McLennan
1996 *Transnational crime; The new security paradigm*. Canberra: Strategic and Defense Studies Centre, ANU. [Working Paper 294.]

MacIntyre, Andrew
1991 *Business and politics in Indonesia*. North Sydney: Allen and Unwin.
2000 'Funny money; Fiscal policy, rent-seeking and economic performance in Indonesia', in: Mushtaq H. Khan and Jomo Kwame Sundaram (eds), *Rent-seeking and economic development; Theory and evidence in Asia*, pp. 248-73. Cambridge: Cambridge University Press.
2001 'Investment, property rights, and corruption in Indonesia', in: Jose E. Campos (ed.), *Corruption; The boom and bust of East Asia*, pp. 25-44. Manila: Ateneo de Manila University Press.
2003 'Institutions and the political economy of corruption in developing countries'. Paper, Workshop on Corruption, Stanford University, 31 January-1 February.

McLeod, Ross H.
2000 'Soeharto's Indonesia; A better class of corruption', *Agenda* 7-2:99-112.
2008a 'Inadequate budgets and salaries as instruments for institutionalising public sector corruption in Indonesia', *South East Asia Research* 16-2:199-223.
2008b 'Survey of recent developments', *Bulletin of Indonesian Economic Studies* 44-2:183-208.

Mahkamah Agung
2008 *Laporan tahunan 2007 Mahkamah Agung Republik Indonesia*. Jakarta: Mahkamah Agung.

Makarenko, Tamara
2003 'The ties that bind; Uncovering the relationship between organized crime and terrorism', in: Dina Siegel, Henk van der Bunt and Damian Zaitch (eds), *Global organized crime; Trends and developments*, pp. 159-73. Dordrecht: Kluwer Academic Publishers.

Malley, Michael
2003 'New rules, old structures and the limits of democratic decentralisation', in: Edward Aspinall and Greg Fealy (eds), *Local power and politics in Indonesia; Decentralisation and democratisation*, pp. 102-16. Singapore: Institute of Southeast Asian Studies.

Manaf, M. Hikman
1999 'The environmental impact of small scale mining in Indonesia', Paper, Third Environmental Cooperation workshop for Sustainable Development on Mining Activities, Cairns, 5 October.

Mann, Michael
1986 'The autonomous power of the state; Its origins, mechanisms and results', in: John A. Hall (ed.), *States in history*, pp. 109-36. Oxford: Blackwell.
Markas Besar Angkatan Laut
2006 'Pendirian sea and coast guard Indonesia (SCGI) sebagai upaya penajaman fungsi penegakan keamanan di laut'. [Manuscript.]
Markas Besar TNI
2003 *Naskah sementara buku petunjuk operasi tentang operasi militer selain perang*. Jakarta: Mabes TNI.
Masaaki, Okamoto
2006 'Broker keamanan di Jakarta; Yang profesional dan yang berbasis massa', in: Okamoto Masaaki and Abdur Rozaki (eds), *Kelompok kekerasan dan bos lokal di era reformasi*, pp. 1-19. Yogyakarta/Kyoto: IRE Press and Center for Southeast Asian Studies.
Mattei, Ugo
1997 'Three patterns of law; Taxonomy and change in the world's legal systems', *American Journal of Comparative Law* 45-1:5-44.
Menuju independensi
1999 'Menuju independensi kekuasaan kehakiman; Position paper'. Jakarta: Indonesian Centre for Environmental Law, Lembaga Kajian dan Advokasi untuk Independensi Peradilan. [Konsorsium Reformasi Hukum Nasional (KHRN) and Lembaga Kajian dan Advokasi untuk Independensi Peradilan (LeIP).]
Merry, Sally E.
1991 'Law and colonialism', *Law and Society Review* 25-4:890-922.
Merryman, John Henry
1984 *The civil law tradition; An introduction to the legal systems of Western Europe and Latin America*. Stanford, Calif.: Stanford University Press.
Mietzner, Marcus
2007 'Party financing in post-Soeharto Indonesia; Between state subsidies and political corruption', *Contemporary Southeast Asia* 29-2:238-63.
2008a 'Comparing Indonesia's party systems of the 1950s and the post-Suharto era; From centrifugal to centripetal inter-party competition', *Journal of Southeast Asian Studies* 39-3:431-53.
2008b 'Soldiers, parties and bureaucrats; Illicit fund-raising in contemporary Indonesia', *South East Asian Research* 16:225-54.
2009a 'Political opinion polling in post-authoritarian Indonesia; Catalyst or obstacle to democratic consolidation?', *Bijdragen tot de Taal-, Land- en Volkenkunde* 165:95-126.
2009b 'Indonesia; Democratic consolidation in Soeharto's shadow', *Southeast Asian Affairs*: 105-23.
2009c 'Indonesia and the pitfalls of low-quality democracy; A case study of the gubernatorial elections in North Sulawesi', in: Andreas Ufen and Marco Bünte (eds), *Democratization in post-Suharto Indonesia*, pp. 124-49. London/New York: Routledge.

Migdal, Joel S.
1988 *Strong societies and weak states; State-society relations and state capabilities in the Third World.* Princeton: Princeton University Press.
2001 *State in society; Studying how states and societies transform and constitute one another.* Cambridge: Cambridge University Press. [Cambridge Studies in Comparative Politics.]
Millie, Julian
1999 'The *Tempo* case; Indonesia's press laws, the *Pengadilan Tata Usaha Negara* and the Indonesian *Negara Hukum*', in: Tim Lindsey (ed.), *Indonesia; Law and society,* pp. 269-78. Leichhardt, NSW: Federation Press. [First edition.]
Mills, C. Wright
1956 *The power elite.* Oxford: Oxford University Press.
Ministry of Finance Malaysia
2007 *Economy report 2006/2007.* Putrajaya: Ministry of Finance.
Mokyr, Joel and John V.C. Nye
2007 'Distributional coalitions; The industrial revolution, and the origins of economic growth in Britain', *Southern Economic Journal* 74-1:50-70.
Montlake, Simon
2008 'Indonesia fights its reputation for graft', *Christian Science Monitor* 3. http://www.csmonitor.com/World/Asia-Pacific/2008/1103/p07s02-woap.html (accessed 28-3-2010).
Moore, Sally Falk
2000 *Law as process; An anthropological approach.* Second edition. Oxford: Currey. [Classics in African Anthropology.]
Mrázek, Rudolf
2002 *Engineers in happy land; Technology and nationalism in a colony.* Princeton, NJ: Princeton University Press.
Mulholland, Jeremy and Ken D. Thomas
2002 'Krisis BPPN dan posisi konglomerat', *Kompas,* 24 January. http://www.unisosdem.org/kliping_detail.php?aid=105&coid=1&caid=29 (accessed 5-6-2009).
Nandy, Ashis
1992 'State', in: Wolfgang Sachs (ed.), *The development dictionary; A guide to knowledge as power,* pp. 264-74. London/New Jersey: Zed.
Nooteboom, Gerben
2003 *A matter of style; Social security and livelihood in upland East Java.* PhD thesis, Radboud University, Nijmegen.
2005 'Competition, collateral damage, or "just" accidents? Three explanations of ethnic violence in Indonesia', *Bijdragen tot de Taal-, Land- en Volkenkunde* 161:565-75.
2008 'Through turbulent times; Diversity, vulnerability and resilience of Madurese livelihoods in East Kalimantan', in: Milan Titus and Paul Burgers (eds), *Rural livelihoods, resources and coping with crisis in Indonesia: A comparative study,* pp. 43-69. Amsterdam: ICAS, Amsterdam University Press.

North, Douglass C.
1990 *Institutions, institutional change and economic performance*. Cambridge: Cambridge University Press.
2005 *Understanding the process of economic change*. Princeton, NJ: Princeton University Press.
North, Douglass C., John Joseph Wallis and Barry R. Weingast
2009 *Violence and social orders; A conceptual framework for interpreting recorded human history*. Cambridge: Cambridge University Press.
O'Rourke, Kevin
2002 *Reformasi; The struggle for power in post-Soeharto Indonesia*. Sydney: Allen and Unwin.
Obidzinski, Krystof
2002 *Logging in East Kalimantan, Indonesia; The historical expedience of illegality*. PhD thesis, University of Amsterdam.
Olivier de Sardan, Jean-Pierre
1999 'A moral economy of corruption in Africa?', *Journal of Modern African Studies* 37-1:25-52.
Olson, Mancur
1971 *The logic of collective action; Public goods and the theory of groups*. Second edition. Cambridge, MA: Harvard University Press.
Pakulski, Jan
2006 'Elite', in: Bryan S. Turner (ed.), *The Cambridge dictionary of sociology*. Cambridge: Cambridge University Press.
Paying for protection
2005 *Paying for protection; The Freeport mine and the Indonesian security forces*. Washington, DC: Global Witness.
PCDC
2007 'Snapshot assessment of Indonesia's public procurement system as at June, 2007; Piloting OECD/DAC procurement JV Baseline Indicator (BLI) Benchmarking Methodology, version 4'. Copenhagen: United Nations Procurement Capacity Development Centre (PCDC).
Peluso, Nancy Lee
2006 'Passing the red bowl; Creating community identity through violence in West Kalimantan, 1967-1997', in: Charles Coppel (ed.), *Violent conflicts in Indonesia; Analysis, representation, resolution*, pp. 106-28. London: Routledge.
Peluso, Nancy Lee and Emily Harwell
2001 'Territory, custom, and the cultural politics of ethnic war in West Kalimantan, Indonesia', in: Nancy Lee Peluso and Michael Watts (eds), *Violent environments*, pp. 83-116. Ithaca, NY/London: Cornell University Press.
Peluso, Nancy Lee and Peter Vandergeest
2001 'Genealogies of the political forest and customary rights in Indonesia, Malaysia, and Thailand', *Journal of Asian Studies* 60-3:761-812.
Pemberton, John
1994 *On the subject of 'Java'*. Ithaca, NY: Cornell University Press.

1999 'Open secrets; Conversations with a Javanese lawyer and a comment', in: Vicente L. Rafael (ed.), *Figures of criminality in Indonesia, the Philippines, and colonial Vietnam*. pp. 193-209. New York: Southeast Asia Program Publications, Cornell University. [Studies on Southeast Asia 25.]

Peoples plantations
2007 'Peoples plantations; Help or hindrance in tackling deforestation?', *Down to Earth* 74 (August).

Perlez, Jane and Raymond Bonner
2005 'The cost of gold, the hidden payroll: below a mountain of wealth, a river of waste', *The New York Times*, 27 December.

Piattoni, Simona (ed.)
2001 *Clientelism, interests, and democratic representation; The European experience in historical and comparative perspective*. Cambridge: Cambridge University Press.

Picarelli, John
2006 'The turbulent nexus of transnational organised crime and terrorism; A theory of malevolent international relations', *Global Crime* 7-1:1-24.

Pierce, Steven
2006 'Looking like a state; Colonialism and the discourse of corruption in Northern Nigeria', *Comparative Studies in Society and History* 48-4:887-914.

Pierre, Jon and Guy Peters
2000 *Governance, politics and the state*. Hampshire: Macmillian.

Pompe, Sebastiaan
2005 *The Indonesian Supreme Court; A study of institutional collapse*. Ithaca, NY: Cornell South-East Asia Program Publications. [Studies on Southeast Asia 39.]

Posner, Richard A.
1974 'Theories of economic regulation', *Bell Journal of Economics* 5:335-58.

Pranoto, Bambang
2005 *Menyiasati KKN sektor konstruksi dan investasi*. Jakarta: Balitbang Pusat, LKJK Indonesia.

Purba, Kornelius
2008 'Corruption Eradication Commission as public enemy no 1', *The Jakarta Post*, 30 April.

Purdey, Jemma
2006 *Anti-Chinese violence in Indonesia, 1996-1999*. Singapore: Singapore University Press.

Purwanto, Bambang
2008 'Korupsi subur di sekolah', *Suara Merdeka*, 16 September. http://antikorupsi.org/indo/content/view/13368/7.

Putnam, Robert D.
1976 *The comparative study of political elites*. Englewood Cliffs, NJ: Prentice-Hall.

Rafick, Ishak
2008 *Catatan hitam lima presiden Indonesia; Sebuah investigasi 1997-2007, mafia ekonomi, dan jalan baru membangun Indonesia*. Jakarta: Ufuk Pub. House.

Raillon, Fransçois

1994 'Can the Javanese do business?', in: Hans Antlöv and Sven Cederroth (eds), *Leadership on Java; gentle hints, authoritarian rule*, pp. 163-85. Richmond, Surrey: Curzon Press. [Studies on Asian Topics 16.]

Ravesteijn, Wim and Jan Kop (eds)

2008 *For profit and prosperity; The contribution made by Dutch engineers to public works in Indonesia; 1800-2000*. Zaltbommel: Aprilis.

Reid, Anthony

1993 *Southeast Asia in the age of commerce, 1450-1680; Expansion and crisis*. New Haven, CT: Yale University Press.

Resink, G.J.

1975 'From the old Mahabharata- to the new Ramayana-order', *Bijdragen tot de Taal-, Land- en Volkenkunde* 131:214-35.

Resosudarmo, Budy (ed.)

2006 *Politics and economics of Indonesia's natural resources*. Singapore: ISEAS.

Rhodes, R.A.W.

1997 *Understanding governance; Policy networks, governance, reflexivity, and accountability*. Buckingham/Philadelphia: Open University Press.

Ridwan, Mad and Guntoro Soewarno

2002 *Bulog Gate; Abdurrahman Gate, Akbargate, Megaskandal*. Jakarta: Global Mahardika Netama.

Rieffel, Lex and Jaleswari Pramodhawardani

2007 *Out of business and on budget; The challenge of military financing in Indonesia*, Washington, DC: Brookings Institution Press and the US-Indonesian Society.

Riggs, Fred Warren

1966 *Thailand; The modernization of a bureaucratic polity*. Honolulu: East-West Center Press.

Rinakit, Sukardi

2005 'Indonesian regional elections in praxis'. Singapore: Institute of Defence and Strategic Studies. [IDSS Commentaries.]

Robison, Richard

1981 'Culture, politics and economy in the political history of the New Order', *Indonesia* 31:1-29.

1986 *Indonesia; The rise of capital*. Sydney: Allen and Unwin.

Robison, Richard and Andrew Rosser

1998 'Contesting reform; Indonesia's New Order and the IMF', *World Development* 26-8:1593-609.

Robison, Richard and Vedi Hadiz

2004 *Reorganising power in Indonesia; The politics of oligarchy in an age of markets*. London: RoutledgeCurzon.

Robison, Richard, Ian Wilson and Adrianus Meliala

2008 '"Governing the ungovernable"; Dealing with the rise of informal security in Indonesia'. Asia Research Centre, Murdoch University, *Policy Brief* 1. http://wwwarc.murdoch.edu.au/wp/pb1.pdf (accessed 19-6-2009).

Roniger, Luis

2004 'Review article; Political clientelism, democracy, and market economy', *Comparative Politics* 36-3:353-75.

Roosa, John
2003 'Brawling, bombing and 'backing', *Inside Indonesia* 73 (January-March). http://www.insideindonesia.org/content/view/334/29/ (accessed 28-3-2010).
2006 *Pretext for mass murder; The September 30th movement and Suharto's coup d'état in Indonesia*. Madison, WI: University of Wisconsin Press.

Rose-Ackerman, Susan
1999 *Corruption and government*. Cambridge: Cambridge University Press.

Rudnyckyj, Daromir
2004 'Technologies of servitude; Governmentality and Indonesian transnational labor migration', *Anthropological Quarterly* 77:407-34.

Rutten, Mario and Carol Upadhya (eds)
1997 *Small business entrepreneurs in Asia and Europe; Towards a comparative perspective*. New Delhi: Sage.

Ryter, Loren
1998 'Pemuda Pancasila; The last loyalist freemen of Suharto's Indonesia?', *Indonesia* 66:44-73.
2005 'Reformasi gangsters', *Inside Indonesia* 82 (April-June). http://www.insideindonesia.org/content/view/177/29/ (accessed 28-3-2010).

Sannen, Ad M.H.
1986 'Mandur and tukang; The functioning of informal subcontractors and building workers in the construction sector of Bandung', in: Peter J.M. Nas (ed.), *The Indonesian city; Studies in urban development and planning*, pp. 220-36. Dordrecht: Foris. [KITLV, Verhandelingen 117.]

Satriyo, Hana A., Adi Abidin, Hari Kusdaryanto, and Luce Agnes Bulosan
2003 'Indonesia rapid decentralization appraisal (IRDA); Third report'. Jakarta: The Asia Foundation.

Saydam, Gouzali
1999 *Skandal Bank Bali tragedi perpolitikan Indonesia*. Jakarta: RajaGrafindo Persada.

Schendel, Willem van
2005 'Spaces of engagement; How borderlands, illicit flows, and territorial states interlock', in: Willem van Schendel and Itty Abraham (eds), *Illicit flows and criminal things; States, borders, and the other side of globalization*, pp. 38-68. Bloomington: Indiana University Press.

Schiller, Anne, and Bambang Garang
2002 'Religion and inter-ethnic violence in Indonesia', *Journal of Contemporary Asia* 32-2:244-54.

Schulte-Bockholt, Alfredo
2006 *The politics of organized crime and the organized crime of politics*. Lanham: Lexington Books.

Schulte Nordholt, Henk
1991 'The jago in the shadow; Crime and order in the colonial state in Java', *Review of Indonesian and Malaysian Affairs (RIMA)* 25-1:74-91.
2002 'A genealogy of violence', in: Freek Colombijn and J. Thomas Lindblad (eds), *Roots of violence in Indonesia; Contemporary violence in historical perspective*, pp. 33-60. Leiden: KITLV Press. [Verhandelingen 194.]

Schulte Nordholt, Henk and Gerry van Klinken
2007a (eds) *Renegotiating boundaries; Local politics in post-Suharto Indonesia*. Leiden: KITLV Press. [Verhandelingen 238.]
2007b 'Introduction', in: Henk Schulte Nordholt and Gerry van Klinken (eds), *Renegotiating boundaries; Local politics in post-Suharto Indonesia*, pp. 1-35. Leiden: KITLV Press. [Verhandelingen 238.]

Scott, James C.
1969 'The analysis of corruption in developing nations', *Comparative Studies in Society and History* 11-3:315-41.
1985 *Weapons of the weak; Everyday forms of peasant resistance*. New Haven, CT: Yale University Press.

Setiono, Bambang and Yunus Husein
2005 'Fighting forest crime and promoting prudent banking for sustainable forest management; The anti-money laundering approach'. Bogor: Center for International Forestry Research. [CIFOR Occasional Paper 44.] http://www.cifor.cgiar.org/Knowledge/Publications/Detail?pid=1881 (accessed 28-0-2010).

Shapiro, Martin
1981 *Courts; A comparative and political analysis*. Chicago: University of Chicago Press.

Shari, Michael and Bruce Einhorn
1998 'Indonesia; Graft won't just vanish', *Business Week Online*, 1 June. [Cover story.]

Shelley, Louise I.
1999 'Transnational organized crime; The new authoritarianism', in: H. Richard Friman and Peter Andreas (eds), *The illicit global economy and state power*, pp. 25-51. New York: Rowman and Littlefield.
2002 'The nexus of organized criminals and terrorists', *International Annals of Criminology* 40-1/2:85-91.

Sidel, John T.
1999 *Capital, coercion and crime; Bossism in the Philippines*. Stanford, CA: Stanford University Press.
2006 *Riots, pogroms, jihad; Religious violence in Indonesia*. Ithaca, NY: Cornell University Press.

Siegel, James
1998 *A new criminal type in Jakarta; Counter-revolution today*. Durham/London: Duke University Press.

Silvey, Rachel
2007 'Unequal borders; Indonesian transnational migrants at immigration control', *Geopolitics* 12-2:265-79.

Simanjuntak, Frenky and Anita Rahman Akbarsyah
2008 *Measuring corruption in Indonesia; Indonesia corruption perception index 2008 and bribery index*. Jakarta: Transparency International Indonesia.

Singapore Department of Statistics
2000 *Singapore population*. Singapore: Singapore Department of Statistics.

Skeldon, Ronald
2000 'Trafficking; A perspective from Asia', *International Migration* 1:7-30.

Slater, Dan
2004 'Indonesia's accountability trap; Party cartels and presidential power after democratic transition', *Indonesia* 78:61-92.
Smith, Daniel Jordan
2006 *A culture of corruption*. Princeton, NJ: Princeton University Press.
Smith, Theodore M.
1971 'Corruption, tradition and change', *Indonesia* 11:21-40.
1975 'Stimulating performance in the Indonesian bureaucracy; Gaps in the administrator's tool kit', *Economic Development and Cultural Change* 23-4:719-38.
Sobary, Mohamad (edited and translated by Keith Foulcher)
1987 *Between 'ngoyo' and 'nrimo'; Cultural values and economic behaviour among Javanese migrants in Tanjung Pinang*. Clayton: Centre of Southeast Asian Studies, Monash University. [Working Paper 43.]
Soetjipto, Tomi
2005 'Indonesia timber war misses top smugglers – Activists', *Reuters* 13 May. http://www.planetark.com/dailynewsstory.cfm/newsid/30784/story.htm (accessed 15-12-2009)
Soewardi Soerjaningrat, R.M.
1913 'Als ik eens Nederlander was...', in: E.F.E. Douwes Dekker, Tjipto Mangoenkoesoemo and R.M. Soewardi Soerjaningrat, *Onze verbanning; Publicatie der officieële bescheiden, toegelicht met verslagen en commentaren, betrekking hebbende op de Gouvernements-Besluiten van den 18en Augustus 1913, nos. 1a en 2a, Regelende de Toepassing van Artikel 47 R.R.*, pp. 67-73. Schiedam: De Indiër.
Sousa, Santos Boaventura de
1992 'State, law and community in the world system; An introduction', *Social and Legal Studies* 1:131-42.
Spaan, Ernst
1994 'Taikongs and calos; The role of middlemen and brokers in Javanese international migration', *International Migration Review* 28-1:93-113.
Stansbury, Neill
2005 'Exposing the foundations of corruption in construction', in: *Global Corruption Report 2005*, pp. 36-50. London: Pluto Press and Transparency International.
Sugiyanti
2008 'Silang sengkarut korupsi buku'. http://www.antikorupsi.org/indo/content/view/13208/2 (accessed 12-9-2010).
Sulaiman, M. Isa and Gerry van Klinken
2007 'The rise and fall of governor Puteh', in: Henk Schulte Nordholt and Gerry van Klinken (eds), *Renegotiating boundaries; Local politics in post-Suharto Indonesia*, pp. 225-52. Leiden: KITLV Press. [Verhandelingen 238.]
Supit, Henky
2004 *Teropong kajian tata kelautan Indonesia*. Jakarta: Yayasan Pendidikan Maritim Indonesia.
Supreme Court of Indonesia
2003 'Policy paper on judicial personnel management reform'. Jakarta: Supreme Court of Indonesia.

Surtees, Rebecca
2003 'Female migration and trafficking in women; The Indonesian context', *Development* 46-3:99-107.

Suryadinata, Leo
1989 *Military ascendancy and political culture; A study of Indonesia's Golkar*. Ohio: Ohio University Center for International Studies. [Monographs in International Studies, Southeast Asia Series 85.]

Susanto, Andreas
2006 'Safety first; Strategies of managing insecurity among Chinese Indonesians in Yogyakarta', in: Juliette Koning and Frans Hüsken (eds), *Rope walking and safety net; Local ways of managing insecurities in Indonesia*, pp. 107-24. Boston, MA/Leiden: Brill.

Synnerstrom, Staffan
2007 'The civil service; Towards efficiency, effectiveness and honesty', in: Ross H. McLeod and Andrew MacIntyre (eds), *Indonesia; Democracy and the promise of good governance*, pp. 159-77. Singapore: Institute of Southeast Asian Studies. [Indonesia Update Series.]

Tacconi, Luca (ed.)
2007 *Illegal logging; Law enforcement, livelihoods and the timber trade*. London: Earthscan.

Tendler, Judith
1997 *Good governance in the tropics*. Baltimore/London: Johns Hopkins University Press.

Thung Ju Lan
1989 'Jaringan sosial elit ekonomi etnis Cina di Indonesia; Studi kasus pengusaha konstruksi di Jakarta', *Masyarakat Indonesia; Majalah Ilmu-Ilmu Sosial Indonesia* 16-2:167-95.

Tilly, Charles
1985 'War making and state making as organized crime', in: Peter Evans, Dietrich Rueschemeyer and Theda Skocpol (eds), *Bringing the state back in*, pp. 169-91. Cambridge: Cambridge University Press.
2003 *The politics of collective violence*. Cambridge: Cambridge University Press.

Tjondronegoro, S.M.P.
1991 'The utilization and management of land resources in Indonesia, 1970-1990', in: Joan Hardjono (ed.), *Indonesia; resources, ecology, and environment*, pp. 17-35. Singapore: Oxford University Press.

Trocki, Carl A.
1998 'Democracy and the state in Southeast Asia', in: Carl A. Trocki (ed.), *Gangsters, democracy, and the state in Southeast Asia*, pp. 7-16. Ithaca, NY: Southeast Asia Program Publications, Cornell University. [Southeast Asia Program Series 17.]

UNICEF
2006 'Children out of sight, out of mind, out of reach'. Jakarta: UNICEF. [Press release, 12 January.]

UNPAN
2002 'Basic data on government expenditure and taxation (1990-2002)'. New York: United Nations Public Administration Programme (UNPAN). http://www.unpan.org/tabid/456/ItemID/181/language/en-US/Default.aspx (accessed 4-3-2010).

Varese, Federico
2001 *The Russian mafia; Private protection in a new market economy*. Oxford: Oxford University Press.
Vásquez-León, Marcela
1999 'Neoliberalism, environmentalism, and scientific knowledge; Redefining use rights in the gulf of California fisheries', in: Josiah M. Heyman (ed.), *States and illegal practices*, pp. 233-60. Oxford: Berg.
Vel, Jaqueline
2005 'Pilkada in East Sumba; An old rivalry in a new democratic setting', *Indonesia* 80:81-108.
Volkov, Vadim
2000a 'Between economy and the state; Private security and rule enforcement in Russia', *Politics and Society* 20-4:483-501.
2000b 'The political economy of protection rackets in the past and present', *Social Research* 67-3:709-44.
2002 *Violent entrepreneurs; The use of force in the making of Russian capitalism*. Ithaca, NY: Cornell University Press.
Wadley, Reed L. and Michael Eilenberg
2005 'Autonomy, identity, and 'illegal' logging in the borderland of West Kalimantan, Indonesia', *The Asia Pacific Journal of Anthropology* 6-1:19-34.
2006 'Vigilantes and gangsters in the borderland of West Kalimantan, Indonesia', *Kyoto Review of Southeast Asia* 7:1-26.
Waldron, Arthur
1990 *The Great Wall; From history to myth*. Cambridge: Cambridge University Press.
Walmsley, Roy
2008 'World prison population list'. London: International Centre for Prison Studies, King's College London. http://www.kcl.ac.uk/depsta/law/research/icps/downloads/world-prison-pop-seventh.pdf (accessed 18-12-2008). [Seventh edition.]
Wardany, Irawaty
2009 'Need a law passed? Not without cash'. *The Jakarta Post*, 25 March. http://www.thejakartapost.com/print/204643 (accessed 17-9-2009).
Warren, Carol and John F. McCarthy (eds)
2008 *Community, environment and local governance in Indonesia*. London: Routledge.
Wells, Michael
1994 'French and American judicial opinions', *Yale Journal of International Law* 19:81-134.
Welsh, Bridget
2008 'Local and national; *Keroyokan* mobbing in Indonesia', *Journal of East Asian Studies* 8-3:473-504.
Wertheim, Willem Frederik
1964 'Sociological aspects of corruption in Southeast Asia', in: Willem Frederik Wertheim (ed.), *East-West parallels; Sociological approaches to modern Asia*, pp. 195-291. The Hague: Van Hoeve.

West, Darrell
2000 *Checkbook democracy*. Boston: Northeastern University Press.
Widoyoko, J. Danang
2007 'Memberantas korupsi di negeri maling; Kritik terhadap strategi pemberantasan korupsi di Indonesia', *Jurnal Renai* 7-2. [Salatiga: Pustaka Percik.]
Widoyoko, J. Danang, Irfan Muktiono, Adnan Topan Husodo, Barly Haliem Noe and Agung Wijaya
2003 *Bisnis militer mencari legitimasi*. Jakarta: Indonesia Corruption Watch and National Democratic Institute.
Widoyoko, J. Danang, Luki Djani, Ade Irawan, Agus Sunaryanto and Febri Katong Hendry
2007 *Saatnya warga melawan korupsi; Citizen report card di sektor pendidikan*. Jakarta: ICW.
Williams, Katherine S.
1994 *Textbook of criminology*. Second edition. London: Blackstone Press.
Wilson, Eric and Tim Lindsey (eds)
2009 *Government of the shadows; Parapolitics and criminal sovereignty*. London: Pluto Press.
Wilson, Ian Douglas
2006 'Continuity and change; The changing contours of organized violence in post-New Order Indonesia', *Critical Asian Studies* 38-2:265-97.
2008 'As long as it's *halal*; Islamic gangsters in Jakarta', in: Greg Fealy and Sally White (eds), *Expressing Islam; Religious life and politics in Indonesia*, pp. 192-210. Singapore: ISEAS.
Winters, Jeffrey A.
1997 'Down with the World Bank', *Far Eastern Economic Review*, 13 February.
Wollenberg, Eva, Jon Anderson and David Edmunds
2001 'Pluralism and the less powerful; Accommodating multiple interests in local forest management', *International Journal of Agricultural Resources, Governance and Ecology* 1-3/4:199-222.
Wong, Diana
2005 'The rumor of trafficking; Border controls, illegal migration, and the sovereignty of the nation-state', in: Willem van Schendel and Itty Abraham (eds), *Illicit flows and criminal things; States, borders, and the other side of globalization*, pp. 69-100. Bloomington: Indiana University Press.
Wongso, Yenwy
2007 'Construction sector gearing up for economic recovery', *The Jakarta Post*, 2 May.
World Bank
1984 *The construction industry; Issues and strategies in developing countries*. Washington, DC: World Bank.
2001 *Indonesia; Country procurement assessment report – reforming the public procurement system*. Jakarta: East Asia and Pacific Region, World Bank Office Jakarta, Operational Services Unit.
2003 *Combating corruption in Indonesia; Enhancing accountability for development*. Jakarta: World Bank, East Asia Poverty Reduction and Economic Management Unit. [20 October.]

2004 *Combating corruption in Indonesia; Enhancing accountability for development*. Jakarta: World Bank Office Jakarta. [http://siteresources.worldbank.org/INTINDONESIA/Resources/Publication/03-Publication/Combating+Corruption+in+Indonesia-Oct15.pdf (accessed 12-11-2009).]

2007 *Spending for development; Making the most of Indonesia's new opportunities; Indonesia public expenditure review*. Jakarta: The World Bank Office. [February.]

2008 *Doing business in 2009*. Washington, DC: World Bank and International Finance Corporation. http://www.doingbusiness.org/features/DB2009Report.aspx (accessed 15-12-2009).

Yuwono, Sutedjo, Maswita Djaja and Ir. Parjoko

2005 *Penghapusan perdagangan orang di Indonesia tahun 2004-2005*. Jakarta: Kementerian Koordinator Bidang Kesejahteraan Rakyat.

Zain, Zainuddin

2006 'Tukar identiti', *Harian Metro*, 13 August.

Ziegenhain, Patrick

2008 *The Indonesian parliament and democratization*. Singapore: ISEAS.

Index